TEST BANK to accompany
Dominick Salvatore's

FOURTH EDITION

MICROECONOMICS

Theory and Applications

Prepared by
Mary H. Lesser
Iona College

New York Oxford
OXFORD UNIVERSITY PRESS
2003

Oxford University Press

Oxford New York
Auckland Bangkok Buenos Aires Cape Town Chennai
Dar es Salaam Delhi Hong Kong Istanbul Karachi Kolkata
Kuala Lumpur Madrid Melbourne Mexico City Mumbai
Nairobi São Paulo Shanghai Taipei Tokyo Toronto

Published by Oxford University Press, Inc.
198 Madison Avenue, New York, New York, 10016
http://www.oup-usa.org

ISBN: 0–19–516290–0

Printing number: 9 8 7 6 5 4 3 2 1

Printed in the United States of America
on acid-free paper

CONTENTS

Chapter 1:

Introduction

Multiple-Choice

Choose the one alternative that best completes the statement or answers the question.

1. Which of the following statements is false?
   A) Limited human wants is the basis for economic choice.
   B) Scarce resources generate costs in production.
   C) Because resources are limited, they are scarce.
   D) Because resources are scarce, there is a need for choice.
   E) None of the statements is false.

   Difficulty: **Easy**

2. Of the following, the one least likely to concern the microeconomist is:
   A) during the last quarter of 1993, the U.S. economy experienced an annual inflation rate of approximately 3.2%.
   B) as the wage rate increases, the amount of hours that an individual is willing to work increases.
   C) the price of oranges increased yesterday because there was a late freeze in Florida.
   D) employment in the steel industry in the United States has declined in recent years.
   E) None of the above is correct.

   Difficulty: **Easy**

3. Economic resources are:
   A) free.
   B) limited and so they command a price.
   C) unlimited and so they command a price.
   D) not free, except for clean air.
   E) None of the above is correct.

   Difficulty: **Easy**

4. Broadly speaking, economic resources will include:
   A) land and natural resources.
   B) labor and the ability of individuals to do work.
   C) iron ore and natural gas deposits.
   D) productive capital such as machinery and factories.
   E) All of the above answers are correct.

   Difficulty: **Easy**

5. To the economist, capital will consist of all of the following except:
   A) a set of mechanic's tools.
   B) an automobile used to deliver newspapers.

C) money.
D) a telecommunications system used by a firm that produces paper clips.
E) inventories.

Difficulty: **Easy**

6. Because human wants are basically unlimited but economic resources are limited, every society must:
A) make choices about what is to be produced, how production is to take place, and for whom output is produced.
B) solve the problem of the distribution of output, but not necessarily the problem of production.
C) determine how output is produced, but not how it is distributed.
D) solve the problem of productive efficiency.
E) (B) and (C) are correct.

Difficulty: **Easy**

7. "In the United States, those households who make more money should pay more taxes." This is an example of:
A) a positive economic statement.
B) an economic fallacy,
C) deductive economic reasoning.
D) stating an economic theory.
E) a normative economic statement.

Difficulty: **Easy**

8. Which of the following best reflects the concept of marginal analysis as used by the economist?
A) The effect on your consumption pattern when you receive a ten percent increase in your income.
B) The satisfaction that you receive when you consume an additional unit of a good.
C) The revenue received by a seller when one more unit of the seller's output is sold.
D) The cost incurred by a firm when an additional unit of output is produced.
E) All of the above are marginal concepts.

Difficulty: **Moderate**

9. When the economist describes the marginal satisfaction received from the consumption of an extra unit of a good, he or she is describing:
A) the overall satisfaction that the consumer receives when the good is consumed.
B) the level of satisfaction where the consumer will be neither better nor worse off if an extra unit of the good is consumed.
C) the change in total satisfaction brought about by the consumption of the extra unit of the good.
D) the change in the extra satisfaction received when an additional unit of the good is consumed.
E) None of the above is correct.

Difficulty: **Moderate**

10. Which of the following is true?
    A) Households are buyers in the market for goods and services and sellers in the market for economic resources.
    B) Households are sellers in the market for goods and buyers in the market for economic resources.
    C) Households are sellers in both the market for goods and the market for economic resources.
    D) Households are buyers in both the market for goods and in the market for economic resources.
    E) Business firms only transact in the market for goods.

    Difficulty: **Easy**

11. According to the circular flow model, all of the following are forms of consumer income <u>except</u>:
    A) wages.
    B) interest.
    C) rent.
    D) profits.
    E) All of the above are forms of consumer income.

    Difficulty: **Easy**

12. The macroeconomist will most likely be interested in all of the following <u>except</u>:
    A) the quantity of money in circulation in the economy.
    B) the relative price ratio between two goods, say bread and coffee.
    C) the rate of change in the general price level in the economy over a particular period of time.
    D) policies that are designed to alter the overall level of output and income within the economy.
    E) All of the above would interest the macroeconomist.

    Difficulty: **Moderate**

13. One of the underlying assumptions of most economic models is that individuals:
    A) try to maximize the overall net benefit to society.
    B) try to promote their own best interest only at the expense of their neighbors.
    C) always put society's best interest above individual interest.
    D) try to pursue their own best interest and maximize net individual welfare.
    E) none of the above are correct.

    Difficulty: **Easy**

14. "If the government raises income taxes, then individuals will save less of their income." This statement is an example of:
    A) a normative economic statement.
    B) a positive economic statement.
    C) an assumption.
    D) (A) and (C) are correct.
    E) (B) and (C) are correct.

    Difficulty: **Moderate**

15. Given an economy that operates within the limits of a price system, prices serve:
    A) to induce buyers to rank their preferences for goods and services.
    B) to finance and pay for the cost of producing the goods and services consumed in the economy.
    C) to ration goods, services, and the factors of the production within the economy.
    D) to allocate goods among alternative uses.
    E) All of the above are correct.

    Difficulty: **Easy**

16. Because human wants are unlimited but the economic resources available to satisfy these wants are limited, every society must:
    A) make choices about what is to be produced, how, and for whom.
    B) make decisions only at the margin.
    C) make decisions to reduce productive efficiency and increase output.
    D) make choices about what is to be produced, but not necessarily how production is to take place or how output will be distributed.
    E) None of the above is correct.

    Difficulty: **Easy**

17. Which one of the following statements is correct?
    A) All economies are mixed economies, to one degree or another.
    B) The United States is a mixed economy.
    C) A mixed economy incorporates some elements of government control or planning.
    D) The former Soviet Union relied almost exclusively on government to make economic decisions.
    E) All of the above are correct.

    Difficulty: **Moderate**

18. When making a choice at the margin, you should consider:
    A) all alternative choices and outcomes.
    B) the effect that the choice you make will have on your neighbors.
    C) only those things that will be changed by the choice.
    D) only the average outcome of the choice.
    E) (A) and (B) are correct.

    Difficulty: **Moderate**

19. If, in your decision-making process, you consider only those things (outcomes) that would be affected by a particular action, then you are:
    A) making a choice at the margin.
    B) making a normative economic judgement.
    C) undertaking positive economic analysis.
    D) engaged in microeconomics but not macroeconomics.
    E) None of the above is correct.

    Difficulty: **Moderate**

20. The large and growing degree of interdependence of the United States in the world economy today:
    A) makes a closed-economy approach to the study of microeconomics unrealistic.
    B) means that U.S. manufacturers are protected from foreign competition.
    C) results in U.S.-made goods being manufactured from only U.S. resources.
    D) is the result of an international vacuum.
    E) All of the above are correct.

    Difficulty: **Easy**

21. One of the unifying themes of microeconomic theory is that:
    A) all individuals work to promote the interests of society as a whole.
    B) all individuals make choices at the margin.
    C) all firms seek only to maximize their profits.
    D) human wants are limited while economic resources are unlimited.
    E) all of the above are correct.

    Difficulty: **Easy**

22. When a region or nation is relatively more efficient in the production of certain goods and services it is said to have a(n) _____ in those goods and services.
    A) relative disadvantage
    B) exchange advantage
    C) comparative advantage
    D) (B) and (C) are correct.
    E) (A) and (C) are correct.

    Difficulty: **Easy**

23. In their work, economists often use economic models. These models:
    A) are tools used in the analysis of economic relationships.
    B) may be a set of economic principles or theories.
    C) may be a single equation or a set of equations expressing a relationship between two or more economic variables.
    D) may be a single graph or a set of graphs expressing the relationship between two economic variables.
    E) All of the above are correct.

    Difficulty: **Easy**

24. Which of the following is <u>not</u> a characteristic of economic theories?
    A) Economic theories may change over time as new evidence is discovered.
    B) Economic theories are based upon abstract ideas, and so they cannot be tested.
    C) Economic theories may be tested by applying economic data to a model.
    D) Economic theories are the basis for economic principles.
    E) None of the above is correct.

    Difficulty: **Easy**

25. Generally speaking, when an economic model achieves or demonstrates an equilibrium, this equilibrium:
    A) will not change if the model's behavioral assumptions are changed.

B) will not change if the assumptions of the model are altered.
C) determines the values that have been hypothesized, given the assumptions of the model.
D) once attained will not change, regardless of any change in the economy; otherwise, it would not be an equilibrium.
E) None of the above is correct.

Difficulty: **Moderate**

26. One of the primary reasons why economists use economic models in their analysis is because a model:
A) permits economic relationships to be quickly and easily specified.
B) makes it possible to predict exact economic relationships.
C) **helps organize and clarify the thinking process about an issue.**
D) incorporates all the inner workings of the real-world economy.
E) None of the above is correct.

Difficulty: **Easy**

27. A normative economic statement:
A) does not exist in economic theory.
B) is based on economic data that has been collected over a period of time.
C) predicts what will occur in the economy at some point in the future.
D) is a statement of what should or should not be.
E) has little relevance in microeconomic theory.

Difficulty: **Easy**

28. Technically speaking, which one of the following would <u>not</u> be considered part of a country's economic resources or factors of production?
A) a bulldozer owned by a firm
B) $500,000 in a firm's saving account
C) the labor force employed by a firm to produce a particular good or service
D) a firm's plant and equipment
E) All of the above are correct.

Difficulty: **Easy**

29. An economy's factors of production or economic resources consist of:
A) its stock of financial wealth.
B) all of the goods produced for household consumption during a given period of time.
C) its stock of financial capital that is used to invest in new plant and equipment.
D) goods and services that are used in the production of output.
E) All of the above are correct.

Difficulty: **Easy**

30. In the absence of government participation and foreign trade, the circular flow model of economic activity shows:
A) that firms supply both the resources and the outputs used in production.
B) that households demand both resources and outputs.
C) that firms supply resources and households demand outputs.

D) that households supply resources and firms supply outputs.
E) the level of aggregate wealth that can be generated by the economic system.

Difficulty: **Easy**

31. Suppose that the country of Alphania operates within a free-enterprise system. The questions of what, how, and for whom are answered by:
A) some central planning committee.
B) the price mechanism.
C) the elected representatives of the people.
D) a mixture of government and private planning.
E) None of the above is correct.

Difficulty: **Easy**

32. Although some goods may be more plentiful than others, all goods are scarce. In a market system, prices serve to:
A) indicate to the government which goods should be produced and which should not.
B) indicate to consumers the goods that they should consume as well as to indicate the quantity that should be consumed.
C) reduce the efficiency with which the market allocated scarce resources.
D) assures that everyone in society gets at least some of the goods produced in the economy.
E) None of the above is correct.

Difficulty: **Easy**

33. The statement that, "The unemployment rate should not be allowed to rise above six percent," is an example of:
A) a normative statement.
B) an economic prediction.
C) an economic assumption.
D) a positive economic statement.
E) None of the above is correct.

Difficulty: **Easy**

34. In a market economy, the major determinant of the allocation of society's scarce resources is:
A) a central planning committee.
B) a central planning committee along with producing firms.
C) both firms and households acting through a central planning committee.
D) both firms and households acting through markets.
E) None of the above is correct.

Difficulty: **Easy**

35. Suppose that resources were plentiful and were therefore not scarce. We can conclude that:
A) even if they were free, there would likely be a shortage of some resources.
B) they would still command some positive prices.
C) the amount of resources that producers want to use in production would not be equal to the amount that they could use.

D) if the resources were free, there would be no shortage of them.
E) the prices of the resources would be negative.

Difficulty: **Moderate**

36. The fraction of national income spent on health care:
A) doubled between 1970 and 2000.
B) in the United States is greater than that in any other country.
C) has increased dramatically over time, and has reduced the income available to spend on other goods and services.
D) has grown dramatically, but infant mortality rates are still higher and life expectancy rates lower in the U.S. than in many other industrial nations.
E) All of the above are correct.

Difficulty: **Easy**

37. Drought in Kansas in 1988 and 1989 did not cause:
A) wheat prices to increase dramatically.
B) American wheat exports to increase.
C) other countries to plant more wheat.
D) a broad range of consumer prices to increase dramatically.
E) farmers' incomes to increase due to substantial price increases and a government subsidy for each bushel of wheat lost to the drought.

Difficulty: **Easy**

38. In the command economy of the former Soviet Union:
A) economic decisions were decentralized.
B) the means of production were owned by the state.
C) economic incentives were lacking or grossly distorted.
D) (B) and (C) are correct.
E) All of the above are correct.

Difficulty: **Easy**

39. The establishment of a market economy in formerly communist countries will require:
A) government control of prices to stabilize the market.
B) transferring productive resources from the state to private ownership.
C) closely regulating international trade to guard against cutthroat competition.
D) maintaining the communist legal system since it is the only system with which businesses in the Commonwealth of Independent States are familiar.
E) (A), (B), and (C) are correct.

Difficulty: **Easy**

40. In the marginal analysis of advertising:
A) the marginal benefits of TV spots exceed the marginal costs of TV spots up to the number of TV spots at which MB=MC.
B) additional TV spots should be purchased so long as the total benefits of advertising increase.
C) the marginal costs of advertising exceed the marginal benefits for all TV spots.

D) the marginal benefits of advertising increase because additional TV spots reach more and more people, and thus are more effective in persuading consumers to buy the product.
E) All of the above are correct.

Difficulty: **Easy**

41. If _____ of advertising at the number of TV spots currently being purchased by a firm, the firm should _____ the number of TV spots it purchases.
A) MB>MC; decrease.
B) MB>MC; increase.
C) MC<MB; increase.
D) MB=MC; decrease.
E) None of the above is correct.

Difficulty: **Moderate**

42. IBM's use of computer parts and components produced overseas:
A) is an example of the internationalization of economic activity.
B) was necessitated by the fact that the parts and components could not be manufactured domestically.
C) caused PC prices to be lower in the U.S. than would have been the case with a PC produced entirely in the U.S.
D) (A) and (B) are correct.
E) (A) and (C) are correct.

Difficulty: **Easy**

43. According to a survey of economists conducted in 1992:
A) most economists agree on propositions which belong to normative economics.
B) most economists agree on propositions which belong to positive economics.
C) most economists agree on propositions which belong both to positive and normative economics.
D) most economists believe that it is almost impossible to distinguish between positive and normative propositions in economics.
E) (C) and (D) are correct.

Difficulty: **Easy**

44. The division of labor refers to:
A) the use of labor for tasks to which it is best suited rather than using other resources such as capital which are less well suited to the task.
B) breaking up a task into a number of smaller tasks which are then assigned to different workers.
C) the separation of workers into opposing camps which will compete with each other and limit wage increases.
D) a government agency with the task of monitoring and reporting on the working conditions of labor.
E) None of the above is correct.

Difficulty: **Easy**

45. According to Nobel Laureate economist Milton Friedman, an economic model:
    A) is tested by the realism of its assumptions.
    B) is tested by the lack of realism of its assumptions.
    C) is tested by its ability to predict and to explain.
    D) (A) and (C) are correct.
    E) None of the above is correct.

    Difficulty: **Easy**

46. Most economists believe that the appropriate methodology of economics is to test a theory by:
    A) its ability to predict accurately.
    B) whether the predictions follow logically from the assumptions.
    C) the internal consistency of its assumptions.
    D) (B) and (C) are correct.
    E) All of the above are correct.

    Difficulty: **Easy**

47. Positive economics is concerned with:
    A) what is.
    B) what ought to be.
    C) the use of statements of "what is" to resolve differences over what ought to be.
    D) the use of statements of "what ought to be" to resolve differences over what is.
    E) the use of combines statements of what is and what ought to be," to formulate policy recommendations.

    Difficulty: **Easy**

48. An increase in the price of milk and a reduction in the price of eggs are signals to farmers to raise more cows and fewer chickens. This is an illustration of answering the question of:
    A) what to produce.
    B) how to produce.
    C) for whom to produce.
    D) Both (A) and (C) are correct.
    E) Both (B) and (C) are correct.

    Difficulty: **Easy**

49. If the satisfaction or benefit that an individual gets from consuming one extra hamburger with a price of \$2 is more than twice as large as the satisfaction of consuming a hot dog with a price of \$1, then the individual would increase net benefits or satisfaction by consuming:
    A) fewer hamburgers and more hot dogs.
    B) more hamburgers and fewer hot dogs.
    C) more of both hamburgers and hot dogs.
    D) fewer of both hamburgers and hot dogs.
    E) Cannot be determined from the information provided.

    Difficulty: **Easy**

50. Suppose that Nation A has a comparative advantage in producing product X and Nation B has a comparative advantage in producing product Y. Assuming that consumers in both nations want both products, trade between the two nations is likely to consist of:
A) Nation A exporting X to Nation B and importing Y from Nation B.
B) Nation A exporting Y to Nation B and importing X from Nation B.
C) Nation A only exporting X to Nation B.
D) Nation A only importing Y from Nation B.
E) None of the above; trade will not take place between the two nations.

Difficulty: **Hard**

Short Answer

Write the word or phrase that best completes each statement or answers the question.

1. **People's material standards of living are much higher now than they were a century ago. Does that mean scarcity is not a problem anymore?**
Answer: It is true that in many places in the world material standards of living are much higher now than in the past. One might even argue that the material impact of scarcity on people's lives is less severe. However, scarcity refers to the inability to satisfy all wants. As long as that cannot be done, choices will have to be made about the alternative uses of resources to satisfy human wants. In other words, there is still a scarcity problem to address.

2. **What does "rationing over time" mean, and how does it apply to the problem of harvesting trees for timber?**
Answer: To ration means to allocate something that is scarce across its alternative uses. Thus, "rationing over time" reflects the fact that future uses constitute alternative uses of resources in addition to competing present uses. Trees may be harvested now for producing lumber or they may be held for that purpose in a future time period. An advantage to delaying harvest is that the trees may grow larger and yield a larger future benefit. Thus, rationing over time may involve some reward for recognizing that there will be wants to satisfy in the future as well as the present.

3. **What does the "function of prices" have to do with the basic questions raised by the existence of scarcity?**
Answer: The function of price to adjust the decisions of people who are attempting to answer basic questions about production and consumption such as: what to produce; and for whom to produce. If decisions about producing a good and selling it to a particular group of consumers do not match the decisions of those consumers about buying the good, shortages or surpluses will appear. These lead, in turn, to price changes, which alter the initial production and consumption decisions.

4. **Explain the view that individuals who attempt to maximize net benefits from their decisions are not selfish.**
Answer: Suppose a person is allocating income across two charities. A rational decision maker could view this as a marginal decision rather than as an all or nothing decision. "Where are the extra benefits to other people of my giving another dollar to the Red Cross or the Salvation Army?" The marginal cost of giving another dollar to the Red Cross is the extra benefit that is foregone at the Salvation Army. The opposite is also true. Thus, maximizing net benefits in this situation has nothing to do with my own material needs.

5. **What difference is there between "specialization" and the "division of labor?" They both create the need for what basic economic act?**
Answer: Specialization refers to the use of labor and other resources in the tasks in which they are most efficient. Division of labor consists of breaking up a task into smaller, more specialized tasks. Both create the need to engage in trade since both create a type of mutual interdependence between people who cannot provide all of the various goods they want for themselves.

6. **What is the basic difference between positive and normative economics?**
Answer: Positive economics studies what is. It is concerned with how an economic system answers the basic question of what, how, and for whom to produce. Normative economics studies what ought to be. Thus, it is concerned with how an economic system ought to answer the basic questions of what, how, and for whom to produce. Normative economics is based on value judgements, and disagreements in this area of economics are more difficult to resolve.

Chapter 2:

Basic Demand and Supply Analysis

Multiple-Choice

Choose the one alternative that best completes the statement or answers the question.

1. Which statement best describes equilibrium price in a competitive market?
   A) The marginal benefit that the individual receives when the last unit of a commodity is consumed just equals the marginal cost of producing that unit.
   B) The quantity bought of a particular commodity equals the quantity sold at every price, so any price could be an equilibrium price.
   C) Consumers receive a higher marginal satisfaction from consuming the last unit of a commodity than it costs to produce the last unit, so firms earn a profit.
   D) In a competitive market, quantity demanded is always equal to quantity supplied regardless of the price.
   E) None of the above is correct.

   Difficulty: **Moderate**

2. Which statement about a market system is <u>not</u> correct?
   A) In a market system, it is necessary for buyers and sellers to be in physical contact with each other for the purpose of the trade.
   B) As trading occurs in a competitive market, both price and quantity move toward equilibrium.
   C) Because of modern communications, buyers and sellers do not have to be in direct contact with each other for the purpose of the trade.
   D) For a market to occur, there must be both buyers and sellers for a commodity.
   E) None of the above is correct.

   Difficulty: **Moderate**

3. Suppose that the XYZ Chemical Company introduces a new fertilizer that increases the yield per acre of green beans. If everything else remains constant, we would expect to see:
   A) a reduction in the supply of green beans.
   B) an increase in the consumption of green beans.
   C) producers allocating less of their land for the production of green beans and more for the production of corn.
   D) a shortage of green beans occurring in the market, so the market price will rise.
   E) None of the above is correct.

   Difficulty: **Hard**

4. One of the more important reasons why the individual consumer's demand curve for a particular good slopes downward and to the right is that when the price of the good falls (with all other things constant):
   A) the consumer's preferences change, so he or she will buy more of the good.

B) consumers will now purchase those additional units of the good that had a lower marginal or extra benefit.
C) the producers of the good will reduce the quantity supplied of their output.
D) the consumer becomes less interested in the relative price of other goods.
E) None of the above is correct.

Difficulty: **Moderate**

5. A movement along any given demand curve for a particular good reflects a changing quantity demanded for the good. The other variable that changes as you move along a demand curve is:
A) the number of buyers in the market for good.
B) the income level of consumers.
C) the prices of the related goods that the consumer might buy.
D) the price of the good itself.
E) the preferences of the consumer.

Difficulty: **Easy**

6. Other things constant, we can expect the demand for a product to decrease if:
A) the number of buyers in the market increases.
B) the price of a complementary good arises.
C) the price of the product arises.
D) the price of a substitute good increases.
E) None of the above will cause a change in the demand for a product.

Difficulty: **Easy**

7. Suppose that chicken and pork are substitute goods. An increase in the price of chicken will, other things constant:
A) cause pork to become relatively less expensive than chicken.
B) cause the demand for pork to fall.
C) cause the quantity demanded of pork to fall.
D) cause pork to become relatively more expensive than chicken.
E) None of the above is correct.

Difficulty: **Moderate**

8. When the price of poultry changes, the quantity demanded of poultry changes, and there is a movement along the demand curve for poultry. Which one of the following statements best explains the movement along the demand curve?
A) As the price of poultry rises, consumers buy more poultry because they can afford less of all other meats.
B) As the price of poultry falls, consumers feel that the opportunity cost of consuming beef has increased.
C) As the price of poultry rises, consumers substitute other meats for poultry, and as the price of poultry falls, consumers substitute poultry for other meats.
D) As the price of poultry falls, consumers substitute other meats for poultry.
E) None of the above is correct.

Difficulty: **Moderate**

9. Other things constant, if the price of apples is below its market equilibrium price, market forces will cause price to rise because:
   A) buyers will bid against each other for the limited quantity of apples, and sellers will realize that they can raise their asking price.
   B) the demand for apples will increase because the price of the commodity is unusually low.
   C) the supply of apples will fall because producers realize that they cannot make a profit at such a low price.
   D) the surplus of grapes on the market will cause some sellers to raise their asking price.
   E) None of the above is correct.

   Difficulty: **Easy**

10. Which of the following statements is <u>not</u> correct?
   A) The interaction of supply and demand determine both the price and amount of a good produced and sold in a competitive market.
   B) Markets may be either informal or formal in their organized structure.
   C) In a market, buyers and sellers of a good do not have to be in direct contact with each other to trade the good.
   D) Most western industrialized nations rely upon markets to allocate resources.
   E) When there is a fall in the market price of a good, the demand curve for the good shifts downward and to the left.

   Difficulty: **Moderate**

11. Suppose that the market for widgets is in equilibrium. We would be correct in concluding that:
   A) there is no shortage of widgets on the market.
   B) the quantity demanded of widgets equals the quantity supplied.
   C) the price is established that clears the market of widgets.
   D) there is no surplus of widgets on the market.
   E) All of the above are correct.

   Difficulty: **Easy**

12. A shift to the right in the market demand curve for Coca-Cola drink might be caused by:
   A) a reduction in the income of consumers.
   B) an increase in the price of Pepsi Cola.
   C) a scientific study that shows Coca-Cola causes kidney stones.
   D) a reduction in the price per can of Coca-Cola.
   E) None of the above is correct.

   Difficulty: **Moderate**

13. If the average income of households in the United States increased by 10% in 2002, we would expect this increase to cause:
   A) an increase in the demand for most goods.
   B) the demand curves for most goods to shift downward and to the left.
   C) a decrease in the demand for a most goods.

D) an increase in the quantity demanded for most goods.
E) None of the above is correct.

Difficulty: **Moderate**

14. Suppose that the Acme Co. experiences an improvement in the production technology that it employs in the production of widgets. This improvement in technology means that the Acme Co. can produce more widgets with the same level of inputs. Other things constant, we would expect to see:
A) a movement up along the supply curve so that a higher equilibrium quantity, as well as a higher price, of widgets is achieved.
B) a leftward shift of the supply curve of widgets so that the Acme Co. offers to sell less at every price.
C) a rightward shift of the supply curve of widgets so that the Acme Co. offers to sell more at every price.
D) no movement of the supply curve but a fall in price and an increase in quantity supplied.
E) None of the above is correct.

Difficulty: **Easy**

15. Suppose that you observe a graph of the demand and supply curves for widgets. You are a little confused, though because the supply curve intersects the vertical (price) axis above the point where the demand curve intersects the axis. In fact, every point on the supply curve is above every point on the demand curve. Such a situation would suggest that:
A) widgets are over-priced, and there will be a shortage on the market.
B) widgets are over-priced, and the quantity demanded will be zero.
C) the good is under-priced, and there will be a surplus on the market.
D) the good is under-priced, and there will be a shortage on the market.
E) these are the demand and supply curves when widgets are a free good.

Difficulty: **Hard**

16. Suppose that you observe the supply and demand curves for a particular commodity, and you are puzzled because the supply curve intersects the horizontal axis (quantity axis) to the right of every point where the demand curve intersects the axis. In fact, every point on the supply curve is to the right of every point on the demand curve. This observation might suggest to you that:
A) the good is a free good.
B) the good is over-priced, and there will be a shortage on the market.
C) the good is under-priced and there will be a shortage on the market.
D) the good is scarce, so some individuals will not be able to consume all they want of the good.
E) There is not enough information provided to determine a correct answer.

Difficulty: **Hard**

17. As the consumer moves along his or her own demand curve for apples:
A) the price of apples remains constant.
B) the quantity of apples bought at different prices remains constant.
C) the amount of apples that the individual wants to buy remains constant at different prices.
D) it is assumed that the price of oranges remains constant.

E) None of the above is correct.

Difficulty: **Easy**

18. As a result of OPEC's oil embargo against the United States in the mid-1970s, the price of gasoline rose sharply. What likely effect did the embargo have on the market demand for motor oil?
A) The supply curve of motor oil shifted downward and to the right.
B) The demand curve for motor oil shifted to the right.
C) The demand curve for motor oil shifted downward and to the left.
D) There was a movement upward along the supply curve for motor oil.
E) Because the markets for the goods are essentially independent of each other, the market for motor oil was not affected.

Difficulty: **Moderate**

19. When we use demand and supply analysis to establish an equilibrium price and quantity for good X, which one of the following will cause the demand curve for good X to shift to the right and the good's price to rise, other things remaining constant?
A) The price of good W, a complementary good, rises.
B) The price of good Y, a substitute good, falls.
C) The price of good Y, a substitute good, rises.
D) Good X is a normal good and there is a decrease in household income.
E) All of the above are correct.

Difficulty: **Moderate**

20. Shifts of the supply curve for a given good can be caused by changes in:
A) the prices of related goods.
B) the prices of the inputs used to produce the goods.
C) the existing state of technology used to produce the good.
D) the number of producers and sellers of the good in the market.
E) All of the above are correct.

Difficulty: **Easy**

21. Suppose that a shortage of corn exists on the grain markets. We would expect this shortage to:
A) put pressure on the price of corn to rise and quantity demanded to fall.
B) put pressure on the price of corn to fall and quantity demanded to rise.
C) put pressure on the price of corn to rise and the quantity demanded to rise also.
D) put pressure on the price of corn to fall and the quantity supplied to rise.
E) None of the above is correct.

Difficulty: **Easy**

22. If the supply curve for good X is positively sloped, then this suggests that:
A) consumers are willing to buy more only at lower prices.
B) producers must receive higher prices in order to cover their marginal cost of producing extra units of the good.
C) producers are making excess profits as the price of a good rises above its equilibrium price.

D) producers face a constant cost of production, so they will charge higher prices in order to make excess profits.
E) None of the above is correct.

Difficulty: **Moderate**

23. As with the demand curve, the various points on the supply curve represent:
A) the maximum price that producers must receive in order to supply a particular quantity of the good.
B) the minimum price that producers must receive in order to supply a particular quantity of the good.
C) alternative price-quantity combinations.
D) the minimum quantity that would be associated with a particular price.
E) None of the above is correct.

Difficulty: **Moderate**

24. Consider the international market for coffee. If the world price of a pound of coffee is below a nation's domestic price, then we would expect the domestic price of a pound of coffee to:
A) move toward the world price of coffee as long as the government places a tariff on the imported coffee.
B) move toward the world price of coffee as long as the nation is able to engage in free trade.
C) be dependent only on the domestic supply and demand of coffee.
D) continue to be below the world price of coffee since governments often are reluctant to incur a trade deficit.
E) None of the above is correct.

Difficulty: **Moderate**

25. Suppose that in the country of Betania, the domestic equilibrium price of beer is greater than the world price. We might expect to see:
A) Betania having some positive quantity of imported beer.
B) domestic producers reducing the price of their beer to a price near or equal to the world price.
C) domestic producers of beer reducing their production.
D) domestic consumers increasing the consumption of their beer.
E) All of the above are correct.

Difficulty: **Moderate**

26. In a world market characterized by free trade, if the price of good X in one country is high relative to the rest of the world, we would expect the price of good X to:
A) fall in that country and rise in the rest of the world as more of the good is imported into the country at the expense of foreign competition.
B) rise as the domestic production increases relative to the rest of the world.
C) fall as domestic producers reduced their prices in order to sell their surplus of the good on the foreign market.
D) remain relatively stable because most likely the government will impose some trade barriers.
E) None of the above is correct.

Difficulty: **Moderate**

27. If the price of natural fibers should suddenly increase, then we would likely observe a textile market in which:
    A) the demand for synthetic fibers increased.
    B) more producers entered the market for synthetic fibers.
    C) the long-run quantity supplied of synthetic fibers increased.
    D) the price of synthetic fibers increased.
    E) All of the above are correct.

Difficulty: **Moderate**

28. Suppose that the government levies a tax on good X. Assuming that the laws of supply and demand hold, the effect of the tax will be:
    A) to increase the price received by sellers for each unit of good X that is sold.
    B) to decrease the price per unit paid by buyers for each unit of good X that is purchased.
    C) to decrease the price received by sellers for each unit of good X sold.
    D) to increase the amount of good X that is sold each month.
    E) not enough information is provided in order to determine an answer.

Difficulty: **Moderate**

29. Suppose that the demand curve for widgets is vertical. An excise tax on widgets will:
    A) be borne by the sellers only.
    B) be borne by consumers only.
    C) be shared by both consumers and sellers.
    D) not generate any revenue for the government because quantity demanded will fall to zero.
    E) None of the above is correct.

Difficulty: **Moderate**

30. Suppose that the government establishes an effective price floor for raw milk. At the established price floor:
    A) the quantity demanded of milk will be greater than the quantity supplied each month.
    B) the quantity demanded will generate a shortage in the market each month.
    C) milk and other dairy products will be available and rationed by the price so that quantity demanded and quantity supplied are equal each month.
    D) the quantity of milk supplied each month will exceed the quantity demanded, and so the market will not achieve an equilibrium.
    E) the quantity sold of milk will be less than the quantity bought.

Difficulty: **Moderate**

31. Suppose that the government imposes a price ceiling on gasoline that is equal to $1.10 per gallon. The market equilibrium price, however, is $1.00 per gallon. We can conclude that:
    A) there will be a constant surplus of gasoline on the market.
    B) there will be neither a surplus nor shortage since the equilibrium price is below the established price ceiling.
    C) there will be a constant shortage of gasoline on the market.
    D) the price of gasoline cannot fall below the price ceiling.

E) None of the above is correct.

Difficulty: **Moderate**

32. Which one of the following would likely not cause the demand curve for electricity to shift to the left?
A) An increase in the price of natural gas occurs.
B) Households using electricity suddenly become more aware of energy conservation and install storm windows.
C) The average household income declines substantially.
D) The use of solar energy for hot water heaters as well as home heating increases following a major technological breakthrough.
E) All of the above are correct.

Difficulty: **Moderate**

33. All of the following leave the supply curve for good X unchanged except:
A) the imposition of a tariff on all imported quantities of good X.
B) a change in the price of substitutes for good.
C) the discovery that substitutes for good X cause insomnia in adults.
D) an increase in the demand for good X.
E) a rise in the equilibrium market price of good X.

Difficulty: **Moderate**

34. In the mid-1960s, the Vatican gave permission for Roman Catholics to eat meat on Fridays rather than only fish. As a result of this decision, the price of chicken and beef rose. We would likely observe:
A) an increase in the price of fish also.
B) the price of fish either rising or falling, depending on the magnitude of the price increases for beef and chicken.
C) a decline in the price of fish.
D) a fall in the price of fish if the price elasticity of demand for fish was equal to one.
E) no change in the price of fish.

Difficulty: **Moderate**

35. The "incidence of a tax" refers to:
A) the burden borne by the entity responsible for collecting a tax.
B) the relative burden of a tax on buyers.
C) the relative burden of a tax on sellers.
D) (B) and (C) are correct.
E) All of the above are correct.

Difficulty: **Easy**

36. Given supply and demand conditions, if an excise tax is collected from demanders rather than suppliers:
A) a greater share of the tax burden will be borne by demanders.
B) a smaller share of the tax burden will be borne by demanders.
C) a greater share of the tax burden will be borne by suppliers.
D) a smaller share of the tax burden will be borne by suppliers.

E) None of the above; the share of the tax borne by suppliers and demanders is not changed by shifting the collection of the tax from demanders to suppliers.

Difficulty: **Moderate**

37. Given the supply of a commodity, the _____ sensitive the quantity demanded is to price, the _____ is the portion of an excise tax paid by consumers.
A) less; greater.
B) less; smaller.
C) more; smaller.
D) (A) and (C) are correct.
E) (B) and (C) are correct.

Difficulty: **Moderate**

38. Given the demand for a commodity, the _____ sensitive the quantity supplied is to price, the _____ is the portion of an excise tax paid by _____.
A) more; smaller; producers.
B) more; greater; producers.
C) less; smaller; producers.
D) less; greater; consumers.
E) None of the above is correct.

Difficulty: **Moderate**

39. Rent controls:
A) have proven to be an effective way to increase the availability of affordable housing.
B) have reduced the rate of abandonment of marginal buildings.
C) are imposed on less than 5 percent of the rental housings in the U.S.
D) exist in only a handful of U.S. cities.
E) None of the above is correct.

Difficulty: **Easy**

40. Rent controls predictably lead to:
A) a shortage of rental housing and lower maintenance conditions.
B) increased construction of rental apartments to deal with shortages.
C) favoritism in the rationing of apartments toward people with low incomes.
D) (A) and (C) are correct.
E) All of the above are correct.

Difficulty: **Easy**

41. Identify the demand and/or supply shifts which could correctly reflect the events described in the following *Wall Street Journal* headline, October 1994: "Aluminum Soars to Four-Year High as Strong Demand, Weak Supply Propel Market."
A) increase in demand and increase in supply
B) increase in demand and decrease in supply
C) decrease in demand and increase in supply

D) decrease in demand and decrease in supply
E) None of the above is correct.

Difficulty: **Moderate**

42. The headline for an article in the *Wall Street Journal* states, "Copper Prices Jump in Response to Shortages." Given the additional information that copper sales were also increasing, which of the following could correctly reflect the events in the copper market?
A) The supply of copper decreased.
B) The supply of copper increased.
C) The demand for copper increased.
D) The demand for copper decreased.
E) (A) and (D) are correct.

Difficulty: **Moderate**

43. In the July 1995 *New York Times* the following headline appeared, "Copper Prices Surge as a Drop in Supply Reflects Brisk Demand." If one knows the correct use of economic terminology, one concludes that:
A) the headline incorrectly used the word "supply" for "inventories."
B) the headline incorrectly implies that an increase in demand causes a decrease in supply.
C) the headline implies that a decrease in supply has taken place, but its incorrect use of economic terminology does not permit the reader to know whether or not this is the intended meaning of the headline.
D) All of the above are correct.
E) None of the above is correct.

Difficulty: **Moderate**

44. In 1994, the U.S. imports of automotive products exceeded the exports. If these imports had been excluded from the U.S. market:
A) U.S. production of automobiles would have expanded, automobile prices would have been unchanged, and U.S. jobs would have been saved.
B) prices of automobiles in the U.S. would have increased substantially.
C) prices of automobiles in the U.S. would have decreased substantially.
D) there would have been no impact on production, employment, or prices in the U.S. automobile market.
E) None of the above is correct.

Difficulty: **Hard**

45. The three basic methods used from the 1930s to the present to prop up farm incomes did not include:
A) price floors maintained by government purchases of surplus agricultural commodities.
B) incentives for farmers to idle part of their land.
C) price ceilings on farm commodities to make the U.S. market less attractive to foreign suppliers of agricultural commodities.
D) a direct subsidy if the market price of certain agricultural commodities fell below a target price.
E) (B) and (D) are correct.

Difficulty: **Easy**

46. In the battle against illegal drug use in the U.S., a successful educational campaign to explain the destructive effects of illegal drugs, in the absence of other changes in market forces, would:
   A) reduce the sale of illegal drugs and lower their price.
   B) reduce the sale of illegal drugs and raise their price.
   C) increase the sale of illegal drugs and lower their price.
   D) increase the sale of illegal drugs and raise their price.
   E) (B) and (D) are correct.

   Difficulty: **Easy**

47. In the battle against illegal drug use in the U.S., subsidies paid to South American farmers which caused them to shift their production from cocoa to other crops, in the absence of other changes in market forces, would:
   A) reduce the sale of illegal drugs and lower their price.
   B) reduce the sale of illegal drugs and raise their price.
   C) increase the sale of illegal drugs and lower their price.
   D) increase the sale of illegal drugs and raise their price.
   E) (C) or (D) are correct.

   Difficulty: **Easy**

48. The increased flow of cocaine to American cities and its falling price is consistent with which of the following explanations?
   A) The demand for cocaine is increasing by a larger amount than the increase in supply of cocaine.
   B) The demand for cocaine is increasing by a smaller amount than the increase in supply of cocaine.
   C) The demand for cocaine is decreasing by a larger amount than the decrease in the supply of cocaine.
   D) The demand for cocaine is decreasing by a smaller amount than the increase in the supply of cocaine.
   E) (B) and (D) are correct.

   Difficulty: **Hard**

49. The nonclearing markets theory suggests that markets do not clear because economic agents:
   A) are trying to increase combined revenues from their activities in related markets.
   B) react both to price signals and quantity signals.
   C) expect a disequilibrium in one market will have desirable spillover effects in a related market.
   D) deliberately create a disequilibrium.
   E) All of the above are correct.

   Difficulty: **Easy**

50. The law of demand states that there is a(n) ______ relationship between price and quantity demanded.
   A) direct.
   B) positive.
   C) inverse.

D) normative.
E) All of the above are correct.

Difficulty: **Easy**

51. If the supply curve is positively sloped, then there is a(n) _____ relationship between price and quantity supplied.
A) negative.
B) positive.
C) inverse.
D) normative.
E) (B) and (D) are correct.

Difficulty: **Easy**

52. If one knows that demand has increased and supply decreased, then one also knows that:
A) equilibrium price has increased and equilibrium quantity increased.
B) equilibrium quantity has decreased and equilibrium price may have increased or decreased or remained the same.
C) equilibrium price has fallen and equilibrium quantity may have increased or decreased or remained the same.
D) equilibrium price has increased and equilibrium quantity may have increased or decreased or remained the same.
E) None of the above is correct.

Difficulty: **Moderate**

53. If one knows that demand has decreased and supply increased, then one also knows that:
A) equilibrium price has increased and equilibrium quantity increased.
B) equilibrium quantity has increased and equilibrium price may have increased or decreased or remained the same.
C) equilibrium price has fallen and equilibrium quantity may have increased or decreased or remained the same.
D) equilibrium quantity has decreased and equilibrium price may have increased or decreased or remained the same.
E) None of the above is correct.

Difficulty: **Moderate**

54. If one knows that demand has increased and supply increased, then one also knows that:
A) equilibrium price has increased and equilibrium quantity increased.
B) equilibrium quantity has increased and equilibrium price may have increased or decreased or remained the same.
C) equilibrium price has fallen and equilibrium quantity may have increased or decreased or remained the same.
D) equilibrium price has increased and equilibrium quantity may have increased or decreased or remained the same.
E) None of the above is correct.

Difficulty: **Moderate**

55. If one knows that demand has increased, then one also knows that:
A) equilibrium price has increased and equilibrium quantity may have increased or decreased or remained the same.
B) equilibrium quantity has decreased and equilibrium price may have increased or decreased or remained the same.
C) equilibrium price has fallen and equilibrium quantity may have increased or decreased or remained the same.
D) equilibrium price has increased and equilibrium quantity increased.
E) None of the above is correct.

Difficulty: **Moderate**

56. If one knows that demand has decreased, then one also knows that:
A) equilibrium price has decreased and equilibrium quantity has increased.
B) equilibrium quantity has increased and equilibrium price may have increased or decreased.
C) equilibrium price has decreased and equilibrium quantity has decreased.
D) equilibrium quantity has decreased and equilibrium price may have increased or decreased.
E) None of the above is correct.

Difficulty: **Moderate**

57. If one knows that supply has increased, then one also knows that:
A) equilibrium price has decreased and equilibrium quantity has increased.
B) equilibrium quantity has increased and equilibrium price may have increased or decreased.
C) equilibrium price has decreased and equilibrium quantity has decreased.
D) equilibrium quantity has decreased and equilibrium price may have increased or decreased.
E) None of the above is correct.

Difficulty: **Moderate**

58. When price is _____ the equilibrium level, firms may detect the existence of a _____ by observing _____ in their inventory levels.
A) below, shortage, increases.
B) below, surplus, decreases.
C) above, shortage, decreases.
D) above, surplus, increases.
E) None of the above is correct.

Difficulty: **Moderate**

59. When price is _____ the equilibrium level, firms may detect the existence of a _____ by observing _____ in their inventory levels.
A) below, shortage, decreases.
B) below, surplus, decreases.
C) above, shortage, increases.

D) above, surplus, decreases.
E) None of the above is correct.

Difficulty: **Moderate**

60. At a price _____ the equilibrium price, quantity _____ is greater than quantity _____ with a resulting _____ in the market.
A) above, demanded, supplied, surplus.
B) below, demanded, supplied, shortage.
C) below, supplied, demanded, shortage.
D) above, supplied, demanded, shortage.
E) None of the above is correct.

Difficulty: **Moderate**

61. At a price _____ the equilibrium price, quantity _____ is greater than quantity _____ with a resulting _____ in the market.
A) above, demanded, supplied, shortage.
B) below, demanded, supplied, surplus.
C) below, supplied, demanded, shortage.
D) above, supplied, demanded, surplus.
E) None of the above is correct.

Difficulty: **Moderate**

62. If price is _____ the equilibrium price, _____ in price will take place with a resulting _____ in quantity demanded and _____ in quantity supplied.
A) below, decreases, increase, decrease.
B) above, decreases, decrease, increase.
C) below, increases, decrease, increase.
D) above, increases, increase, decrease.
E) None of the above is correct.

Difficulty: **Moderate**

63. If price is _____ the equilibrium price, _____ in price will take place with a resulting _____ in quantity demanded and _____ in quantity supplied.
A) below, decreases, increase, decrease.
B) above, decreases, increase, decrease.
C) below, decreases, decrease, increase.
D) above, increases, increase, decrease.
E) None of the above is correct.

Difficulty: **Moderate**

64. A change in which of the following will <u>not</u> cause a shift of the demand curve?
A) consumer tastes
B) consumer incomes
C) prices of substitute goods
D) technology

E) the number of consumers in the market

Difficulty: **Easy**

65. A change in which of the following will cause a shift in the supply curve?
A) price of the good itself
B) consumer preferences
C) consumer income
D) prices of inputs
E) the number of consumers in the market

Difficulty: **Easy**

66. A movement upward along a supply curve in response to a change in price is a(n):
A) increase in supply.
B) increase in quantity supplied.
C) decrease in supply.
D) decrease in quantity supplied.
E) None of the above is correct.

Difficulty: **Easy**

67. An increased price of steel will cause:
A) a decrease in the demand for autos.
B) a decrease in the supply of autos.
C) an increase in the demand for autos.
D) an increase in the supply for autos.
E) no changes in the demand for or supply of autos.

Difficulty: **Easy**

68. A leftward shift of a demand curve represents a(n):
A) increase in demand.
B) increase in quantity demanded.
C) decrease in demand.
D) decrease in quantity demanded.
E) (C) and (D) are correct.

Difficulty: **Easy**

69. A rightward shift of a supply curve represents a(n):
A) increase in supply.
B) increase in quantity supplied.
C) decrease in supply.
D) decrease in quantity supplied.
E) None of the above is correct.

Difficulty:

70. When a price ceiling is set at a level where it affects the market, the result is:
A) a shortage.
B) a surplus.

C) excess supply.
D) that quantity supplied is greater than quantity demanded.
E) (B), (C), and (D) are correct.

Difficulty: **Easy**

71. When a price floor is set at a level where it affects the market, the result is:
A) a shortage.
B) a surplus.
C) an excess supply.
D) that quantity supplied is greater than quantity demanded.
E) **(B), (C), and (D) are correct.**

Difficulty: **Easy**

72. The effects of rent controls in New York City do <u>not</u> include which of the following?
A) non-price rationing of apartments for rent
B) lower maintenance
C) reduced supply of non-rent controlled co-ops
D) a very low vacancy rate for rent-controlled apartments
E) None of the above is correct.

Difficulty: **Moderate**

Short Answer

Write the word or phrase that best completes each statement or answers the question.

1. What is the "ceteris paribus assumption," and why is it used?
Answer: The term refers to the simplifying assumption made to isolate the relationship that exists between the price of the good and the quantity demanded. Other variables influence the demand for a good, but if one is to understand this crucial relationship it is necessary to ignore, temporarily, the effect that other variables have on the amount of a good that a person desires to purchase.

2. When a market is in equilibrium, why do demanders have no incentive to try to purchase a larger quantity of the good they are buying at the existing price?
Answer: An equilibrium is reached when, at the existing price, demanders are purchasing the quantity they wish to purchase. Even if additional units were available at the same price, the demanders would not purchase them because the extra benefit to them from additional units is less than the existing price; i.e., their demand curve shows that extra benefits of units beyond the equilibrium quantity are worth less to them than the current price. What is important to them is that they can actually purchase the quantity that their demand curve indicates at the existing price.

3. If one knows that the demand for hamburgers has increased and the supply of hamburgers has increased, but one does not know how large the increases are, it is possible, to predict the direction of change in only price or quantity. Explain.
Answer: If one knows that both demand and supply have increased, then one knows that both curves have shifted to the right. The intersection of the new demand and supply curves must be to the right of the original equilibrium quantity. Equilibrium quantity will increase, although without knowing the size of the shifts one cannot say how large the

increase is. The new demand and supply curve may intersect at a higher or lower price depending on the relative size of the shifts. One cannot predict the direction of change in equilibrium price unless one knows the relative size of the shifts.

4. **If a country which engages in no international trade begins to import good X and export good Y, other things remaining the same, what happens to the domestic price of X and Y? Why does it happen?**
Answer: As more of good X is imported its price will fall, and as more of good Y is exported its price will rise. The foreign demanders will begin to compete with domestic demanders for good Y and will bid up its price. Foreign suppliers will begin to compete with domestic suppliers of good X and will bid its price down.

5. **Explain why apartment building owners will decrease the amount of maintenance work they perform on an apartment building when rent controls are imposed. What will the consequences be for the number of apartments available for rent in the long run?**
Answer: Owners are trying to reduce the cost of maintaining the building in the effort to maintain a competitive rate of return on their investment. The failure to perform adequate maintenance will shrink the existing supply of apartments, and the below-normal rate of return on investment in apartment buildings will discourage the construction of new buildings. The long-run result will be that the number of apartments available for rent will either shrink or grow at a slower pace than would be the case without rent controls in place.

6. **The increased flow of cocaine into American cities, and the falling price of cocaine indicate that the drug war is being lost. Explain.**
Answer: Drug policy is intended to decrease the demand for cocaine and decrease its supply. However, levels of cocaine use and cocaine price suggest that, at best, the supply curve is moving outward faster than the demand curve for cocaine is shifting inward. It is possible that the demand curve for cocaine is also shifting outward but at a slower pace than the supply shift. In any case, a higher level of cocaine use is a relatively unambiguous indicator of how badly the drug war is going.

Chapter 3:

Consumer Preferences and Choice

Multiple-Choice

Choose the one alternative that best completes the statement or answers the question.

1. When studying the theory of consumer behavior, economists assume that the consumer tries to:
A) maximize total level of income, given relative prices.
B) maximize utility, given income and prices.
C) minimize the rate at which the consumer is willing to trade one good for another.
D) minimize the level of disutility associated with the consumption of various goods.
E) None of the above is correct.

Difficulty: **Easy**

2. Suppose that there are only two goods on the market, X and Y. Also, suppose that the price of good X is $15 per unit while the price of a unit of Y is $45. The trade-off between goods X and Y is:
A) one unit of X for 1/3 units of Y.
B) one unit of X for one unit of Y.
C) three units of X for one unit of Y.
D) (A) and (C) are correct.
E) (A) and (B) are correct.

Difficulty: **Moderate**

3. Given prices and income, the budget line of the typical consumer shows:
A) that as the consumer spends more on one good, he or she spends less on other goods.
B) that a trade-off faces the consumer in the consumption of goods.
C) that the consumer faces a limit to the quantity of goods that he or she can purchase.
D) that total income equals total spending on all goods.
E) All of the above are correct.

Difficulty: **Easy**

4. When economists describe the utility of a certain good, they are referring to:
A) the demand for the good.
B) the satisfaction gained by an individual when the good is consumed.
C) the usefulness of the good to an individual when the good is consumed.
D) the rate at which consumers are willing to trade one good for another.
E) None of the above is correct.

Difficulty: **Easy**

5. Suppose that a consumer is faced with several bundles of goods and is asked to rank the goods in order of preference. The most important, if not the only, determinant of the ranking will be:
   A) the absolute prices of each bundle, given consumer income.
   B) the price of each bundle relative to every other bundle.
   C) both the income of the consumer and the relative prices of each bundle.
   D) the utility received from the consumption of each bundle relative to other bundles.
   E) None of the above is correct.

   Difficulty: **Moderate**

6. Suppose you are given three bundles of goods, and these are bundles X, Y, and Z. Then you are asked to rank the bundles in order of your preferences, which one of the ordering is <u>not</u> possible?
   A) X is indifferent to Y, Y is preferred to Z, so X is preferred to Z.
   B) Y is preferred to X, X is indifferent to Z, so Y is indifferent to Z.
   C) Z is preferred to X, X is preferred to Y, so Z is preferred to Y.
   D) X is indifferent to Y, Y is indifferent to Z, so X is indifferent to Z.
   E) All of the above are correct.

   Difficulty: **Moderate**

7. When an extra glass of wine is consumed, the total utility gained from the consumption changes by an amount equal to:
   A) the price of the extra glass of wine.
   B) the average utility of all goods consumed.
   C) the total utility gained from the consumption of the wine divided by the number of glasses of wine consumed.
   D) the marginal utility gained or lost when the additional glass of wine is consumed.
   E) zero, because total utility is at a maximum.

   Difficulty: **Moderate**

8. When you consume extra slices of apple pie (assuming that you like it), after some point the change in total utility caused by the consumption of each extra slice:
   A) falls because of the law of diminishing marginal utility.
   B) rises because of the law of demand.
   C) rises because total utility must be rising or else you would not consume an extra slice.
   D) falls because of the negative relationship between price and quantity.
   E) None of the above is correct.

   Difficulty: **Easy**

9. Suppose that you consume two goods, A and B, and the marginal utility of the last unit of A consumed is six times as great as the marginal utility of the last unit of B consumed. The price of A, though, is only three times the price of B. This disequilibrium between the amounts of A and B consumed can be resolved by:
   A) consuming less of good A and more of good B.
   B) increasing the consumption of both A and B.
   C) consuming more of good A and less of good B.
   D) decreasing the consumption of both A and B.

E) refusing to pay three times more for an extra unit of A than you pay for an extra unit of B.

Difficulty: **Moderate**

10. A curve that shows a constant level of utility as an individual consumes different combinations of two goods, X and Y, is the:
A) budget line.
B) demand curve.
C) marginal utility curve.
D) indifference curve.
E) total utility curve.

Difficulty: **Easy**

11. Typical indifference curves exhibit all of the following characteristics <u>except</u> that:
A) as the consumer moves down and along any of his or her indifference curves, the slope of the curve changes and becomes flatter.
B) the indifference curves are negatively sloped, and this indicates that consumers are willing to substitute one good for another.
C) as the consumer substitutes one good for another along an indifference curve, the overall level of total utility changes.
D) higher indifference curves correspond to higher levels of total utility.
E) the indifference curves cannot intersect each other.

Difficulty: **Moderate**

12. Suppose that you consume two goods, A and B, and that $MU_A/P_A = 1.5$ and $MU_B/P_B = 3.5$. With a given income and prices, the consumer should:
A) purchase less of good A and more of good B.
B) purchase more of good A and less of good B.
C) stop his or her purchases because an equilibrium has been achieved.
D) purchase all of good A and none of good B.
E) purchase all of good B and none of good A because the law of diminishing marginal utility holds.

Difficulty: **Moderate**

13. If the consumer is initially in equilibrium with some combination of goods X and Y, a decrease in the price of one good:
A) shifts the budget line toward the origin, so the consumer moves to a lower indifference curve.
B) lowers the real income of the consumer, so less of both goods can be consumed.
C) rotates the budget line toward the origin and the consumer moves to a lower indifference curve.
D) shifts the budget line and indifference curve outward, so the consumer's overall utility level remains unchanged.
E) rotates the budget line outward and away from the origin, and the consumer moves to a higher indifference curve.

Difficulty: **Moderate**

14. If there was some way that you could measure the total utility generated for your friend when he consumes peaches, and you observed your friend's total utility increasing, you could conclude that:
    A) marginal utility is positive.
    B) marginal utility is zero.
    C) marginal utility is negative.
    D) the slope of the total utility curve is increasing at an increasing rate.
    E) None of the above is correct.

    Difficulty: **Moderate**

15. Suppose that you are considering the purchase of two goods, X and Y. You may consume 7 units of X and 5 units of Y. The prices of both X and Y are $1 per unit, and you only have $15 to spend. The total utility generated from consuming 7 units of X is 70 and the total utility generated from consuming 5 units of Y is 50. Given this information, and assuming that you want to maximize your total utility, you should:
    A) buy all X and no Y.
    B) buy all Y and no X.
    C) buy less X and more Y.
    D) buy less Y and more X.
    E) there is not enough information provided to make a decision.

    Difficulty: **Hard**

16. Leon Jones is a rational individual and so he is a utility maximizer. Leon has a budget of $270 that he plans to allocate by purchasing 5 units of good X at a price of $30 per unit and 6 units of Y at a price of $20 per unit. If the marginal unity of the 5th unit of good X is 30 utils and the marginal utility of the 6th unit of Y is 40, Leon should:
    A) buy fewer units of Y and more units of X.
    B) buy X and Y as initially planned.
    C) buy fewer units of X and more units of Y.
    D) buy the same units of Y but fewer units of X.
    E) not enough information is provided to make a decision.

    Difficulty: **Hard**

17. Suppose that a consumer chooses a point on one of his or her indifference curves that represents a combination of two goods, X and Y, such that the marginal utility of X (MU_X) is 3 and the marginal utility of Y (MU_Y) is 1. The marginal rate of substitution of X for Y at that point is:
    A) 1/3.
    B) 3/1.
    C) 3Y/X.
    D) Y/3X.
    E) Cannot be determined from the information provided.

    Difficulty: **Moderate**

18. John Jones likes beer and pretzels. He chooses a combination of beer and pretzels such that MU_P equals 3 and MU_B equals 2 (P represents pretzels and B represents beer). The marginal rate of substitution of pretzels for beer is:
    A) 3/2.

B) 2/3.
C) 3/5.
D) 2/5.
E) 5/3.

Difficulty: **Moderate**

19. Suppose that your marginal rate of substitution of Coca-Cola for Pepsi-Cola is constant and equal to 1. If the price of Coca-Cola is $.50 per unit while the price of Pepsi-Cola is $.65 per unit, utility maximizing behavior on your part would be to:
A) divide your weekly expenditures on soft drinks between Coke and Pepsi, but always consume at least one more bottle of Coke than Pepsi.
B) reach a corner solution on your indifference map and purchase no Pepsi; all of your soft drink expenditures are allocated to Coca Cola.
C) reach a corner solution on your indifference map and purchase no Coke; all of your soft drink expenditures are allocated to Pepsi Cola.
D) divide your weekly expenditures on soft drinks between Coke and Pepsi, but always consume at least one more bottle of Pepsi than Coke.
E) not enough information is provided to reach a conclusion.

Difficulty: **Hard**

20. Suppose that fourteen-year-old Susan receives a weekly allowance of $10. She allocates this allowance on pizza and root beer. The price of a small pizza is $5.00 and the price of a bottle of root beer is $.50. If Susan's budget line is plotted with root beer on the horizontal axis, then which one of the following statements is correct?
A) The slope of Susan's budget line is –2.
B) The budget line intercepts the vertical axis at 5 pizzas.
C) The slope of Susan's budget line is +1.
D) The budget line intercepts the horizontal axis at 10 bottles of root beer.
E) The slope of Susan's budget line is -.10.

Difficulty: **Moderate**

21. John likes cheeseburgers and french-fries. His marginal utility from an extra cheeseburger is six utils and his marginal utility from an extra order of French-fries is four utils. If the price of a cheeseburger is $1.50 and the price of an order of fries is $.50, then in order to maximize his utility, John should:
A) consume more cheeseburgers and fewer fries.
B) maintain his current consumption bundle of cheeseburgers and french fries.
C) consume more fries and fewer cheeseburgers.
D) reduce his consumption of fries but leave his consumption of cheeseburgers unchanged.
E) Not enough information is provided about John's preference function in order to reach a conclusion.

Difficulty: **Moderate**

22. You observe your friend consuming goods X and Y and exhausting her income. You friend is consuming X and Y in amount such that her $MU_X/P_X = 17$ and $MU_Y/P_Y = 23$. Assuming that your friend is attempting to maximize her utility, you should recommend that she:
A) consume more of good Y and less of good X.

B) consume more of good X and less of good Y.
C) consume more of both good X and good Y.
D) consume less of both good X and good Y.
E) None of the above is correct.

Difficulty: **Moderate**

23. Jan likes boiled shrimp and crab soup, she purchases these items in amounts such that the marginal utility of the last order of shrimp eaten is 60 utils and the marginal utility of the last bowl of soup eaten is 30 utils. If the price of an order of shrimp is $3 and the price of an order of soup is $2, and she exhausts her income, Jan should:
A) spend more of her money on crab soup and less on shrimp.
B) spend less of her money on both shrimp and crab soup.
C) spend more of her money on shrimp and less on crab soup.
D) increase her consumption of both shrimp and soup.
E) None of the above is correct.

Difficulty: **Moderate**

24. Indifference curve analysis has a major advantage over marginal utility analysis because:
A) indifference curve analysis requires weaker assumptions about consumer behavior and activity.
B) the indifference curve model allows us to directly observe consumers' reactions to price changes.
C) we know whether an individual is on his indifference curve but we don't know how to accurately measure utility.
D) we can assign exact numbers to indifference curve analysis but we can't in marginal utility analysis.
E) All of the above are correct.

Difficulty: **Easy**

25. Suppose that John's marginal rate of substitution of good X for good Y is less than the price of good X relative to good Y. If quantities of good Y are measured on the vertical axis and quantities of good X are measured on the horizontal axis in John's budget constraint diagram, and assuming that John's budget will permit, he will:
A) buy more of good X and move down his budget line.
B) buy more of good X and move up his budget line.
C) buy more of good Y and move down his budget line.
D) buy more of good Y and move down his budget line.
E) not enough information is provided to determine an answer.

Difficulty: **Moderate**

26. Suppose that John's marginal rate of substitution of good X for good Y is greater than the relative price of good X in terms of good Y. Assuming that a diagram of John's budget constraint reflects quantities of good Y measured on the vertical axis and quantities of good X measured on the horizontal axis and also assuming that John's budget will permit, he will:
A) buy more of good X and move down the budget line.
B) buy more of good X and move up the budget line.
C) buy more of good Y and move down the budget line.

D) buy more of good Y and move up the budget line.
E) None of the above is correct.

Difficulty: **Moderate**

27. Suppose that Henry's indifference map is such that his indifference curves are concave to the origin and higher curves lie farther from the origin. If Henry faces given prices for goods X and Y, and he has a limited money income, we can conclude that:
A) Henry will attain an equilibrium when he spends all of his money on either X or Y.
B) a tangency point between one of Henry's indifference curves and his budget line will represent a minimization of utility, not a maximization.
C) a corner solution will generate Henry's consumption optimum.
D) Henry's budget line will be tangent to one of his indifference curves from above, not below.
E) All of the above are correct.

Difficulty: **Moderate**

28. Joe's marginal rate of substitution of good X for good Y is equal to 6. If the price of good X is $1 per unit and the price of good Y is $.60 per unit, then Joe:
A) will change his consumption of goods X and Y until the marginal rate of substitution of X for Y is 5.
B) will substitute the less expensive Y for the more expensive X.
C) will substitute the more expensive X for the less expensive Y.
D) will continue to consume the same bundle of X and Y because he is in an equilibrium.
E) None of the above is correct.

Difficulty: **Moderate**

29. Suppose that commodity X is an economic "bad", while commodity Y is an economic good. Then an indifference curve between X and Y, with X plotted on the horizontal axis and Y plotted on the vertical, will:
A) not exist.
B) be upward sloping with higher indifference curves to the left.
C) be downward sloping with higher curves to the right.
D) be a vertical line with some positive horizontal intercept on the X-axis.
E) show that more of X is preferred to less as long as all other things remain the same.

Difficulty: **Hard**

30. If an indifference map for goods X and Y (X is plotted on the horizontal axis and Y is plotted on the vertical) plots as a vertical line with a positive intercept, this suggests that:
A) the consumer has a definite marginal rate of substitution between goods X and Y.
B) the consumer can achieve higher levels of satisfaction by consuming more of X even if no Y is consumed.
C) if the consumer gives up some X, then he or she is worse off no matter how much Y he consumes.
D) given income and prices, a budget line will generate a corner solution in which only X is consumed.
E) All of the above are correct.

Difficulty: **Hard**

31. For an indifference curve that is convex to the origin, the marginal rate of substitution between the two goods:
A) diminishes as more and more of one good is substituted for another good.
B) is the slope of an indifference curve.
C) is the ratio of the marginal utilities of the two goods.
D) is equal to the relative price ratio when a consumer is in equilibrium.
E) All of the above are correct.

Difficulty: **Moderate**

32. Suppose that in some way, we could measure an individual's utility received when a good was consumed. We can conclude that:
A) all goods will be consumed up to the point where the marginal utility of each extra good consumed is zero.
B) the consumer's marginal rate of substitution between any two goods would be the numerical value of the ratio of their marginal utilities.
C) the marginal utility of all goods would be equal when a consumer reached an optimal combination, given income and prices.
D) the consumer could not attain an optimal combination of goods because the amount of numbers that would need to be analyzed would be too overwhelming.
E) None of the above is correct.

Difficulty: **Moderate**

33. Suppose that an individual's money income increases by 10 percent, the price of good X increases by 6 percent, the price of good Y increases by 9 percent, and all income is spent on these two goods. The budget constraint for this individual will:
A) shift outward from the origin and exhibit a change in slope.
B) exhibit a parallel shift away from the origin.
C) shift inward toward the origin because the prices of both goods have increased in proportion to each other.
D) exhibit a parallel shift outward from the origin.
E) None of the above is correct.

Difficulty: **Moderate**

34. The typical household will maximize its utility by selecting that consumption bundle and allocating its expenditures among goods within the bundle so that:
A) the total utility of all goods is maximized.
B) the marginal utility of the last dollar spent on some goods is greater than the last dollar spent on other goods.
C) the marginal utility gained from spending the last dollar on each good is equal.
D) the marginal utility of the last dollar spent on each good is equal.
E) it is impossible to tell because we cannot get a cardinal measure of utility.

Difficulty: **Easy**

35. When X and Y are being consumed, an individual consumer will achieve an equilibrium when:

A) the marginal rate of substitution for an indifference curve equals the relative price ratio of the goods.
B) $MU_X/MU_Y = P_X/P_Y$.
C) the indifference curve is tangent to the budget line.
D) the marginal utility gained from spending the last dollar on each good is equal.
E) All of the above are correct.

Difficulty: **Moderate**

36. Suppose that you observe an individual's indifference map and the indifference curves are L-shaped with higher levels of utility indicated by curves to the right. Such curves suggest that:
A) the two goods being consumed are prefect substitutes for each other.
B) the consumer does not exhibit rational behavior in consumption.
C) it is possible to have a higher level of utility by having more of one of the goods and no less of the other.
D) the goods are perfect complements for each other.
E) the indifference curves will be concave to the origin.

Difficulty: **Moderate**

37. When the consumer faces two goods and a given income, the absolute value of the slope of his budget line is the:
A) the ratio of the prices of the two goods.
B) income of consumers divided by the price of each good.
C) ratio of this year's income to last year's income.
D) ratio of different levels of income relative to her given income.
E) None of the above is correct.

Difficulty: **Easy**

38. For any given budget line, an increase in the price of one good while all other goods remain constant:
A) increases the amounts of both goods that the consumer can purchase.
B) causes the budget line to rotate about the intercept on the axis of the good with the constant price, and the rotation is toward the origin.
C) shifts the budget line away from the origin.
D) shifts the budget line toward the origin.
E) None of the above is correct.

Difficulty: **Easy**

39. An increase in the amount of money income received by the consumer:
A) shifts the budget line outward since more of both goods can be consumed if prices remain constant.
B) rotates the budget line outward since more of at least one good can be consumed.
C) shifts the budget line toward the origin.
D) rotates the budget line toward the origin since less of at least one good is consumed.
E) None of the above is correct.

Difficulty: **Easy**

40. If you consume two goods, X and Y, and $MU_X > MU_Y$, then we can conclude that:
A) you will not buy any of good Y.
B) you will not be consuming the two goods in their optimal quantities.
C) you will buy more of good X and less of good Y.
D) you are willing to pay more for good X than for good Y.
E) None of the above is correct.

Difficulty: **Moderate**

41. All of the following statements are incorrect <u>except</u>:
A) Once the consumer attains a point on the budget line, he remains at that point because total utility is maximized.
B) The consumer's optimal consumption basket will be on or below his budget line.
C) The consumer maximizes his or her utility by choosing the consumption bundle satisfying the budget constraint at the point where the ratio of the marginal utility to price is the same for all goods.
D) The fact that consumers experience diminishing marginal utility from consuming additional units if a good has little, if anything, to do with the negative slope of the demand curve for good.
E) When the marginal utility of a good is increasing, the demand curve for the good is horizontal.

Difficulty: **Moderate**

42. If good X is plotted on the horizontal axis and good Y is plotted on the vertical axis, then an increase in the price of good X from $10 to $15 per unit while the price of good Y remains unchanged at $15 per unit causes the budget line to:
A) rotate about the horizontal intercept on the X-axis so less Y can be bought if no X is purchased.
B) rotate about the horizontal intercept on the X-axis, so more Y can be purchased if no X is bought.
C) rotate about the vertical intercept on the Y-axis, so more X can be purchased if no Y is purchased.
D) rotate about the vertical intercept on the Y-axis so that less X can be purchased for each additional unit of Y purchased.
E) None of the above is correct.

Difficulty: **Moderate**

43. Suppose that you observe a preference map where quantities of good Y are measured on the vertical axis and quantities of good X are measured on the horizontal axis. If indifference curves in the preference map are horizontal lines, then we can conclude that:
A) good X has negative utility in consumption.
B) good Y has positive utility in consumption, so it is an economic good.
C) good X is an economic good.
D) good Y is an economic bad.
E) None of the above is correct.

Difficulty: **Hard**

44. When we make the assumption that utility can be ordinarily measured, we assume all of the following <u>except</u> that:
A) the consumer is able to rank his preferences.
B) the consumer is able to measure the total and marginal utility received when a basket of goods and an additional unit of the good is consumed.
C) the consumer's preferences are transitive.
D) the consumer is not satiated with the amount of goods being consumed, so more goods will be preferred to fewer goods.
E) None of the above is correct.

Difficulty: **Moderate**

45. Suppose that you observe an individual's preference map and you see only one indifference curve. That curve bisects the 90°-angle formed by the intersection of the horizontal and vertical axes. If good X is measured on the horizontal axis and good Y is measured on the vertical axis, then we conclude that:
A) good X has negative but increasing marginal utility.
B) good Y has positive but diminishing marginal utility.
C) good Y has zero marginal utility.
D) good X is an economic good.
E) None of the above is correct.

Difficulty: **Hard**

46. Indifference curves are usually:
A) negatively sloped.
B) nonintersecting.
C) convex to the origin.
D) All of the above are correct.
E) (A) and (B) are correct.

Difficulty: **Easy**

47. Suppose that money income increases but prices remain the same. We would expect to see:
A) a decrease in the slope of the budget line.
B) an increase in the intercept(s) of the budget line but no change in its slope.
C) a reduction in the intercept(s) of the budget line but no change in its slope.
D) a rotation of the budget line about its vertical intercept.
E) None of the above is correct.

Difficulty:

47. Suppose that an individual has a given income and purchases two goods, X and Y. If the quantity of good X is measured on the horizontal axis and the quantity of good Y is measured on the vertical axis, and if P_X is the price of good X while P_Y is the price of good Y, then the slope of the budget line is:
A) $-P_X/P_Y$.
B) $-(X/Y)$.
C) $P_Y + P_X$.

D) $-P_Y/P_X$.
E) None of the above answers are correct.

Difficulty: **Easy**

48. An assumption of indifference curve analysis is that preferences are transitive, this means:
A) that indifference curves are convex to the origin.
B) that indifference curves are concave to the origin.
C) that indifference curves are L-shaped.
D) that indifference curves cannot cross each other.
E) that indifference curves have a positive slope.

Difficulty: **Moderate**

49. Global products:
A) are introduced simultaneously in most countries and have little or no local variations.
B) are evidence of the diverging trend in tastes around the world.
C) are successful because significant variations in style are developed in order to introduce such products in so many markets.
D) have proven successful despite the spectacular failure of products such as the Gillette Sensor Razor introduced globally in 1990.
E) None of the above is correct.

Difficulty: **Easy**

50. Utility-maximizing consumers make decisions subject to which of the following constraints?
A) output prices
B) income
C) time
D) All of the above are correct.
E) None of the above is correct.

Difficulty: **Easy**

51. The impact of government warnings about a possible cancer risk from diet sodas is properly reflected in which of the following components of constrained utility maximization?
A) price of goods
B) the budget line
C) indifference curves
D) All of the above are correct.
E) None of the above is correct.

Difficulty: **Moderate**

52. Suppose that water is represented on the horizontal axis of a graph representing constrained utility maximization, and other goods are represented on the vertical axis. If government enacts a system of rationing which limits the number of gallons of water each individual may purchase at any price, and is successful in preventing anyone from getting around the restriction (e.g., by purchasing water at a higher price on the black market), then:

A) the shape of the buyer's indifference curves will change until the buyer's ration of water is consistent with achieving the same level of total utility as was achieved before the rationing was introduced.
B) the budget line for the buyer will become horizontal at the quantity of water allowed to each buyer under the rationing policy.
C) the buyer will maximize utility subject to the new constraints of the problem and will be better off, i.e., will reach a higher indifference curve than that reached before rationing was introduced.
D) the buyer will maximize utility subject to the new constraints of the problem wand will be worse off, i.e., will reach a lower indifference curve than that reached before rationing was introduced.
E) (A) and (B) are correct.

Difficulty: **Moderate**

53. Suppose that gasoline is represented on the horizontal axis of a graph representing constrained utility maximization, and other goods are represented on the vertical axis. If government enacts a system of rationing which limits the number of gallons of gasoline each individual may purchase at any price, and is successful in preventing anyone from getting around the restriction (e.g. by purchasing gasoline at a higher price on the black market), then:
A) the budget line for the buyer will become horizontal at the quantity of gasoline allowed to each buyer under the rationing policy.
B) the budget line for the buyer will become vertical at the quantity of gasoline allowed each buyer under the rationing policy.
C) the slope of the budget line will not be affected by the successful introduction of rationing.
D) the indifference curves will rotate until they are tangent with the budget line at the quantity of gasoline allowed for each buyer under the rationing system.
E) None of the above is correct.

Difficulty: **Moderate**

54. If government introduces rationing of a good:
A) the constraints under which individual utility maximization takes place are changed.
B) individuals have an incentive to purchase the good at a higher price in the black market.
C) the rationing is more likely to be binding or restrictive on high-income people than low-income people.
D) None of the above is correct.
E) All of the above are correct.

Difficulty: **Moderate**

55. The Theory of revealed preference:
A) has practical uses in the study of economic phenomena because it leads to the understanding that consumer tastes can be inferred or revealed by observing actual choices in the market place.
B) was developed by Paul Samuelson and John Hicks.
C) is important, in part, because as an alternative we cannot be sure that consumers will provide trustworthy answers to direct questions about their preferences.
D) is based, in part, on the idea that if a consumer purchases a collection of commodities described as market basket A rather than another collection described as market basket

B, even though market basket A is not cheaper than B, we can assume that the consumer prefers A to B.
E) All of the above are correct.

Difficulty: **Moderate**

56. In the derivation of an indifference curve through revealed preference, the "zone of ignorance" consists of:
A) an area beneath the budget line.
B) an area, relative to the actual combination of commodities chosen by the consumer, consisting of combinations of commodities containing more of one good and an equal or greater amount of the other good.
C) all combinations of commodities represented by points on the budget line other than the actual combination chosen by the consumer.
D) all points not included in (A), (B), and (C).
E) (A) and (C) are correct.

Difficulty: **Moderate**

57. If a consumer purchases market basket A rather than market B:
A) even though A is not cheaper than B, we can infer that the consumer prefers A to B.
B) even though A is not cheaper than B, we can infer that the consumer prefers B to A.
C) even though B is not cheaper than A, we can infer that the consumer prefers B to A.
D) (B) and (C) are correct.
E) no inference may be drawn regarding the preferences of the person for A and B.

Difficulty: **Hard**

58. Which of the following is <u>not</u> an assumption made in the theory of revealed preference?
A) The tastes of the customer are unchanged over the period of the analysis.
B) The consumer's tastes are consistent, so that if the consumer purchases basket A rather than basket B, the consumer will prefer A to B.
C) The consumer's tastes are intransitive, so that if the consumer prefers A to B and B to C, it does not necessarily follow that the consumer will prefer A to C.
D) The consumer will be introduced to purchase any basket of commodities if its price is lowered sufficiently.
E) All of the above are correct.

Difficulty: **Moderate**

59. Consumers seek to:
A) maximize marginal utility.
B) minimize total satisfaction.
C) maximize total utility.
D) purchase all units of a good with positive marginal utility.
E) All of the above are correct.

Difficulty: **Easy**

60. The principle of diminishing marginal utility states that as a person consumes additional units of a good:
A) total utility must decrease.
B) increases in total utility eventually become smaller.
C) total utility decreases as marginal utility increases.
D) extra utility decreases but the size of increases in satisfaction do not.
E) extra utility is not affected until total utility is at a maximum.

Difficulty: **Easy**

61. Which of the following statements is <u>not</u> correct?
A) The "saturation point" occurs where total utility is at a maximum.
B) The "saturation point" occurs where marginal utility is zero.
C) The "saturation point" is reached by consuming all units of a good for which marginal utility is greater than or equal to zero.
D) Beyond the "saturation point" total utility decreases.
E) The "saturation point" represents the level of consumption of a good at which total utility is zero.

Difficulty: **Easy**

62. Which of the following statements is <u>not</u> correct?
A) Total utility increases over the range where marginal utility is positive.
B) Marginal utility increases until total utility is at a maximum and then marginal utility decreases.
C) Total utility is at a maximum when marginal utility is zero.
D) Marginal utility eventually becomes negative.
E) Total utility falls when marginal utility is negative.

Difficulty: **Moderate**

Quantity	Total Utility	Marginal Utility
1	25	25
2	42	17
3	57	
4	65	8
5	71	6
6	71	0
7	65	-6
8		-15
9	32	-18
10	11	-21
11	-20	-31
12	-62	-42

63. In the table above, the "saturation point" occurs at which quantity?
A) 1.
B) 3.
C) 6.

D) 11.
E) 12.

Difficulty: **Easy**

64. In the table above, the missing total utility and marginal utility figures are:
A) 80, 42.
B) 59, 60.
C) 71, 9.
D) 50, 15.
E) None of the above is correct.

Difficulty: **Moderate**

In the following marginal utility schedule, the person's income I = \$8. Also, P_a *= \$1 and* P_b *= \$2.*

# of Units	MU_a	MU_b
1	35	22
2	25	20
3	16	17
4	10	15
5	5	14
6	1	9

65. The consumer should purchase how many units of good A?
A) 1.
B) 2.
C) 3.
D) 4.
E) 6.

Difficulty: **Moderate**

66. The consumer should purchase how many units of good B?
A) 1.
B) 2.
C) 3.
D) 4.
E) 5.

Difficulty: **Moderate**

The marginal utility schedule of a person is represented below. The person's income I = \$24. Also, P_a *= \$2 and* P_b *= \$4.*

# of Units	MU_a	MU_b
1	9	16
2	6	12
3	3	8
4	2	4
5	1	2

67. The consumer should purchase how many units of good A?
A) 1.
B) 2.
C) 3.
D) 4.
E) 5.

Difficulty: **Moderate**

68. The consumer should purchase how many units of good B?
A) 1.
B) 2.
C) 3.
D) 4.
E) 5.

Difficulty: **Moderate**

The marginal utility schedule of a person is represented below. The person's income I = $8. Also, P_a *= $2, and* P_b *= $0.50.*

# of Units	MU_a	MU_b
1	40	15
2	30	8
3	20	7
4	10	5
5	5	3
6	2	2.5

69. The consumer should purchase how many units of good A?
A) 2.
B) 3.
C) 4.
D) 5.
E) 6.

Difficulty: **Moderate**

70. The consumer should purchase how many units of good B?
A) 2.
B) 3.
C) 4.
D) 5.
E) 6.

Difficulty: **Moderate**

71. The indifference curves for a "neuter" good are _____ in a case where the neuter good is measured on the horizontal axis.
A) horizontal
B) vertical

C) L-shapes
D) negatively sloped and straight
E) convex to the origin

Difficulty: **Moderate**

72. If the set of indifference curves for a person is negatively sloped and straight, then the MRS of good X for good Y is _____ as more of X and less of Y is chosen.
A) zero
B) infinite
C) constant
D) increasing
E) decreasing

Difficulty: **Moderate**

73. If two goods are perfect substitutes, then the indifference curves for these two goods are:
A) horizontal.
B) vertical.
C) L-shaped.
D) negatively sloped and straight.
E) convex to the origin.

Difficulty: **Moderate**

74. Which of the following shapes for indifference curves <u>cannot</u> generate corner solutions to the utility maximization?
A) horizontal
B) vertical
C) negatively sloped and straight
D) L-shaped
E) concave to the origin

Difficulty: **Moderate**

75. Which of the following conditions will generate a corner solution?
A) Indifference curves are flatter or steeper than the budget line.
B) Indifference curves are not as flat or steep as the budget line.
C) Indifference curves and L-shaped.
D) Only (A) and (C) are correct.
E) All of the above are correct.

Difficulty: **Moderate**

76. If the MRS between two goods is zero, then:
A) the goods are perfect complements.
B) having more of one good without having more of the other does not increase the individual's satisfaction.
C) the indifference curve for the two goods is L-shaped.
D) the proportion in which the goods will be purchased is the same regardless of relative price.

E) All of the above are correct.

Difficulty: **Moderate**

77. If utility is cardinally measurable, then constrained utility maximization requires that consumer income be expended for goods X and Y such that:
A) $MU_x = MU_y$.
B) $(MU_x)(P_x) = (MU_y)(P_y)$.
C) $MU_x / P_x = MU_y / P_y$.
D) $MU_x / P_y = MU_y / P_x$.
E) None of the above is correct.

Difficulty: **Moderate**

78. Which of the following statements regarding cardinal and ordinal utility theory is not correct?
A) Cardinal utility means that an individual can assign a specific number of utils to the consumption of various quantities of a good.
B) Ordinal utility means that the utility received from consuming various quantities of a good can be ranked but a specific number of utils cannot be assigned to each quantity.
C) Cardinal utility is a stronger assumption.
D) Ordinal utility is a weaker assumption.
E) Cardinal utility is a superior theory.

Difficulty: **Moderate**

79. Which of the following statements is false?
A) A rapid convergence of tastes is taking place in the world today.
B) Tastes in the United States affect tastes around the world.
C) Tastes abroad strongly influence tastes in the United States.
D) All of the above are true.
E) (A) and (B) are true.

Difficulty: **Easy**

80. The increasing popularity of pre-cooked or ready-to-eat foods is evidence that consumers face a _____ constraint.
A) budget
B) price
C) time
D) income
E) tastes

Difficulty: **Easy**

Short Answer

Write the word or phrase that best completes each statement or answers the question.

1. **Ordinal utility theory has weaker assumptions but it is a stronger theory than cardinal utility theory. Explain.**
Answer: Ordinal theory can explain consumer behavior with the assumption that a person only ranks various bundles according to the satisfaction received from them. To explain consumer behavior, cardinal theory requires the person to assign a specific amount of satisfaction to each bundle where the amounts assigned reflect not only the ranking but also how much more a person prefers one bundle to another. Ordinal utility requires a less rigorous kind of ordering but explains the same behavior. Accomplishing the same task with a less stringent assumption makes the theory stronger.

2. **Why does the use of indifference curves not imply that, in light of all relevant information, a consumer is indifferent about which bundle of goods he or she consumes?**
Answer: The bundle of goods a person desires most to consume is influenced by a number of variables. For example, relative prices influence which combination of goods he or she wishes to consume. A person is not indifferent between purchasing a bundle with more of good A and less of good B or a bundle with more of good B and less of good A if the relative price of good A has just increased.

3. **What is the marginal rate of substitution between perfect complements and what is the shape of the indifference curve? Explain.**
Answer: MRS = 0 because the goods cannot be traded off as alternative sources of utility. The goods must be used together to yield any satisfaction and in this case they must be used together in a fixed proportion. The indifference curve cannot be downward sloping, which describes goods as alternative sources of utility. Neither can the indifference curves be flat or vertical, implying that increased use of one good without increased use of the other yields greater utility. L-shaped indifference curves indicate that fixed proportions must be maintained to reach higher levels of total utility.

4. **Why don't L-shaped indifference curves generate "corner solutions?"**
Answer: The term corner solution does not describe the shape of the indifference curve. Rather, it suggests that moving to one end or the other of the budget constraint and expending one's entire budget on only one good will maximize utility. L-shaped curves yield consumption combinations of fixed proportions, not combinations that exclude the consumption of one of the goods.

5. **What is the shape of a budget constraint when one of the goods is rationed by government so that a person my purchase only a fixed quantity of the good regardless of its price? What is the likely effect of the restriction on the decisions of a person who receives very little satisfaction from the good?**
Answer: The budget line becomes vertical or horizontal at the quantity of the good that the government permits the person to buy per time period. For a person who receives little satisfaction from the good, it is likely that the point of tangency between the budget line and the person's indifference curves will not change and the person will not experience a reduction in total utility.

6. **Explain why the condition for consumer utility maximization with the marginal utility approach is equivalent to that with the indifference curve approach.**

Answer: The condition for consumer utility maximization with the marginal utility approach is that the last dollar spent on each good should be equal, which is shown as $MU_X/P_X = MU_Y/P_Y$ (and so on for all goods purchased). Using the indifference curve approach, the equilibrium point occurs where the indifference curve is tangent to the budget constraint, which means at the point where the two curves have the same slope. The slope of the indifference curve is MU_X/MU_Y, and the slope of the budget line is P_X/P_Y, so in equilibrium $MU_X/MU_Y = P_X/P_Y$ and it can be shown that by rearranging terms this is equal to $MU_X/P_X = MU_Y/P_Y$.

Chapter 4:

Consumer Behavior and Individual Demand

Multiple-Choice

Choose the one alternative that best completes the statement or answers the question.

1. Suppose that you receive an income of $100 per week, and all of this income is allocated to the consumption of two goods, X and Y. If the price of good X is $50 and the price of good Y is $10, and the quantity of good X is plotted on the horizontal axis while quantities of Y are plotted on the vertical axis, then:
   A) you will buy ten units of good Y every week.
   B) you will buy two units of good X every week.
   C) the slope of your budget line is –5 and it has a vertical intercept of 10 units of Y.
   D) the slope of your budget line is –2 and it has a horizontal intercept of +2.
   E) the slope of your budget line is +5 and has a horizontal intercept of 2 units of X.

   Difficulty: **Moderate**

2. A consumer has an income of $200 per week and faces given prices in the market. If income increases to $250 per week, we observe:
   A) an outward, parallel shift of her budget line.
   B) a rotation of the budget line about the intercept of the good with the lowest price.
   C) an inward, parallel shift of the budget line.
   D) the budget line to become less steep as real income falls.
   E) None of the above is correct.

   Difficulty: **Easy**

3. If, during the year, all prices rise by ten percent and your employer gives you a ten percent cost of living raise, then:
   A) the relative price ratio between goods will change, and you will change your consumption patterns.
   B) your budget line will shift inward toward the origin because you can buy less of all goods.
   C) you will be able to buy more of some goods while at the same time buying no less of some others.
   D) overall, you will be able to buy more goods and services at new price level.
   E) None of the above is correct.

   Difficulty: **Moderate**

4. Suppose that you observe the price of widgets falling and at the same time, consumers are actually buying fewer widgets. All other things remaining the same you would be correct in concluding that:
   A) such an observation was theoretically impossible.
   B) widgets must be a very strong luxury good since consumers do not want them when they are inexpensive.

C) the good is normal and the income effect is equal to the substitution effect.
D) the good is inferior and the negative income effect dominates the positive substitution effect.
E) None of the above is correct.

Difficulty: **Moderate**

5. If you observe a positively sloped income-consumption curve for goods X and Y when their prices are constant, then:
A) both X and Y are inferior goods.
B) the Engel curve for one of the goods will be horizontal.
C) at least one of the goods must be normal.
D) the substitution effect between X and Y is positive.
E) None of the above is correct.

Difficulty: **Hard**

6. When you derive an income-consumption curve from an individual's preference map, you are assuming that:
A) nominal income remains constant.
B) real income remains constant.
C) the relative price ratio between goods remains constant.
D) at least one of the bundles represented on the preference map contains a "bad."
E) the substitution effect of a price change is positive.

Difficulty: **Moderate**

7. The income-consumption curve, for an individual with a given indifference map, is the locus of points where:
A) money income remains constant, but prices change.
B) relative prices remain constant but money income changes.
C) the rate at which an individual consumer is willing to trade one good for another remains constant.
D) (A) and (B) are correct.
E) (B) and (C) are correct.

Difficulty: **Moderate**

8. The relationship between the amount of a commodity that an individual consumes during a given period of time with changes in money income can be illustrated by:
A) an Engel curve.
B) an income-consumption curve.
C) a price-consumption curve.
D) an indifference curve.
E) a budget line.

Difficulty: **Easy**

9. Which of the following statements is false?
A) The Engel curve is derived from the income-consumption curve.
B) The Engel curve shows the quantity of the good that a person would consume at different prices of that good.

C) The Engel curve shows the quantity of the good that a person would consume at different income levels.
D) The $MRS_{XY} = P_X/P_Y$ at every point on the Engel curve.
E) Engel curves can sometimes show the relationship between income and expenditures on various goods rather than the quantity purchased of those goods.

Difficulty: **Easy**

10. If the income-consumption curve for two goods, X and Y, bends back on itself and takes a negative slope, then:
A) both of the goods must be inferior.
B) the income effect for both goods is zero.
C) there is no substitution effect when the price of either X or Y changes.
D) the Engel curve for both of the goods will be horizontal.
E) at least one of the goods must be inferior.

Difficulty: **Hard**

11. If the Engel curve for good X is positively sloped but is increasing at a decreasing rate, then the good most likely:
A) is an inferior good.
B) will exhibit a relatively small substitution effect when its price changes.
C) is a luxury good.
D) can be classified as a necessity because some amount will always be bought regardless of the income level.
E) None of the above is correct.

Difficulty: **Hard**

12. Assuming that money income per unit of time is plotted on the vertical axis and the quantity of good X purchased per unit of time is plotted on the horizontal axis, then an Engel curve that slopes upward indicates that good X is:
A) a necessity.
B) an inferior good.
C) a luxury good.
D) a normal good.
E) There is not information to decide.

Difficulty: **Easy**

13. The income effect for a particular good shows that:
A) a decrease in the price of a good increases the purchasing power of a consumer's money income.
B) when the price of a good rises, consumers are able to buy more of other goods because of an increase in the purchasing power of their money income.
C) if a good is inferior, a decrease in the purchasing power of money income results in less of the good being consumed.
D) if the consumer's money income rises, she buys less of a normal good and more of an inferior good.
E) None of the above is correct.

Difficulty: **Easy**

14. If your money income falls and you increase your demand for hamburger, this suggests that hamburger is a(n):
A) normal good.
B) substitute good.
C) complementary good with steak.
D) inferior good.
E) necessity.

Difficulty: **Easy**

15. Suppose that steak is a normal good. The demand for steak will most likely increase when:
A) the price of steak falls, other things constant.
B) the income of consumers rises.
C) the price of pork, a substitute good, falls.
D) the price of catsup, a complementary good, rises.
E) consumers expect the price of steak to fall in the future.

Difficulty: **Easy**

16. Suppose that good X is normal and that you determine an income-consumption curve for goods X and Y. When good X is measured on the horizontal axis and good Y is measured on the vertical, you would expect good X to:
A) have many close substitute goods.
B) have an Engel curve that is positively sloped.
C) exhibit little change in demand when consumer income changes.
D) exhibit a reduction in the amount consumed when consumer income increases.
E) have only a few close substitutes.

Difficulty: **Easy**

17. When the relative price ratio between goods X and Y changes, the change will affect the quantity demanded of the goods. The quantity demanded of the (now) relatively cheaper good will rise while the quantity demanded of the relatively more expensive good will fall. Assuming that the purchasing power of the consumer's income is the same after the price change as it was before, the change in quantity demanded is a result of:
A) the income effect between goods X and Y.
B) the slope of the Engel curve for either good X or Y.
C) the shape of the income-consumption curve for goods X and Y.
D) the substitution effect between goods X and Y.
E) None of the above is correct.

Difficulty: **Easy**

18. Suppose that the price of X falls. If we adjust for changes in the relative price ratio and X is normal, then there will be an increase in the quantity demanded of X. The reason for this increase in quantity demanded, even though relative prices are held constant is:
A) the income effect.
B) the fact that good X must have a negatively sloped Engel curve.
C) the substitution effect.

D) the pure price effect.
E) the income and substitution effects.

Difficulty: **Easy**

19. The diminishing marginal rate of substitution between goods A and B is based on the notion that:
A) the satisfaction received from various bundles of goods decreases as a consumer moves down an indifference curve.
B) the more of good A and the less of good B that a household has, the less it will be willing to give up some of good A to get more of good B.
C) as the prices of good A and B decrease, the household will be forced to move to a lower indifference curve.
D) the more of good A and the less of good B that a consumer has, the more willing he or she will be to give up some of good A to obtain an additional unit of good B.
E) None of the above is correct.

Difficulty: **Moderate**

20. When the price of a particular good falls, an individual will always be induced to purchase more of the good because of:
A) the substitution effect and sometimes the income effect of the price change.
B) the income effect of the price change.
C) both the income and substitution effect of the price change.
D) the substitution effect but never the income effect of the price change.
E) None of the above is correct.

Difficulty: **Moderate**

21. Suppose that you observe an indifference map that consists only of L-shaped indifference curves. You can conclude that:
A) the goods are perfect substitutes for each other.
B) the income effect of a change in price will always be less than the substitution effect.
C) the substitution effect between the two goods will be positive but less than one.
D) the substitution effect between the two goods will be zero.
E) there will be neither an income nor a substitution effect when there is a change in real income.

Difficulty: **Hard**

22. The income-consumption curve for goods X and Y shows how:
A) total consumption varies inversely with income.
B) consumption bundles change as both income and relative prices change.
C) consumption bundles change as income remains constant but the relative price ratio changes.
D) consumption bundles change as income changes and relative prices are held constant.
E) None of the above is correct.

Difficulty: **Easy**

23. When good Y is plotted on the vertical axis and good X on the horizontal axis, the price-consumption curve for good X shows:
A) how a change in the relative price ratio will cause a parallel shift in the budget line.
B) how the purchase of a good will increase as its price increases.
C) how the consumption bundles change as relative prices change, given that money income is held constant.
D) how the consumption bundles change as real income and relative prices change.
E) how the consumption bundles change as real income and relative prices change.

Difficulty: **Easy**

24. If the relative price ratio between goods X and Y changes but money income does not, the resulting change in household consumption is shown by:
A) the income-consumption curve.
B) the consumer's indifference map.
C) the price-consumption curve.
D) changes in the consumer's budget line.
E) None of the above is correct.

Difficulty: **Easy**

25. When a household experiences a change in money income with no change in relative prices, the resulting change in the consumption bundles is shown by:
A) the price-consumption curve.
B) movements along a given budget line.
C) the household's indifference map.
D) the income-consumption curve.
E) (B) and (C) are correct.

Difficulty: **Easy**

26. In order to derive the individual's demand curve for good X, the:
A) price of good X is changed, resulting in a rotation of the budget line and a new point of consumer equilibrium.
B) price of good X is changed, resulting in a parallel shift of the budget line and a new point of consumer equilibrium.
C) consumer's income is changed, resulting in a parallel shift of the budget line and a new point of consumer equilibrium.
D) consumer's income is changed, resulting in a rotation of the budget line and a new point of consumer equilibrium.
E) None of the above is correct.

Difficulty: **Easy**

27. Suppose that the income effect of a price change for good X is zero but the substitution effect is not. You can conclude that:
A) the demand curve for good X will be horizontal.
B) the demand curve for good X will be downward sloping.
C) the demand curve for good X will be vertical.
D) the effect of a change in price of X cannot be determined because there is no income effect.

E) None of the above is correct.

Difficulty: **Moderate**

28. When economists generate an Engel curve for a typical household consuming good X, it is necessary to :
A) permit the price of good X to change while holding all other prices and household income constant.
B) increase the household's income and reduce the price of good X while holding all other prices constant.
C) increase or decrease household income while holding all prices constant and observing the change in the consumption of good X.
D) increase the price of good X and increase the prices of all other goods and observe the change in the household's consumption of good X.
E) None of the above is correct.

Difficulty: **Easy**

29. Suppose that the weekly consumption of milk is measured on the horizontal axis while spending on all other goods is measured on the vertical axis. If milk is a normal good, then its income-consumption curve will most likely be:
A) positively sloped.
B) horizontal.
C) negatively sloped.
D) vertical.
E) not enough information is provided to determine an answer.

Difficulty: **Moderate**

30. Suppose that a consumer purchases only two goods, X and Y. In order to isolate the substitution effect of a price decrease in good X, it is necessary to:
A) ensure that the consumer's money income is held constant.
B) reduce the consumer's money income by the same percent as the decrease in the price of good X.
C) increase the consumer's money income by a certain amount.
D) reduce the consumer's real income to the point where he is neither better nor worse off than before the price decrease.
E) None of the above is correct.

Difficulty: **Moderate**

31. One of the ways in which consumer's surplus can be measured is to use:
A) an Engel curve.
B) a price-consumption curve.
C) a demand curve.
D) an indifference curve and a budget line.
E) a total utility curve.

Difficulty: **Easy**

32. The substitution effect shows that if an individual could continue buying the same amount of goods after a price increase as before and yet still maintain the same level of utility:
A) when the price of one good rises, consumers buy more of that good and less of others.
B) when the price of a good falls relative to other goods, consumers buy less of that good and more of others.
C) when the price of a good rises, consumers buy less of that good and more of all other goods.
D) when the price of a good falls, consumers buy less of all goods.
E) None of the above is correct.

Difficulty: **Moderate**

33. Which one of the following statements is <u>false</u>?
A) The substitution effect of a change in a good's own price upon the quantity demanded of the good is always negative.
B) The net effect upon quantity demanded of the change in a price of a good incorporates both the income effect and the substitution effect.
C) The net effect of the change in a good's price on other goods depends on whether the income effect or the substitution effect dominates.
D) The downward sloping demand curve for a normal good depends on both the income effect and the substitution effect.
E) The substitution effect of a change in a good's own price upon the quantity demanded of the good may be either positive or negative.

Difficulty: **Moderate**

34. If apples are a normal good and the price of a pound of red delicious apples rises, then:
A) the income effect encourages the consumer to buy more of the good and the substitution effect encourages him to buy less.
B) the income effect encourages the consumer to buy less of the good and the substitution effect encourages him to buy more.
C) both the income and substitution effects encourage the consumer to buy more of the good.
D) both the income and substitution effects encourage the consumer to buy less of the good.
E) None of the above is correct.

Difficulty: **Moderate**

35. When economists describe consumer surplus, they mean:
A) the marginal utility received by consumers from consuming an extra unit of a good.
B) the total utility received by consumers from consuming an extra unit of a good.
C) the price that consumers have to pay for an additional unit of a good.
D) the difference between what a consumer would be willing to pay for an extra unit of a good and what he or she actually pays.
E) None of the above is correct.

Difficulty: **Easy**

36. Generally speaking, consumer surplus can be expressed as the:
A) price of a good times the number of units of the good that is sold.
B) value of an extra unit of a good to be consumed.

C) difference between the value of a good to a consumer and the price that he or she has to pay in order to purchase the good.
D) price that a consumer is willing to pay for the good.
E) None of the above is correct.

Difficulty: **Easy**

37. An expenditure index is calculated by:
A) dividing relative prices during a given year by the relative prices during some base year.
B) multiplying total income in a given year by the total income in some specified base year.
C) dividing total spending on all goods during a particular year by total spending on all other goods during some specified base year.
D) dividing total spending on all goods during some specified base year by total spending on all goods during some given year.
E) None of the above is a correct way to calculate an expenditure index.

Difficulty: **Easy**

38. Suppose that an expenditure index (E) has a value greater than one. This suggests that:
A) overall consumer spending on all goods has increased from the base year to the current year.
B) overall consumer spending on all goods has fallen from the base year to the current year.
C) overall consumer spending during the base year was greater than overall consumer spending during the current year.
D) there was no significant change in overall consumer spending from the base year to the current year.
E) None of the above is correct.

Difficulty: **Moderate**

39. In order to obtain a Laspayres index, the economic analyst must divide the cost of a market basket of goods:
A) bought in the base year at current prices by current income.
B) bought in the current year are current prices by the cost of the same goods during the base year at base year prices.
C) bought in the base year at current prices by the cost of the same basket at base year prices.
D) bought in the current year at base year prices by a similar basket bought in the base year at current prices.
E) None of the above is correct.

Difficulty: **Easy**

40. If the value of the ratio of current income compared to income in some base year is 1.85, and the value of the Laspayres index for the current year and the same base year is 1.60, we can conclude that:
A) the average household is worse off because purchasing power has fallen.
B) the consumer is thought to be better off during the current year than in the base year.
C) the consumer is neither better off nor worse off in the current year relative to the base year because we cannot compare ratios of current income to base income and a Laspayres index.

D) prices have increased faster during the current year than has income.
E) None of the above is correct.

Difficulty: **Moderate**

41. If Ex(90) represents total expenditures on goods and services in 1990, Ex (93) represents total expenditures on goods and services in 1993, L_S is used to designate the Laspayres index, and P_a is used to designate the Paasche index, then we can conclude that:
A) if L_S < [Ex(93)/Ex(90)], then the consumer is better off in 1993 when compared to 1990.
B) if L_S > [Ex(93)/Ex(90)], then the consumer is better off 1993 when compared to 1990.
C) if P_a < [Ex(93)/Ex(90)], then nothing definite can be said about consumer well being.
D) if P_a < [Ex(93)/Ex(90)], then the consumer is better off in 1993 when compared to 1990.
E) (A) and (C) are correct.

Difficulty: **Hard**

42. Suppose that the government levies a tax on automobile tires and then returns the average tax paid to each family in the form of an annual grant. This tax would most probably:
A) not have an effect on the consumption of automobile tires because the net effect on the consumer will be zero.
B) cause the average consumer to buy fewer tires because of the substitution effect.
C) cause the average consumer to buy more tires because of the income effect, assuming that automobile tires are a normal good.
D) have essentially no effect on the demand for automobile tires because the income and substitution effects will offset each other.
E) None of the above is correct.

Difficulty: **Hard**

43. Suppose that good X is a normal good. We can conclude that:
A) the demand curve for good X is vertical.
B) the demand curve for good X is upward sloping.
C) the demand curve for good X is downward sloping.
D) the demand curve for good X is horizontal.
E) None of the above is correct.

Difficulty: **Easy**

44. If the indifference map between goods X and Y consists of L-shaped indifference curves, you would correctly conclude that:
A) the income effect of a price change in either good is positive.
B) the goods are perfect substitutes for each other.
C) either good X or good Y must be a free good.
D) the substitution effect of a price change in either good is zero.
E) None of the above is correct.

Difficulty: **Hard**

45. Suppose that the indifference curves between goods X and Y are vertically parallel to each other. We can conclude that:
A) either X or Y is an inferior good.
B) either X or Y will be a Giffen good.
C) there will be no income effect when the price of one of the goods changes.
D) both goods are inferior.
E) there will be no substitution effect when the price of one of the goods changes.

Difficulty: **Hard**

46. Suppose that you really want a soft drink, and you are willing to pay $.75 in order to consume one. However, you stop at a roadside service station and buy a drink from a machine and pay only $.50. Which of the following statements is <u>false</u>?
A) The total utility of the soft drink that you purchase is positive.
B) You enjoy a consumer surplus of $.25 when you purchase the drink.
C) The marginal utility of the soft drink is greater than zero.
D) You do not receive any consumer surplus when you purchase the soft drink.
E) You value the soft drink that you purchase by more than the drink costs you.

Difficulty: **Easy**

47. The regularity observed in the proportion of income spent on food across various income levels:
A) has in recent years almost disappeared.
B) suggests that food is no longer a necessity but a luxury.
C) suggests that in poorer nations a higher proportion of income is spent on food than in richer nations.
D) is also observed on the proportion of income spent on almost all other goods and services.
E) None of the above is correct.

Difficulty: **Moderate**

48. Engel's Law is the name given to the following observed regularity:
A) the proportion of income spent on food decreases as income rises.
B) the proportion of income spent on food increases as income rises.
C) the proportion of income spent on food is constant as income rises.
D) the proportion of income spent on insurance and pensions is higher among high income families.
E) the proportion of income spent on insurance and pensions is lower among low income families.

Difficulty: **Easy**

49. Lump sum distributions of pension money:
A) are permitted when people change jobs, are ejected from retirement systems due to the sale of a company, or when taking early retirement.
B) are usually rolled into Individual Retirement Accounts, according to a 1993 Labor Department study.
C) are preferred by employers because it saves them the cost of administering a retirement system.

D) are leading toward a retirement crisis because a significant portion of such distributions are being spent for a variety of purposes rather than being reinvested to generate a retirement income.
E) (A), (C), and (D) are correct.

Difficulty: **Moderate**

50. In the effort to reduce alcohol use by youths:
A) the minimum legal age for purchasing and drinking alcohol has been raised in many states in the effort to shift the demand curve for alcohol use by young people to the left.
B) federal alcohol taxes have been raised with understanding that they will have a disproportionate impact on the purchase of youths because of their limited disposable income.
C) federal policies have been implemented to raise the real price (nominal price adjusted for inflation) of alcoholic beverages to their 1951.
D) All of the above are correct.
E) None of the above is correct.

Difficulty: **Easy**

51. The imposition of a larger excise tax on gasoline, placing it more in line with the gas taxes in Europe and Japan, combined with a general tax rebate unrelated to gasoline consumption.
A) would be pointless because it is a self-contradictory policy, i.e., encouraging and discouraging gasoline use.
B) is an effort to make use of the income effect of a price change while avoiding the deflationary effects of a tax increase.
C) will increase our dependency on foreign soil.
D) will reduce the total consumption gasoline in the U.S.
E) will lead to increased gasoline consumption because consumers will have a direct incentive to use the tax rebate to purchase luxury cars with lower gas mileage.

Difficulty: **Moderate**

52. It is becoming increasingly _____ to define what is an "American" car because _____.
A) easier; Americans make it clear that that is what they want to purchase.
B) difficult; the American Automobile Labeling Act of 1992 prevents producers from revealing the extent of their use of foreign-made parts.
C) easier; the use of foreign-made parts in automobiles assembled in the U.S. has almost disappeared over the past 10 years.
D) difficult; the United Automobile Workers Union views cars assembled in Mexico and Canada which include some American made parts as "American" cars.
E) None of the above is correct.

Difficulty: **Moderate**

53. In the characteristics approach to consumer theory:
A) the characteristics ray is derived from consumer income.
B) the tangency of the characteristics ray and an indifference curve identifies the utility maximizing combination of characteristics.
C) the efficiency frontier contains the utility maximizing combinations of characteristics.

D) an increase in the price of one good will shift the budget line outward.
E) None of the above is correct.

Difficulty: **Moderate**

54. In the characteristics approach to consumer theory, the "feasible region":
A) lies outside the characteristics ray for each good.
B) includes the "efficiency frontier."
C) contains only combinations of characteristics which will maximize utility.
D) cannot be increased in size by a change in the price of a good, but can be increased in size by a change in income.
E) All of the above are correct.

Difficulty: **Moderate**

55. In the characteristics approach to consumer theory, the budget line is the same as the:
A) feasible region.
B) characteristics ray.
C) efficiency frontier.
D) indifference curves.
E) None of the above is correct.

Difficulty: **Moderate**

56. In the characteristics approach to consumer theory, the tangency of the _____ and the _____ defines the utility maximizing combination of characteristics.
A) efficiency frontier; characteristics ray.
B) characteristics ray; feasible region.
C) feasible region; efficiency frontier.
D) indifference curves; efficiency frontier.
E) None of the above is correct.

Difficulty: **Moderate**

57. The advantages of the characteristics approach to consumer theory over the traditional demand theory do not include:
A) the easy explanation of substitution among goods in terms of some common characteristics.
B) the easy introduction of a third good to the analysis by drawing a new characteristics ray.
C) showing quality changes by rotating the indifference curves for a good.
D) developing "hedonic" prices.
E) All of the above are correct.

Difficulty: **Moderate**

58. A "hedonic" price:
A) is the implicit price of a particular characteristic of a good.
B) is the explicit price of a particular good.
C) may be discovered by observing the difference between the price of two goods which are otherwise identical except for a particular characteristic.

D) is easier to estimate for services than for physical goods.
E) (A) and (C) are correct.

Difficulty: **Moderate**

59. Which of the following statements regarding the consumer price index is incorrect?
A) The consumer price index has a downward bias.
B) Underestimates of the rate of inflation based on the consumer price index costs the U.S. government billions of dollars in higher cost-of-living adjustments to social security recipients.
C) Alan Greenspan, chairman of the Federal Reserve System, argues that the consumer price index understates the rate of inflation by 0.5 to 1.5 percent.
D) Computing the correct consumer price index requires the elimination of the effect of warehouse clubs and the purchase of generic drugs on the index.
E) All of the above are incorrect.

Difficulty: **Moderate**

60. In an Edgeworth box diagram, mutual gains from trade:
A) are possible if at the initial distribution of good X and good Y, the MRS between good X and Y for the two individuals are different.
B) are possible if at the initial distribution of good X and good Y, the MRS between good X and Y for the two individuals are equal.
C) are exhausted when trading brings the MRS between good X and Y for the two individuals to the same proportionate share of the goods at the time of the initial distribution, e.g., if one trader has twice has many units of X and Y at the initial distribution, then his MRS between X and Y will be double that of the other trader.
D) exist up to a point at which trading has caused the MRS between good X and Y for the two individuals to be as far apart as possible.
E) (B) and (D) are correct.

Difficulty: **Moderate**

61. Which of the following are measured on the vertical and horizontal axes of an Edgeworth box diagram for exchange?
A) utility received from each good
B) prices of each good
C) quantities of each good
D) money income of each trader
E) None of the above is correct.

Difficulty: **Moderate**

62. If mutual gains from trade are possible, then the initial distribution of goods X and Y between two traders is such that the two traders are at a point in the Edgeworth box at which:
A) the indifference curves of the two traders do not intersect.
B) the indifference curves of the two traders intersect and are not tangent to each other.
C) the indifference curves of the two traders are tangent to each other.
D) the indifference curves of the two traders have the same sloe but are not tangent to each other.

E) None of the above is correct.

Difficulty: **Moderate**

63. Assume that mutual gains from trade are possible at the initial distribution of goods X and Y between Individual A and Individual B, and that a position where no gains from trade are possible is reached by staying on the same indifference curve of Individual B. Which of the following statements is correct?
A) Individual A and Individual B gain from the movement to the new position.
B) Individual A gains from the movement to the new position.
C) Individual B gains from the movement to the new position.
D) Neither Individual A nor Individual B gain from the movement to the new position.
E) It is not possible to determine who gains from the information given.

Difficulty: **Hard**

64. If x and y refer to quantities of commodities X and Y, and "1" and "0" refer to period 1 and the base period, which of the following ratios is an expenditure index?
A) $\mathbf{x_1P_{x1} + y_1P_{y1} / x_0P_{x0} + y_0P_{y0}}$
B) $x_0P_{x1} + y_0P_{y1} / x_0P_{x0} + y_0P_{y0}$
C) $x_1P_{x1} + y_1P_{y1} / x_1P_{x0} + y_1P_{y0}$
D) $x_1P_{x1} + y_1P_{y1} / x_0P_{x1} + y_0P_{y1}$
E) None of the above is correct.

Difficulty: **Moderate**

65. If x and y refer to quantities of commodities X and Y, and "1" and "0" refer to period 1 and the base period, which of the following ratios is a Laspayres index?
A) $x_1P_{x1} + y_1P_{y1} / x_0P_{x0} + y_0P_{y0}$
B) $\mathbf{x_0P_{x1} + y_0P_{y1} / x_0P_{x0} + y_0P_{y0}}$
C) $x_1P_{x1} + y_1P_{y1} / x_1P_{x0} + y_1P_{y0}$
D) $x_1P_{x1} + y_1P_{y1} / x_0P_{x1} + y_0P_{y1}$
E) None of the above is correct.

Difficulty: **Moderate**

66. If x and y refer to quantities of commodities X and Y, and "1" and "0" refer to period 1 and the base period, which of the following ratios is a Paasche index?
A) $x_1P_{x1} + y_1P_{y1} / x_0P_{x0} + y_0P_{y0}$
B) $x_0P_{x1} + y_0P_{y1} / x_0P_{x0} + y_0P_{y0}$
C) $\mathbf{x_1P_{x1} + y_1P_{y1} / x_1P_{x0} + y_1P_{y0}}$
D) $x_1P_{x1} + y_1P_{y1} / x_0P_{x1} + y_0P_{y1}$
E) None of the above is correct.

Difficulty: **Moderate**

67. Which of the following is a Paasche index?
A) The ratio of period 1 quantities at period 1 prices to base year quantities at base year prices.

B) The ratio of base year quantities at period 1 prices to base year quantities at base year prices.
C) The ratio of period 1 quantities at period 1 prices relative to period 1 quantities at base year prices.
D) The ratio of period 1 quantities at base year prices to base year quantities at period 1 prices.
E) None of the above is correct.

Difficulty: **Moderate**

Use the data below to find the index.

Period	Q_x	P_x	Q_y	P_y
0 (base)	6	$1	5	$2
1	5	$2	10	$1

68. What is the expenditure index for period 1?
A) 0.80
B) 1.06
C) 1.17
D) 1.25
E) 1.44

Difficulty: **Moderate**

69. What is the Laspayres index for period 1?
A) 0.80
B) 1.06
C) 1.17
D) 1.25
E) 1.44

Difficulty: **Moderate**

70. What is the Paasche index for period 1?
A) 0.80
B) 1.06
C) 1.17
D) 1.25
E) 1.44

Difficulty: **Moderate**

71. If "E" is the expenditure index, "L" is the Laspayres index, and "P" is the Paasche index, which of the following demonstrates that an individual is definitely better off in period 1 than in the base year?
A) E less than L, and E greater than or equal to P.
B) E greater than L, and E less than P.
C) E is equal to L, and E is equal to P.

D) E greater than L, and E greater than or equal to P.
E) None of the above is correct.

Difficulty: **Moderate**

72. Assuming that money income per unit of time is plotted on the vertical axis and the quantity of a good purchased per unit of time is plotted on the horizontal axis, an Engel curve which rises rapidly indicates that the good:
A) is a luxury good.
B) is a necessity.
C) is an inferior good.
D) is purchased in decreasing amounts as income rises.
E) cannot be classified as being a luxury, necessity, or inferior good.

Difficulty: **Moderate**

73. Assuming that money income per unit of time is plotted on the vertical axis and the quantity of a good purchased per unit of time is plotted on the horizontal axis, an Engel curve with a negative slope indicates that the good:
A) is a luxury good.
B) is a necessity.
C) is an inferior good.
D) is purchased in constant amounts as income rises.
E) (B) and (D) correct.

Difficulty: **Moderate**

74. The classification of a good as inferior or normal:
A) depends only on how a specific consumer views the particular good.
B) may change if a person's income level changes.
C) is important because inferior goods come to be viewed as economic "bads."
D) depends on whether the indifference curves are negatively or positively sloped.
E) (A) and (B) are correct.

Difficulty: **Easy**

75. The demand curve for a good is derived from the:
A) Engel curve.
B) price-consumption curve.
C) income-consumption curve.
D) efficiency frontier curve.
E) None of the above is correct.

Difficulty: **Easy**

76. In the real world, the substitution effect is likely to:
A) be much larger than the income effect.
B) dominate the income effect because most goods have suitable substitutes.
C) dominate the income effect because consumers purchase many goods spending only a small fraction of their income on any one good.

D) be larger than the income effect but there are exceptions.
E) All of the above are correct.

Difficulty: **Moderate**

77. A good is a "Giffen good" if the:
A) substitution effect is larger than the income effect when the price of a normal good falls.
B) substitution effect is larger than the income effect when the price of an inferior good falls.
C) substitution effect is smaller than the income effect when the price of an inferior good falls.
D) substitution effect is smaller than the income effect when the price of a normal good falls.
E) None of the above is correct.

Difficulty: **Moderate**

78. Which of the following statements is correct?
A) All Giffen goods are inferior goods.
B) All inferior goods are Giffen goods.
C) All inferior goods have negatively sloped demand curves.
D) The substitution effect is negative for a Giffen good.
E) All of the above are correct.

Difficulty: **Moderate**

79. The Giffen paradox refers to the fact that:
A) the Engel curve for a Giffen good is negatively sloped.
B) the income effect for a Giffen good is negative.
C) the income-consumption curve for a Giffen good is negatively sloped.
D) the demand curve for a Giffen good is positively sloped.
E) None of the above is correct.

Difficulty: **Easy**

80. Giffen goods:
A) are commonplace in the real world.
B) cannot exist in the real world because substitution effects would have to be zero for a Giffen good to exist.
C) are rare but research supports Robert Giffen's claim that potatoes in nineteenth century Ireland are an example of the Giffen paradox.
D) are unlikely to exist because inferior goods are usually narrowly defined goods for which sufficient suitable substitutes are available.
E) (C) and (D) are correct.

Difficulty: **Moderate**

81. Which of the following is <u>not</u> a factor in the increasing substitution between domestic and foreign goods?
A) falling transportation costs
B) international information revolution
C) global advertising campaigns by multinationals

D) increase in international travel
E) rapidly diverging tastes internationally

Difficulty: **Moderate**

82. The increasing degree of substitution between domestic and foreign goods has not:
A) made government more likely to step in and restrict foreign competition in areas of rapidly increasing substitution.
B) impacted the market for homogeneous goods such as a particular grade of steel.
C) impacted the market for industrial products with precise specifications such as computer chips.
D) created markets in which a small price difference can lead quickly to a large shift in sales.
E) reduced intraindustry trade in differentiated products.

Difficulty: **Moderate**

83. Assume that nonfood items are measured on the vertical axis and food items are measured on the horizontal axis. Which of the following statements about the impact of food stamps on the budget line of poor families is not correct?
A) The budget line shifts to the right.
B) The top portion of the budget line contains a horizontal segment.
C) A cash transfer of equal dollar value to the foodstamps generates the same budget line but not the same utility maximizing combination of food and nonfood items.
D) The budget line representing the cash transfer will make more combinations of food and nonfood items attainable than the budget line representing a transfer of the same dollar value in foodstamps.
E) All of the above are correct.

Difficulty: **Moderate**

84. Which is a correct statement regarding the impact of cash transfers versus foodstamps of the same dollar amount on utility maximization?
A) A cash subsidy will always be worse than food stamps.
B) Foodstamps will always be worse than a cash subsidy.
C) A cash subsidy will always be no worse than foodstamps and may be better.
D) A cash subsidy will always be no better than foodstamps and may be worse.
E) Foodstamps and cash transfers of the same dollar value will always leave the recipient at the same level of utility maximization.

Difficulty: **Moderate**

85. Assume that nonfood items are measured on the vertical axis and food items are measured on the horizontal axis. Which is a correct statement regarding the relative impact on the MRS between food and non-food items of cash transfers versus foodstamps of the same dollar amount when the recipient is in the new consumer equilibrium?
A) The MRS between food and nonfood items will remain the same or fall depending on the intensity of the recipient's preference for food.
B) The MRS between food and nonfood items will remain the same or increase depending on the intensity of the recipient's preference for food.
C) The MRS between food and nonfood items will always remain the same regardless on the intensity of the recipient's preference for food.

D) The MRS between food and nonfood items will always fall regardless of the intensity of the recipient's preference for food.
E) The MRS between food and nonfood items will always increase regardless of the intensity of the recipient's preference for food.

Difficulty: **Moderate**

86. Assume that nonfood items are measured on the vertical axis and food items are measured on the horizontal axis. Which is a correct statement regarding the relative impact on the MRS between food and non-food items of cash transfers versus foodstamps of the same dollar amount when the recipient is in the new consumer equilibrium?
A) The MRS of food for nonfood items will always be greater than the ratio of food price to nonfood price regardless of the intensity of the recipient's preference for food.
B) The MRS of food for nonfood items will always be smaller than the ratio of food price to nonfood price regardless of the intensity of the recipient's preference for food.
C) The MRS of food for nonfood items will always be equal to the ratio of food price to nonfood price regardless of the intensity of the recipient's preference for food.
D) The MRS of food for nonfood items will always be equal to or greater than the ratio of food price to nonfood price regardless of the intensity of the recipient's preference for food.
E) The MRS of food for nonfood items will always be equal to or less than the ratio of food price to nonfood price regardless of the intensity of the recipient's preference for food.

Difficulty: **Moderate**

87. Which of the following is a correct statement regarding the relative impact of cash transfers versus food stamps of the same dollar amount when the recipient is in consumer equilibrium?
A) A cash transfer will always result in the recipient purchasing more food than if the recipient receives food stamps.
B) A cash transfer will always result in the recipient purchasing less food than if the recipient receives food stamps.
C) A cash transfer will always result in the recipient purchasing an equal or greater amount of food than if the recipient receives food stamps.
D) A cash transfer will always result in the recipient purchasing an equal or lesser amount of food than if the recipient receives food stamps.
E) The recipient will purchase the same amount of food whether the transfer is in cash or in food stamps.

Difficulty: **Moderate**

88. Given that a person is willing to pay $600 for the first television to put in his home, $400 for the second, $300 for the third, and $200 for the fourth, and the market price he must pay for a television set is $300. What will be his total benefit from purchasing television sets?
A) $800.
B) $900.
C) $1200.
D) $1300.
E) $1500.

Difficulty: **Moderate**

89. Given that a person is willing to pay $600 for the first television to put in his home, $400 for the second, $300 for the third, and $200 for the fourth, and the market price he must pay for a television set is $300. What will be the amount of his consumer surplus from purchasing television sets?

A) $300.
B) $400.
C) $600.
D) $1000.
E) $1300.

Difficulty: **Moderate**

90. Given that a person is willing to pay $600 for the first television to put in his home, $400 for the second, $300 for the third, and $200 for the fourth, and the market price he must pay for a television set is $300. What will be the maximum total dollar amount he would be willing to pay for the number of television sets he wishes to purchase rather than do without all television sets, i.e., make an all or nothing decision about this good?

A) $600.
B) $900.
C) $1000.
D) $1200.
E) $1300.

Difficulty: **Moderate**

91. The water-diamond paradox refers to:

A) the fact that people act irrationally about luxury goods, such as diamonds, by seriously overvaluing them.
B) the irony that people in wealthy countries spend so much more of their income on diamonds than on water when they should be doing the opposite.
C) the fact that water is so cheap while diamonds are so expensive.
D) the fact that a nonessential always ends up reducing the availability of really essential goods like water.
E) None of the above is correct.

Difficulty: **Easy**

92. Regarding the water-diamond paradox, which of the following is correct?

A) The utility of the last unit of water we consume is much lower than the utility of the last unit of diamonds.
B) The total utility received from water is greater than the total utility received from diamonds, but the marginal utility received from diamonds is greater than the marginal utility received from water.
C) Price reflects marginal utility not total utility.
D) We pay as low a price for all units of water as we are willing to pay for the last nonessential unit of water.
E) All of the above are correct.

Difficulty: **Easy**

Short Answer

Write the word or phrase that best complete each statement or answers the question.

1. **If the federal excise tax on gasoline was increased by $3.00 per gallon, but consumers received an income tax rebate of $3.00 for every gallon of gasoline they purchased, how would their consumption behavior be affected? Explain.**
Answer: Their behavior probably would not change much because the tax rebate is linked to gasoline usage. They get back exactly what they pay in tax so, except for the time delay, gasoline obviously still has the same relative price. For the tax and rebate to reduce their gasoline consumption, the rebate has to be general, i.e., not connected to gasoline usage.

2. **Why is it highly unlikely that one will ever find "clothing" to be an inferior good?**
Answer: The good is defined so broadly that there are no adequate substitutes to move to as a person's income rises. Thus as income rises, a person is not likely to buy less clothing (an inferior good) although he or she may not buy proportionally more clothing (a necessity).

3. **Use indifference curve analysis to explain the circumstances in which food stamps will not be better than a cash subsidy from the point of view of the food stamp recipient.**
Answer: If the food stamp recipient has a strong preference for food, then the restricted subsidy will not prevent the recipient from reaching the same point on a higher indifference curve than a cash subsidy would allow. The food stamp subsidy leaves a horizontal segment at the top of the budget line if nonfood items are measured on the vertical axis and food items on the horizontal axis. The limitation of the food stamps does not affect the decisions of a person for whom the tangency of indifference curves and budget line is lower on the budget constraint.

4. **What difference will there be in the slopes of the Engel curves for food and entertainment in a very poor country?**
Answer: The Engel curve for food in a very poor country is likely to be much steeper than the Engel curve for entertainment because food is a necessity while entertainment is a luxury good. A steep Engel curve suggests that increases in income lead to proportionately smaller increases in the purchases of the good. That is the case with food in a poor country.

5. **Why is water, which is essential for life, so cheap, while diamonds, which are not essential, so expensive?**
Answer: This water-diamond paradox exists because the price of a good reflects the value of the marginal unit. Water is so plentiful relative to our wants that the last unit of water consumed is not very valuable to us. That the total benefit of water to us is higher than the total value of diamonds is clear if one asks which you would give up completely in order to have the other good.

6. **Explain the slope of demand curve for a "Giffen" good.**
Answer: A Giffen good has a positively sloped demand curve. As price increases a person wishes to buy more of the good. Although no example has actually been found, such a demand curve would reflect what happens when a good is an inferior good and the income effect of a price change not only works opposite to the substitution effect but also is larger than the substitution effect.

Chapter 5:

Market Demand and Elasticities

Multiple-Choice

Choose the one alternative that best completes the statement or answers the question.

1. Although economists usually ignore the sign of the price elasticity of demand coefficient because they are more interested in the magnitude of the number, the price elasticity coefficient will always be a negative number because:
A) the price and quantity demanded of a good are always negatively related.
B) the demand curve slopes downward.
C) when the price of a good increases, the quantity demanded falls.
D) a change in price and a change in quantity demanded occur in the opposite direction.
E) All of the above are correct.

Difficulty: **Easy**

2. Along any downward-sloping linear demand curve:
A) the price elasticity of demand varies along the curve.
B) the price elasticity of demand is constant at every point along the demand curve.
C) demand is price elastic for prices below the midpoint of the demand curve.
D) demand is price inelastic for prices above the midpoint of the demand curve.
E) None of the above is correct.

Difficulty: **Easy**

3. Along any downward-sloping linear demand curve:
A) the price elasticity of demand is constant.
B) demand is elastic for prices above the midpoint of the demand curve and inelastic for prices below the midpoint.
C) the elasticity of demand is zero at the midpoint of the demand curve.
D) demand is elastic below the midpoint of the curve and inelastic above the midpoint.
E) None of the above is correct.

Difficulty: **Easy**

4. Which of the following possibilities results in an increase in total consumer expenditures?
A) Demand is unitary elastic and price falls.
B) Demand is elastic and price rises.
C) Demand is inelastic and price falls.
D) Demand is inelastic and price rises.
E) None of the above is correct.

Difficulty: **Moderate**

5. The market demand curve for a particular good:
A) shows that a positive relationship exists between price and quantity demanded.

B) is the horizontal sum of all individual consumer demands for the good.
C) shows that in the market, there will never be a positive consumer surplus.
D) does not reflect the law of demand, as do individual demand curves.
E) None of the above is correct.

Difficulty: **Easy**

6. The market demand curve for a commodity will shift for all of the following reasons <u>except</u>:
A) the income of consumers changes.
B) the preferences of consumers change.
C) the number of consumers change.
D) the price of the commodity changes.
E) All of the above are correct.

Difficulty: **Easy**

7. If the price elasticity of demand for a particular good is greater than zero but less than one, then the:
A) percentage change in quantity demanded is greater than the percentage change in price.
B) price is above midpoint of the demand curve if the demand curve is linear.
C) percentage change in quantity demanded equals the percentage change in price.
D) percentage change in quantity demanded is less than the percentage change in price.
E) price is at the midpoint of the demand curve if the demand curve is linear.

Difficulty: **Moderate**

8. Which of the following will affect a good's price elasticity of demand?
A) the number of substitute goods available to the consumer
B) the tastes and preferences of consumers
C) the ease of substitution between goods
D) the period of time available to adjust to a price change
E) All of the above are correct.

Difficulty: **Easy**

9. Sometimes coffee growers in Brazil have destroyed some or all of their coffee crop in order to keep it from going to market. The best explanation for this type of action on the part of the growers is that they believed that:
A) the demand for coffee had an elasticity coefficient greater than zero but less than one.
B) the demand for coffee had an elasticity coefficient greater than one.
C) there was an international shortage of coffee.
D) coffee was an inferior good.
E) they faced an inelastic supply of coffee.

Difficulty: **Hard**

10. If you observe that the market demand curve for carrots is expressed by the equation QP=3, then the elasticity of demand for carrots is:
A) 1/3.
B) 3.

C) 1.
D) ½.
E) Cannot be determined from the information provided.

Difficulty: **Hard**

11. If the demand curve is a rectangular hyperbola then its general equation is:
A) Q = CP.
B) P = CQ.
C) Q = P/C.
D) Q = C/P.
E) P = C/Q.

Difficulty: **Moderate**

12. For a linear demand curve, total expenditures are maximum:
A) at its geometric midpoint.
B) at its vertical intercept.
C) at its horizontal intercept.
D) where price is maximum.
E) where quantity is maximum.

Difficulty: **Easy**

13. Everything else held constant, a firm seeking to increase its revenues would lower its price if the current price was:
A) at the midpoint of its demand curve.
B) below the midpoint of its demand curve.
C) above the midpoint of its demand curve.
D) at the horizontal intercept of its demand curve.
E) None of the above is correct.

Difficulty: **Moderate**

14. The market demand curve for day old fish is given by the equation PQ = 5. If the price of fish falls, then this reduction leads to:
A) an increase in the total revenue received by sellers.
B) a reduction in the total amount spent on day old fish.
C) an increase in the supply of day old fish.
D) no change in the total spending on fish.
E) None of the above is correct.

Difficulty: **Hard**

15. In which of the following cases will the total revenue fall?
A) Demand is inelastic and product price decreases.
B) Demand is elastic and product price decreases.
C) Demand is inelastic and product price increases.
D) Demand is unitary elastic and product price decreases.
E) Total spending does not fall in any of the above cases.

Difficulty: **Moderate** Page in Text: **141**

16. If the market demand curve for a particular good is given by the equation PQ = 1, and the price of this good rises, we would expect to see:
A) the total amount spent on the good to fall.
B) an increase in the total amount spent on the good.
C) the total amount spent on the good to remain unchanged.
D) the total amount spent on the good fall to zero.
E) None of the above is correct.

Difficulty: **Hard**

17. The total revenue received by sellers of widgets increases if:
A) the demand for widgets is inelastic and the seller raises prices.
B) the demand for widgets is unitary elastic and the sellers lower prices.
C) the demand for widgets is elastic and the seller lowers prices.
D) (A) and (B) are correct.
E) (A) and (C) are correct.

Difficulty: **Moderate**

18. When the value of a good's price elasticity of demand is greater than one, then:
A) a reduction in price causes a reduction in total revenue received by sellers.
B) an increase in price causes a reduction in the total revenue received by the sellers.
C) an increase in price causes an increase in the total revenue received by the sellers.
D) an increase in price causes no change in the total revenue received by the sellers.
E) None of the above is correct.

Difficulty: **Moderate**

19. If the percentage in price change is greater than the percentage change in quantity demanded of good X, then when price increases:
A) total revenue falls since demand is inelastic.
B) total revenue increases since demand is elastic.
C) there is no change in total revenue since demand is unitary elastic.
D) total revenue remains unchanged since demand is inelastic.
E) None of the above is correct.

Difficulty: **Moderate**

20. All of the following statements are false <u>except</u>:
A) demand is more elastic in the short run than in the long run.
B) the time period available for adjustment to changes in a good' price does not affect the elasticity of demand for the good.
C) the longer the time period consumers have to adjust to price changes, the more elastic will be the demand for the product.
D) the long-run demand curve for a product reflects the same elasticity as does the product's short-run demand curve.
E) in the long run, the demand curve for all goods are horizontal.

Difficulty: **Moderate**

21. If the percentage increase in the quantity demanded of good X is larger than the percentage decrease in the price of good Y, then the cross elasticity of demand between goods X and Y is:
    A) greater than zero but less than one.
    B) negative.
    C) equal to zero; X and Y are independent goods.
    D) greater than one.
    E) not enough information is provided to determine an answer.

    Difficulty: **Moderate**

22. If the number of apples sold falls from 700 bushels to 500 bushels when the price of oranges falls from $5 to $4 per bushel, then the cross elasticity of demand between apples and oranges is:
    A) 1.5, and so the goods are substitutes.
    B) –1.6, and so the goods are complements.
    C) 1.8, and so the goods are complements.
    D) –1.3, and so the goods are substitutes.
    E) So close to zero that apples and oranges are essentially independent of each other.

    Difficulty: **Moderate**

23. If you wanted to measure the relative responsiveness of the quantity demanded of good X when the price of a related good, say good Y, changed, then:
    A) you would use the same (or direct) price elasticity of demand for good X.
    B) since the price of good X doesn't initially change, its price elasticity of demand is equal to one.
    C) You would first have to consider the elasticity of supply for good X.
    D) You would have to calculate the cross elasticity of demand between goods X and Y.
    E) You would also need to calculate the income elasticity of demand for both good X and Y.

    Difficulty: **Easy**

24. Suppose that no relationship exists between goods X and Y, and so the demand for one is not affected by the demand for the other. The cross elasticity of demand when the price of good Y increases is:
    A) positive.
    B) greater than zero but less than one.
    C) greater than one.
    D) equal to zero.
    E) negative and less than –1.

    Difficulty: **Easy**

25. When any two goods are complementary, the cross elasticity of demand between the two goods is:
    A) greater than zero.
    B) equal to zero.
    C) less than zero.
    D) greater than zero but less than one.

E) may be either positive or negative.

Difficulty: **Easy**

26. Suppose that good X is a luxury. We would expect the income elasticity of demand for good X to be:
A) positive but less than one.
B) negative and greater than –1.
C) zero.
D) positive and greater than +1.
E) some value between –1 and +1.

Difficulty: **Moderate**

27. Suppose that a 5 percent increase in your income causes your purchases of widgets to fall from 10 to 7 units per time period. Your income elasticity of demand for widgets is:
A) -10.
B) –6.
C) –5.
D) +6.
E) +10.

Difficulty: **Moderate**

28. Suppose that you own an appliance store and that your main product is washing machines. If you reduce the price of washing machines by 30 percent and the quantity demanded increases by 35 percent, then you can conclude that the demand for washing machines is:
A) inelastic, and your total revenue is falling.
B) elastic, and your total revenue is rising.
C) inelastic, so there is no change in your total revenue.
D) elastic, so your total revenue is falling.
E) unitary elastic, so total revenue remains unchanged.

Difficulty: **Moderate**

29. The most likely reason why the demand for gasoline is more price elastic in the long run than in the short run is that, in the long run:
A) the law of demand does not hold.
B) individuals' incomes rise in order to offset rising prices.
C) as time passes, the cost of producing gasoline falls.
D) individuals respond to the price change by adjusting the amount of miles that they drive, the amount of public transportation that they consume, and the type of automobile that they purchase.
E) None of the above is correct.

Difficulty: **Moderate**

30. Suppose that the price elasticity of demand for widgets is 1.5 and their price falls from $2.10 to $1.90 per dozen. We would expect the quantity demanded of widgets to:
A) rise by less than 10 percent.
B) rise by about 15 percent.
C) fall by more than 10 percent.

D) fall by about 20 percent.
E) rise by about 20 percent.

Difficulty: **Moderate**

31. If the demand curve for soybeans is horizontal, then the price elasticity of demand for soybeans is:
A) 1.0.
B) zero.
C) approaching positive infinity.
D) somewhere between zero and one.
E) high relative to the elasticity of demand for corn.

Difficulty: **Hard**

32. Suppose you are the Director of the Metropolitan Atlanta Rapid Transit Authority and want to increase your revenues. When a study indicates that the price elasticity of demand for public transport services is -.73, in order to raise revenues, other things constant, you should:
A) raise the transit fares even though the number of riders will fall.
B) raise the transit fares because ridership will not change.
C) reduce your fares because the number of riders will increase and so will your revenue.
D) leave your fares unchanged since people using public transportation are obviously not responsive to price.
E) buy new buses and subway trains because the new models are more appealing to riders.

Difficulty: **Hard**

33. Some goods have close substitutes, others do not. Think about the ease or difficulty of substituting one good for another. After looking at the product classes below, select the most likely ranking of the products from highest to lowest price elasticity of demand.
A) Magnavox television sets, television sets, stereo television sets, color television sets.
B) Color television sets, television sets, stereo television sets, Magnavox television sets.
C) Magnavox television sets, stereo television sets, color television sets, television sets.
D) Stereo television sets, television sets, Magnavox television sets, color television sets.
E) It is impossible to say anything about the relative elasticities without knowing relative prices.

Difficulty: **Hard**

34. Generally speaking, the long-run demand curve for good X, when compared to the short-run demand curve:
A) will be perfectly elastic.
B) will be perfectly inelastic.
C) will have the same elasticity in the short run as in the long run.
D) will have a price elasticity of demand that approaches one in the long run.
E) will be more elastic than the short-run curve.

Difficulty: **Moderate**

35. Which pair of the following would likely have a positive cross elasticity of demand?
A) chicken and beef
B) peanut butter and jelly
C) gasoline and motor oil
D) mouthwash and automobile tires
E) beer and pretzels

Difficulty: **Moderate**

36. If the cross elasticity of demand of margarine with respect to the price of butter is 1.53%, then:
A) a 1% decrease in the price of butter leads to a 1.53% increase in the demand for margarine.
B) a 1% increase in the price of butter leads to a 1.53% increase in the demand for margarine.
C) a 1% increase in the price of margarine leads to a 1.53% decrease in the demand for margarine.
D) a 1% decrease in the price of margarine leads to a 1.53% increase in the demand for margarine.
E) None of the above is correct.

Difficulty: **Hard**

37. For any firm facing a downward-sloping linear demand curve, its marginal revenue:
A) decreases each time that the firm raises its price.
B) increases each time that the firm lowers its price.
C) is at a minimum at the midpoint of the demand curve.
D) is greater for prices above the midpoint of the demand curve than it is for prices below the midpoint.
E) reaches a maximum when the firm's total revenue is maximized.

Difficulty: **Moderate**

38. If a firm has a demand curve that plots as a rectangular hyperbola, we conclude that the price elasticity of demand faced by this firm is:
A) approaching positive infinity at every point on the curve.
B) the primary reason why total revenue changes when prices are lowered and quantity demanded increases.
C) constant and equal to one at every point on the curve.
D) approaching, or equal to, zero at every point on the curve because there is only a slight change in total revenue when price is reduced.
E) cannot be measured or expressed as a geometric relationship as is the case when the demand curve is linear.

Difficulty: **Moderate**

39. If a firm sells 10,000 units of output at a market price of $20 per unit, then its total revenue is:
A) $20,000.
B) $200,000.
C) $100,000.
D) $2,000,000.

E) $2,000.

Difficulty: **Easy**

40. All of the following statements about marginal revenue are correct <u>except</u>:
A) it falls and is less than price if prices fall with increased output.
B) it is always equal to the unit price of the output if price is constant.
C) it is equal to zero when a firm's demand curve is horizontal and price is constant.
D) it is equal to zero when total revenue is maximized.
E) it is negative when total revenue falls.

Difficulty: **Moderate**

41. Suppose that firm faces a downward-sloping linear demand curve. When the firm begins to change its price:
A) total revenue will fall when the firm reduces prices that are higher than that associated with the midpoint of the demand curve.
B) total revenue will not change if prices are below the midpoint of the demand curve.
C) total revenue will fall if the firm increases its prices when those prices are higher than that associated with the midpoint of the demand curve.
D) total revenue will rise if the firm lowers prices when those prices are below the midpoint of the demand curve.
E) None of the above is correct.

Difficulty: **Moderate**

42. For a firm facing a downward-sloping linear demand curve, the marginal revenue gained when an additional unit of output is sold is:
A) the product of the new price and the new quantity.
B) the price at which the extra unit is sold minus a loss in revenue because each unit previously sold is now sold at a lower price.
C) equal to the price of the output.
D) rises as long as demand is elastic.
E) None of the above is correct.

Difficulty: **Moderate**

43. The marginal revenue curve associated with a firm's downward-sloping linear demand curve:
A) lies below the demand curve at every level of output sold except for the first unit.
B) is not affected by shifts in the firm's demand curve.
C) shows a positive relationship between price and quantity demanded.
D) lies below the horizontal axis as long as total revenue is rising.
E) is at a maximum when total revenue is at a maximum.

Difficulty: **Moderate**

44. Suppose that a firm faces a downward-sloping demand curve and it cuts its price from $9 per unit of output to $8 per unit of output. As a result of the price change, quantity demanded increases from 2 to 3 units. The marginal revenue received by this firm from the last unit of output sold is:
A) $18.
B) $24.

C) $6.
D) $42.
E) None of the above is correct.

Difficulty: **Moderate**

45. Suppose that a firm can sell 50 units of output at a price of $100 per unit and 75 units of output when price drops to $90 per unit. The marginal revenue generated by this price reduction is:
A) $70.
B) $1,750.
C) $5,000.
D) $10.
E) None of the above is correct.

Difficulty: **Moderate**

46. Suppose that a firm sells 20 units of output at a particular price and receives total revenue of $800. If the firm reduces its price, sales go up to 25 units and total revenue rises to $845. We can conclude that:
A) the firm is operating above the midpoint of its demand curve.
B) the marginal revenue received from the sale of the last unit is $45.
C) the demand for the product is price elastic.
D) total revenue has not yet reached a maximum.
E) All of the above are correct.

Difficulty: **Moderate**

47. Suppose that a firm with a downward-sloping linear demand curve operates at a point on that curve. If price is reduced slightly from $1.00 to $.99, an additional unit is sold. If the price elasticity of demand is 4, what is the marginal revenue generated by the last unit sold?
A) $.01
B) $.746
C) $.995
D) $1.00
E) None of the above is correct.

Difficulty: **Moderate**

48. If you have the relation MR = P(1 – 1/?), where P is product price and ? is the price elasticity of demand. If the price of a product at a particular quantity is $8 per unit, and ? is 1, what can be said about total revenue when the last unit is old at $8?
A) Total revenue is increasing because the price elasticity of demand is a positive number.
B) Total revenue is at a maximum.
C) Total revenue is increasing but at a decreasing rate.
D) Total revenue is decreasing at an increasing rate.
E) Nothing can be said about total revenue because we do not know how many units of output are being sold at $8.

Difficulty: **Moderate**

49. If the price elasticity of demand is 2 and the last unit of a product is sold at a price of $10, what is the marginal revenue generated by this last unit?
A) $10.
B) $1.
C) $2.
D) $5.
E) $8.

Difficulty: **Moderate**

50. Suppose that you used regression analysis to statistically estimate the demand function for widgets. Your estimated function is

$$Q = P_w^{-2.5} P_x^{3.1} P_z^{-1.7} Y^{1.7}$$

where: P_w = the unit price of widgets, P_x = the unit price of good X, P_z = the unit price of good Z, Y = the consumer's money income.
From this information you would be correct in concluding that:
A) the demand curve for widgets is downward sloping.
B) the price elasticity of demand for widgets is –2.5.
C) widgets and good X are rather good substitutes.
D) widgets can be considered a luxury good.
E) All of the above are correct.

Difficulty: **Hard**

51. All of the following goods will likely have a positive cross elasticity of demand <u>except</u>:
A) coffee and tea.
B) wax paper and aluminum foil.
C) Coca-Cola and Pepsi-Cola.
D) hamburgers and french fries.
E) corn flakes and raisin bran.

Difficulty: **Moderate**

52. The relationship among marginal revenue, price, and the price elasticity of demand can be expressed as:
A) MR = P(1/ ?).
B) MR = P(1 - 1/ ?).
C) MR = P(1 + 1/ ?).
D) MR = P(1 + ?).
E) None of the above is correct.

Difficulty: **Moderate**

53. Suppose that the quantity demanded falls from 100 to 90 units when the price of good X increases from $45 to $55 per unit. The price elasticity of demand is:
A) 2.25
B) 1.75
C) 1.00
D) 0.53

E) 0.04

Difficulty: **Moderate**

54. Suppose that the quantity demanded of some good rises from 2 to 3 units when the price of the good falls from $10 to $9 per unit. We can conclude that:
A) the demand for the good is inelastic.
B) the demand for the good is elastic.
C) the demand for the good is perfectly inelastic.
D) the demand for the good possesses unitary elasticity.
E) the demand for the good is perfectly elastic.

Difficulty: **Moderate**

55. Assume that a recent market study indicates that the price elasticity of demand for fresh salmon is 2.5. If there is a thirty percent decrease in the price per pound of salmon, we can conclude that the quantity demanded of this fish will:
A) increase by 45 percent.
B) increase, but by some percentage less than the percent change in price.
C) increase by 75 percent.
D) also increase by 30 percent.
E) increase by 250 percent.

Difficulty: **Moderate**

56. Along any downward-sloping linear demand curve:
A) the price elasticity of demand is constant.
B) the price elasticity of demand is zero at the midpoint of the curve.
C) demand is elastic below the midpoint of the curve.
D) demand is elastic above the midpoint of the curve and inelastic below the midpoint.
E) the price elasticity of demand is less than one above the midpoint of the curve.

Difficulty: **Moderate**

57. Suppose that the price of a particular good rises from $15 to $20, and the quantity demanded of the good falls from 1,500 to 1,000 units. The arc elasticity of demand is:
A) 1.4.
B) 2.6.
C) 3.9.
D) 0.8.
E) 1.0.

Difficulty: **Moderate**

58. Suppose that the price of good X increases by ten percent and that as a result, the quantity demanded falls by four percent. We can conclude that:
A) the demand for good X is elastic with an elasticity coefficient of 4, so total spending by consumers for good X will rise.
B) the demand for good X is elastic with an elasticity coefficient of 0.4, so total spending by consumers for good X will rise.

C) the demand for good X is inelastic with an elasticity coefficient of 0.4, so total spending by consumers for good X will rise.
D) the demand for good X is inelastic with an elasticity coefficient of 4, so total spending by consumers for good X will fall.
E) None of the above is correct.

Difficulty: **Moderate**

59. When you calculate the price elasticity of demand for a particular good, you are calculating the ratio of:
A) a percentage change in quantity demanded to a percentage change in price.
B) a percentage change in price to a percentage change in quantity demanded.
C) a change in demand to a change in price.
D) a change in price to a percentage change in quantity demanded.
E) None of the above is correct.

Difficulty: **Easy**

60. Suppose that the price elasticity of demand for tickets to the movie theatre is 2.0. If the price should suddenly rise by 15 percent because fewer movies are now made in Hollywood, the quantity demanded for movie tickets will:
A) fall by 15 percent.
B) increase by 20 percent.
C) fall by 10 percent.
D) increase by 15 percent.
E) fall by 30 percent.

Difficulty: **Moderate**

61. Assume that you are the president and CEO of the Widget Corporation. You want to increase the quantity of widgets that your company sells by 10 percent. Your marketing department estimates that the price elasticity of demand for widgets is –0.50. Assume that your marketing department has correctly estimated the price elasticity of demand for widgets, in order for you to increase your sales by 10 percent, you must:
A) lower the price of widgets by 5 percent.
B) lower the price of widgets by 10 percent.
C) increase the price of widgets by 20 percent because demand is inelastic.
D) lower the price of widgets by 20 percent.
E) None of the above is correct.

Difficulty: **Moderate**

62. Which of the following statements is true?
A) The price elasticity for Marlboro cigarettes is much larger than that for cigarettes in general.
B) The price elasticity of demand for a commodity is smaller the greater are the number of substitutes.
C) The demand for coffee is more elastic than the demand for salt.
D) All of the above are true.
E) None of the above is true.

Difficulty: **Moderate**

63. Suppose that the price elasticity of demand for good Y has been estimated (correctly) at 2. After a 10 percent increase in the demand for good Y, buyers would continue to purchase the same quantity of the good as before if the price was about:
A) 5 percent higher.
B) 10 percent higher.
C) 5 percent lower.
D) 10 percent lower.
E) None of the above is correct.

Difficulty: **Hard**

64. If the ABC Corp. increased the amount of its spending on advertising, this increase would likely cause:
A) the demand curve for the firm's product to shift to the right, but the price elasticity of demand would remain unchanged.
B) the demand curve for the firm's product to shift to the left.
C) the demand curve for the firm's product to shift to the right, and the new demand curve would be relatively more inelastic than the initial demand curve.
D) (B) and (C) are possible.
E) (A) and (C) are possible.

Difficulty: **Hard**

65. The arc elasticity method is most often used by economists to estimate the price elasticity of demand when:
A) they believe the demand for the product under analysis to be elastic.
B) they believe the demand for the product under analysis to be inelastic.
C) it is impossible to derive the demand curve for the product.
D) the demand curve for the product is linear.
E) the economists have only two observations on product price and quantity.

Difficulty: **Easy**

66. Which of the following has not contributed to the decline of sales at McDonald's?
A) Higher relative price of McDonald's products.
B) Excessive expansion of McDonald's restaurants abroad.
C) Increased competition from other fastfood chains.
D) Slowed growth of personal income.
E) A decrease in the proportion of 15- to 29-year-olds in the total population.

Difficulty: **Easy**

67. Estimates of the short run and long run price elasticity of demand in the U.S. for a number of goods are given below. Based on what these estimates reveal about the opinions of demanders, which good(s) appear to lack suitable substitutes even in the long run?

COMMODITY	SHORT RUN	LONG RUN
Foreign travel	-0.14	-1.77
Gasoline	-0.2	-0.6
Jewelry and	-0.41	-0.67

watches		
Tobacco products	-0.46	-1.89
Wine	-0.88	-1.17
Clothing	-0.9	-2.9

A) foreign travel and gasoline
B) wine and clothing
C) gasoline and jewelry and watches
D) foreign travel only
E) clothing only

Difficulty: **Moderate**

68. Correct values for income elasticity of demand may be calculated by using the percentage change in expenditures on a commodity in place of the percentage change in the quantity purchased only if:
A) the price of the commodity has been held constant.
B) the quantity purchased of the commodity has been held constant.
C) income has been held constant.
D) the income elasticity has a positive sign.
E) All of the above are correct.

Difficulty: **Hard**

69. In a celebrated court case regarding DuPont Corporation and the market for cellophane:
A) the court held that DuPont's seventy-five percent cellophane market share was clear evidence that DuPont had monopolized the market for cellophane.
B) the cross elasticity of demand between cellophane and other flexible packaging materials was sufficiently high to indicate that DuPont's market share in the relevant market was only twenty percent.
C) DuPont's share of the flexible packaging market indicated that it had monopolized that market.
D) the court held that, although DuPont had monopolized the flexible packaging market, the cross elasticity of demand between flexible packaging and cellophane justified DuPont's actions.
E) None of the above is correct.

Difficulty: **Moderate**

70. Given that the cross elasticity of demand for beer with respect to wine is 0.31 and with respect to spirits is 0.15, one may conclude from this information that:
A) only wine is a substitute for beer.
B) only spirits are a substitute for beer.
C) wine and spirits are both substitutes for beer, but wine is a better substitute.
D) wine and spirits are both substitutes for beer, but spirits are a better substitute.
E) Neither wine nor spirits are substitutes for beer.

Difficulty: **Moderate**

71. Given that income elasticity of demand for beer is –0.09, for wine is 5.03, and for spirits is 1.21, one may conclude from this information that:
A) beer is a luxury good, and wine and spirits are inferior goods.
B) **wine and spirits are luxury goods, and beer is an inferior good.**
C) if income increases ten percent, then demand for beer will drop 0.09 percent.
D) spirits are a stronger inferior good than wine.
E) wine and spirits are both substitutes for beer.

Difficulty: **Moderate**

72. Traditional marketing approaches to estimate demand curves do <u>not</u> include:
A) interviews or questionnaires.
B) consumer clinics.
C) market experiments.
D) regression analysis.
E) All of the above are correct.

Difficulty: **Easy**

73. Which of the following is <u>not</u> a weakness of marketing approaches to estimating market demand?
A) biased results from untrustworthy answers
B) small sample size
C) only long run responses are measured
D) permanent loss of customers
E) All of the above are weaknesses of marketing approaches to estimating market demand.

Difficulty: **Easy**

74. Micromarketing:
A) involves narrowing a marketing strategy to the individual store or consumer.
B) involves the use of detailed point-of-sale information on demographic and economic characteristics of customers.
C) is practiced by companies, such as Waldenbooks, to automatically send you information on new books in a field in which you have already shown an interest.
D) has been made possible by technological change.
E) All of the above are correct.

Difficulty: **Easy**

75. Elasticities of demand for electricity, with regard to: the price of electricity; per capita income; the price of gas; and the number of customers in the market, are: -0.974; 0.714; 0.159, and 1.000, respectively. Given this information, which of the following is incorrect?
A) Electricity is an inferior good.
B) The market demand curve for electricity is negatively sloped.
C) Electricity is a necessity.
D) Gas is a substitute for electricity.
E) Market demand grows proportionately with an increase in the number of customers in the market.

Difficulty: **Hard**

76. To calculate the contribution which increases in per capita income will make to the forecasted growth in demand for electricity:
   A) multiply the income elasticity of demand for electricity by the expected growth in per capita income.
   B) divide the income elasticity of demand for electricity by the expected growth in per capita income.
   C) add the income elasticity of demand for electricity to the expected growth in per capita income.
   D) divide the expected growth in per capita income by the income elasticity of demand for electricity.
   E) subtract the income elasticity of demand for electricity from the expected growth in per capita income.

   Difficulty: **Hard**

77. Elasticities of demand for electricity, with regard to: the price of electricity; per capita income; the price of gas; and the number of customers in the market, are: -0.974; 0.714; 0.159; and 1.000, respectively. Using the assumption of respective growth rates of 2%, 11%, 5%, and 3% for each of these variables, what would one forecast as the rate of growth in demand for electricity?
   A) 11.65%.
   B) 5.25%.
   C) 6.63%.
   D) 9.7%.
   E) 7.4%.

   Difficulty: **Hard**

78. Elasticities of demand for electricity, with regard to: the price of electricity; per capita income; the price of gas; and the number of customers in the market, are: -0.665; 0.580; 0.127; and 1.23, respectively. Using the assumption of respective growth rates of 3%, 15%, 7%, and 5% for each of these variables, what would one forecast as the rate of growth in demand for electricity?
   A) 7.5%.
   B) 13.75%.
   C) 2.6%.
   D) 10.65%.
   E) 6.44%.

   Difficulty: **Hard**

79. If the demand curve is a negatively sloped straight line, which of the following statements is correct?
   A) Marginal revenue is zero at the unitary elastic point.
   B) Total revenue is maximized where marginal revenue is zero.
   C) Total revenue increases and marginal revenue decreases over the range of output from zero to the unitary elastic point.
   D) Total revenue decreases and marginal revenue decreases at output levels beyond the unitary elastic point.
   E) All of the above are correct.

   Difficulty: **Moderate**

80. For the United States, the price elasticity of demand for imports:
A) is equal to the ratio of the percentage change in quantity of U.S. imports to the percentage change in the price of U.S. imports.
B) applies to cases where the foreign-currency price of the import changes.
C) applies to cases where the exchange rate between the U.S. dollar and other currencies changes.
D) of manufactured goods is estimated to be approximately equal to 1 in the short run and in the long run.
E) All of the above are correct.

Difficulty: **Moderate**

81. For the United States, the price elasticity of demand for exports:
A) is equal to the ratio of the percentage change in quantity of U.S. exports to the percentage change in the price of U.S. exports.
B) applies to cases where the foreign-currency price of the export changes.
C) applies to cases where the exchange rate between the U.S. dollar and other currencies changes.
D) of manufactured goods is estimated to be low in the short run and high in the long run.
E) All of the above are correct.

Difficulty: **Moderate**

82. Estimates of the price elasticity of demand for imports of manufactured goods for the United States indicate that if the U.S. dollar decreases in value in foreign exchange markets, then relative to their initial level, the dollar value of imports will:
A) be unchanged in the short run and the long run.
B) be unchanged in the short run and will increase in the long run.
C) decrease in the short run and increase in the long run.
D) increase in the short run and decrease in the long run.
E) decrease in short run and in the long run.

Difficulty: **Moderate**

83. Estimates of the price elasticity of demand for exports of manufactured goods for the United States indicate that if the U.S. dollar decreases in value in foreign exchange markets, then relative to their initial level, the dollar value of exports will:
A) decrease in the short run and the long run.
B) decrease in the short run and will increase in the long run.
C) increase in the short run and decrease in the long run.
D) increase in the short run and decrease in the long run.
E) be unchanged in short run and increase in the long run.

Difficulty: **Moderate**

84. For the United States, which of the following statements regarding the income elasticity of demand for imports is <u>not</u> correct?
A) The income elasticity of demand for imports is equal to the ratio of the percentage change in quantity of U.S. imports to the percentage change in U.S. income.
B) The income elasticity of demand for imports is estimated to be greater than one.

C) The income elasticity of demand for imports indicates that for the U.S. imports are a normal good.
D) The income elasticity of demand for imports for the United States is much lower than for all other industrialized countries.
E) All of the above are correct.

Difficulty: **Moderate**

85. In a market with a very large number of sellers of a homogeneous product, the demand curve for the output of any one firm is:
A) a vertical line.
B) a negatively sloped line.
C) a positively sloped line.
D) a horizontal line.
E) Demand has no meaning at the level at the level of one firm in a market with many sellers.

Difficulty: **Moderate**

Short Answer

Write the word or phrase that best complete each statement or answers the question.

1. **What are bandwagon, snob, and Veblen effects and how do they affect the demand curve?**
Answer: The bandwagon effect occurs when price falls and quantity demanded increases, and the fact that some people are buying more of the good causes others to purchase more of the good in order to be fashionable. The bandwagon effect causes the demand curve to be flatter or more elastic than it would be otherwise. The snob effect has the opposite effect on demand. As price falls and quantity demanded increases, some buyers reduce their purchases or stop buying the good in order to stand out and be different. This causes the demand curve to be steeper or more elastic.

2. **Why is a demand curve that reflects unitary elastic demand for good X at all prices a rectangular hyperbola?**
Answer: The area defined by any point on a rectangular hyperbola is of an equal size. Thus, the area of price x quantity is the same no matter what price is chosen. This means that total expenditures of demanders is the same regardless of price. According to the total expenditures test for elasticity, if the total expenditure on good X is unchanged when its price changes, then the demand for good X must be unitary elastic, i.e., the percentage change in quantity demanded is equal (but of the opposite sign) to the percentage change in price that brought it about.

3. **The estimated price elasticity of demand for natural gas use in the home is relatively high, i.e., -1.40 in the short run and –2.10 in the long run. How is this possible given that it takes up a non-trivial portion of household budgets?**
Answer: Price elasticity of demand for goods is determined by a number of variables of which percentage of household budget spent on the good is only one. In the case of natural gas, it is possible that there are relatively close substitutes which can be accessed without too much difficulty, especially in the long run, e.g., electricity. It may also be relatively easy to economize on the use of natural gas in some geographic regions in the long run.

4. **The court used cross elasticities in arriving at the decision, a number of years ago, that DuPont had not monopolized the market for cellophane even though it had 75% of the market. Explain.**
Answer: Cross elasticities reveal how sensitive the demands for goods are to price changes in other goods. High cross elasticities suggest strong substitute relationships between goods and help to define what goods may be considered to be part of a single market composed of differentiated goods. This relationship was found to exist between cellophane and other flexible packing materials. DuPont had only a 20% market share in the market for flexible packing materials including cellophane.

5. **Given that the U.S. price elasticity of demand for imports of manufactured goods is 1.06 in the short run and the long run, and the foreign price elasticity of demand for exports of manufactured goods is 0.48 in the short run and 1.67 in the long run, a drop in the value of the dollar on foreign exchange markets is likely to cause the U.S. trade deficit in manufactured goods to worsen at first. Explain.**
Answer: These elasticities indicate that a drop in the value of the dollar will in the short run leave U.S. expenditures on foreign manufactured goods almost unchanged. However, they also indicate that a drop in the value of the dollar will in the short run cause foreign expenditures on U.S. manufactured goods to fall. This leads to a larger trade deficit in manufactured goods. In the long run, however, the drop in the value of the dollar will cause U.S. spending on foreign manufactured goods to remain the same but will substantially increase foreign spending on U.S. manufactured goods.

6. **Explain the "Veblen" effect.**
Answer: The Veblen effect refers to the effects on market demand of what Thorstein Veblen called "conspicuous consumption." Showing off is part of what a person engaged in conspicuous consumption is doing. Thus, if price of the good falls and others can afford it more readily, the person practicing conspicuous consumption will not wish to buy the good. Such consumers cause the market demand curve to be less elastic than would other wise be the case.

Chapter 6:

Choice Under Uncertainty

Multiple-Choice

Choose the one alternative that best completes the statement or answers the question.

1. The applicability of traditional economic theory is limited by the fact that it is based on the assumption of:
   A) a riskless world.
   B) rational behavior.
   C) consumer optimization of utility.
   D) perfect information.
   E) All of the above.

   Difficulty: **Easy**

2. The situation in which there is only one possible outcome to a decision and this outcome is known precisely is:
   A) risk.
   B) uncertainty.
   C) rationality.
   D) certainty.
   E) None of the above is correct.

   Difficulty: **Easy**

3. The situation in which there is more than one possible outcome to a decision and the probability of each specific outcome is known or can be estimated is:
   A) risk.
   B) uncertainty.
   C) rationality.
   D) certainty.
   E) None of the above is correct.

   Difficulty: **Easy**

4. The situation in which there is more than one possible outcome to a decision and the probability of each specific outcome is not known or even meaningful is:
   A) risk.
   B) uncertainty.
   C) rationality.
   D) certainty.
   E) None of the above is correct.

   Difficulty: **Easy**

5. The difference between risk and uncertainty is whether or not:
   A) there are more than one of possible outcomes.
   B) the outcomes are certain.
   C) the probability of the possible outcomes can be known or estimated.
   D) All of the above.
   E) (A) and (C) are true.

   Difficulty: **Moderate**

6. Tossing a coin is an example of a situation of:
   A) risk.
   B) uncertainty.
   C) rationality.
   D) certainty.
   E) None of the above is correct.

   Difficulty: **Easy**

7. Investing in a stock is an example of a situation of:
   A) risk.
   B) uncertainty.
   C) rationality.
   D) certainty.
   E) None of the above is correct.

   Difficulty: **Easy**

8. Drilling for oil in an unproven field is an example of a situation of:
   A) risk.
   B) uncertainty.
   C) rationality.
   D) certainty.
   E) None of the above is correct.

   Difficulty: **Easy**

9. In general, the risk associated with a decision or action:
   A) increases with the number of possible outcomes.
   B) increases with the range of possible outcomes.
   C) cannot be measured.
   D) Both (A) and (B) are true.
   E) None of the above is true.

   Difficulty: **Easy**

10. One of several alternative courses of action that a decision maker can take to achieve a goal is called a(n):
    A) state of nature.
    B) payoff matrix.
    C) strategy.
    D) outcome.

E) None of the above.

Difficulty: **Easy**

11. A condition in the future that will have a significant effect on the degree of success or failure of a chosen course of action, but over which the decision maker has little or no control is called a(n):
A) state of nature.
B) payoff matrix.
C) strategy.
D) outcome.
E) None of the above.

Difficulty: **Easy**

12. A payoff matrix shows the possible outcomes or results of each _____ under each _____.
A) state of nature; strategy
B) strategy; state of nature
C) state of nature; decision
D) course of action; decision
E) course of action; strategy

Difficulty: **Easy**

13. Which of the following statements is <u>false</u>?
A) Coca-Cola changed its recipe in 1985 in order to ward off the challenge from Pepsi-Cola, which had been chipping away at Coke's market lead over the years.
B) When the new Coke was introduced, there was nothing short of a consumer revolt against it.
C) Even with both new Coke and Classic Coke selling side by side, Coca-Cola still lost market share to Pepsi.
D) Most marketing experts are convinced that Coca-Cola underestimated consumers' loyalty to the old Coke.
E) The example of Coca-Cola and its introduction of new Coke shows that even a well-conceived strategy is risky.

Difficulty: **Easy**

Use the data below to answer questions 14 – 17:

Investment	State of Economy	Probability	Outcome of Investment
	Boom	0.25	$1000
A	Normal	0.50	500
	Recession	0.25	200
	Boom	0.25	$500
B	Normal	0.50	300
	Recession	0.25	100

14. The expected value of Investment A is:
    A) $1000.
    B) $550.
    C) $500.
    D) $250.
    E) Cannot be determined from the information provided.

    Difficulty: **Moderate**

15. The expected value of Investment B is:
    A) $500.
    B) $225.
    C) $200.
    D) $50.
    E) Cannot be determined from the information provided.

    Difficulty: **Moderate**

16. Which of the following statements is true?
    A) Investment A is less risky than Investment B.
    B) Investment B is less risky than Investment A.
    C) Both Investment A and Investment B have the same degree of risk.
    D) The riskiness of either investment cannot be calculated from the information provided.
    E) None of the above is true.

    Difficulty: **Moderate**

17. An individual should choose:
    A) Investment A because it is less risky.
    B) Investment B because it is less risky.
    C) Investment B if its lower risk compensates for its lower expected outcome.
    D) Investment A if its lower risk compensates for its lower expected outcome.
    E) None of the above; the individual would be indifferent between the two investments.

    Difficulty: **Moderate**

18. A particular strategy or decision has a lower risk if:
    A) there is a smaller probability that the actual outcome will deviate significantly from the expected value.
    B) the probability distribution of its outcomes is tighter or less dispersed.
    C) the standard deviation has a small value.
    D) All of the above are true.
    E) and (B) are true.

    Difficulty: **Moderate**

19. Which of the following statements is <u>false</u>?
   A) Risk analysis can be used to analyze crime deterrence.
   B) Studies have shown that the rate of robberies and burglaries is positively related to the gains and inversely related to the costs of criminal activity.
   C) According to some research, increasing the efficiency of the police in apprehending criminals and the imposition of stiffer sentences discourages crime.
   D) By increasing the penalty, law enforcement agencies can reduce the cost of enforcement.
   E) All of the above are true.

   Difficulty: **Moderate**

20. Most individuals are:
   A) risk seekers.
   B) risk averters.
   C) risk neutral.
   D) risk lovers.
   E) unaware of risk.

   Difficulty: **Easy**

21. Individuals who choose a more risky investment can be described as:
   A) risk seekers.
   B) risk averters.
   C) risk neutral.
   D) risk lovers.
   E) Both (A) and (D) are true.

   Difficulty: **Easy**

22. Individuals who are indifferent to risk are called:
   A) risk seekers.
   B) risk averters.
   C) risk neutral.
   D) risk lovers.
   E) unaware of risk.

   Difficulty: **Easy**

23. Most individuals are _____ because they face diminishing marginal utility of money.
   A) risk seekers.
   B) risk averters.
   C) risk neutral.
   D) risk lovers.
   E) unaware of risk.

   Difficulty: **Easy**

24. Which one of the following best describes a risk-neutral person?
   A) The risk-neutral person will always hedge his bets.
   B) The risk-neutral person is concerned only with return and not risks.
   C) The risk-neutral person will balance his risk-averse and his risk-seeking behavior over the year.

D) The risk-neutral person does not have a well-defined preference function.
E) None of the above is correct.

Difficulty: **Moderate**

25. An individual for whom the marginal utility of money diminishes will have a total utility of money curve that is:
A) concave.
B) convex.
C) a straight line.
D) downward sloping.
E) horizontal.

Difficulty: **Easy**

26. Suppose an individual is offered the opportunity to engage in a bet in which a fair coin is tossed. If "heads" comes up, the individual wins $1000. If "tails" comes up, the individual loses $1000. If an individual is risk averse, the expected utility of the bet for the individual is:
A) zero.
B) positive.
C) negative.
D) $1000.
E) indeterminate.

Difficulty: **Easy**

27. Even if the expected monetary return from a project is positive, it may not be undertaken by an individual who is:
A) a risk seeker.
B) risk averse.
C) risk neutral.
D) a risk lover.
E) None of the above; all individuals, regardless of their risk preferences, will undertake such a project.

Difficulty: **Easy**

28. When risk is taken into account, individuals are assumed to seek to maximize:
A) expected monetary return.
B) actual monetary return.
C) utility.
D) expected utility.
E) the standard deviation of the outcomes.

Difficulty: **Easy**

29. The change in America's tastes in favor of gambling is due to:

A) the boom in legal gambling.
B) the increased presence of organized crime in gambling.
C) an absence of other forms of leisure activities.
D) a change in the age distribution of the population.
E) the presence of more poor people in the population.

Difficulty: **Easy**

30. The individual who purchases insurance is willing to pay a _____ amount of money to avoid the _____ risk of incurring a _____ loss.
A) small; small; small
B) large; large; large
C) small; large; large
D) small; small; large
E) None of the above is correct.

Difficulty: **Easy**

31. In economics, we assume that most people take risks:
A) because it is exciting to do so.
B) only when they are forced to do so.
C) if their indifference between goods X and Y are positively sloped.
D) if they are compensated for taking the risks.
E) None of the above is correct.

Difficulty: **Easy**

32. In many coastal areas of the United States, private insurance companies will not write flood insurance, and so the Federal government underwrites the insurance. The most likely reason why private firms will not insure against flooding is that:
A) the individual risks of flooding are not independent of each other.
B) insurance companies are basically unfair to people living in coastal areas.
C) at least once a year some part of the mainland coast will be hit by a major hurricane, so flooding somewhere is unavoidable.
D) the individual risks of property owners are independent of each other.
E) None of the above is correct.

Difficulty: **Moderate**

33. The fact that some people who buy insurance against property losses will also gamble on horse races suggests that:
A) economists cannot analyze the behavior of gamblers.
B) there is some excitement and positive utility in gambling.
C) most people are, in fact, not risk averse.
D) the expected gain from gambling is equal to the expected loss from an unexpected adverse event.
E) None of the above is correct.

Difficulty: **Moderate**

34. It is possible for an individual investor to reduce risk in her portfolio through asset diversification. By this we mean:
A) having only riskless assets in her portfolio.
B) including several different types of assets in her portfolio.
C) avoiding those assets whose prices are too high at the time of purchase.
D) the investor is trying to insure against risk, not reduce it.
E) None of the above is correct.

Difficulty: **Easy**

35. Suppose that you are offered a raffle ticket for $10. There will be 1,000 tickets sold, and the payoff will be $5,000. What is your expected return from this raffle?
A) $5,000
B) $500
C) $-5
D) $-10
E) $0

Difficulty: **Moderate**

36. Suppose that you have a business that generates $4,000 income, per month, for you. If your business should be totally or partially destroyed, your income would fall to $500 per month. If the likelihood of your business being destroyed is .8, what is the expected value of your business income?
A) $2,000
B) $1,200
C) $2,450
D) $5,200
E) $3,450

Difficulty: **Moderate**

37. Gambling:
A) has similar effects to a very progressive tax, i.e., takes a larger percentage of the income of high income earners than of low income earners.
B) has grown in the U.S. to a greater extent as a consequence of efforts of state and local governments to raise more money without increasing taxes.
C) acts as a substantial net stimulus to the economy as suggested by the experience of Atlantic City, New Jersey.
D) absorbs only a small fraction of the income of Americans when compared to Americans' expenditures on movie theatres and recorded music.
E) All of the above are correct.

Difficulty: **Moderate**

38. Indifference curves used in the analysis of how risks (measured on a vertical axis) and returns (measured on a horizontal axis) are balanced in an optimum portfolio:
A) are negatively sloped and are steeper for more risk averse investors.
B) are positively sloped and are steeper for more risk averse investors.
C) are negatively sloped and are flatter for more risk averse investors.
D) are positively sloped and are flatter for more risk averse investors.

E) indifference curves cannot be successfully employed in the analysis.

Difficulty: **Moderate**

39. In the use of utility theory to explain the selection of an optimum portfolio, the efficiency opportunity set:
A) shows the various combinations of return and risk that assure the investor equal satisfaction.
B) shows various combinations of return and risk that are obtainable with a mixed portfolio.
C) is used with indifference curves to identify the optimum portfolio.
D) (A) and (C) are correct.
E) (B) and (C) are correct.

Difficulty: **Moderate**

40. The maximum amount that an individual would be willing to pay to avoid a risk is called the:
A) risk premium.
B) insurance gap.
C) maximum premium.
D) expected value.
E) None of the above is correct.

Difficulty: **Easy**

41. An individual who is willing to gamble faces a total utility function that is:
A) concave.
B) convex.
C) horizontal.
D) vertical.
E) None of the above is correct.

Difficulty: **Easy**

42. Which of the following statements is true?
A) In the real world we often observe individuals purchasing insurance and also gambling.
B) An individual may be a risk avoider for declines in income and a risk seeker for increases in income.
C) The total utility of money curve may be concave at low levels of money income and convex at high levels of income.
D) All of the above are true.
E) None of the above is true.

Difficulty: **Easy**

43. If an indifference curve is drawn relating expected income (on the vertical axis) to the variability of expected income (on the horizontal axis), the more risk averse the individual the:
A) flatter the indifference curves.
B) steeper the indifference curves.
C) closer the indifference curves will be to each other.
D) farther apart the indifference curves will be from each other.

E) None of the above is true.

Difficulty: **Easy**

44. If an indifference curve is drawn relating expected income (on the vertical axis) to the variability of expected income (on the horizontal axis), the less risk averse the individual the:
A) flatter the indifference curves.
B) steeper the indifference curves.
C) closer the indifference curves will be to each other.
D) farther apart the indifference curves will be from each other.
E) None of the above is true.

Difficulty: **Easy**

45. An individual can reduce risk or uncertainty by:
A) gathering more information.
B) diversification.
C) risk spreading.
D) insurance.
E) All of the above.

Difficulty: **Easy**

46. Consumers who consult publications such as *Consumer Reports* before making purchases are attempting to reduce their risk or uncertainty by:
A) gathering more information.
B) diversification.
C) risk spreading.
D) insurance.
E) All of the above.

Difficulty: **Easy**

47. A consumer who invests in a number of independent projects instead of a single one is attempting to reduce his or her risk or uncertainty by:
A) gathering more information.
B) diversification.
C) risk avoidance.
D) insurance.
E) All of the above.

Difficulty: **Easy**

48. For diversification to be effective in reducing risks, there must be:
A) a large number of projects.
B) a small number of projects in the same sector of the economy.
C) negative correlation between the projects.
D) a large number of projects with positive correlation among them.
E) a small number of projects with perfect positive correlation among them.

Difficulty: **Easy**

49. If there is _____ correlation between two projects, then investing in both of them will not reduce the risk at all.
A) imperfect positive
B) imperfect negative
C) perfect negative
D) perfect positive
E) zero

Difficulty: **Easy**

50. Suppose that an individual wishes to reduce the risk in his or her portfolio of stocks. This can be accomplished by:
A) buying a large number of different stocks.
B) buying a small number of stocks in firms in the same industry.
C) buying a large number of shares of stock in the same firm.
D) All of the above.
E) (A) and (C) are true.

Difficulty: **Easy**

51. The maximum price that an individual is willing to pay for insurance is equal to the:
A) risk premium.
B) difference between the expected value of a loss and a certain sum that provides the individual with the same utility.
C) expected value of the loss.
D) All of the above.
E) (A) and (B) are true.

Difficulty: **Easy**

52. Suppose that an individual owns a house worth $250,000 and faces a probability of 1 in 100 or 1 percent that the house will burn down in any given year. How much would a risk-averse homeowner be willing to pay for a fire insurance policy?
A) $1,000
B) $2,500
C) $2,500 or more
D) between $1,000 and $2,500
E) Cannot be determined from the information provided.

Difficulty: **Moderate**

53. Suppose that an individual owns a house worth $250,000 and faces a probability of 1 in 100 or 1 percent that the house will burn down in any given year. If there were 100 such homeowners, how much would an insurance company be willing to charge for a fire insurance policy?
A) $1,000
B) $2,500
C) $2,500 plus some allowance for the firm's operating expenses
D) between $1,000 and $2,500
E) Cannot be determined from the information provided.

Difficulty: **Moderate**

54. As a result of competition among insurance companies, the insurance premium usually _____ the risk premium.
A) exceeds
B) is less than
C) is equal to
D) depends on
E) has no relationship to

Difficulty: **Moderate**

55. Insurance companies do not offer insurance against non-diversifiable risks such as:
A) hurricanes.
B) flooding.
C) war.
D) terrorist attacks.
E) All of the above.

Difficulty: **Easy**

56. Portfolios that include foreign securities usually have:
A) lower overall volatility than those with U.S. securities only.
B) higher dollar returns than those with U.S. securities only.
C) foreign-exchange risk.
D) All of the above.
E) (A) and (B) are true.

Difficulty: **Easy**

57. The covering of a foreign-exchange risk is called:
A) hedging.
B) arbitrage.
C) risk spreading.
D) All of the above.
E) (A) and (B) are true.

Difficulty: **Easy**

58. Hedging can be accomplished with:
A) a forward contract.
B) a futures contract.
C) a portfolio of stocks.
D) All of the above.
E) (A) and (B) are true.

Difficulty: **Easy**

59. Compared to forward contracts, futures contracts are:

A) more liquid.
B) less liquid.
C) only for currencies.
D) (A) and (B) are true.
E) (A) and (C) are true.

Difficulty: **Easy**

60. Futures markets exist in:
A) currencies.
B) stocks.
C) interest rates.
D) commodities.
E) All of the above.

Difficulty: **Easy**

Short Answer

Write the word or phrase that best completes each statement or answers the question.

1. **Explain the difference between risk and uncertainty.**
Answer: Risk refers to a situation where there is more than one possible outcome to a decision and the probability of each specific outcome is known or can be estimated. Uncertainty is the case when there is more than one possible outcome to a decision and where the probability of each specific outcome occurring is not known or even meaningful. Although this distinction is theoretically important, the usual convention is to use the two terms interchangeably.

2. **Most individuals are risk averters because they face diminishing marginal utility of money. Explain.**
Answer: Risk averters are individuals who seek to minimize risks. For such individuals, the marginal utility of money diminishes, which means that the amount of utility they would gain from winning a particular amount of money is less than the amount of utility they would lose from losing the same amount of money. Thus even if the expected value in money terms of a bet were zero (as with a fair bet), for risk averters the expected utility would be negative and they would not take the bet.

3. **Why might the same individual both purchase insurance and gamble?**
Answer: In the real world we often observe individuals purchasing insurance and also gambling. This behavior may seem contradictory, but can be explained by the shape of the total utility of money curve. The curve may be concave (with diminishing marginal utility of money) at lower levels of income and convex (so that the marginal utility of money increases) at higher levels of income. An individual with an income at or near the point of inflection on the total utility curve (where the curve changes from being concave to being convex) will find it advantageous to both purchase insurance (spending a small amount to insure against the small chance of a large loss) and to gamble (purchase a lottery ticket for a small amount of money for the small chance of a large win).

4. **What can an individual do to reduce risk or uncertainty?**

Answer: An individual can reduce risk or uncertainty by (1) gathering more information (for example, investors can obtain information about the riskiness of a bond by checking its rating from agencies like Moody's or Standard & Poor); (2) diversification or risk spreading (an individual should invest in a number of projects whose returns have negative correlation); and (3) insurance (the individual can pay for someone else to assume the risk).

5. **Why is diversification more than just engaging in a large number of projects?**
Answer: The object of diversification is to reduce risk. To do so an investor must engage in projects that are not closely related. If there is perfect negative correlation between two projects (like a seesaw; if one is up the other is down) then risk can be entirely eliminated by engaging in both activities. If there is perfect positive correlation between the two, the risk will not be reduced at all. If one considers a portfolio of stocks as an example, one is not achieving diversification if one has a large number of stocks in different companies all of which are in the same industry; investors who held portfolios that were heavy in technology firms learned this lesson the hard way in recent years!

6. **Why wouldn't an insurance company offer coverage against terrorist acts?**
Answer: Insurance companies do not offer insurance against non-diversifiable risks (meaning those risks which cannot be reduced or eliminated through diversification) because they cannot spread their risks. Most insurance companies are reluctant to offer coverage for terrorist acts because they cannot calculate the risk and thus cannot set appropriate premiums.

Chapter 7:

Production Theory

Multiple-Choice

Choose the one alternative that best completes the statement or answers the question.

1. A firm's production function can best be described as being:
   A) a unique relationship between input and outputs showing the maximum level of output that can be produced from a particular set of inputs, given existing technology.
   B) a relationship that describes how inputs are transformed into outputs in the short run but not in the long run.
   C) a relationship measuring the cost of producing various levels of output, given input prices and input requirements.
   D) a unique relationship measuring the opportunity cost of using inputs in one production technique rather than another.
   E) None of the above correctly describes a production function.

   Difficulty: **Easy**

2. When the typical firm uses inputs to produce an output, the marginal, average, and total products can be calculated. The curves reflecting these products:
   A) relate input requirements, input prices, and outputs.
   B) tell the producer whether or not production is taking place efficiently.
   C) describe the relationship between physical inputs and outputs when production is efficient.
   D) tell the producer the level of input usage and output that should be produced in order to maximize the firm's profit.
   E) can be used in economic analysis only in the long run.

   Difficulty: **Moderate**

3. For the firm producing in the short run, its total, marginal, and average product curves will exhibit all of the following relationships except:
   A) when total product is rising, average and marginal product may be either rising or falling.
   B) when marginal product is negative, total product and average product are falling.
   C) when marginal product is at a maximum, average product equals marginal product, and total product is rising.
   D) when average product is at a maximum, marginal product equals average product and total product is rising.
   E) when total product begins to increase at a decreasing rate, marginal product begins to fall.

   Difficulty: **Moderate**

4. Which one of the following is <u>not</u> a characteristic of the firm's short-run average, marginal, and total product curves?

A) When average product is zero, total product is at a maximum.
B) When marginal product is less than average product, average product is falling.
C) When marginal product is zero, total product is at a maximum and average product is falling.
D) When marginal product is rising, average product is less than marginal product.
E) When total product is falling, marginal product is negative.

Difficulty: **Moderate**

5. Suppose that the Smith Company has a fixed plant and variable units of labor as its only inputs into its production process. If increasing amounts of the variable factor, labor, are added to the fixed factor, then we can expect all of the following to occur <u>except</u>:
A) the average product of labor to reach a maximum when the marginal product is zero.
B) the marginal product of labor to reach a maximum earlier than the total product.
C) the average product of labor to continue rising as long as marginal product of labor is greater than average product.
D) the total product of labor to be at a maximum when the marginal product of labor it zero.
E) the total product of labor to begin increasing at a decreasing rate when diminishing marginal physical returns to labor set in.

Difficulty: **Moderate**

6. Firms produce in the short run, while the long run is the firm's planning horizon. For a firm, the short run is that period of time:
A) when all factors of production are variable.
B) when at least one factor of production is fixed.
C) the lasts less than one year.
D) when the firm's plant size can be adjusted.
E) None of the above is correct.

Difficulty: **Easy**

7. Suppose that you plot a total product curve and then draw a line that it tangent to the curve. The tangent line will be steepest when:
A) average product is at a maximum.
B) marginal product is zero.
C) total product is at a maximum.
D) marginal product is at a maximum.
E) total product is falling.

Difficulty: **Moderate**

8. In the long run, a firm may experience increasing, constant, or decreasing returns to scale. One reason often given for increasing returns to scale is that:
A) it becomes very difficult to manage a large firm.
B) inputs are often not perfectly divisible.
C) as a firm gets larger, it is able to purchase inputs in larger quantities and at lower per unit prices.
D) as the firm gets larger and has a larger plant size, its fixed costs increase.
E) the law of diminishing returns no longer holds.

Difficulty: **Moderate**

9. The Riley Company uses a variable input in the production of its output. The marginal product of the variable input used by the Riley Company:
   A) increases as long as more of the input is used.
   B) is the same as the average product of the variable input at each level of output.
   C) falls, reaches a minimum, and then rises as the level of output is expanded.
   D) is the change in total output that occurs when an additional unit of the variable input is used.
   E) None of the above is correct.

   Difficulty: **Moderate**

10. Suppose that the ABC Company uses a fixed and variable input to produce its output. As long as the total output of the firm is increasing the marginal product of the:
    A) fixed input is zero.
    B) variable input is zero.
    C) fixed input is negative.
    D) variable input is increasing.
    E) variable input is greater than zero.

    Difficulty: **Moderate**

11. As more of a variable factor of production is combined with a firm's fixed factor, beyond some level of output the marginal product of the variable factor:
    A) rises continuously as long as total output is rising.
    B) falls as long as total output is increasing at a decreasing rate.
    C) reaches a maximum and remains constant.
    D) increases at a decreasing rate as long as total output is increasing.
    E) None of the above is correct.

    Difficulty: **Easy**

12. The law of diminishing returns in production theory:
    A) is a physical law about the technology of production.
    B) shows that output can always be expanded by adding one more unit of the variable input to some amount of fixed input.
    C) reaches a maximum and remains constant.
    D) (A) and (B) are correct.
    E) (A) and (C) are correct.

    Difficulty: **Easy**

13. For a firm in production with its marginal product equal to its average product, total product:
    A) is at a maximum.
    B) is positive and rising.
    C) is decreasing at an increasing rate.
    D) is decreasing at a decreasing rate.
    E) does not exhibit the law of diminishing returns.

    Difficulty: **Moderate**

14. Suppose that in your firm, the number of machines and your plant size are fixed. If you hire ten workers, you can produce 180 units of output per day; however, if you hire eleven workers, your output increases to 187 units per day. Given this information, you can correctly conclude all of the following <u>except</u>:
A) the average product when ten workers are hired is 18.
B) when the eleventh worker is hired, average product of labor is greater than the marginal product.
C) the firm has passed the point of diminishing returns to labor.
D) the marginal product of the eleventh worker is 10 units of output.
E) total product has not yet reached a maximum.

Difficulty: **Moderate**

15. An isoquant provides a complete listing of:
A) the location of the intersection of all isoquants with their corresponding input ratios.
B) all possible input combinations capable of producing a given level of output.
C) production techniques that produce all levels of output.
D) all possible levels of capital needed to produce a given quantity for a fixed capital-labor ratio.
E) None of the above is correct.

Difficulty: **Easy**

16. Any point on an isoquant represents a correspondence between an output level and:
A) a particular production technique.
B) the prices that have to be paid to the factors of production.
C) the supply of the various factors of production.
D) the price that the producer will be able to charge for the output produced by the firm.
E) None of the above is correct.

Difficulty: **Easy**

17. Any particular isoquant in an isoquant map shows different combinations.
A) of outputs produced by a given constant capital-to-labor ratio.
B) of inputs capable of producing increasing levels of output.
C) of inputs capable of producing a given level of output.
D) of output levels produced by a fixed level of inputs.
E) None of the above is correct.

Difficulty: **Easy**

18. Those production techniques that require more of both inputs correspond to higher levels of output, and so they are represented on an isoquant map by movements:
A) inward to lower isoquants because resources are limited.
B) downward and to the right along an isoquant.
C) upward and to the left along a particular isoquant.
D) outward to higher and higher isoquants.
E) along and changes in the shape of a particular isoquant.

Difficulty: **Moderate**

19. Select the answer which best completes the following statement: "An isoquant shows the different combinations...":

A) of outputs produced by a given level of inputs."
B) of output that can be produced using different input combination ratios."
C) of inputs capable of producing increasing levels of outputs."
D) of inputs that can be used to produce a given level of output."
E) of inputs and outputs among which the producer is indifferent."

Difficulty: **Easy**

20. Given any particular isoquant curve in an isoquant map, a specific point on the curve establishes a correspondence between an output level and:

A) a particular production function.
B) the price that can be charged for the output.
C) the marginal rate of technical substitution.
D) the ratio of the prices of the inputs.
E) None of the above is correct.

Difficulty: **Easy**

21. The reason why isoquants are drawn convex to the origin is that:

A) the marginal product of both inputs remains constant as more units of the inputs are used.
B) the production function reflects decreasing returns to scale.
C) the marginal rate of technical substitution falls as more of one input is substituted for the other.
D) the production function reflects constant returns to scale.
E) at least one of the inputs used in the production process must remain fixed.

Difficulty: **Easy**

22. Given an isoquant map with amounts of capital plotted on the vertical axis and amounts of labor plotted on the horizontal axis, the absolute value of the slope of any isoquant is:

A) MP_K/MP_L.
B) P_K/P_L.
C) MP_L/MP_K.
D) increasing at a decreasing rate.
E) None of the above is correct.

Difficulty: **Moderate**

23. Suppose that we use only two inputs, capital (K) and labor (L), in our production process. If these two inputs were perfect substitutes in production, then our isoquant map would consist of isoquants that are:

A) convex to the origin.
B) straight lines.
C) concave to the origin.
D) concave from above.
E) right angles, so one or both factors may be redundant.

Difficulty: **Hard**

24. When you follow a recipe and bake a Mississippi mud cake, you cannot alter the ingredients because if you do, you will have a Mississippi mess. The production function for these cases can best be represented by isoquants that are:
A) strictly concave to the origin.
B) straight lines.
C) right angles.
D) vertical lines with higher quantities to the right.
E) None of the above is correct.

Difficulty: **Hard**

25. Suppose that the marginal rate of substitution of labor for capital falls as more labor is substituted for capital. We will have isoquants that are:
A) straight lines.
B) concave to the origin.
C) strictly convex to the origin.
D) right angles.
E) None of the above is correct.

Difficulty: **Hard**

26. Suppose that we have the Cobb-Douglas production function and that it takes the form:

$$Q = AK^{b}L^{1-b}$$

where Q = quantity of output produced; K = quantity of capital used in production; L = quantity of labor used in production; b = a parameter such that $0 < b < 1$. We can conclude that this production function generates:
A) isoquants that are upward sloping to the right.
B) isoquants that are right angles with higher isoquants to the right.
C) isoquants that are concave to the origin with higher isoquants to the right.
D) isoquants that are convex to the origin with higher isoquants to the right.
E) None of the above is correct.

Difficulty: **Hard**

27. You are given the Cobb-Douglas production function that takes the form:

$$Q = AK^{.3}L^{.7}$$

where Q = quantity of output produced; K = quantity of capital used in production; L = quantity of labor used in production. We can conclude that:
A) this production function is homogeneous of degree 1.
B) the production function exhibits constant returns to scale.
C) the production function exhibits diminishing returns to labor.
D) if labor increases by 1 percent, output increases by .7 percent.
E) All of the above are correct.

Difficulty: **Hard**

28. If you are given a Cobb-Douglas production function that takes the form:

$$Q = AK^{b}L^{1\text{-}b}$$

Where Q = quantity of output produced; K = capital used in production; L = labor used in production; b = a parameter such that $0 < b < 1$; then the output elasticity of labor is:

A) greater than one since the output elasticity for capital for capital is less than one.
B) less than one and equal to b.
C) a parameter that increases and becomes greater than one as more labor is used in production.
D) equal to 1 only if b is equal to zero.
E) cannot be determined from the above information.

Difficulty: **Hard**

29. Suppose that you are given a Cobb-Douglas production function that takes the form:

$$Q = J^{a} K^{b} L^{c}$$

where Q = the quantity of output produced in units; J, K, L = some quantities of physical inputs used in production; a, b, c = some estimated parameters with the characteristics that $0 < a, b, c < 1$ (each of the parameters lies in the unit interval between zero and 1) and $a + b + c > 1$. You would be correct if you concluded that:

A) at least one of the inputs exhibits increasing returns to factors, and the production function itself exhibits constant returns to scale.
B) each of the inputs exhibits decreasing returns to factors but the production function itself exhibits decreasing returns to scale.
C) each of the factors exhibits diminishing returns to factors and the production function itself exhibits decreasing returns to scale.
D) each of the inputs exhibits constant returns to the factors, so the production function itself exhibits constant returns to scale.
E) None of the above is correct.

Difficulty: **Hard**

30. Suppose that you are given the following information about an estimated production function in the printing industry:

$$Q = AK^{.46}L^{.62}$$

where Q = the quantity of output produced in physical units; A = some positive estimated parameter; K = capital input usage in physical units L = labor input usage in physical units. You would be correct if you concluded that:

A) if labor is increased by 10 units, output increases by 6.2 units.
B) the output elasticity for capital is equal to (1 - .46).
C) the production function exhibits constant returns to scale.
D) neither capital nor labor exhibit diminishing returns to the factors.
E) the production function exhibits decreasing returns to scale.

Difficulty: **Hard**

31. To say that a production function is homogeneous of degree one means that the function:
A) exhibits increasing returns to scale once all inputs are increased by more than one percent.
B) exhibits decreasing returns to scale because each of the inputs in the function must have some exponent less than one.
C) exhibits constant returns to scale because the sum of the exponents is one.
D) will generate an isoquant map that consists of straight lines, either vertical or horizontal.
E) None of the above is correct.

Difficulty: **Moderate**

32. In the real world, most firms seem to exhibit near:
A) increasing returns to scale.
B) constant returns to scale.
C) decreasing returns to scale.
D) both increasing and decreasing returns simultaneously.
E) increasing returns to scale at very large scales of operation.

Difficulty: **Easy**

33. Suppose that you observe an isoquant map and you notice that the distance between isoquants diminishes but as you move further from the origin to higher curves, you are increasing output by some constant amount (50 units, perhaps). The most likely explanation for this is:
A) the production function that generates the isoquant map is homogeneous to degree one.
B) the inputs used in the production process are perfect substitutes for each other.
C) the production function is encountering increasing returns to scale.
D) there is some fixed proportion in which the inputs must be combined in order to get a constant increase in output.
E) the production function is encountering decreasing returns to scale.

Difficulty: **Moderate**

34. If you observe an isoquant map where the isoquants become further and further apart even though the change in quantity remains constant as you move from one isoquant to another, then the level of output changes proportionately less than does the change in inputs. The best explanation for this is:
A) the production function that generates such an isoquant map takes the form Q = A(jK + mL).
B) the production function exhibits increasing returns to scale, so as inputs double, output more than doubles.
C) the production function exhibits diminishing returns to the factors of production (capital and labor) as more of the inputs are used, so each produces less and less.
D) the production function exhibits decreasing returns to scale.
E) None of the above explains the isoquant map.

Difficulty: **Moderate**

35. According to the product cycle model:
A) firms that first introduce an innovation will maintain their export market and their domestic market even though foreign imitators pay lower wages and generally face lower costs.

B) firms that first introduce an innovation eventually lose their export market and even their domestic market to foreign imitators who pay lower wages and generally face lower costs.
C) firms that first introduce an innovation eventually lose their export market and even their domestic market to foreign imitators who pay higher wages and generally face higher costs.
D) firms that first introduce an innovation may eventually lose their export market to foreign imitators who pay lower wages and generally face lower costs but will maintain their domestic market.
E) None of the above is correct.

Difficulty: **Easy**

36. Which one of the following statements best describes the law of diminishing marginal (physical) returns?
A) As more and more units of the variable input are added to a fixed input, total product begins to decline after some point.
B) When equal amounts of a variable input are added to a decreasing amount of a fixed input, the resulting increments of output that they produce begin to fall beyond some point.
C) When all inputs are increased by equal amounts, given the technique of production, output will increase by smaller and smaller proportions.
D) For proportional increases in all inputs, total output begins to fall after some point is reached.
E) None of the above is correct.

Difficulty: **Moderate**

37. If the total product curve is tangent to a ray from the origin, it must also be true that:
A) total product is at a maximum.
B) marginal product is negative.
C) total product is decreasing.
D) average product is at a maximum.
E) marginal product is greater than average product.

Difficulty: **Moderate**

38. If we draw a line from the origin and it is tangent to the total product curve, then this line has to be steepest when:
A) marginal product is at a maximum.
B) marginal product is rising.
C) average product is at a maximum.
D) average product is rising.
E) total product is at a maximum.

Difficulty: **Moderate**

39. If the XYZ Company introduces a new, improved technique of production, then other things constant, we would expect to see the company:
A) produce more output with the same level of inputs.
B) produce the original level of output with fewer inputs.
C) reduce the per unit cost of production.

D) be able to produce new products as well as their original products.
E) to be able to do any or all of the above.

Difficulty: **Moderate**

40. All of the following statements are correct <u>except</u>:
A) If technological advancement enables a firm to produce a new product line, then the new product line would have to be described by a new isoquant map.
B) The innovations that a firm undertakes will greatly affect its competitiveness both domestically and in the foreign market.
C) Rivalry among domestic firms will not usually lead to either new product or process innovations.
D) Generally speaking, it is easier to introduce and establish a market for a new product group than it is to change the market for an established, known product.
E) According to the product cycle model, firms that first introduce an innovation will lose their export market as well as their domestic market to foreign producers who can pay lower wages.

Difficulty: **Moderate**

41. In the U.S. economic system, most new innovations:
A) are quickly embraced by other producers who are anxious to improve their production technique.
B) die from lack of adequate planning.
C) are quickly exported to foreign producers.
D) will not affect the cost of producing goods in the long run.
E) do not directly affect the competitiveness of domestic firms.

Difficulty: **Moderate**

42. All of the following statements about the movement along an isoquant are true <u>except</u>:
A) as you move along the isoquant, the slope of a ray from the origin intersecting different points along the isoquant changes.
B) as you move along the isoquant, the quantity of one input used in production rises while the quantity of the other input used falls.
C) as you move along the isoquant, the marginal rate of technical substitution for both input increases.
D) as you move along the isoquant, the marginal rate of technical substitution rises for one input but falls for the other.
E) as you move along an isoquant, the level of output produced remains constant.

Difficulty: **Moderate**

43. All of the following statements are incorrect <u>except</u> that:
A) a fixed-proportion production function will generate higher levels of output if one factor is held constant at a particular level and the other in increased.
B) a fixed-proportion production function generates an isoquant map with isoquants that are concave from above.
C) a variable proportion production function generates an isoquant map with isoquants that are right angles.
D) in order to increase output with a fixed-proportion production function, it is necessary to increase all at the same time.

E) a Cobb-Douglas production function generates a marginal product curve for labor that initially rises and then begins to fall when diminishing returns set in.

Difficulty: **Moderate**

44. When we calculate the marginal rate of technical substitution, it is equal to:
A) MPL/MPK.
B) the rate at which producers are willing to substitute labor for capital (or vice versa).
C) the absolute value of the slope of an isoquant.
D) the amount of one input, say capital, that a firm can give up by using one additional unit of labor and remain on the same isoquant so that output does not change.
E) All of the above are correct.

Difficulty: **Moderate**

45. Suppose that firm X experiences decreasing returns to scale and that it increases all inputs by 15 percent. We would expect to see:
A) the output produced by firm X to rise by more than 15 percent.
B) the output produced by firm X to rise by 15 percent.
C) the output produced by firm X to increase but by less than 15 percent.
D) None of the above is possible.
E) All of the above are possible.

Difficulty: **Moderate**

46. In the late 18th century, Thomas Malthus argues in his *Essay on the Principles of Population* that:
A) population growth would create pressure for people to innovate and thus lead, in the long run, to substantial improvements in their standard of living.
B) the industrial revolution had proven that people could rely on technological innovations to generate substantial increases in material living standards over the next century, but he failed to recognize the social costs that such improvements would entail.
C) rapid population growth could reduce the average and marginal product of labor sufficiently to keep people always near starvation.
D) market economies could expect pollution to make their cities essentially uninhabitable within a century and thus drive more people to live in slum dwellings in overcrowded cities.
E) None of the above is correct.

Difficulty: **Easy**

47. The label of "the dismal science" given to economies in the late 18th and early 19th century was due to the fact that:
A) economics was very poorly developed as a discipline and was unable to contribute anything worthwhile to our understanding of a market system.
B) economists believed that recessions were very common even though such economic downturns were always followed by economic recovery and further growth.
C) economists were extremely anti-technology at the time and criticized technological improvements emerging from the industrial revolution.
D) economists suggested that population growth in the face of fixed stocks of land and other nonhuman resources could doom humanity to a subsistence standard of living.

E) All of the above are correct.

Difficulty: **Easy**

48. The predictions of Thomas Mathus and many other practitioners of "the dismal science" in the late 18th and early 19th centuries regarding changes in material standards of living proved to be:
A) correct in the long run.
B) incorrect because they were grounded in an inappropriate application of the law of diminishing marginal returns to a long run question.
C) correct for most of the world although in a few places the outcome has been temporarily put off by government intervention in agricultural markets.
D) correct because they were grounded in an appropriate application of the law of diminishing marginal utility to a long run question.
E) None of the above is correct.

Difficulty: **Easy**

49. The predictions of Thomas Malthus and many other late 18th and 19th century practitioners of the dismal science" regarding changes in material standards of living:
A) proved to be incorrect because of substantial increases in the quantities of non-human resources.
B) proved to be incorrect because of a decrease in the growth of population in industrial nations.
C) proved to be incorrect because significant improvements in technology greatly increased productivity.
D) (A), (B), and (C) are correct.
E) None of the above is correct because Malthus and others predicted substantial growth in incomes over the long run.

Difficulty: **Easy**

50. The production isoquant representing the use of time and gasoline (the inputs) to a travel a specific number of miles (the output):
A) will be a fixed-proportions production function.
B) will always have a marginal rate of technical substitution equal to 1.
C) will be negatively sloped and convex to the origin in the relevant range.
D) will not be convex to the origin because as speed is increased gas mileage decreases.
E) (A) and (B) are correct.

Difficulty: **Moderate**

51. The reorganization of General Motors that took place in the first half of the 1990s suggests that it had previously been operating in the region of _____.
A) increasing returns to scale.
B) constant returns to scale.
C) decreasing returns to scale.
D) increasing marginal product.
E) no conclusions regarding scale may be inferred from GM's actions.

Difficulty: **Moderate**

52. Many experts believe that the market share of Chrysler compared to that of Ford and General Motors during the period of the early 1990s suggests that it had been operating in the region of:
    A) increasing returns to scale.
    B) constant returns to scale.
    C) decreasing returns to scale.
    D) increasing marginal product.
    E) None of the above is correct.

    Difficulty: **Moderate**

53. General Motor's problems in the early 1990s were the consequence of:
    A) a bloated workforce and management.
    B) having too many divisions and models.
    C) using high-cost suppliers.
    D) low capacity utilization.
    E) All of the above are correct.

    Difficulty: **Moderate**

54. Survey data suggests that the most important method of acquiring product and process innovations is by:
    A) reverse engineering.
    B) independent research and development by the firm.
    C) licensing technology by the firms that originally developed the technology.
    D) hiring employees of innovating firms.
    E) patent disclosures.

    Difficulty: **Moderate**

55. The Xerox Corporation's experience with Japanese competition from the early 1970s to the early 1990s suggests that:
    A) once a loss of market share to an aggressive foreign competitor has begun, the only way to stop the trend is to ask government to protect the domestic market with tariffs and other import restrictions.
    B) competitive benchmarking missions will simply transfer more information to foreign competitors and yield a continued loss of market share.
    C) foreign competitors always initiate their entry into a new market at the high end where profits per unit are highest.
    D) reorganization, quality-control efforts, employee involvement, end involvement of suppliers in early stages of product design will actually be counterproductive rather than helpful.
    E) None of the above is correct.

    Difficulty: **Moderate**

56. Relative to its international competitive position a decade earlier, in the early 1990s the United States maintained a dominant position in which industry?
    A) pharmaceuticals
    B) computers
    C) telecommunications
    D) motor vehicles

E) aerospace

Difficulty: **Easy**

57. Relative to its international competitive position a decade earlier, in the early 1990s the United States had lost a dominant position in which of the following industries?
A) telecommunications
B) computers
C) aerospace
D) All of the above are correct.
E) The United States did not lose a dominant position in any industries, but did lose in areas in which it had previously shared world leadership.

Difficulty: **Easy**

58. Which of the following statements regarding computer sided design (CAD) and manufacturing (CAM) is not correct?
A) CAD and CAM reduce the optimal lot size or production run for products.
B) CAD and CAM shorten the time required to develop and introduce new products.
C) CAD and CAM are a revolutionary change in manufacturing taking place all over the world.
D) CAD and CAM are based on superiority in computer software and computer networks.
E) All of the above are correct.

Difficulty: **Easy**

59. New digital factories:
A) at present are emerging only in a narrow range of industries specializing in the production of sophisticated electronics equipment.
B) customize products down to one unit while achieving mass-production speed and efficiency.
C) are being brought online by the Japanese at a very rapid pace.
D) are based on technical capabilities which can already be easily copied by foreign competitors.
E) None of the above is correct.

Difficulty: **Easy**

60. Which of the following is not a part of the cost of production for someone who owns their own auto shop, including tools and building?
A) Wages paid to workers.
B) Rental expense for the owner's use of the owner's building.
C) Forgone earnings of the money invested in tools.
D) A salary paid to the owner of the auto shop.
E) All of the above are a part of the cost of production.

Difficulty: **Moderate**

61. Which of the following is <u>not</u> a postulate of "managerial theories of the firm"?
A) Firms pursue multiple goals.
B) Firms seek to maximize market share.
C) Firms are profit maximizers.

D) Firms seek to maximize growth.
E) Firms attempt to minimize uncertainty.

Difficulty: **Moderate**

62. Iron ore deposits are an example of what type of input?
A) labor
B) capital
C) investment goods
D) natural resources
E) None of the above is correct.

Difficulty: **Easy**

63. The ability to see opportunities to combine resources in a more efficient way is an example of which type of input?
A) human resources
B) capital
C) investment goods
D) natural resources
E) None of the above is correct.

Difficulty: **Easy**

64. In the short run:
A) all inputs are variable.
B) no inputs are variable.
C) some inputs are variable.
D) all inputs are fixed.
E) (B) and (D) are correct.

Difficulty: **Easy**

65. Fixed inputs:
A) do not exist in the long run.
B) cannot be varied.
C) can be varied only with excessive cost during the time period under construction.
D) exist only in the short run.
E) All of the above are correct.

Difficulty: **Easy**

66. "Stock" is a concept used in economics to:
A) describe things which are measured over time.
B) describe things which are measured at one point in time.
C) refer to the claim that owners of a firm have against another firm's assets.
D) describe the rate at which a good is being produced and placed in inventory.
E) All of the above are correct.

Difficulty: **Easy**

67. Which of the following is not a firm in the economic sense?
A) Corporation.
B) Partnership.
C) Proprietorship.
D) Foundation.
E) All of the above are firms in the economic sense.

Difficulty: **Easy**

Use the product functions to answer the following questions.

L	TP	AP_L	MP_L
1	5	5	5
2	12		7
3		6	6
4	23	5.57	
5	27	5.4	4
6	30		3
7		4.57	
8	33	4.12	1

68. The missing total product figures (TP) are:
A) 18 and 32.
B) 17 and 31.
C) 16 and 30.
D) 14 and 32.
E) None of the above is correct.

Difficulty: **Moderate**

69. The missing average product figures (AP) are:
A) 7 and 5.
B) 12 and 9.4.
C) 6 and 5.
D) 8 and 4.
E) None of the above is correct.

Difficulty: **Moderate**

70. The missing marginal product figures (MP) are:
A) 4 and 2.
B) 4.5 and 1.5.
C) 5 and 1.
D) 5 and 2.
E) None of the above is correct.

Difficulty: **Moderate**

71. The point of diminishing returns begins to operate after how many units of labor are used?
A) 1.
B) 2.

C) 3.
D) 4.
E) 5.

Difficulty: **Moderate**

72. A horizontal line drawn across a production isoquant map where capital is measured on the vertical axis and labor on the horizontal axis:
A) allows one to derive a total product function for one variable input from the production function for two variable inputs.
B) reveals what happens to total product while holding constant the input measured on the vertical axis and adding more of the input measured on the horizontal axis.
C) may be placed lower on the vertical axis to derive a lower total product function for labor.
D) may be placed lower on the vertical axis to demonstrate that the total product of labor will decrease when a given amount of labor has less capital to work with.
E) All of the above are correct.

Difficulty: **Moderate**

73. A firm will operate in the region of the isoquant map:
A) where isoquants are negatively sloped.
B) where isoquants are positively sloped.
C) outside the area defined by the ridge lines.
D) outside the area defined by the points on the isoquants where the $MRTS_{LK}$ is zero or infinite.
E) All of the above are correct.

Difficulty: **Moderate**

74. Which of the following statements about ridge lines is not correct?
A) A ridge line specifies the minimum amount of capital required to produce the levels of output indicated by the various isoquants.
B) A ridge line specifies the minimum amount of labor required to produce the levels of output indicated by the various isoquants.
C) Outside the region defined by ridge lines, the slopes of the isoquants are negative.
D) A ridge line contains all of the points on the isoquants where the $MRTS_{LK}$ is infinite.
E) A ridge line contains all of the points on the isoquants where the $MRTS_{LK}$ is zero.

Difficulty: **Moderate**

75. Which of the following statements is <u>not</u> correct?
A) Decreasing returns to scale refers to the long run when all inputs are variable.
B) Diminishing returns refers to the short run when at least one input is fixed.
C) Diminishing returns in the short run is consistent with constant, increasing, or decreasing returns to scale.
D) Decreasing returns to scale and diminishing returns both occur in the short run and the long run.

E) All of the above are correct.

Difficulty: **Moderate**

76. Which of the following statements regarding innovation is <u>not</u> correct?
   A) Product innovation refers to the introduction of new or improved products.
   B) Process innovation refers to the introduction of new or improved methods of producing.
   C) The product cycle model suggests that firms that fail to be the first to introduce an innovation can expect to lose out in the competition with domestic and foreign competitors.
   D) Japanese firms were successful in the 1970s and 1980s in competing with American companies because the Japanese firms stressed process innovations rather than product innovations.
   E) Most innovations are incremental involving more or less continuous small improvements in products or processes.

   Difficulty: **Moderate**

Short Essays

Give a brief answer to each of the following questions.

1. **A business entrepreneur says, "I added so many people to my factory that our production of street sign posts actually fell! I must have finally reached the point of diminishing returns. No wonder my profits are down." What is wrong with this statement?**
   Answer: The point of diminishing returns, or diminishing marginal product, is reached not when total product falls but when marginal product falls. The entrepreneur passed the point of diminishing returns at which marginal product is positive but decreasing, and extended his use of the variable input so much that marginal product was negative. The profit maximizing use of the variable input takes place beyond the point of diminishing returns but before marginal product is zero. The firm's profits probably began to fall long before marginal product became negative.

2. **What is the economic region of production and how does one find it on a production isoquant map?**
   Answer: The economic region of production occurs where the marginal products of labor and capital are declining but positive. That means that a firm has not combined so much capital with so little labor, or so much labor with so little capital, that the marginal product of capital or labor is negative. Ridge lines, which consist of all the points on the production isoquants at which the marginal rate of technical substitution between labor and capital is zero or infinity, define the economic region of production, i.e., where the slope of the production isoquant is negative.

3. **What economic law explains why the marginal product curve intersects the average product curve from above at the peak of the average product curve?**
   Answer: It is not an economic law which explains this phenomenon but rather the behavior of averages. AP is simply an averaging of marginal product numbers. Since MP numbers rise and fall, so will their average. Once the MP numbers peak and begin to fall (a consequence of diminishing returns), they will eventually fall sufficiently to meet their own rising average. Once they fall below their own average, the falling MP numbers will begin to "pull" their own average

down. To the extent that any economic law is involved with this phenomenon, it is the law of diminishing returns.

4. **"Diminishing returns and decreasing returns to scale mean the same thing because they both mean that output is increasing but at a slower rate." Explain what is wrong with this statement.**
Answer: Both diminishing returns and decreasing returns to scale have to do with using more input and generating smaller increases in output. However, diminishing returns applies only in cases where at least one output is fixed, and the eventual smaller increases in output are due to one input being fixed. If all inputs are variable, that cause of smaller increases in output no longer applies. Decreasing returns to scale allows all inputs to be variable, i.e., the long run, but still yields increases in output that are proportionately smaller than the increases in the use of all outputs.

5. **"Innovations usually come from scientific breakthroughs which bring about rapid and dramatic change. Thus, technological change is always big news." Are these comments correct?**
Answer: Generally speaking, these comments are not correct. Most innovations are incremental and involve small changes in existing products or production processes. They commonly involve commercial utilization of ideas that have been around for a long time. Thus, they are not tied very tightly to breakthroughs, although dramatic change is possible.

Chapter 8:

Costs of Production

Multiple-Choice

Choose the one alternative that best completes the statement or answers the question.

1. When the ABC Corp. uses factors of production to produce a particular output, the implicit cost of alternative outputs that could have been produced with the factors is the:
   A) total accounting cost of using the factors.
   B) opportunity costs of using the factors.
   C) explicit costs only of using the factors.
   D) total production cost of using the factors.
   E) None of the above is correct.

   Difficulty: **Easy**

2. Suppose that you have $25,000 in a certificate of deposit earning 10 percent per year. IF you withdraw the $25,000 and invest in starting a new business, the:
   A) firm will show a positive profit after the first year of operation because less money was borrowed.
   B) explicit costs increase since the financial capital would have to be borrowed otherwise.
   C) opportunity cost of the funds should be included in the proprietor's total cost of doing business.
   D) opportunity cost of the invested funds is zero because no physical capital is used.
   E) None of the above is correct.

   Difficulty: **Moderate**

3. John resigned from his $50,000 per year job as an assistant buyer for a large corporation and withdrew $120,000 from his savings account in order to start his own business. The $120,000 in savings was earning 10 percent interest per year while it was in the bank. After John's first year in business, his accountant told him that his cost of operation, excluding his salary, was $60,000, and the total revenue earned by the firm was $122,000. When all of the costs are included, at the end of the first year of operation, John has a profit of:
   A) $62,000.
   B) $10,000.
   C) -$62,000.
   D) $0 (John broke even).
   E) Not enough information is provided to determine an answer.

   Difficulty: **Moderate**

4. It's just what you've been waiting for! General Motors has offered you a job when you complete your college studies at a starting salary of $30,000 per year. Lately, however, you have been thinking about going into business for yourself. You would have to borrow $200,000 from the bank at 10 percent interest per year, and your estimated labor costs (as

well as other variable expenses) will be $175,000. During the first year in business, your best estimate is that your total revenue will be $220,000. Based on this information, you should:

A) refuse the General Motors offer and start your own business because you will have a profit of $25,000.
B) refuse the General Motors offer and start your own business because you will have a profit of $52,000.
C) accept the General Motors offer because your calculations show you with a business loss of -$35,000.
D) accept the General Motors offer because your calculations show you with a business loss of -$5,000.
E) It really does not matter what you do because the results of either action will be the same in the long run.

Difficulty: **Moderate**

5. When a proprietor invests his own financial capital to start a business, the:
A) opportunity cost of the invested funds is zero since no physical capital is used.
B) opportunity cost of the funds should not be included in the proprietor's total cost of doing business.
C) accounting cost increase since the financial capital would have to be borrowed otherwise.
D) firm's accounting profit will be less than its economic profits.
E) None of the above is correct.

Difficulty: **Easy**

6. As a college student, you certainly have to pay explicit (out-of-pocket) costs, especially if you are paying your way through college. However, you also incur an opportunity cost when you attend college. This opportunity cost is:
A) the cost of new books, rather than used books, that you purchase.
B) the cost of meals and lodging that you must pay.
C) the income that you give up by not working full-time.
D) the incidental costs (entertainment, ball games, etc.) that you pay to enhance your enjoyment of your college experience.
E) None of the above is correct.

Difficulty: **Easy**

7. A fireman has a primary duty extinguishing fires; however, the individual could be providing other services or producing physical goods in either government or the private sector. The cost of the fireman providing fire protection as opposed to another service would best be classified as a(n):
A) accounting cost.
B) opportunity cost.
C) variable cost.
D) fixed cost.
E) overhead cost.

Difficulty: **Easy**

8. The absolute value of the slope of a firm's isocost line is equal to the ratio of:
A) the amount of one input used relative to the amount of others used.

B) the marginal products of the inputs.
C) the prices of inputs.
D) the marginal product of a particular input relative to its price.
E) None of the above is correct.

Difficulty: **Easy**

9. The highest attainable level of output, given a firm's operating budget, input prices, and the state of technology, is found where:
A) the firm's isocost line intersects the highest isoquant.
B) the isocost line intersects the either the vertical or horizontal axis, depending on the relative price of the inputs.
C) that point where the firm's isoquants intersects with each other.
D) the firm's isocost line is tangent to an isoquant.
E) None of the above is correct.

Difficulty: **Moderate**

10. Other things contant, the firm's optimal production technique and input combination is found where the:
A) firm's isocost line intersects an isoquant.
B) isocost line is tangent to the horizontal axis.
C) point where two of the isoquants intersect.
D) isoquant and isocost lines are tangent to each other.
E) None of the above is correct.

Difficulty: **Moderate**

11. Suppose that a firm initially faces a given operating budget and given input prices. A change in the relative prices of the inputs used in production, other things constant, causes the:
A) isocost line to shift to the right.
B) isocost line to shift to the left.
C) isoquants to shift closer together.
D) isocost line to rotate and change the absolute value of its hope.
E) isoquants to shift to the right or to the left.

Difficulty: **Moderate**

12. The total fixed costs faced by a firm operating in the short run:
A) fall as more and more output is produced.
B) remain constant regardless of the level of output produced.
C) are equal to the cost of using the variable inputs.
D) increases as more output is produced.
E) None of the above is correct.

Difficulty: **Easy**

13. Suppose that you operate the Widget Company and decide, due to a weak demand for widgets, to shut your plant down for three months while you reduce your inventory. Which one of the following best describes your firm's costs?
A) Total variable costs are zero but fixed cost are positive, so total costs are positive.

B) Total fixed costs are zero but fixed total variable costs may be positive, so total costs may be positive.
C) Total fixed, total variable, and total cost are zero since nothing is being produced.
D) Total fixed and total variable costs may be positive, so total cost may be positive.
E) None of the above describes the firm's costs.

Difficulty: **Moderate**

14. As more output is produced in the short run, more variable inputs are added to a given amount of fixed. After some point, we expect continued increases in output to cause:
A) essentially no change in average fixed costs.
B) average variable cost to stop falling, reach a minimum, and then begin to rise.
C) average total cost to stop rising, reach a maximum, and then begin to fall.
D) marginal cost to continue its decline throughout all ranges of output.
E) average fixed cost to fall, reach a minimum, and then begin to rise.

Difficulty: **Moderate**

15. Suppose that rubber is the primary input in the production of golf balls. If the price of rubber increases while all other things remain constant, we can expect that:
A) the marginal and average variable cost curves to shift upward but not the average total or average fixed cost curves.
B) the average total and average variable cost curves to shift upward, but the marginal and average fixed cost curves will shift downward.
C) the marginal, average variable, and average fixed cost curves to shift upward, but the average total cost curve will remain stationary.
D) the marginal, average variable, and average total cost curves will shift upward, but the average fixed cost curve will not shift.
E) the total cost curve to make a parallel shift downward.

Difficulty: **Hard**

16. When a firm enters the market and hires any of the factors of production, the cost of hiring the factors is:
A) an implicit cost to the firm.
B) a variable cost to the firm.
C) an explicit cost to the firm.
D) a fixed cost to the firm.
E) None of the above is correct.

Difficulty: **Easy**

17. In a short-run production function, once production encounters diminishing returns, the total variable cost curve will:
A) begin to fall at an increasing rate.
B) begin to increase at a decreasing rate.
C) begin to rise at an increasing rate.
D) become less steep and approach a horizontal line if quantity of output is measured on the horizontal axis.
E) begin to fall at a decreasing rate.

Difficulty: **Moderate**

18. Given a firm's total cost curve, the point where a straight line from the origin is tangent to the total cost curve suggests that average total cost:
A) is at a minimum point.
B) is greater than average variable cost.
C) is equal to marginal cost.
D) is neither rising nor falling.
E) All of the above are correct.

Difficulty: **Moderate**

19. When we examine an isocost line, the line tells us:
A) the minimum cost of producing a given level of output.
B) those sets of production processes that are all of equal cost.
C) the change in the relative marginal productivities of inputs as inputs are substituted for each other.
D) all different production processes that can be used to produce a given level of output.
E) None of the above is correct.

Difficulty: **Moderate**

20. Given a production function, an operating budget, and input prices, the firm produces any given level of output at minimum cost when it:
A) adjusts the use of all inputs until the ratio of the marginal product of each input to its price is equal to the ratios of the marginal products of all inputs to their prices.
B) produces that level of output associated with minimum average total cost.
C) produces that level of output where marginal cost is at a minimum.
D) hires all of the factors of production up to the point where their respective marginal products are equal to zero.
E) None of the above is correct.

Difficulty: **Easy**

21. Suppose that a firm uses two variable inputs in its production process, labor and capital. If the wage rate rises relative to the interest rate, the firm would be inclined to:
A) produce a given level of output using a more labor-intensive production technique.
B) substitute labor for capital because with a given budget, a certain amount of labor must be used, so less is left to spend on capital.
C) produce a given level of output using a more capital-intensive production technique.
D) do nothing since with a given isocost line, total cost cannot change.
E) reduce its use of capital until the ratio of the marginal product of capital to its price equals the ratio of the marginal product of labor to its price.

Difficulty: **Moderate**

22. Suppose that the price of labor is the wage rate (w) per unit of labor and the price of capital is the rental rate of capital (r) per unit. If we have a total operating budget of TC, and we use L units of labor and K units of capital, then with capital plotted on the vertical axis and labor on the horizontal:
A) the isocost line is expressed as $TC = rK + wL$.

B) if no labor is used, the maximum amount of capital that can be used is TC/r.
C) the slope of the isocost line is –(w/r).
D) if no capital is used, the maximum amount of labor that can be used is TC/w.
E) All of the above are correct.

Difficulty: **Moderate**

23. Consider the output and cost schedule for producing widgets:

OUTPUT	0	1	2	3	4	5	6	7
TOTAL COST	$36	45	51	60	66	73	81	92

Which one of the following statements is false?
A) The average fixed cost of producing the 4th unit of output is $9.
B) The average total cost of producing 7 units of output is $13.14.
C) The total variable cost of producing 5 units of output is $37.
D) The average variable cost of producing 3 units of output is $24.
E) The total cost of producing 6 units of output is $81.

Difficulty: **Moderate**

24. You work for the XYZ Company and are in charge of establishing a new office facility for the company. You will have $1,000 per week to spend on computers and labor. You can hire labor at a rate of $10 per hour or $400 per week. You can lease computers (not very sophisticated) for $40 per day or $200 per week. An equation for the isocost constraint within which you must operate is:
A) $1,000 = $200K + $400L.
B) $1,000 = $40K + 10L.
C) $1,000 = $400K + $200L.
D) $1,000 = $200K + $200L.
E) Cannot be determined from the information provided.

Difficulty: **Moderate**

25. Suppose that you observe a firm in production using only two inputs, capital (K) and labor (L). If the price of capital is r per unit and the price of labor is w per unit, and you note that $MP_K/r > MP_L/w$, then you would be correct in recommending that:
A) the firm, if possible, substitutes capital for labor along an isoquant until a tangency point between the highest attainable isoquant and the firm's isocost line is reached.
B) the firm shuts down and produces nothing.
C) the firm, if possible, substitutes labor for capital along an isoquant until a tangency point between the highest attainable isoquant and the firm's isocost line is reached.
D) the firm reduces its cost of production by reducing its productive capacity.
E) the firm attempts to increase its output so that the marginal product of capital will decrease, other things remaining the same.

Difficulty: **Moderate**

26. Assume that the producer uses two inputs in his or her production process. If the two inputs are capital (K) and labor (L), which one of the conditions represents a level of output produced at minimum cost?

A) $P_K (MP_K) = P_L (MP_L)$

B) $MP_K/P_K = MP_L/P_L$

C) $P_L/MP_K = P_K/MP_L = 1$

D) $MP_K/P_L = MP_L/P_K$

E) None of the above is correct.

Difficulty: **Moderate**

27. The Widget Corp. is combining inputs capital (K) and labor (L) in production such that $MP_K/MP_L = P_K / P_L$. If the price of labor rises relative to the price of capital, then the firm will:

A) use more capital and less labor because now $MP_K / MP_L > P_K / P_L$.

B) use more labor and less capital because now $MP_K / MP_L < P_K / P_L$.

C) use more capital and less labor because now $MP_K / MP_L < P_K / P_L$.

D) use more labor and less capital because now $MP_K / MP_L > P_K / P_L$.

E) None of the above is correct.

Difficulty: **Moderate**

28. In order to maximize output subject to a given cost or minimize cost subject to a given output, the same conditions apply. These conditions may be expressed as:

A) $MP_K = MP_L$.

B) $MP_L / MP_K = P_K / P_L$.

C) $MP_L / MP_K = P_L/P_K$.

D) $MP_L / P_K = MP_K / P_L$.

E) None of the above is correct.

Difficulty: **Moderate**

29. Given a U-shaped long-run average total cost curve, the tangency point between a particular short-run average total cost curve and the LAC curve:

A) never occurs at the output level where LAC = LMC.

B) is always at the output level where LAC = LMC.

C) represents the most efficient way to use a given plant.

D) represents the most efficient way to produce the level of output involved.

E) None of the above is correct.

Difficulty: **Moderate**

30. Suppose that a firm uses two inputs, capital (K) and labor (L), and that the price of labor increases relative to the price of capital. The effect on the firm's isocost line is to:

A) increase the convexity of the curve relative to origin.

B) change the absolute value of the slope because the relative input price ratio changed.

C) shift the curve inward toward the origin.

D) shift the curve outward away from the origin.
E) None of the above is correct.

Difficulty: **Moderate**

31. Suppose that firm A is operating under conditions of constant returns to scale. Assuming that input prices remain constant in the long run, the long-run average total cost curve for the firm:
A) will be a horizontal line.
B) will be U-shaped.
C) will slope downward throughout the relevant range of output.
D) will slope upward throughout the relevant range of output.
E) will slope downward over a very large range of output, but it will eventually turn upward.

Difficulty: **Moderate**

32. Suppose that you hire two inputs (X and Y) to produce an output. However, the more of either X or Y that you use, the less each additional unit of the input produces. You decide to maximize your output for a given operating budget, and the price of X is $2 per unit while the price of Y is $4 per unit. Suppose that you choose a combination of X and Y such that the marginal product of X is 8 units and the marginal product of Y is 12 units. Which of the following should you do?
A) Buy more of input Y and less of input X.
B) Buy more of both inputs because their marginal products are still positive.
C) Buy more of input X and less of input Y.
D) Buy less of both inputs because you must be overspending your operating budget.
E) The current input mix of X and Y is optimal, so don't do anything.

Difficulty: **Moderate**

33. Short-run average cost usually rises beyond some level due to:
A) economies of scale.
B) the law of diminishing returns.
C) diseconomies of scale.
D) constant returns to scale.
E) an increase in the price of inputs.

Difficulty: **Moderate**

34. For the firm in the long run, the expansion path:
A) is the various combinations of inputs capable of producing a given level of output.
B) is the various combinations of inputs that can be purchased for a given expenditure level.
C) is the locus of least-cost combinations of inputs that will be selected when input prices remain constant.
D) is the locus of alternative combinations of different levels of output that can be produced with a certain input ratio.
E) is the locus of tangency points between isocost and isoquant lines with a changing marginal rate of technical substitution between the inputs.

Difficulty: **Easy**

35. Suppose that in the production of widgets, there is only one production process (input ratio) possible. Also suppose that there are constant returns to scale to the process faced by the firm. We can conclude that the expansion path:
A) is a straight line and it passes through the origin.
B) increases at a decreasing rate.
C) increases at an increasing rate.
D) is a vertical line.
E) bends back on itself.

Difficulty: **Moderate**

36. If a firm builds a new plant or changes its scale of operation, its options for change in the short run are determined by:
A) whether or not the firm is experiencing increasing or decreasing returns to scale.
B) the shape of its long-run average cost curve.
C) its short-run average total cost curve.
D) its long-run marginal cost since this reflects the change in cost of producing additional units of the output.
E) None of the above is correct.

Difficulty: **Moderate**

37. If a firm knows its production function and knows the prices of the inputs used to produce its output, then the firm can determine:
A) the minimum cost of producing each level of output.
B) its total cost curve.
C) the minimum cost of producing a specific level of output.
D) its lowest-cost production methods.
E) All of the above are correct.

Difficulty: **Moderate**

38. The distinction between the long run and the short run is that in the long run:
A) the opportunity costs of production are higher than in the short run.
B) some inputs are fixed, while in the short run, all inputs are fixed.
C) the firm can adjust all of its inputs completely, while in the short run it can adjust only some of its inputs.
D) there will be some fixed cost of production.
E) None of the above is correct.

Difficulty: **Moderate**

39. If a production technique uses only capital and labor as its only inputs into the production process, then a decrease in the wage rate paid to labor may cause:
A) the firm's total cost curve to shift downward.
B) the relative cost of using labor to fall.
C) the firm to change its production technique.
D) a substitution of labor for capital.
E) All of the above are possibilities.

Difficulty: **Hard**

40. The smallest quantity at which the LAC curve reaches its minimum is called the:
A) point of diminishing returns.
B) the expansion path.
C) SATC.
D) minimum efficient scale (MES).
E) point of increasing returns to scale.

Difficulty: **Easy**

41. Assume that a firm is adding more units of labor to some amount of a fixed input. Which statement is <u>not</u> correct?
A) $AVC = w(1/AP_L)$, where w is a constant wage rate.
B) TC = TVC + AFC.
C) TVC is a function of the level of output produced by the firm.
D) $MC = w(1/MP_L)$, where w is a constant wage rate.
E) AVC = ATC – AFC.

Difficulty: **Moderate**

42. Given a firm's long-run expansion path when all input prices and technology are held constant, it is possible to:
A) derive the firm's long-run total cost curve.
B) determine the optimal level of output that the firm should produce.
C) determine the profit that is earned by the firm in the long run.
D) determine whether or not the isoquants associated with the path are right angles or straight lines.
E) None of the above is correct.

Difficulty: **Easy**

43. When a firm experiences decreasing returns to scale:
A) the long-run average cost curve rises as output expands.
B) it should expand its scale of operation because production efficiency can be increased.
C) proportionate increases in all inputs change output by the same proportion.
D) the long-run average cost curve decreases as output expands.
E) the long-run average cost curve is a horizontal line.

Difficulty: **Easy**

44. A firm's short-run marginal cost curve takes its particular shape from:
A) a state of technology that is assumed constant.
B) the shape of the firm's marginal product curve.
C) the law of diminishing returns to the variable factor of production.
D) the firm's production function.
E) All of the above are correct.

Difficulty: **Moderate**

45. All of the following statements are false <u>except</u>:
A) marginal cost shows how much fixed cost changes when output changes.

B) marginal cost equals average variable cost when average variable cost is at its minimum.
C) as long as average total cost is decreasing, marginal cost is increasing.
D) marginal cost equals average total cost when average total cost is at its maximum.
E) as more and more output is produced, the gap between average total cost is at its maximum.

Difficulty: **Moderate**

46. For the typical firm operating in the short run, the relationship between the marginal cost and average total cost curve is such that:
A) if marginal cost is greater than average total cost, then average total cost must be falling.
B) if average total cost is greater than marginal cost, then marginal cost must be falling.
C) if average total cost is less than marginal cost, the marginal cost must be rising.
D) if marginal cost equals average total cost, average total cost must be falling.
E) if marginal cost and average total cost are equal, then total cost must have reached a maximum.

Difficulty: **Moderate**

47. The reason why the marginal cost curve reaches a minimum and then turns upward is that:
A) after some point, each extra unit of a variable input that is used in production produces less extra output.
B) the total cost of production reaches a minimum and then begins to rise.
C) the average variable cost curve reaches a minimum and then turns upward.
D) the price of the inputs used in production increase as more inputs are used.
E) the average fixed cost of production decreases but at an increasing rate.

Difficulty: **Easy**

48. All of the following statements are incorrect <u>except</u>:
A) economies of scope are not related to the size of the firm.
B) economies of scope arise only when a firm produces a single output or product.
C) economies of scope can be used to describe the efficiencies achievable with greater size in such areas as marketing, corporate finance, and product distribution.
D) economies of scope are the same as economies of scale.
E) economies of scope are present only in the short run.

Difficulty: **Moderate**

49. All of the following statements are correct <u>except</u>:
A) as a firm moves up along its learning curve, the average cost of production decrease.
B) the existence of a learning curve for a firm implies that individuals "learn by doing", and so they become more efficient.
C) the movement down and along a firm's learning curve will shift the LAC curve downward, other things constant.
D) a firm's learning curve develops over a period of time.

E) generally a firm's learning curve is convex to the origin when average total cost is plotted on the vertical axis and cumulative total output is plotted on the horizontal axis.

Difficulty: **Moderate**

50. All of the following will cause a decline along a firm's learning curve except:
A) that the firm experiences few interruptions in its production process.
B) that it is relatively easy for a firm to transfer knowledge from the production of one product to the production of another.
C) that as workers perform their job duties, they become more efficient in production.
D) that firms with an easy turnover of workers continually get new, fresh workers to use in production.
E) All of the above will cause a decline in a firm's learning curve.

Difficulty: **Moderate**

51. Today, firms often use foreign sources of inputs used in the production process. When this happens, the firms:
A) purchase and assemble the final product within the same general region of the market for the final output.
B) are producing in a static business environment.
C) always have their goal as higher profits.
D) are pursuing a policy of protectionism of domestic industries.
E) None of the above is correct.

Difficulty: **Moderate**

52. All of the following can contribute to international economies of scale for firms except:
A) designing a core product for the entire world economy.
B) purchasing raw materials on a world rather than a regional basis.
C) coordinating production in a low-cost manufacturing are and then completing the final assembly in a higher-cost area near its final market.
D) effectively forecasting demand for the product.
E) undertaking demand management of their product market on a regional rather than a global basis.

Difficulty: **Moderate**

53. Which of the following is an opportunity cost of attending college?
A) room and board
B) foregone interest on an explicit cost
C) tuition
D) books
E) All of the above.

Difficulty: **Easy**

54. If most college students are foregoing similar wage incomes in order to attend schools which vary substantially in the tuition, book and supply fees they charge, then the _____ costs of attending college will vary more substantially than the _____ costs.
A) implicit; explicit
B) explicit; implicit

C) implicit; tuition, book and supply fees
D) explicit; tuition, book and supply fees
E) None of the above is correct.

Difficulty: **Easy**

55. The foregone interest on explicit cost of tuition is _____ of attending college.
A) an implicit cost and an opportunity cost
B) an explicit cost and an opportunity cost
C) an implicit cost but not an opportunity cost
D) an explicit cost but not an opportunity cost
E) Not a cost.

Difficulty: **Moderate**

56. The actual estimated marginal cost function for corn production on Iowa farms:
A) is very steep but flattens out as the minimum point of AVC is approached.
B) is relatively flat, but once marginal cost begins to increase it increases rapidly.
C) is relatively flat across all output levels.
D) is somewhat unique in that no other industries have marginal costs which behave in a similar fashion.
E) None of the above is correct.

Difficulty: **Moderate**

57. Assume that production isoquants and isocost lines have been used to identify the optimal quantity of time and gasoline to use in traveling a specific distance. If the government requires that a traveler drive at a:
A) slower speed, the total cost of the trip will decrease.
B) faster speed, the total cost of the rip will increase.
C) slower speed, the total cost of the trip will increase.
D) (B) and (C) are correct.
E) Speed does not affect the cost of the trip.

Difficulty: **Moderate**

58. Available data on long run average cost (LAC):
A) suggest that constant costs are a common phenomenon.
B) suggest that a large number of industries have L-shaped or nearly L-shaped LAC curves.
C) are consistent with U-shaped LAC curves.
D) Only (A) and (B) are correct.
E) All of the above are correct.

Difficulty: **Moderate**

59. Which of the following statements are supported by the data given below?

LONG-RUN AVERAGE COST (LAC) OF SMALL FIRMS
AS A PERCENTAGE OF LAC OF LARGE FIRMS

INDUSTRY	PERCENTAGE
Hospitals	129

Commercial banking	
Demand deposits	116
Installment loans	102
Electric power	112
Airline (local service)	100
Railroads	100
Trucking	95

A) Small hospitals operate in the rising portion of their LAC curve.
B) The LAC curve is mildly U-shaped in the trucking industry.
C) The LAC of small firms is generally much higher than for large firms with the possible exception of hospitals.
D) Constant costs are not common in the industries represented.
E) All of the above are correct.

Difficulty: **Moderate**

60. Analysis of the learning curve for the L-1011 aircraft produced by Lockheed between 1970 and 1984 in the United States reveals that:
A) there was a learning rate of about 10% up to the production of the 100th aircraft.
B) the learning rate increased to about 20% after the production of the 100th aircraft..
C) after producing 150 of the aircraft the rate of production increased dramatically.
D) organizational forgetting can occur, resulting in a significant slowdown in the rate of production.
E) None of the above is correct.

Difficulty: **Moderate**

61. International economies of scale:
A) refer to the increasing costs resulting from a firm's efforts to integrate its entire system of manufacturing operations around the world.
B) account for a sharp drop over the past decade in international trade in parts and components.
C) are important but are not required to remain competitive.
D) are exploited subject to the need to retain those aspects of the operation which are essential to a firm's competitive position over subsequent product generations.
E) All of the above are incorrect.

Difficulty: **Moderate**

62. The ease with which a firm can substitute one input for another in production, or elasticity of substitution, is measured by:
A) the percentage change in (Input B/Input A) with respect to the percentage change in (Price of Input B/Price of Input A).
B) the percentage change in (Input A/Input B) with respect to the percentage change in (Price of Input B/Price of Input A).

C) the percentage change in (Output A/Output B) with respect to the percentage change in (Price of Output B/Price of Output A).
D) the percentage change in (Output B/Output A) with respect to the percentage change in (Price of Output B/Price of Output A).
E) All of the above will provide the same measure of elasticity of substitution.

Difficulty: **Hard**

63. According to the data in the table, which of the following statements is correct?

ELASTICITY OF SUBSTITUTION IN JAPANESE MANUFACTURING INDUSTRIES

Elasticity of Substitution Between...

	Elasticity of Substitution Between...		
Industry	**Nonskilled labor/capital**	**Skilled labor/capital**	**Nonskilled labor/skilled labor**
Food	0.14	0.62	0.38
Pulp and paper	0.76	0.75	1.32
Metal products	0.99	0.86	1.72
Machinery			
Non-electrical	0.31	0.56	1.44
Electrical	0.52	0.6	0.96
Precision instruments	0.67	0.62	1.15

A) The isoquant between nonskilled labor and capital in the food industry is almost L-shaped suggesting little possibility of factor substitution in production.
B) Elasticity of substitution between nonskilled and skilled workers for metal products suggests a steep isoquant and little possibility of substituting nonskilled for skilled workers.
C) Except in the food industry, it is harder to substitute nonskilled for skilled labor than to substitute nonskilled or skilled labor for capital.
D) Only (B) and (C) are correct.
E) All of the above are incorrect.

Difficulty: **Hard**

64. The opportunity cost doctrine:
A) suggests that implicit costs may be ignored if they remain positive over a long period of time.
B) states that a firm cannot earn sufficient revenue to meet explicit and implicit costs and consequently should attempt to meet its opportunity costs instead.
C) states that for a firm to retain any input for its own use, it must include, as a cost, the opportunity cost that the input could earn in its best alternative use.
D) states that private costs of producing are always greater than the opportunity costs of producing.

E) None of the above is correct.

Difficulty: **Easy**

65. If a firm uses an input which it already owns in its production process, such as capital equipment purchased and paid for in an earlier time period, then in the current time period the firm's cost of producing under the accounting definition must be:
A) greater than its opportunity costs.
B) less than its opportunity costs.
C) equal to its opportunity costs.
D) negative.
E) None of the above is correct.

Difficulty: **Moderate**

66. Marginal cost is equal to:
A) MP_L/W.
B) W/MP_L.
C) W x MP_L.
D) TVC/L.
E) $1/MP_L$.

Difficulty: **Moderate**

67. The Average Total Cost of producing is equal to:
A) AVC + AFC.
B) AVC + MC.
C) AFC + MC.
D) W/AP_L.
E) (C) and (D) are correct.

Difficulty: **Moderate**

68. At the least-cost input combination of labor and capital, which of the following is correct?
A) $MRTS_{LK} = r/w$.
B) $MP_L/MP_K = r/w$.
C) $MP_L = MP_K$.
D) The absolute slope of the isocost line is equal to the $MRTS_{LK}$.
E) All of the above are correct.

Difficulty: **Moderate**

69. Given that w is the per unit price of labor and r is the per unit price of capital, if the rate at which labor can be substituted for capital in production is smaller than the rate at which labor can be substituted for capital in the market, then:
A) $MRTS_{LK} < w/r$, and the firm should use less labor and more capital.
B) $MRTS_{LK} < w/r$, and the firm should use less capital and more labor.
C) $MRTS_{LK} > w/r$, and the firm should use less labor and more capital.

D) $MRTS_{LK} > w/r$, and the firm should use less capital and more labor.
E) the firm will increase its costs if it attempts to equalize these rates.

Difficulty: **Moderate**

70. The planning horizon refers to:
A) the limit to production decisions which exists if firms have a fixed input.
B) the situation in which all inputs are fixed and firms are combining inputs in fixed proportions.
C) the length of time into the future beyond which it is simply impossible to make cost minimizing decisions.
D) the long run.
E) None of the above is correct.

Difficulty: **Easy**

71. Which of the following statements regarding Long Run Marginal Cost (LMC) is <u>not</u> correct?
A) LMC is given by the slope of the LTC curve.
B) The LMC curve intersects the LAC curve at the minimum point of LAC.
C) If the LAC curve is U-shaped, then the LMC curve is U-shaped.
D) The LMC is U-shaped because of the law of diminishing returns.
E) All of the above are correct.

Difficulty: **Moderate**

72. An L-shaped LAC for an industry indicates that economies of scale:
A) prevail over a large range of output, and only large firms can survive in the industry over the long run.
B) are quickly exhausted and only small firms can survive in the industry over the long run.
C) are quickly exhausted, constant returns to scale prevail over a large range of output, and small and large firms can survive in the industry over the long run.
D) do not exist, but rather constant returns to scale prevail over a large range of output allowing small and large firms to survive in the industry over the long run.
E) None of the above is correct.

Difficulty: **Moderate**

73. Economies of scope:
A) necessitate the breakup of firms into smaller firms in order to achieve minimum cost production.
B) are present if it is cheaper for a single firm to produce various jointly, than for separate firms to produce the same products independently.
C) are present if it is more expensive for a single firm to produce various products jointly, than for separate firms to produce the same products independently.
D) may have caused the breakup of AT&T into smaller companies in 1995.
E) (A) and (D) are correct.

Difficulty: **Moderate**

74. Which of the following is <u>not</u> a source of economics of scope?
A) products that can be produced with common production facilities

B) a second product which allows the firm to utilize by-products generated by producing the first product
C) improved marketing strategies
D) specializing administration duties so that each product has administrative resources which can be applied to it exclusively
E) All of the above are sources of economies of scope.

Difficulty: **Moderate**

75. The learning curve:
A) illustrates cost savings from increasing cumulative total output over many time periods.
B) illustrates cost savings from increasing output per time period.
C) illustrates cost savings from increasing output per time period and across time periods.
D) drops at a slower rate, the smaller the rate of employee turnover.
E) (C) and (D) are correct.

Difficulty: **Easy**

76. Which of the following statements regarding pricing policy and the learning curve is correct?
A) If a firm believes that the learning curve is flat, it should keep unit prices very low.
B) If a firm believes that the learning curve is steep, it should keep unit prices very low.
C) Steep learning curves suggest that pricing policy cannot affect the pace at which costs of producing decrease for a firm in a given time period.
D) Steep learning curves suggest that pricing policy cannot affect the pace at which costs of producing decrease for a firm across time periods.
E) (C) and (D) are correct.

Difficulty: **Moderate**

77. In the range of output where the increasing use of the variable input leads to decreasing TP:
A) TVC is decreasing.
B) TVC is constant.
C) TVC is increasing.
D) TVC is no longer affected by employment decisions.
E) (B) and (D) are correct.

Difficulty: **Moderate**

78. The smaller is the minimum efficient scale (ME) the _____ is the prevalence of economies of scale and the _____ the number of firms that can operate efficiently in the industry.
A) larger; larger
B) larger; smaller
C) smaller; larger
D) smaller; smaller
E) None of the above is correct; the MES is a short-run concept and has no effect on economies of scale.

Difficulty: **Moderate**

79. In an industry with a U-shaped LAC curve, as the firm size expands:
A) the forces for increasing returns to scale operate first to lower SATC curves, and then the forces for decreasing returns to scale appear and begin to raise SATC curves.
B) the forces for increasing returns to scale and the forces for decreasing returns to scale may have effects initially, but the former usually dominates the latter in early stages and thereby raises the ATC curves.
C) the forces for increasing returns to scale and the forces for decreasing returns to scale may have effects initially, but both disappear once the firm reaches the optimal scale of plant.
D) the forces for increasing returns to scale and the forces for decreasing returns to scale may have effects initially, but the former dominates the latter in early stages and thereby lowers the ATC curves.
E) None of the above is correct.

Difficulty: **Moderate**

80. A "natural monopoly" would be the result of a situation in which _____ prevailed over a very large range of output.
A) decreasing input prices
B) constant returns to scale
C) decreasing returns to scale
D) increasing returns to scale
E) government regulation

Difficulty: **Easy**

Short Answer

Write the word or phrase that best completes each statement or answers the question.

1. **"I own my own auto repair business and have been doing extremely well. I use a building I inherited from my uncle so I don't have to pay any rent, and I can use some of my own tools so I don't have to pay for them either. I am even making enough to pay myself the wage I earned at my old job." How well is this person doing in economic terms?**
Answer: Not very well since he is ignoring some important implicit costs in his business. He could be renting out the building he inherited and could use his tools for another purpose or even possibly sell them. In any case, he apparently has no accounting losses, but in economic terms he is suffering losses, i.e., below normal rates of return, in his business.

2. **"All average cost curves are U-shaped because of the law of diminishing returns." Is this true? Explain.**
Answer: There are two exceptions to this statement. They are the average fixed cost curve and the long-run average cost curve. AFC is not U-shaped because fixed costs are not affected by the law of diminishing returns. LAC may be U-shaped, but this is due to increasing and decreasing returns to scale which are experienced when all inputs are variable and the law of diminishing returns does not apply.

3. **What difference is there between the rate at which labor can be substituted for capital in production and in the market?**

Answer: In production the marginal rate of technical substitution between labor and capital is technologically determined. It depends on how the marginal productivity of labor and capital behave as the K/L ratio is changed. The rate at which L can be substituted for K in the market is the ratio of the wage rate (w) to the rental price of capital (r). If one wants to purchase more units of capital, one will have to give up, i.e., trade off, the purchase of units of labor. When these two rates are equated, the firm is using a cost-minimizing combination of L and K.

4. **"Economies of scope simply means that as a firm gets bigger, its average cost of producing falls." Evaluate this statement.**
Answer: Economies of scope have no direct connection to economies of scale. Firms may remain the same size and yet reorganize their use of resources to allow them to produce more than one good at a lower cost. Full service banking in which banks provide checking deposits, currency exchange, loans, and data processing is a way of providing all those services at a lower cost way than if they were provided by different firms. These cost savings exist separate and apart from the cost savings of producing a given product on a larger scale.

5. **"This guy's learning curve isn't even flat, it goes uphill!" This is an insult. Why?**
Answer: Learning curves slope downward to the right indicating that, as experience is accumulated, the average cost of producing decreases. A flat learning curve implies that experience teaches you nothing about how to reduce costs. An upward-sloping learning curve implies that experience causes one to have higher costs, i.e., one loses knowledge as experience accumulates.

Chapter 9:

Price and Output Under Perfect Competition

Multiple-Choice

Choose the one alternative that best completes the statement or answers the question.

1. In the market period, price and quantity are determined by:
   A) the actions of both buyers and sellers.
   B) the actions of only the buyers.
   C) the producers since they can control the amount of output that is placed on the market.
   D) forces other than supply and demand because the supply curve is completely inelastic.
   E) None of the above statements is correct.

   Difficulty: **Moderate**

2. Economists define the market period as being that time period in which:
   A) some inputs into the production process are re-fixed and some are variable.
   B) the output supply curve is perfectly elastic.
   C) the output supply curve slopes upward and to the right.
   D) all inputs into the production process are fixed, so output is fixed.
   E) the output supply curve is a horizontal line.

   Difficulty: **Easy**

3. Suppose that a firm operates in a perfectly competitive market so that it is a price taker. If the firm wants to maximize its profits, it should increase (or decrease) its output up to the level where:
   A) price equals the average total cost of producing the last unit.
   B) price equals the marginal cost of producing the last unit.
   C) the difference between price and the average total cost of producing the last unit of output is maximized.
   D) the difference between price and the marginal cost of producing the last unit of output is maximized.
   E) the difference between marginal cost and marginal revenue is maximized.

   Difficulty: **Easy**

4. For the firm operating in a perfectly competitive market, profit maximization is attained at that level of output where:
   A) the price of the product is equal to the marginal cost of producing the last unit sold.
   B) the marginal revenue generated when the last unit is sold is equal to the cost of producing the last unit.
   C) the slope of the total revenue curve is equal to the slope of the total cost curve.
   D) the vertical distance between the total revenue curve and the total cost curve is maximized.

E) All of the above statements are correct.

Difficulty: **Moderate**

5. When economists study perfectly competitive markets as well as other market structures, they examine:
A) only the behavior of producers.
B) the behavior of both buyers and sellers as the prices and quantities of goods are determined.
C) only the consumption behavior of buyers.
D) only the effect on government actions on the performance of both competitive and imperfectly competitive markets.
E) None of the above is a correct statement.

Difficulty: **Moderate**

6. When a market is perfectly competitive on both the buying and selling side, individual buyers and sellers:
A) can buy or sell all that they want at the prevailing market price.
B) are price takers in the market price.
C) assume that they cannot affect market price.
D) regard the price of the good as being given to them.
E) All of the above are correct statements.

Difficulty: **Moderate**

7. For a business firm, total profits are maximized where:
A) the total revenue curve is parallel to the total cost curve, as long as total revenue is greater than total cost.
B) the total cost curve and the total revenue curve intersect each other.
C) the total revenue curve and the total cost curve are parallel to each other.
D) the marginal revenue curve gained from the last unit of a good sold adds more to total revenue than it cost to produce the last unit.
E) None of the above statements is correct.

Difficulty: **Easy**

8. If production takes place in the short run, the perfectly competitive firm maximizes profits by producing that level of output where:
A) MR > MC.
B) the vertical distance between the TR curve and the TC curve is greatest, assuming that TR > TC.
C) the price received from selling another unit of output exceeds the cost of producing that unit.
D) TR = TC.
E) None of the above is correct.

Difficulty: **Easy**

9. A firm operating under the conditions of perfection is better off producing in the short run rather than not producing as long as it can produce some level of output and receive a price where:

A) marginal cost is greater than average variable cost.
B) average fixed cost are minimized.
C) total fixed cost are zero.
D) price is greater than marginal cost.
E) total revenue can be increased.

Difficulty: **Moderate**

10. During the summer in the rural South, roadside stands selling farm fresh produce pop up as often as afternoon thunderstorms. Suppose that you operate one of these produce stands and you have some tomatoes that are almost too ripe to sell. You will have to throw them away when you close. It is almost dusk and two cars drive up to your stand and begin to inspect your products. Even though it cost you something to produce the tomatoes, what price should you charge if you want to maximize your profits?
A) That price where marginal cost equals marginal revenue.
B) That price which gives you the greatest profit per pound of tomatoes.
C) That price at which you will be certain of selling all of your tomatoes.
D) That price which maximizes your total revenue.
E) There is not enough information provided to determine a price.

Difficulty: **Hard**

11. Which one of the following statements correctly describes some characteristic of a perfectly competitive market?
A) Under perfect competition, each firm is a price taker.
B) Under perfect competition, there are many buyers and sellers in the market.
C) Under perfect competition, there are no barriers to entry into the market.
D) Under perfect competition, each seller produces and sells products that are perfect substitutes.
E) All of the above are characteristics of perfectly competitive markets.

Difficulty: **Moderate**

12. Suppose that you own a firm that operates in a perfectly competitive market. The level of output that you select to produce is associated with a price that is less than your average variable cost. At this level of output, you are:
A) losing not only all of your fixed cost but some of your variable cost as well.
B) better off by producing some positive level of output because you will generate some positive revenue for your firm.
C) covering all of your fixed cost and some of your variable cost.
D) producing the level of output that minimized your losses.
E) None of the above is a correct statement.

Difficulty: **Moderate**

13. Which one of the following is <u>not</u> a characteristic of a perfectly competitive market?
A) There is freedom of entry into and exit from the market.
B) Each firm can produce all that it wants to and not affect the market price of the good.
C) The market demand curve is perfectly elastic and thus is horizontal.
D) Each firm in the market produces a product that is a perfect substitute for the products of other firms.

E) There is no advertising in a perfectly competitive market.

Difficulty: **Moderate**

14. Suppose that you produce corn and sell your product in a perfectly competitive market. You are a price taker in the market for corn, and by this we mean:
A) that in order to sell additional bushels of corn, you must reduce your asking price.
B) you can increase your output and sell the increase at the prevailing market price without affecting the price.
C) the demand curve that you face for corn is downward sloping.
D) at the prevailing market price, you will be able to sell an infinite amount of corn.
E) if you raise your asking price above the prevailing market price of corn, your total revenue will go up but you sales will go down.

Difficulty: **Moderate**

15. Suppose that you own the XYZ Co. and produce widgets. You operate in a perfectly competitive output market. Currently your production is 2,000 widgets per time period, and you sell them on the market at the prevailing price of $3 per unit. Your company incurs a total cost of $12,000, total fixed cost of $4,000, and a marginal cot of $3. In order to maximize your profits or minimize your losses, you should:
A) shutdown and produce no widgets in order to minimize your losses.
B) expand your output in order to increase your total revenue.
C) reduce your output to 1,000 widgets in order to reduce your total cost of production to $6,000.
D) continue producing 2,000 widgets in the short run but not in the long run.
E) Not enough information is provided to make a decision.

Difficulty: **Moderate**

16. Suppose that the price received by a firm operating in a competitive market for its output equals marginal cost and is less than the average variable cost of producing the output. The firm should:
A) reduce its total cost of production to zero and thus minimize its losses.
B) shift the demand curve for its product towards the origin.
C) reduce its losses to the amount of its total variable costs.
D) reduce the amount of its losses to its total fixed costs.
E) reduce its output to the level where total cost equals total revenue and just break even.

Difficulty: **Moderate**

17. If you own the ABC Co., and the demand for your product slopes downward and to the right, we can conclude that the ABC Co.:
A) operates in a perfectly competitive market.
B) can sell all that it wants to at the established market price.
C) will not be able to maximize profits because price and revenue are subject to change.
D) is not a price taker in the market because it must lower its price in order to sell additional units of output of its product.
E) operates in a market in which there are no barriers to entry or exit for potential competitors.

Difficulty: **Moderate**

18. In a perfectly competitive market, the demand curve for the firm is determined by:
A) the firm's marginal cost of producing an extra unit of output.
B) the price that is established by the firm.
C) the market demand for and supply of the product.
D) the average total cost of producing a particular level of output.
E) the average variable cost of producing a particular level of output.

Difficulty: **Moderate**

19. For the typical perfectly competitive firm operating in the short run, it should reduce its output to zero if:
A) the price that it receives for its output is greater than its marginal cost.
B) the price that it receives for its products is less than average total cost.
C) the price that it receives for its product is less than average fixed cost.
D) the price that it receives for its product is less than average variable cost.
E) total cost is less than total revenue.

Difficulty: **Moderate**

20. In a perfectly competitive market, the typical firm cannot affect the price of the output that it sells, and so the firm maximizes its profits or minimizes any losses (assuming that P > AVC and the firm produces at all) by producing that level of output where:
A) MC < P.
B) MC > P.
C) MC = P.
D) P > MC = AVC.
E) P = MR.

Difficulty: **Easy**

21. If the price faced by a competitive firm is less than its average total cost but greater than its average variable cost when it produces a particular level of output, the firm:
A) is making a positive profit and should continue to produce.
B) is incurring a loss in the short run, but it should continue to produce in order to minimize its loss.
C) is breaking even, and so it should continue to produce a positive level of output.
D) is incurring a loss and should shut down its plant immediately in order to minimize its loss.
E) None of the above is correct.

Difficulty: **Moderate**

22. When a firm in perfect competition is maximizing its profits and produces that level of output where price, marginal revenue, marginal cost, average total cost, long-run marginal cost, and long-run average total cost are all equal, the firm:
A) earns an economic profit, and this is greater than the return required to keep the firm in business.
B) earns an economic profit that can be continued in the long run.
C) is in a long-run equilibrium and is just breaking even.
D) incurs a loss and will shut down in the long run.

E) serves to signal other competing firms to enter the market.

Difficulty: **Moderate**

23. Suppose that the typical firm in a competitive market faces average variable costs that remain constant regardless of the level of output that it produces. This firm's short-run supply curve is:
A) that rising portion of its marginal cost curve that lies above minimum average variable cost.
B) the same as its average variable cost curve.
C) the rising portion of the average total cost curve that is less than marginal cost.
D) reflecting a positive relationship between price and quantity supplied.
E) the segment of its average variable cost curve that is less than marginal cost.

Difficulty: **Hard**

24. The XYZ Co. produces widgets and operates in a competitive output market. The market price of widgets is $17 per unit, and the firm incurs a per unit total cost of $11. The marginal cost equals the price per unit cost of producing the widgets, and so the firm should:
A) expand its output in order to maximize its profits.
B) maintain its current level of output because profits are being maximized.
C) reduce output in order to maximize profits.
D) reduce output to zero and only incur a loss equal to its total fixed cost.
E) None of the above alternatives is correct.

Difficulty: **Moderate**

25. Given a competitive market, equilibrium price and quantity are established in the upward sloping supply curve and the downward sloping demand curve. If there is an increase in the demand for a product, which one of the following will occur in the short run?
A) There will be some firms that leave the market because they are not as efficient as other firms.
B) There will be an increase in the equilibrium price and an increase in the equilibrium quantity.
C) There will be an increase in the prices of the inputs used in production.
D) There will be an increase in equilibrium quantity but a decrease in equilibrium price.
E) There will be an increase in the number of firms in the market.

Difficulty: **Hard**

26. Given the assumption about the freedom of entry and exit for a perfectly competitive market, we can conclude that in the long run, the typical firm will operate where:
A) price equals short-run average total cost which equals long-run average total cost.
B) price equals short-run marginal cost and long-run total cost.
C) price equals short-run average total cost and long-run marginal revenue.
D) long-run average total cost is rising.
E) None of the above is correct.

Difficulty: **Moderate**

27. The supply curve for a perfectly competitive industry is the horizontal sum of all individual producer's supply curve if:
   A) the industry is characterized by increasing costs.
   B) the supply of inputs to the individual producers is perfectly inelastic.
   C) the industry does not experience increasing costs of production as the market output expands.
   D) the number of firms in the industry is held constant.
   E) the supply of inputs to the industry is completely elastic so that as more firms enter, the cost of the inputs does not rise.

   Difficulty: **Moderate**

28. Suppose that a firm operates under perfect competition and faces an upward sloping long-run supply curve for its output. This type of supply curve would occur:
   A) only if the firm experienced increasing returns to scale.
   B) if the firm was in a decreasing cost industry.
   C) if the industry was operating in the general range of decreasing returns to scale.
   D) if the firm was in an increasing cost industry.
   E) if the firm was in a constant cost industry.

   Difficulty: **Moderate**

29. In a competitive market, the firm's short-run supply curve is simply the:
   A) rising segment of its average total cost curve.
   B) that segment of its marginal cost curve that lies above minimum average variable cost.
   C) that segment of the average total cost curve that lies above the marginal cost curve.
   D) the same as its marginal revenue curve.
   E) None of the above is correct.

   Difficulty: **Moderate**

30. Suppose that for a perfectly competitive firm in an increasing cost industry, output price rises above the long-run equilibrium price. We would expect to see:
   A) the prices of the inputs that the firm uses begin to rise.
   B) the prices of the inputs that the firm uses remain constant and industry output to increase.
   C) market price to eventually return to its initial equilibrium price.
   D) the long-run supply curve for the industry to be horizontal.
   E) None of the above is correct.

   Difficulty: **Hard**

31. Input X is a variable input into the production of widgets. If the price of input X increases, then we would expect to see (assuming that widgets are sold in a competitive market and other things remain constant):
   A) the fixed cost of producing widgets to increase.
   B) the demand curve for widgets to shift to the left.
   C) the short-run supply curve of widgets to shift upward and to the left.
   D) the short-run supply curve of widgets to shift outward and to the right.

E) equilibrium price to fall and equilibrium quantity to rise.

Difficulty: **Hard**

32. Suppose that a firm in a perfectly competitive market operates and encounters the following market conditions: Total fixed cost = $1,000; Total cost = $3,500; Marginal cost = $1. The firm sells 3,000 units of output at a market price of $1 per unit. Based on this information, you may correctly conclude that:

A) the firm is breaking even on every unit of output that it sells because at its output level, MC = P.
B) the firm should reduce its output and increase product price in order to expand profits.
C) the firm is producing the correct amount since MC = P, and it is earning a positive profit.
D) the firm incurs a loss but it should continue to produce because all variable and some fixed costs are covered.
E) the firm suffers a loss and should shut down.

Difficulty: **Moderate**

33. I like zaflings, but not many other people do. In fact, if I purchased a box of zaflings they would be very expensive because the cost of producing a small amount would be high. However, if I can change the attitudes (tastes and preferences) of some of my friends so that they, too, like zaflings, then production can increase, per unit production costs will fall, and it will make it cheaper for me to buy zaflings. This observation is best described as:

A) an external diseconomy of scale.
B) increasing returns to the factors of production.
C) diminishing returns to the factors of production.
D) an external economy of scale.
E) an economy of being established.

Difficulty: **Moderate**

34. When we say that a perfectly competitive firm is simply a quantity adjuster in the market, we are saying essentially that:

A) the firm is not concerned with its cost of production.
B) the firm will achieve maximum profits or minimum losses through the adjustment of quantity of output produced but not changes in price.
C) a firm's decision regarding quantity is independent of the forces of supply and demand.
D) a firm's decision is independent of the prevailing market price for the product that it produces.
E) None of the above is correct.

Difficulty: **Hard**

35. The Jones Co. is a perfectly competitive firm and it produces output incurring a total cost of $6,000, a total variable cost of $4,500, and a marginal cost of $2.75 for the last unit produced. If these costs are incurred at an output level of 8,000 units which are sold at the market price of $2.25 per unit, the Jones Co. should:

A) reduce its output because a loss is being incurred.
B) expand its output because it is not maximizing profit.
C) reduce its output because it is not maximizing its profit.
D) maintain its current level of output because profits are being maximized.

E) do none of the above.

Difficulty: **Moderate**

36. Brown Brothers' Farm operates in a perfectly competitive market and produces soybeans. Suppose that the market price of soybeans is $2.50 per bushel when 5,000 bushels are produced and offered for sale. At this output level, the firm incurs an average total cost of $3 per bushel, and marginal cost equals average total cost. Average variable cost is $2 per bushel of soybeans. To achieve an optimum output level, Brown Brothers' Farm should:

A) maintain its current level of output because it is optimum.
B) reduce its output but continue to produce.
C) increase its output in order to increase its total revenue.
D) shut-down and produce nothing so that the farm loses only its fixed costs.
E) try to shift its average total cost curve down so that the firm at least breaks even.

Difficulty: **Moderate**

37. When a firm operates in a perfectly competitive market, any price below the minimum average variable cost of production is the firm's:

A) shut down price.
B) profit-maximizing price.
C) market price.
D) selling price.
E) break-even price.

Difficulty: **Moderate**

38. For a firm operating in a competitive market, its long-run marginal cost curve is flatter than its short-run marginal cost curve because the:

A) firm can adjust more factors of production in the long run than in the short run.
B) firm can control its product's market price in the long run.
C) cost of inputs used by the firm fall over the long run.
D) firm experiences economies of scale throughout the relevant range of production in the long run.
E) law of diminishing returns to the factors of production is operating in the long run.

Difficulty: **Moderate**

39. In order for the firm operating in a perfectly competitive market to supply any output in the long run:

A) the firm must cover all of its fixed cost of production.
B) the firm must not incur a loss in the long run.
C) the firm must show some positive economic profit where TR > TC.
D) the price received from selling an extra unit of output must not be less than the long-run per unit cost of producing the good.
E) None of the above is correct.

Difficulty: **Moderate**

40. The perfectly competitive firm in the long run:

A) earns a positive profit since TR > TC.
B) may produce even if it is suffering a loss.

C) does not have a shut down price.
D) earns only a normal profit.
E) None of the above is correct.

Difficulty: **Moderate**

41. In a perfectly competitive market, if market price is greater than long-run average cost, we would expect:
A) the firm to lower its level of output and price to rise.
B) new firms to enter the industry and market price to fall.
C) some firms will leave the industry and market price to rise.
D) the typical firm in the industry to earn a profit just sufficient to cover all costs of production.
E) All of the existing firms in the industry to expand their productive capacity.

Difficulty: **Moderate**

42. All of the following statements are false <u>except</u>:
A) for a competitive firm in the long run, if P = LMC, the firm should produce as long as P < LAC.
B) for a competitive firm in the long run, with P = LMC, the firm should temporarily shut down if LAC > P.
C) in the long run, a competitive firm leaves the industry if market price is lower than the long-run average cost of production.
D) for a competitive firm in the long run, its supply curve is steeper than its short-run supply curve.
E) In the long run, a firm in perfect competition may earn an economic profit.

Difficulty: **Moderate**

43. Suppose that a constant-cost, perfectly competitive industry producing a normal good is in a long-run equilibrium. Other things constant, a permanent increase in consumer incomes will likely cause:
A) only an increase in the market price of the good.
B) an increase in both the market price and the quantity supplied of the product.
C) a decrease in the market price of the product but increases in quantity supplied.
D) only an increase in the quantity supplied of the product.
E) None of the above is correct.

Difficulty: **Moderate**

44. Suppose that a constant-cost, perfectly competitive industry producing a normal good is in a long-run equilibrium. Other things constant, a permanent decrease in consumer incomes will likely cause:
A) a reduction in the quantity supplied of the product, but not the product price.
B) a reduction in both the price and quantity supplied of the product.
C) a decrease in the quantity supplied of the product but an increase in the product price.
D) a decrease in the price of the product but an increase in the quantity supplied.
E) None of the above is correct.

Difficulty: **Moderate**

45. Suppose that the Glum Company is in a perfectly competitive market and that the price of its output is $25 per unit. If the firm produces 1,000 units per week at an average total cost of $25 per unit and average cost falls as more output is produced, then in order to maximize its profits, the Glum Company should:
A) reduce its output since marginal cost must be greater than price.
B) increase its output.
C) shut down in order to minimize losses.
D) maintain the current level of output.
E) do none of the above.

Difficulty: **Hard**

46. The Widget Company produces and distributes its output in a perfectly competitive market. If its marginal costs are rising but market price is greater than the average variable cost as well as the cost of producing an extra unit of output, the Widget Company should:
A) maintain its current level of output because the last unit that it produces brings in more than it costs to produce.
B) expand its current output in order to increase its profits.
C) reduce its level of output in order to increase its profits.
D) reduce its level of current output in order to minimize its losses.
E) expand its current level of output in order to reduce its losses.

Difficulty: **Moderate**

47. New firms will enter a competitive industry in the long run if:
A) some firms in the industry can cover their variable but not all of their fixed costs.
B) some firms in the industry are able to control their product's price.
C) the typical firm in the industry earns a positive economic profit.
D) the typical firm in the industry just covers its total cost of production.
E) None of the above will affect the entry of new firms.

Difficulty: **Moderate**

48. If a country's demand for good A is relatively inelastic and the government imposes a tariff on the good, we would expect:
A) no change in the price of the good.
B) a smaller consumption effect than would be the case if demand was more elastic.
C) a very large change in the level of output produced.
D) the demand curve for the product to shift outward and to the right.
E) None of the above is likely to occur.

Difficulty: **Moderate**

49. Suppose that the government imposes a general sales tax on all goods sold in a competitive market. Next, in order to offset the effect of the sales tax, the government gives a tax rebate in the form of a general income subsidy. The result will be that:
A) society's overall social welfare will not have changed.
B) there will be neither a consumption nor production effect.
C) there will be an external diseconomy of scale in the production of the good.

D) the deadweight welfare loss of the tax will still remain.
E) None of the above to occur.

Difficulty: **Hard**

50. Suppose that it costs a firm $3 to produce an extra unit of output, and this unit is sold on the market for $7. This difference between the marginal cost of production and the price of the good is the:
A) consumers' surplus.
B) producer's surplus on the extra unit produced.
C) total revenue for the unit of the good that is sold.
D) marginal revenue for the extra unit of the good that is sold.
E) None of the above is correct.

Difficulty: **Easy**

51. An economist defines the exchange rate between two countries as the:
A) amount of one currency that must be given up in order to obtain one unit of another currency.
B) difference between total exports and total imports within a country.
C) price at which the sales and purchases of foreign goods takes place.
D) ratio of import prices to export prices for a particular economy.
E) None of the above is correct.

Difficulty: **Easy**

52. When an allocation of resources in a competitive market is efficient in consumption:
A) it is not possible to reallocate goods consumed among individuals in order to make one person better off without making someone else worse off.
B) consumers will be at some point either on or below their demand curve for the product.
C) by rearranging the allocation of consumer goods, someone can be made better off without making someone else worse off.
D) it can never be efficient in production.
E) None of the above is correct.

Difficulty: **Moderate**

53. In a perfectly competitive system, producer's surplus is:
A) always greater than consumer's surplus.
B) always equal to consumer's surplus.
C) a cost to society since it does not accrue to consumers.
D) the part of the revenue a firm receives which is not necessary to induce it to produce a given quantity.
E) an explicit cost of production like wages and rents.

Difficulty: **Moderate**

54. Suppose that the production and distribution of widgets takes place in a perfectly competitive market. If, in an attempt to raise revenue, the government places a sales tax of X% on each widget that is sold, then:
A) the market will achieve an efficient allocation of resources and widgets more quickly.

B) widgets will be produced up to a point where the marginal cost of producing the last widget is greater than the marginal valuation of consuming it.
C) the price of widgets will equal the marginal cost of producing the last widget.
D) widgets will be produced at the quantity where the marginal valuation of consuming the last widget is greater than the marginal cost of producing that widget.
E) None of the above is correct.

Difficulty: **Hard**

55. Which of the following statements regarding the stock market as an example of a perfectly competitive market is <u>incorrect</u>?
A) The individual demanders and suppliers of stock have no perceptible effect on price.
B) All stocks with each company category are differentiated.
C) The frequency of sale for a particular type of stock indicates resources are mobile.
D) Information on prices and quantities of stocks traded is readily available.
E) All of the above are correct statements.

Difficulty: **Moderate**

56. The stock market:
A) provides a good example of the efficient market hypothesis because large profits can be made by efficient entrepreneurs.
B) provides a good example of the efficient market hypothesis because the price of stock at any point in time usually reflects all publicly known information about the stock.
C) provides a poor example of the efficient market hypothesis because mere expectations of losses can cause a stock price to fall.
D) provides a poor example of the efficient market hypothesis because price adjustments are too rapid for ordinary investors.
E) (A) and (D) are correct.

Difficulty: **Moderate**

57. The linking of international stock markets:
A) has sharply increased opportunities for portfolio diversification.
B) has created the danger that a crisis in one stock market will quickly spread to other stock markets around the world.
C) has reduced the New York Stock Exchange's ability to anticipate changing economic conditions.
D) has reduced the New York Stock Exchange's importance as a central source of capital for American corporations.
E) All of the above are correct.

Difficulty: **Moderate**

58. The supply curve of oil from tar sands:
A) has shifted outward despite the loss of government subsidies for synthetic fuel projects.
B) has shifted outward due to technological innovation.
C) suggests that the cost of extracting oil from tar sands over a wide range of output is below the market price of oil.
D) is now relatively flat.

E) All of the above are correct.

Difficulty: **Moderate**

59. A study by Lloyd Reynolds has shown that the U.S. cotton textile industry in the years between the world wars was almost perfectly competitive. Which of the following statements about that industry is <u>false</u>?
A) Cotton textiles were practically homogeneous.
B) There were many buyers and sellers of cotton cloth.
C) Entry into and exit from the industry were easy.
D) Firms did not leave the industry in spite of the low returns.
E) All of the above occurred.

Difficulty: **Moderate**

60. Lloyd Reynolds found that the U.S. cotton textile industry was essentially a perfectly competitive market between World Wars I and II. He also found that the rate of return for investment in the textile industry was about 6% in the South and 1% in the North, while the average rate of return for all manufacturing industries in the U.S. was about 8%. Which of the following combination of events actually occurred as predicted by the perfect competition model?
A) The capacity of the textile industry declined by 33% from 1925-1938, and most of the textile firms that closed were in the South.
B) The capacity of the textile industry expanded by 33% from 1925-1938, and most of the textile firms that closed were in the South.
C) The capacity of the textile industry declined by 33% from 1925-1938, and most of the textile firms that were closed were in the North.
D) The capacity of the textile industry expanded by 33% from 1925-1938, and most of the textile clubs that closed were in the North.
E) The capacity of the textile industry expanded by 33% from 1925-1938 because government subsidies were used to prevent any closures from occurring.

Difficulty: **Moderate**

61. In the U.S., the newest method of allocating the use of the airwaves is(are):
A) the auctioning of licenses to private bidders.
B) a lottery for private companies with qualified winners selected by chance to receive licenses.
C) merit hearings to award licenses to entities which will best serve local communities.
D) All of the above methods have been employed extensively since 1927.
E) None of the above because government has not controlled the allocation of the airwaves since 1946.

Difficulty: **Moderate**

62. In an auction, the so-called "winner's curse":
A) arises when the average of all bids is substantially below to the true value of the item being auctioned and the winner consequently pays more for the item than was necessary to "win" it away from the other bidders.
B) arises when the average of all bids is equal to the true value of the item being auctioned and the winner pays too much for the item relative to its true market bidders.

C) arises when the winner of an auction pays too little for an item, resells it at a substantial gain, and then pays a heavy tax on the arbitrage profits earned.
D) refers to the case where someone bidding in a sealed auction (only one secret bid is made) ends up losing the item to another bidder because he believes that no other bidder has the resources to make a similar bid.
E) None of the above is correct.

Difficulty: **Moderate**

63. Which of the following is not a characteristic of a perfectly competitive market?
A) many buyers and many sellers
B) heterogeneous output
C) perfect mobility of resources
D) perfect mobility of resources
E) All of the above are characteristics of a perfectly competitive market.

Difficulty: **Easy**

64. The economist's concept of competition as it appears in the perfect competition theory:
A) stresses the impersonality of the market.
B) is used to depict a situation in which one producer does not care and is not affected by what other producers are doing.
C) is used to depict a situation in which there is no need to engage in advertising.
D) is diametrically opposite to the everyday usage of the term which stresses the notion of rivalry.
E) All of the above are correct.

Difficulty: **Easy**

65. Which of the following statements about the market period is not correct?
A) It is also referred to as the very short run.
B) It is the time period in which no input can be varied.
C) It must be a very short period of time such as one week or less.
D) It is the period in which the output supply curve is vertical.
E) If fresh vegetables can be delivered only once a week to a town, then the market period is one week in length.

Difficulty: **Moderate**

66. In the market period:
A) demand alone determines price.
B) supply determines price and quantity.
C) there is a perfectly elastic market supply curve.
D) costs of production affect the market price.
E) All of the above are correct.

Difficulty: **Easy**

67. Assuming P = MC, which of the following describes a situation in which a firm should not shut down in the short run?
A) P > ATC > AVC.
B) ATC > P > AVC.

C) P = ATC > AVC.
D) All of the above are correct.
E) Only (A) and (C) are correct.

Difficulty: **Moderate**

68. Suppose that tobasco sauce is produced in an increasing cost situation. Other things remaining the same, a change in consumer preferences which leads to a permanent increase in demand for tobasco sauce will cause:
A) an increase in market price and a decrease in market quantity.
B) an increase in market price and market quantity.
C) only an increase in market quantity.
D) only an increase in market price.
E) All of the above could be correct depending on the behavior of costs as the industry changes size.

Difficulty: **Moderate**

69. The United States imports Absolut Vodka from Sweden. If the supply curve of Absolut is perfectly elastic, then an increase in the tastes and preferences of Americans for the product will likely cause:

1. a reduction in the monthly supply of vodka produced in the U.S.
2. an increase in the monthly quantity supplied of Absolut.
3. A decrease in the monthly quantity supplied of Absolut.
4. An increase in the price of a bottle of Absolut.

A) 1 only.
B) 2 only.
C) 3 only.
D) 1 and 3 are correct.
E) 2 and 4 are correct.

Difficulty: **Hard**

70. An excise tax on a normal good will fall entirely on sellers of the good if:
A) the demand for the good is perfectly inelastic and the supply curve is upward sloping.
B) the supply of the good is perfectly inelastic and the demand curve is downward sloping.
C) the supply curve is upward sloping and the demand curve is downward sloping.
D) the supply of the good is perfectly elastic while the demand for the good is perfectly inelastic.
E) Not enough information is provided in order to determine an answer.

Difficulty: **Moderate**

71. The price elasticity of supply is measured by a ratio of:
A) a change in supply to a change in price.
B) a percentage change in price to a percentage change in quantity supplied.
C) a percentage change in quantity supplied to a percentage change in price.
D) a change in supply to a percentage change in price.
E) None of the above is correct.

Difficulty: **Easy**

72. Elasticity of supply measures the degree of responsiveness of the:
A) quantity supplied of a good to a change in the price of that good.
B) price of a good to a change in the quantity supplied of that good.
C) price of a good to a change in the price of the inputs used to produce that good.
D) price of a good to a change in the supply of that good.
E) supply of a good to a change in the demand for that good.

Difficulty: **Easy**

73. For a constant cost industry, the adjustment to an increase in demand:
A) falls increasingly on price as the market moves through the market period, to the short run, and then the long run.
B) falls increasingly on quantity as the market moves through the market period, to the short run, and then the long run.
C) falls first on quantity and then on price as the market moves through the market period, to the short run, and then the long run.
D) falls immediately on quantity which remains stable through the market period, to the short run, and then the long run.
E) None of the above is correct.

Difficulty: **Moderate**

Use the per unit cost table below to answer questions 74 - 77.

Per Unit Cost Schedules of a Firm

Q	ATC	MC
12	21.66	15
13	21.54	20
14	21.86	26
15	22.6	33
16	23.75	41
17	25.29	50

74. What are the total profits of the firm if it maximizes profits and the market price of the good is $41.00?
A) $267.07.
B) $270.76.
C) $276.00.
D) $380.00.
E) $656.00.

Difficulty: **Moderate**

75. What are the total profits of the firm if it produces 17 units of output and the market price of the good is $41.00?
A) $267.07.
B) $270.76.
C) $276.00.

D) $429.93.
E) $697.00.

Difficulty: **Moderate**

76. At which output level will the firm maximize profit per unit of output?
A) 12
B) 13
C) 14
D) 15
E) 16

Difficulty: **Moderate**

77. Given the unit per cost table, the firm maximizes total profits by:
A) producing the output level which minimizes ATC.
B) producing the output level that minimizes MC.
C) producing the output level where price exceeds ATC by the greatest amount possible.
D) maximizing profit per unit.
E) None of the above is correct.

Difficulty: **Moderate**

78. Which of the following statements regarding long-run equilibrium in perfectly competitive industry is <u>not</u> correct?
A) P = LMC = LAC.
B) P = LMC demonstrates that productive efficiency is achieved in the long run.
C) P = LMC demonstrates that allocative efficiency is achieved in the long run.
D) Output is produced at lowest cost and represents the best use of the economy's resources.
E) All of the above are correct.

Difficulty: **Moderate**

79. Which of the following statements regarding cost curves of perfectly competitive firms is correct?
A) Perfectly competitive firms need not have identical cost curves.
B) The minimum point on the LAC curves of perfectly competitive firms must occur at the same cost per unit.
C) Competition in input markets assures that all perfectly competitive firms have identical minimum average costs and zero economic profits when the industry is in long run equilibrium.
D) The lowest point on the LAC curve of each firm is the same for firms that have inputs with different productivities.
E) All of the above are correct.

Difficulty: **Moderate**

80. Which of the following statements regarding the behavior of costs is correct?
A) External economies are reached as the firm moves upward along a given LAC curve and results in an upward shift in the firm's per unit cost curves.

B) External diseconomies result from a decrease in input prices as an industry expands and cause a downward shift in the firm's per unit cost curves.
C) External economies are achieved as the firm moves downward along a given LAC curve and results in a downward shift in the firm's per unit cost curves.
D) External economies result from a decrease in input prices as the industry expands and cause a downward shift in the firm's per unit cost curves.
E) None of the above is correct.

Difficulty: **Moderate**

81. Assume that: (1) in the absence of international trade the domestic equilibrium price of wheat is $4.00 per bushel; (2) wheat is available on the international market at $2,00 per bushel; and, (3) this nation's demand for imports of wheat is small in relation to the total world supply of exports of wheat. Given these assumptions and allowing the importation of wheat, which of the following statements is not correct?
A) The foreign supply of wheat to this nation is horizontal at the domestic market price of $4.00 per bushel.
B) Domestic consumers purchase more wheat.
C) The domestic production of wheat will decrease.
D) Resources in the domestic economy will be shifted into the production of goods in which the nation has a comparative advantage.
E) All of the above are correct.

Difficulty: **Moderate**

82. The area between the marginal cost curve and the horizontal axis up to the chosen output level of the firm is:
A) the firm's producer surplus.
B) the buyer's consumers surplus.
C) the opportunity cost of the variable inputs used by the firm.
D) the firm's profits from the production of the good up to that output level.
E) the amount that it is not necessary for the firm to receive in order to induce the firm to produce at that output level.

Difficulty: **Hard**

83. At the equilibrium output level in a perfectly competitive market:
A) consumer surplus is maximized.
B) producer surplus is maximized.
C) consumer surplus plus producer surplus is maximized.
D) changes in output would not affect the total of consumer and producer surplus.
E) All of the above are correct.

Difficulty: **Moderate**

84. Deadweight loss:
A) results from the imposition of an excise tax unless the tax is rebated.
B) consists of the loss of consumer surplus to producers.
C) consists of the loss of producer surplus to consumers.
D) consists of the loss of producer and consumer surplus to the government collecting the tax.

E) None of the above is correct.

Difficulty: **Moderate**

85. Which of the following statements regarding the impact of a tariff is not correct?
A) The consumption effect of a tariff is the resulting decrease in domestic consumption.
B) The production effect of a tariff is the resulting decrease in domestic production.
C) The trade effect of a tariff is the resulting decreasing in imports.
D) The revenue effect of a tariff is the resulting revenue collected by the government.
E) All of the above are correct.

Difficulty: **Moderate**

86. Which of the following statements regarding the effects of a tariff is not correct?
A) A tariff leads to a reduction in consumer surplus.
B) A tariff leads to a reduction in domestic producer surplus.
C) A tariff leads to a transfer of consumer surplus to domestic producers.
D) A tariff causes deadweight loss.
E) All of the above are correct.

Difficulty: **Moderate**

87. Which of the following statements comparing and contrasting the effects of an excise tax on a domestically produced good and a tariff on an imported good is not correct?
A) Both excise taxes and tariffs cause deadweight loss.
B) Both excise taxes and tariffs reduce consumption.
C) Both excise taxes and tariffs transfer consumer surplus to producers.
D) Both excise taxes and tariffs generate revenue for government.
E) Both excise taxes and tariffs raise the price that consumers pay for a good.

Difficulty: **Moderate**

Short Essays

Give a brief answer to each of the following questions.

1. **"When a firm is at its 'breakeven point' it is not breaking even." Evaluate this statement.**
Answer: A breakeven point is the minimum point of the ATC curve. Profit-maximizing firms producing at that point earn normal profits or a competitive rate of return. To many people, breaking even means zero accounting profits, i.e., the firm is not earning accounting profits ("in the black"), but is not experiencing accounting losses ("in the red"). From an economic view, zero accounting profits cannot be "breaking even" because in the long run it is not a sustainable position. Firms will leave an industry where they are earning below normal accounting profits much less zero accounting profits.

2. **"Firms experiencing decreasing returns to scale are experiencing increasing cost. Thus, they are in an increasing cost industry." Explain what is wrong with this statement.**
Answer: It confuses different sources of cost increases for firms. Decreasing returns to scale are internal to an industry. Firms experience higher costs because of the inefficiencies of being big, but input prices are assumed to be constant. An increasing cost industry is one

in which the source of cost increases is external to the industry. As the industry expands, it bids up the price of an input and the firms experience increasing cost even in cases where the firms are the same size as before.

3. **If a country begins importing good X that it also currently produces, the production of other goods in the domestic economy will increase. Explain.**
Answer: The increase in imports will cause some decreases in the domestic production of good X. This will release some resources for use in the production of other goods after a period of adjustment.

4. **"Perfect competition isn't very competitive. There are never any profits because nobody ever tries to get ahead of anybody else." Evaluate this statement.**
Answer: Perfect competition is not very competitive if competition is taken to be rivalry. On the other hand, it is so "competitive" in another common sense of the word that economic profits are immediately eliminated by the competitive entry of new firms. As to no one ever trying to get ahead, again this is true to the extent that it implies the absence of rivalry. However, firms do try to improve their own situation by responding appropriately to changes in demand or supply conditions. Firms do earn profits or keep losses to a minimum by such actions.

5. **"In the market period, price is demand determined, so supply has no influence on price." Evaluate this statement.**
Answer: It is correct insofar as the supply curve is vertical in the market period, and the quantity supplied is constant no matter what the price of the good. In such cases, price is determined by the position of the demand curve. On the other hand, the relative position of the vertical market supply curve does affect the price of the good. What is absent is the interaction between supply and demand behaviors which causes supply behavior to change, i.e., a change in quantity supplied in response to a change in price.

6. **Why can the perfect competition model be applied to the stock market?**
Answer: Although the stock market is not what first comes to mind when one thinks about perfect competition, the model is applicable. Consider the characteristics of that market: (1) in most cases, there are so many buyers or sellers of a stock that individual buyers or sellers have no perceptible influence on price; (2) all stocks within each company category are largely homogenous; (3) frequency of sale of a specific type of stock suggests that resources are mobile in this market; and, (4) information on prices and quantities is readily available.

7. **When is it a curse to win in a competitive market? (Hint: Beware of the "winner's curse.")**
Answer: In an auction, if the average of the bids for an item is a correct estimate of the true market value of the item, then the winner is paying more than the good is worth. That is the curse.

Chapter 10:

Price and Output Under Pure Monopoly

Multiple-Choice

Choose the one alternative that best completes the statement or answers the question.

1. Which one of the following is <u>not</u> a characteristic of a monopolist's marginal revenue curve?
   A) The marginal revenue curve shows the monopolist the profit-maximizing level of output to produce.
   B) When total revenue is decreasing as prices fall, the marginal revenue lies below the horizontal axis.
   C) Assuming that both the demand and marginal revenue functions are continuous, both the demand and marginal revenue curves begin as the same point on the vertical axis.
   D) When the demand and marginal revenue functions are continuous, the marginal revenue curve lies below the demand curve for all levels of output.
   E) The marginal revenue curve is twice as steep as the demand curve.

   Difficulty: **Moderate**

2. The ABC Corp. is considered a pure monopolist, and so it must:
   A) take as given the price of the product that is established in the marketplace.
   B) be the only buyer of a factor of production.
   C) be the only producer of a product for which there are no close substitutes.
   D) face only a few competitors that produce similar, but not identical, products.
   E) face a demand curve for its product that is horizontal.

   Difficulty: **Easy**

3. Suppose that the Jones Corp. is a pure monopolist and is not worried about the potential entry of new firms into the market. The marginal revenue for the Jones Corp. is equal to:
   A) the price at which an extra unit of output is sold minus the loss in revenue because the original output is now sold at the lower price.
   B) the price of the additional units sold times the number of units sold at the original price.
   C) the price of the additional units sold.
   D) the original quantity sold minus the price of the extra units sold.
   E) None of the above is correct.

   Difficulty: **Moderate**

4. The Lambert Corp. is a profit-maximizing monopolist and the marginal revenue that it earns on an additional unit of output sold is less than the price charged for that unit. The reason for this difference between marginal revenue and product price is that:
   A) the marginal cost of producing additional units of output increases, and so price must also rise.
   B) the monopolist is the only seller in the market, and so it can charge whatever price it wants to charge.

C) the amount of output produced by the monopolist does not affect the price of the product.
D) in order to sell an additional unit of output, the Lambert Corp. must lower the price not only on the additional unit of output but on all previous units as well.
E) None of the above is correct.

Difficulty: **Moderate**

5. For the monopolistic producer in the short run, if P > AVC, the output level is established at that quantity where:
A) P > LAC.
B) P = ATC.
C) MC = MR.
D) P = MC.
E) P < MR.

Difficulty: **Moderate**

6. For any firm, the degree of control that it has over the price of its product is a measure of the firm's:
A) capital usage.
B) profitability potential.
C) efficiency in production.
D) cost in terms of lost social welfare.
E) monopoly power.

Difficulty: **Easy**

7. Suppose that a monopolist is unregulated and that the barriers to entry into the market are complete. The total revenue curve of the monopolist:
A) increases but at a decreasing rate as more and more output is sold.
B) is a horizontal line at the established market price of the firm's product.
C) increases at an increasing rate as more and more output is sold.
D) decreases at a decreasing rate once total revenue is maximized.
E) is a straight line sloping upward and to the right as more and more output is sold.

Difficulty: **Moderate**

8. If a monopolist faces an elastic demand curve, then its marginal revenue is:
A) equal to zero at all levels of output.
B) positive at all levels of output.
C) equal to one at all levels of output.
D) negative at all levels of output.
E) falling at a constant rate as price falls.

Difficulty: **Moderate**

9. Suppose that a monopolist is charging a price of $15 at a particular point on its demand curve. At this price of $15, the price elasticity of demand is .5, and so its marginal revenue is:
A) $15.
B) $1.

C) $0.
D) $-15.
E) There is not enough information provided to calculate the firm's marginal revenue.

Difficulty: **Moderate**

10. For the monopolist, the best level of output occurs at that point where:
A) total revenue is at a maximum.
B) total revenue equals short run total cost.
C) the total revenue and the short run total cost curves are parallel.
D) the short run total cost is minimized.
E) None of the above is correct.

Difficulty: **Moderate**

11. Suppose that the government imposes a per unit tax on the output produced by a monopolist. We would expect the tax to cause the monopolist's:
A) short-run average total cost curve to shift upward.
B) short-run average total cost and short-run marginal cost curves to shift upward because the tax is like a fixed cost.
C) short-run average total cost curve and short-run marginal cost curve to shift upward because the tax is like a variable cost.
D) the total sales of the monopolist to be unaffected by the monopolist's behavior in the market.
E) None of the above is correct.

Difficulty: **Hard**

12. Suppose that a monopolist faces two identical demand curves for his product when he subdivides his overall market into two submarkets. If the monopolist tries to practice third-degree price discrimination, he will:
A) increase his profits in one market and not reduce them in the other.
B) increase overall total revenue and profits in both markets.
C) charge a higher price in the market with the less elastic demand.
D) be unable to increase either total revenue or total profits.
E) increase sales in one market and face no reduction in sales in the other.

Difficulty: **Moderate**

13. Suppose that a profit-maximizing monopolist is unregulated. The monopolist produces 9,000 units of output and the marginal revenue associated with this output level is $14. If the output level increases to 10,000 units, we can conclude that:
A) the marginal revenue associated with the increase is $27.
B) the marginal revenue associated with the new level of output is also $14.
C) the marginal revenue associated with this new level of output must be less than $14.
D) the price required to sell this increases level of output must be less than $14.
E) the marginal cost of producing the last unit of output is $14.

Difficulty: **Moderate**

14. A monopolist facing a downward-sloping linear demand curve produces an output level of 10,000 units and sells them at a price of $40 each. At this output and price level, the demand curve has a price elasticity of demand coefficient equal to one. The marginal revenue received from selling the last of the 10,000 units is equal to:
A) $40.
B) $-0.
C) $20.
D) $1.
E) some amount greater than zero.

Difficulty: **Moderate**

15. Suppose that a monopolist is able to block entry into the market. The firm earns an average profit (at some particular level of output) which is equal to the vertical distance between:
A) the demand curve and the marginal revenue curve.
B) the total cost curve and the total revenue curve.
C) the demand curve and the marginal revenue curve.
D) the marginal cost curve and the marginal revenue curve.
E) the demand curve and the average total cost curve.

Difficulty: **Hard**

16. A natural monopoly occurs when the firm:
A) experiences decreasing returns to scale throughout the relevant range of production.
B) has some type of patent protection for either its output or its production process.
C) has complete or exclusive control over some raw material used in the production process.
D) experiences economies of scale and decreasing long-run average cost over a sufficiently large range of outputs.
E) is able to enjoy economies of being established that would not be available to a new entrant into the market.

Difficulty: **Moderate**

17. Suppose that a monopolist faces a downward-sloping linear demand curve. We can conclude that its total revenue curve is:
A) a linear function of the amount of output produced and the price at which the output is sold.
B) the same as the monopolist's demand curve.
C) a rising function of output which increases at a decreasing rate, reaches a maximum at the mid-point of the demand curve, and then falls.
D) negatively sloped and has a slope that is equal to twice that of the linear demand curve.
E) a linear function from the origin with a slope equal to product price.

Difficulty: **Moderate**

18. All of the following statements about the monopolist's marginal revenue function are correct <u>except</u>:
A) average revenue is greater than marginal revenue when the quantity of output produced is greater than one.
B) if the price elasticity of demand is equal to one, marginal revenue equals zero.
C) it is possible for marginal revenue to be negative.

D) marginal revenue is the slope of the firm's total revenue curve.
E) for the monopolist, marginal revenue and price are equal.

Difficulty: **Moderate**

19. Suppose that a monopoly operates with two plants, each with different cost functions. SMC_1 designates the marginal cost of production in plant one and SMC_2 designates the marginal cost of production in plant two. This multiplant monopolist should allocate production between the two plants so that:
A) $SMC = SATC_1 = SATC_2$.
B) $SMC_1 = SMC_2 = P$.
C) $MR = SMC_1 + SMC_2$.
D) $MR = SMC_1 = SMC_2$.
E) $TR - (TC_1 + TC_2) = 0$.

Difficulty: **Moderate**

20. Suppose that you are a monopolist and that you produce widgets. You are able to market your product such that you charge the maximum price that each buyer is willing to pay. You are engaging in:
A) first degree price discrimination.
B) second degree price discrimination.
C) third degree price discrimination.
D) fourth degree price discrimination.
E) not being a nice person.

Difficulty: **Moderate**

21. It is quite common for public utilities (natural monopolies) to engage in:
A) predatory pricing.
B) first degree price discrimination.
C) second degree price discrimination.
D) monopoly pricing.
E) fourth degree price discrimination.

Difficulty: **Moderate**

22. The Clarke Corporation engages in third degree price discrimination. The Clarke Corporation, which sells its product in two markets (market A and market B), will maximize profit by producing a total output level where:
A) $MC_A + MC_B = MR$.
B) $MR_A = MR_B = MR = MC$.
C) $MR_A = MR_B = P$.
D) $MR = MC_A - MC_B$.
E) None of the above is correct.

Difficulty: **Moderate**

23. Suppose that you observe that a monopolist reduce its price from $50 to $40 per unit, and as a result, total sales increases. You would be correct if you concluded that:
A) the firm's total profits fell.
B) the firm is operating in the inelastic range of its demand curve.
C) the marginal revenue from the price reduction is less than $40.
D) the total revenue of the firm went up.
E) the marginal revenue from the price reduction is somewhere between $50 and $40.

Difficulty: **Moderate**

24. The monopolist can produce that output level which maximizes its profits where all but one of the following is true:
A) marginal cost equals price.
B) average revenue equals average total cost.
C) marginal revenue equals marginal cost.
D) marginal revenue average total cost.
E) price equals average total cost.

Difficulty: **Moderate**

25. Suppose that you are a monopolist and that you can produce your output at no cost (an unrealistic assumption, but just suppose). The price that you should charge in order to maximize your profit would be that price where demand is:
A) perfectly elastic.
B) unitary elastic.
C) inelastic.
D) elastic but not perfectly elastic.
E) perfectly inelastic.

Difficulty: **Moderate**

26. Suppose that the monopolist maximizes its profits when MR = MC = ATC. We can conclude that its profits:
A) just cover the firm's cost of production, so no excess profits are being made.
B) are negative because total revenue is less than total cost.
C) are not being maximized because total revenue would increase by more than total cost if output was expanded.
D) are positive because total revenue is greater than total cost.
E) Not enough information is provided to determine an answer.

Difficulty: **Moderate**

27. Suppose that the marginal cost of an additional ton of aluminum produced by the Germans is the same whether the aluminum is used domestically or exported. If the price elasticity of demand for aluminum is greater abroad than in Germany, then other things constant, which one of the following statements is correct?
A) The Germans will sell aluminum in the export market at a lower price than they will sell it in the domestic market.
B) The Germans will be unable to sell all of their aluminum in both the domestic and the export market, so they will reduce their overall output.
C) The Germans will sell more aluminum abroad than they will sell domestically.
D) The Germans will sell more aluminum domestically than they will sell abroad.

E) The Germans will set a higher price abroad for their aluminum than they will set domestically.

Difficulty: **Moderate**

28. Suppose that the monopolist produces that level of output that maximizes its profits. The vertical distance between the monopolist's average total cost curve and the demand curve at the level of output produced is:

A) the average per unit profit associated with the level of output produced.
B) the total profit earned by the firm.
C) maximized when the price charged by the firm equals the marginal cost of producing the last unit.
D) the same as the vertical distance between the firm's total revenue curve and its total cost curve at the level of output produced.
E) the average fixed cost per unit of output.

Difficulty: **Moderate**

29. Suppose that the profit-maximizing monopolistic establishes the level of output that it produces at that level where price and marginal cost are equal. The monopolist could:

A) increase total profit by expanding the level of output.
B) increase its total profits by reducing its price below marginal cost.
C) increase its profits by reducing output and increasing product price.
D) increase its profits by reducing both output and price.
E) None of the above is correct.

Difficulty: **Moderate**

30. Suppose that the ABC Co. is a monopolist and its demand curve is greater than its average total cost curve. If the ABC Co. is producing that level of output where marginal revenue is greater than marginal cost, it could increase its profits by:

A) reducing output and increasing price.
B) increasing price but leaving output unchanged.
C) reducing price and increasing output.
D) increasing output and leaving price unchanged.
E) reducing both price and output.

Difficulty: **Moderate**

31. The Acme Corporation is a monopolist, and it tries to adjust price and output in order to maximize its profits. If the Acme Corp. experiences increases in the price of some of its primary inputs and at the same time the demand for some of its product falls, then we can conclude that:

A) both product price and output will increase because of shifting demand and cost curves.
B) output will fall but we cannot be sure what will happen to product price.
C) both the price and output will fall.
D) price will fall and output will increase as the firm adjusts to changes in demand and cost.
E) the Acme Corp. will, in all likelihood, shut down.

Difficulty: **Hard**

32. Suppose that the Acme Co. is a monopolist and produces widgets. The price established for widgets is $6 each but the AVC at the level of output produced is $9. In fact, the Acme Co.'s AVC curve lies above its demand curve at all possible levels of output. The Acme Co. should:
A) change its level of output and produce that amount where MC = MR.
B) shut down and lose only its fixed costs.
C) reduce the price of widgets and increase the number produced and offered for sale.
D) increase the price of widgets and reduce the number produced.
E) leave the price alone, but reduce the quantity produced.

Difficulty: **Moderate**

33. Select the answer that correctly completes the following statement: "The possibility of earning excess (or economic) profits over a long period of time exists…
A) for the firm in perfect competition but not for the monopolist."
B) for both the perfect competitor and the pure monopolist."
C) for neither the pure monopolist nor the perfect competitor."
D) for the pure monopolist but not for the perfect competitor."
E) for both the pure monopolist and the perfect competitor only if the time period is longer than one year."

Difficulty: **Moderate**

34. The ACME Co., a public utility, charges each consumer a different price for each kilowatt hour of electricity used. The ACME Co. lowers the rate for the consumer who uses more and more kilowatt-hours. If the utility practices price discrimination in an attempt to extract all consumers' surplus, the type of price discrimination being practiced is:
A) first degree price discrimination.
B) second degree price discrimination.
C) third degree price discrimination.
D) fourth degree price discrimination.
E) pure price discrimination.

Difficulty: **Moderate**

35. The pure monopolist may earn excess (economic) profits in the long run; however, the perfectly competitive firm will not. The best reason to explain the differences in long run profit is that:
A) the monopolist has some control over the price that it charges for its product, but the competitor does not.
B) the pure monopolist produces its optimal output level more efficiently (and hence at a lower per unit cost) than does the competitive firm.
C) the government permits the pure monopolist to earn excess profits but it prevents the competitive firm from entering economic profits in the long run.
D) firms can enter or leave a competitive industry at will but there are barriers to prevent entry into a pure monopoly.
E) None of the above is correct.

Difficulty: **Moderate**

36. When the monopolist and the perfect competitor are compared, the monopolist does not use society's scarce resources as efficiently as the competitor. The reason for this is that the monopolist:
    A) does not produce enough of the product, and so its profit maximizing output does not minimize average total cost.
    B) does not equate MC = MR when determining its optimal output level.
    C) charges a price for its output that is too high.
    D) able to practice price discrimination, and this harms society.
    E) may be large enough to have more than one plant in operation at the same time, and this causes an overuse of resources.

    Difficulty: **Moderate**

37. Suppose that a monopolist and a perfectly competitive industry face the same cost and demand conditions. We will observe that the monopolist:
    A) produces a larger output and charges a higher price than does the competitive industry.
    B) produces a smaller output and charges a higher price than does the competitive industry.
    C) produces a smaller output and charges a lower price than does the competitive industry.
    D) produces the same output as the competitive industry but charges a higher price.
    E) None of the above is correct.

    Difficulty: **Moderate**

38. Suppose that the ACME Co. has to purchase a license from the local city government in order to sell its product. We would expect:
    A) the firm's price to be closer to the monopoly price than to the competitive price.
    B) the firm to have some degree of monopoly power.
    C) the entry into the market to be more restricted than it would be if no license was required.
    D) the ACME Co. to face a downward-sloping demand curve for its product.
    E) All of the above are correct.

    Difficulty: **Moderate**

39. Many areas of the nation have electric power provided by a single supplier. The supplier of electricity is essentially a monopoly. If the natural monopoly was suddenly broken up and the production and distribution of electric power became more competitive, we would probably see:
    A) an increase in the price of electricity.
    B) an increase in the average cost of producing electricity.
    C) an increase in the marginal cost of producing electricity.
    D) a decrease in the efficiency of electric power production.
    E) All of the above to occur.

    Difficulty: **Hard**

40. Suppose that a monopolist sells the same good to two different groups of consumers at the same time and at different prices. The firm is engaging in:
    A) price discrimination.
    B) predatory pricing.
    C) competitive pricing.

D) average cost pricing.
E) the dumping of its product.

Difficulty: **Easy**

41. Suppose that you, your younger brother, and your grandmother go to a movie and you pay a higher price than either of the other two. The theater is most likely engaging in:
A) competitive pricing because without the difference in prices, some individuals would not go to the movies.
B) first degree price discrimination because you want to see the movie more than does your grandmother or brother.
C) second degree price discrimination.
D) third degree price discrimination because the elasticity of demand for movies is generally higher for older people and children.
E) unfair pricing practices because each individual in the theater consumes the same product.

Difficulty: **Moderate**

42. When a competitive industry is monopolized, a cost is imposed on society. This social cost arises because:
A) the monopoly producer reduces the amount of output that is produced.
B) the value placed by society on an additional unit of the good produced is greater than the cost of society of producing an extra unit of the good.
C) the price charged by the monopolist rises relative to the competitive producer.
D) the market price is greater than the marginal cost of producing an extra unit of the good.
E) All of the above are valid reasons.

Difficulty: **Moderate**

43. When compared to the perfect competitor, the monopolist allocates resources less efficiently. An indication of this allocative inefficiency is that the monopolist:
A) earns a greater economic (excess) profit in the long run than does the competitive firm.
B) sets a price that is above the marginal cost of producing the last unit of output sold.
C) has no incentive to reduce his cost of production.
D) does not have an incentive to use the most productive technology.
E) All of the above are correct.

Difficulty: **Moderate**

44. Suppose that the XYZ Co. sells widgets in batches of 500 each. If the XYZ Co. charges a lower price for each additional batch of widgets, then it is engaging in:
A) price leadership.
B) first degree price discrimination.
C) second degree price discrimination.
D) third degree price discrimination.
E) None of the above is correct.

Difficulty: **Easy**

45. When a competitive industry is monopolized, it is quite possible that the monopolist will earn monopoly (economic) profits and carry these profits into the long run. These monopoly profits:
A) will lead to more research, innovation, and product development.
B) are present because the monopolist operates more efficiently and can enjoy more economies of scale than does the competitive firm.
C) are a redistribution of income from consumers to the monopolist; they are like a privately collected tax.
D) will always be to the eventual benefit of consumers.
E) represent a net welfare loss to society.

Difficulty: **Moderate**

46. If a regulated monopoly uses a two-part tariff in establishing its price:
A) users pay a fixed amount for access to the service and then pay the marginal cost for units of the good or service used.
B) users pay the total cost of producing the units of the service consumed and then pay a predetermined rate of return to the firm.
C) users pay the marginal cost of producing the units of the service consumed and then pay a predetermined rate of profit to the firm.
D) the firm will always make an economic profit.
E) users of the good or service will experience an increase in their consumer surplus.

Difficulty: **Moderate**

47. All of the following are characteristics of a two-part tariff pricing strategy except:
A) the user of the good or service must initially pay a membership or access fee in order to be able to use the service.
B) one part of the tariff is determined by the marginal cost associated with producing the firm's level of output.
C) one part of the tariff is equal to the price of the product that is sold.
D) society's social welfare (as measured by consumers' surplus) will be greater with a two-part tariff than without the tariff.
E) any monopoly profits earned as a result of the tariff will be less than would be the case if the firm could engage in unregulated monopoly pricing.

Difficulty: **Moderate**

48. Suppose that a firm in Country A produces widgets and sells those widgets both domestically and well as in Country B. If the firm persistently charges a lower price in Country B for widgets than in Country A because the price elasticity of demand is lower in Country B, then the firm is engaging in:
A) first degree price discrimination.
B) dumping of widgets in Country B.
C) predatory pricing.
D) second degree price discrimination.
E) marginal cost pricing.

Difficulty: **Easy**

49. Which of the following is an example of predatory dumping?
A) Country A always sells good B in Country C at a lower price than it does charges for good B domestically.
B) Firm A charges its consumers an access fee in order to use a product or service and then sets product price equal to the marginal cost of producing its level of output.
C) From time to time, one country sells good A in another country at a price below its domestic cost of production.
D) Country A temporarily sells good B at a price below its cost of production to buyers in Country C in an attempt to drive the producers of good B in Country C out of business.
E) None of the above is an example.

Difficulty: **Moderate**

50. Which of the following was not a method employed by the Aluminum Company of America (Alcoa) to maintain its monopoly power in the market for aluminum?
A) The acquisition of key patents on technology for producing aluminum.
B) Entering into long-term contacts with producers of bauxite encouraging them to sell bauxite only to Alcoa and other American firms.
C) Entering into agreements with foreign producers of aluminum not to export aluminum into each other's markets.
D) Purchasing electricity only from power companies that agreed not to sell energy for the production of aluminum to any other firm.
E) Expanding productive capacity in anticipation of any increase in demand and pricing aluminum in such a way as to discourage new entrants.

Difficulty: **Moderate**

51. Alcoa's monopoly of the aluminum market:
A) has been preserved essentially to the present day.
B) was permanently ended by court decisions in 1912.
C) was ended after World War II when Alcoa was not allowed to purchase government-finance aluminum plants built during the war.
D) was ended by Russia's heavy export of aluminum in the early 1990s.
E) None of the above is correct.

Difficulty: **Easy**

52. Since January of 1994, world aluminum prices have:
A) decreased as growing international competition led to rounds of price cutting.
B) decreased by 50% due to Russia's expansion of aluminum exports.
C) decreased as a consequence of shrinkages in world demand due to recessions in major industrial countries.
D) increased due to international agreements to cut the production of aluminum voluntarily.
E) (A) and (B) are correct.

Difficulty: **Easy**

53. The international market for diamonds:
A) has until recently been highly competitive.

B) has effectively been dominated for decades by DeBeers Consolidated Mines Company.
C) has been controlled by a cartel dominated by Russia since 1887.
D) has been suffering from a record drop in sales of diamond jewelry in 1995.
E) None of the above is correct.

Difficulty: **Easy**

54. The Central Selling Organization:
A) markets about 75% of the world's supply of diamonds.
B) has been used for decades by DeBeers Consolidated Mines Company to control the international market for diamonds.
C) is an international cartel which in the past has flooded the market to punish cartel members for trying to sell diamonds independently of the cartel.
D) is currently facing demands from Russia to increase its share of the CSO's uncut rough diamond sales.
E) All of the above are correct.

Difficulty: **Moderate**

55. In the market for taxi services in New York, "medallions":
A) are used to protect taxi customers from exploitation by unscrupulous taxi cab drivers.
B) serve to expand the total volume of taxi services by assuring a high quality of services and thereby stimulating demand for taxi services.
C) have dropped in value over time due to a substantial expansion in the umber of medallions issued.
D) limit the number of cabs which can cruise the streets for customers but are not required for cabs responding to radio calls.
E) All of the above are correct.

Difficulty: **Moderate**

56. The market value of taxi "medallions":
A) reflects the relative scarcity of taxis.
B) would drop to zero if they were freely granted by municipal governments.
C) reflects the present value of the future stream of earnings resulting from ownership of the medallion.
D) have been affected in New York by the sharp increase in the number of radio cabs which occurred during the 1980s.
E) All of the above are correct.

Difficulty: **Moderate**

57. If taxi medallions are originally issued by a municipality for a nominal fee and the relative price of medallions increases and then remains stable over time:
A) only the original owner of the medallion earns monopoly profits by owning the medallion.
B) all successive owners of the medallion will earn monopoly profits as a consequence of owning the medallion.
C) monopoly profits will never be earned even by the original owner of the medallion.
D) medallion owners will make monopoly profits while owning the medallion but will suffer equal sized losses when they sell the medallion.

E) medallion owners will lobby municipal government to issue more medallions in the hope that it will stimulate demand for medallions and raise their price.

Difficulty: **Moderate**

58. Which of the following statements regarding taxi medallions is <u>not</u> correct?
A) Windfall gains from owning taxi medallions will be earned when the original owner sells the medallion at a higher relative price than he paid for it when he it was originally issued by the government.
B) Windfall gains from owning taxi medallions may be earned by the second owner if unanticipated increases in market demand for taxi services occur.
C) Municipal governments can do nothing to prevent windfall gains to private owners from the sale of medallions once the medallions have been issued.
D) Expanding the supply of taxi services other than those provided exclusively by taxis with medallions will cause the price of medallions to fall or at least to increase less rapidly.
E) All of the above are correct.

Difficulty: **Moderate**

59. Empirical estimates of the social cost of monopoly power in the U.S. economy may be _____ because _____.
A) underestimated; they do not incorporate the impact of x-inefficiency
B) underestimated; there are many cases of blatant monopoly power being exercised across a wide range of product markets which researchers have chosen to ignore
C) overestimated; they do not incorporate the impact of rent seeking
D) overestimated; they are limited to measuring the size of the welfare loss triangle
E) All of the above are correct.

Difficulty: **Moderate**

60. In 1996, Con Edison charged different prices per kilowatt-hour used in New York City for different categories of customers and for different quantities of electricity purchased. The former is an example of _____ and the latter an example of _____.
A) second degree price discrimination; peak-load pricing
B) third degree price discrimination; second degree price discrimination
C) second degree price discrimination; third degree price discrimination
D) first degree price discrimination; second degree price discrimination
E) peak-load pricing; third degree price discrimination

Difficulty: **Moderate**

61. The issuance of coupons which give discounts on the purchase of breakfast cereal is a way to practice:
A) first degree price discrimination.
B) second degree price discrimination.
C) third degree price discrimination.
D) peak-load pricing.
E) competitive pricing but it is not a form of price discrimination.

Difficulty: **Hard**

62. Peak-load pricing:

A) is a form of price discrimination because it involves selling output at two different prices.
B) is a form of second degree price discrimination because it involves selling different quantities of output at different prices.
C) is a form of third degree price discrimination because it involves selling different quantities of output at different prices.
D) is not price discrimination because it is based on differences in cost.
E) is not price discrimination because customers are willing to pay the different prices, i.e., peak-load and non-peak-load prices.

Difficulty: **Moderate**

63. In 1993, The Eastman Kodak Company of Rochester, New York, charged that the Fuji Photo Company of Japan was using its excessive profits from its near monopoly in photographic supplies in Japan to dump photographic supplies in the United States. Eastman Kodak argued that Fuji intended to undermine the competitive position of Eastman Kodak and other U.S. competitors. Kodak's charges actually described more than one form of dumping, but failed to make any distinctions between them. What forms of dumping are these?
A) persistent and predatory dumping
B) persistent and sporadic dumping
C) predatory and sporadic dumping
D) persistent, sporadic, and predatory
E) None of the above, because Fuji does not charge different prices for photographic supplies in Japan and the U.S.

Difficulty: **Moderate**

64. Profitable bundling in the sale of two goods to two buyers requires that:
A) the seller be able to practice discrimination.
B) both buyers attach the same value to the first good and the same value to the second good.
C) one buyer attach greater value to one of the goods and lesser value to the other good in comparison to the valuations of the other buyer.
D) one buyer attach greater value to both goods than the other buyer.
E) both buyers attach the same value to one good but a different value to the second good.

Difficulty: **Moderate**

Given the assumption that the supplier may not engage in price discrimination, use the information in the table below to answer the following questions. The table shows the maximum price each theater would be willing to pay to lease each film separately or as a bundle.

	Theatre 1	Theatre 2
Movie A	$14,000	$10,000
Movie B	$3,000	$6,000

65. Without bundling, the maximum revenue that the lessor can obtain from each theatre for leasing the films is _____.
A) $20,000.
B) $17,000.
C) $16,000.

D) $13,000.
E) $9,000.

Difficulty: **Moderate**

66. With bundling, the maximum revenue which the lessor can obtain for leasing the films is:
A) $20,000.
B) $17,000.
C) $16,000.
D) $13,000.
E) $9,000.

Difficulty: **Moderate**

67. Which of the following changes would make profitable bundling impossible in the example given above?
A) Theatre 1 values Movie A at $12,000.
B) Theatre 2 values Movie A at $12,000.
C) Theatre 1 values Movie A at $9,000.
D) Theatre 2 values Movie B at $7,000.
E) Theatre 2 values Movie B at $9,000.

Difficulty: **Moderate**

68. Microsoft Corporation has been accused by its competitors of engaging in numerous acts that are described as monopolizing behavior. Of the following actions, which have been at least partially barred by a consent agreement that Microsoft signed with the U.S. Justice Department?
A) Stealing ideas and reworking competitors' programs.
B) Charging unfairly low prices for its application programs by using the profits made on the sale of its operating software where it has a near monopoly.
C) Spreading fear and warning potential customers that competitors' software programs may not be around in a few years.
D) Preempting competitors' products by announcing products years before they are actually introduced and thus discouraging customers from purchasing competing products.
E) Requiring PC manufacturers to pay Microsoft a fee for every PC they produce even if the manufacturer does not install the Microsoft operating system.

Difficulty: **Moderate**

Use the table below to answer questions 69 - 73.

P($)	Q	TR($)	MR($)	STC($)	MC($)	ATC
9	1	9	9	10	10	10
8	2	16	7	12	2	6
7	3			17	5	5.67
6	4	24	3	23	6	5.75
5	5	25	1	30	7	6
4	6	24	-1	38	8	6.33
3	7	21	-3	47	9	6.71

69. The missing total and marginal revenue figures are:
A) $21 and $5.
B) $23 and $6.
C) $20 and $4.
D) $22 and $6.
E) None of the above is correct.

Difficulty: **Moderate**

70. Assume that the demand function given is for a good that will cure baldness. While out in a stroll one day, you happen to find 7 units of this good but neither you nor anyone else is able to reproduce it. Thus you are a pure monopolist with no costs of producing to consider in making profit-maximizing decisions. Further assume that you cannot price discriminate. How many units of this good will you sell, at what price will you sell them, and what will your monopoly profits be?
A) 3 units, $9, $27
B) 4 units, $3, $12
C) 5 units, $5, $25
D) 6 units, $4, $24
E) 7 units, $9, $63

Difficulty: **Hard**

71. Assume that the demand function given is for a good that will cure baldness. While on a stroll one day, you happen to find 7 units of this good but neither you nor anyone else is able to reproduce it. Further assume that you can practice first degree price discrimination. How many units of this good will you sell and what will your monopoly profits be?
A) 7 units, $21.
B) 7 units, $42.
C) 5 units, $25.
D) 5 units, $35.
E) 3 units, $4.

Difficulty: **Hard**

72. Assume that the cost functions in the table above represent a pure monopolist selling a cure for baldness where the cure is assumed to be a reproducible good. Assume further that the demand for this cure for baldness is represented by the demand function also given in the table above. What is the pure monopolist's profit maximizing output level?
A) 3
B) 4
C) 5
D) 6
E) 7

Difficulty: **Moderate**

73. What are the monopoly profits received by the profit maximizing monopolist?
A) $1.00
B) $4.00
C) $5.00
D) $14.00

E) None of the above is correct.

Difficulty: **Moderate**

74. The causes of monopoly do not include:
A) a firm owning or controlling the entire supply of a raw material required to produce a good.
B) a patent for the exclusive right to produce a commodity.
C) economies of scale sufficiently large to leave a single firm supplying the entire market.
D) monopolies created by government franchise.
E) developing a new product which is a close substitute for the output of a firm which dominates another market.

Difficulty: **Moderate**

75. The reasons why a monopolist does not have unlimited market power include:
A) the need for the monopolist to compete for consumer dollars with the sellers of all other commodities.
B) the existence of imperfect substitutes.
C) threat of potential competitors and international competition.
D) (B) and (C) are correct.
E) All of the above are correct.

Difficulty: **Moderate**

76. The "?" is price elasticity of demand, then marginal revenue for a monopolist is:
A) P(1 + ?).
B) zero if ? is equal to infinity.
C) greater than price when |?| > 0.
D) P (1 + 1/ ?).
E) None of the above is correct.

Difficulty: **Moderate**

77. If a pure monopolist is charging a profit maximizing price of $10 for a good, and ? = -1.25 at that price, and the firm is unable to successfully engage in price discrimination, then what is the monopolist's marginal revenue?
A) $1.25
B) $2.00
C) $2.50
D) $8.00
E) None of the above is correct.

Difficulty: **Moderate**

78. Which of the following statements regarding the supply of output from a monopolist is correct?
A) A monopolist could supply the same quantity of commodity at different prices depending on the price elasticity of demand.
B) There is no unique relationship between price and output for a monopolist.
C) Under monopoly, costs affect supply decisions.
D) (A) and (B) are correct.

E) All of the above are correct.

Difficulty: **Moderate**

79. Which of the following statements regarding the long-run equilibrium of a monopolist is correct?
A) P > LAC means there is allocative inefficiency.
B) P < LMC means there is distributional inefficiency.
C) LAC is not equal to LMC means there is production inefficiency.
D) P = LMC > LAC.
E) All of the above are correct.

Difficulty: **Moderate**

80. Which of the following is a measure of the social cost of monopoly?
A) All decreases in consumer surplus due to monopoly pricing and output decisions.
B) All consumer surplus that is transferred from consumers to monopoly sellers.
C) All producer surplus gained by monopoly sellers.
D) All decreases in consumer surplus that are not transferred to monopolists, and all areas of producer surplus that are lost due to monopoly output restrictions.
E) (A) and (B) are correct.

Difficulty: **Moderate**

81. A multiplant monopoly in long-run equilibrium will:
A) utilize plants whose SATC curve form the lowest point of the LAC.
B) produce where SATC = SMC = LAC = LMC.
C) restrict output to achieve monopoly profits by restricting the number of plants built rather than utilizing all plants at levels where ATC is at its minimum point.
D) operate some of its plants at output levels where minimum SATC production is not achieved if that is the only way that the profit maximizing monopoly output level for the entire multiplant monopoly can be achieved.
E) All of the above are correct.

Difficulty: **Moderate**

82. Which of the following correctly describes sporadic dumping?
A) Selling goods abroad at a lower price than in the home market due to differences in elasticity of demand across the two markets.
B) The temporary sale of a commodity at a lower price abroad in order to drive competitors out of business.
C) The temporary sale of a commodity at a lower price abroad in order to unload an unforeseen and temporary surplus without having to reduce domestic prices.
D) A form of dumping that may benefit consumers more than it hurts producers.
E) (C) and (D) are correct.

Difficulty: **Moderate**

83. The "harassment thesis" refers to:
A) the efforts of foreign producers to harass domestic suppliers until they agree to give up a part of their market share rather than lose all of it to foreign producers.

B) the fact that simply threatening to file a dumping complaint discourages imports and leads to higher domestic production and profits.
C) the fact that industrial countries have a persistent tendency to dump agricultural products arising from their farm-support programs.
D) the efforts of governments to "persuade" other governments that they should voluntarily restrict exports or expect to have mandatory import restrictions imposed to keep them out.
E) None of the above is correct.

Difficulty: **Moderate**

84. The behavior known as "tying":
A) consists of a requirement by the seller that the consumer who buys or leases one of the firms' products also purchases another product needed in the use of the first product.
B) is a form of two-part tariff whereby the monopolist can charge a price higher than marginal cost for supplies and thus extract more of the consumer surplus from the heavier users of equipment purchased from the monopolist.
C) is sometimes used to ensure that the correct supplies are used for the equipment to function properly or to ensure quality.
D) (B) and (C) are correct.
E) All of the above are correct.

Difficulty: **Easy**

85. When Xerox required the firms which leased its copiers to use paper purchased from Xerox, Xerox was engaged in:
A) a behavior similar to IBM's when IBM required users of its computers to also use IBM punchcards.
B) a form of price discrimination.
C) tying.
D) Only (A) and (C) are correct.
E) All of the above are correct.

Difficulty: **Moderate**

86. Which of the following statements about "bundling" is <u>not</u> correct?
A) It is a form of tying.
B) It is a form of price discrimination.
C) Its use requires that customers have different tastes.
D) It enables a monopolist to earn higher profits.
E) None of the above is correct.

Difficulty: **Moderate**

87. "Financial aid leveraging" by private colleges is a form of:
A) first degree price discrimination.
B) second degree price discrimination.
C) third degree price discrimination.
D) peak-load pricing.
E) competitive pricing but it is not a form of price discrimination.

Difficulty: **Moderate**

88. Assume that the LAC curve is above the D curve at all output levels for a monopoly firm. Which of the following would permit the firm to remain in existence in the long run?
    A) The monopolist produces a normal good and persuades government to stop subsidizing consumer income.
    B) The monopolist can expand its firm and lower its short run costs sufficiently to begin earning profits.
    C) The monopolist can engage in price discrimination.
    D) The monopolist can introduce the patented cost saving technology, which it has been suppressing up to now, as a part of its profit-maximizing scheme.
    E) (B), (C) and (D) are correct.

    Difficulty: **Hard**

89. Assume there is a monopoly seller of oil filters for automobile engines, and that the monopolist has invented a filter which can be produced at the same cost but it will last for 10,000 miles instead of 5,000 miles of driving. Assume also that the firm's short run cost curves are horizontal lines, i.e., MC = AC. Which of the following statements is not correct?
    A) The introduction of the invention will reduce the monopolist's profits because it will cut its sales in half.
    B) The cost of producing the service that oil filters provide, i.e., miles of oil filtered driving, is substantially lower with the new filter.
    C) If the monopolist introduces the invention, the short run cost curves for the oil filter "service" which the monopolist sells will fall by a larger amount than the profit maximizing monopoly service.
    D) If the monopolist introduces the invention, the total revenues of the monopolist at the new profit maximizing output level will fall.
    E) All of the above are correct.

    Difficulty: **Moderate**

90. Under which of the following circumstances would a monopoly seller of widgets earning monopoly profits suppress the introduction of an invention that enabled the firm to produce widgets that last 50% longer at the same cost?
    A) The monopolist expects that its total revenues will be lower after the introduction of the invention.
    B) The monopolist expects to sell a smaller quantity of widgets after the introduction of the invention.
    C) The monopolist does not expect to be able to patent the invention.
    D) The monopolist does not expect an outward shift of the demand curve for widgets after the invention is introduced.
    E) All of the above are correct.

    Difficulty: **Moderate**

Short Essays

Give a brief answer to each of the following questions.

1. **A pure monopolist can always earn monopoly profits because it has captured the entire market, "i.e., it faces the market demand curve." Evaluate this statement.**

Answer: A pure monopolist does face the market demand curve and therefore has a source of gains which perfect competitors lack. However, even with that advantage it is still possible for the demand curve to lie below the SATC curve at every output level leaving the pure monopolists with losses. The firm faces the demand curve, but it does not control it. Thus, it may try to increase demand through advertising and other devices, but in the end the monopoly firm will have to pick from among the price-quantity combinations on the demand curve itself.

2. **Explain why a pure monopolist does not have a supply curve.**
Answer: This is not intended to suggest that there is no connection between cost and the quantity offered for sale. In perfect competition that connection is clear because for a given price the marginal cost determines the quantity offered for sale. In pure monopoly, cost still affects supply decisions, but there is no unique relationship between price and quantity supplied, i.e., no supply curve, because a particular quantity will be offered for sale at different prices depending on demand elasticity conditions.

3. **The social cost of monopoly does not include the monopoly profits earned by the firm, but it does include the spending a monopolist does lobbying government to give it monopoly power. Explain.**
Answer: The monopoly profits are extracted at the expense of consumer surplus and thus represent a redistribution of benefits from consumers to the monopolist. However, these benefits are not lost altogether as is the case with the deadweight loss triangle. The expenditures on lobbying are a part of social cost because they represent resources used up to accomplish the transfer. They could be used for other purposes if they were not being used for this purpose. They are not wasted from the monopolist's viewpoint, but they are wasted from a social viewpoint.

4. **Explain how grocery coupons work as a form of third degree price discrimination.**
Answer: This form of price discrimination involves selling the same good at different prices in separated markets with different price elasticities. Coupons allow those who are willing to go to the trouble to clip them and use them to purchase the good at a lower price. Presumably, people who are willing to do this are more sensitive to price and have more elastic demand than other consumers.

5. **When would it be rational for a monopoly seller of lightbulbs to suppress an invention which allowed him to introduce a new lightbulb which costs the same to produce, but which lasts for ten years instead of six months?**
Answer: It might be rational if the monopolist believed that he could not successfully patent the new lightbulb and would lose monopoly power by introducing the good. This assumes that the profits from the sales of the new bulb before competitors entered the market would not be sufficient to compensate for the loss of monopoly power over the long run.

6. **"Dumping may be beneficial to the economy." Explain.**
Answer: Of the three forms of dumping, i.e., persistent, predatory, and sporadic, a strong case can be made for using trade restrictions to counter predatory dumping because its intended effect is to eliminate domestic competition and then charge a monopoly price in the domestic market. Persistent and sporadic dumping do not have the same purpose. They are part of a strategy for foreign producers to extract monopoly profits from their own markets, and consequently they produce a benefit to other countries by making goods available at a lower price than would otherwise exist.

Chapter 11:

Price and Output Under Monopolistic Competition and Oligopoly

Multiple-Choice

Choose the one alternative that best completes the statement or answers the question.

1. All of the following are predicted by the theory of monopolistic competition except:
   A) the monopolistically competitive firm does not find it profitable to engage in advertising.
   B) when the monopolistically competitive industry achieves a long-run equilibrium, price is greater than marginal cost at the equilibrium quantity.
   C) under monopolistic competition, customers have a variety of products from which to choose.
   D) when the monopolistically competitive firm is in a long-run equilibrium, price is greater than minimum average total cost.
   E) the typical firm in monopolistic competition tries to differentiate its product.

   Difficulty: **Moderate**

2. When the typical monopolistically competitive firm advertises its product, one of its objectives is to:
   A) increase the elasticity of the demand curve for its product.
   B) reduce the overall cost of production, and so expand profits.
   C) make the product more like that of its competitors.
   D) shift the demand curve for its product to the right and capture some of its competitors' market.
   E) None of the above is correct.

   Difficulty: **Moderate**

3. The typical monopolistically competitive industry resembles:
   A) monopoly because the typical firm has a downward sloping demand curve.
   B) monopoly because it is very difficult for new firms to enter the industry.
   C) perfect competition because in the long run, it produces that level of output associated with the minimum point of its LAC curve.
   D) perfect competition because the typical firm determines its optimal level of output where P = MR = MC.
   E) perfect competition because the industry produces a standardized product.

   Difficulty: **Moderate**

4. The typical firm in a monopolistically competitive industry resembles perfectly competitive firms in that firms in both industries:
   A) earn no excess or economic profit in the long run.

B) face a downward-sloping demand curve for their products.
C) produce standardized products.
D) in the long run, operate at the minimum points on their respective average total cost curves.
E) face no freedom of entry into and exit from the industry.

Difficulty: **Moderate**

5. The monopolistically competitive firm in the long run produces an output associated with some point on the falling segment of its LAC curve. Even though this level of output is not produced as efficiently as under perfect competition, economists are not that concerned because:
A) consumers are not really that interested in productive efficiency.
B) advertising permits the firm to sell more, and so it is able to produce more.
C) consumers may gain by having a wide variety of products from which to choose.
D) the potential entry of new firms assures that the given level of output is produced efficiently.
E) in the long run, consumers' surplus is maximized.

Difficulty: **Moderate**

6. Suppose that the typical firm in a monopolistically competitive industry earns an economic profit and new firms enter. This entry will eventually cause:
A) the firm's demand curve to shift to the right.
B) the firm's average total cost curve to shift upward.
C) the industry demand curve to shift to the left.
D) the firm's demand curve to shift downward and to the left.
E) None of the above is correct.

Difficulty: **Easy**

7. When monopolistic competition, in a long-run equilibrium, is compared to the long-run equilibrium of perfect competition, the monopolistically competitive industry produces:
A) a smaller variety of products but at a lower per unit cost.
B) a larger variety of products but at a higher per unit cost.
C) a larger variety of products but at a lower per unit cost.
D) a smaller variety of products but at a higher per unit cost.
E) products that are practically perfect substitutes for each other.

Difficulty: **Moderate**

8. One of the primary similarities between perfectly competitive markets and monopolistic competition is that:
A) it is relatively easy for firms to enter or leave the market.
B) each type of market produces standardized products.
C) the demand curve faced by each type of market is horizontal.
D) nonprice competition occurs in both markets.
E) in a long-run equilibrium, both firms operate at the minimum point on their respective LAC curves.

Difficulty: **Moderate**

9. The short-run supply curve for a monopolistically competitive firm:
   A) is the same as the supply curve for the competitive firm.
   B) is given by the rising portion of its SMC curve that is above AVC.
   C) cannot be determined.
   D) can be determined only if factor prices remain constant.
   E) exhibits unitary elasticity throughout.

   Difficulty: **Moderate**

10. Which one of the following defines the short-run equilibrium for the monopolistically competitive firm that is making a profit?
   A) P = MC.
   B) P = SAC = SMC.
   C) MR = MC and P > ATC.
   D) MR > MC and P > ATC.
   E) P = MC = MR > ATC.

   Difficulty: **Moderate**

11. Which one of the following is <u>not</u> a characteristic of monopolistic competition?
   A) There are many firms are in the industry.
   B) The typical firm does not engage in advertising.
   C) A large variety of similar products are available on the market.
   D) The typical firm faces a downward-sloping demand curve for its product.
   E) The typical firm has some control over product price.

   Difficulty: **Easy**

12. In a monopolistically competitive industry, firms differentiate their products since this gives each seller a small amount of monopoly power. The reason each firm has some degree of monopoly power is that:
   A) the products of all of the firms in the industry are different.
   B) the typical firm has complete control over the price of its product.
   C) the typical firm faces a downward-sloping demand curve.
   D) there will always be some excess capacity in the monopolistically competitive firm.
   E) None of the above is correct.

   Difficulty: **Easy**

13. One of the differences between a perfectly competitive firm and a monopolistically competitive firm in a long-run equilibrium is that:
   A) under perfect competition, excess profits are zero in the long run, but the monopolistically competitive firm can earn positive excess profits.
   B) LAC = LMC under perfect competition but not under monopolistic competition.
   C) LMC = MR under perfect competition but not under monopolistic competition.
   D) SAC = LAC under perfect competition but not under monopolistic competition.
   E) SMC = LMC under perfect competition but not under monopolistic competition.

   Difficulty: **Moderate**

14. When a monopolistic competitor is in a long-run equilibrium, the price that will be charged by the firm is most likely to be:

A) somewhere between the perfect competitor's price and that of the monopolist.
B) greater than the monopolist's price.
C) greater than the long-run average cost or else the typical firm would not remain in business.
D) lower than the perfect competitor's price.
E) None of the above is correct.

Difficulty: **Moderate**

15. One of the results of the monopolistically competitive industry is that the industry will, when in a long-run equilibrium, possess excess productive capacity. This excess capacity is demonstrated by the difference between:
A) the long-run and the short-run equilibrium output rate.
B) minimum short-run average total cost and the long-run average cost at the equilibrium level of output.
C) the output where long-run average total cost is at a minimum and the long-run average total cost associated with the actual level of output for the monopolistically competitive industry.
D) long-run marginal cost and short-run marginal cost at the equilibrium level of output.
E) None of the above is correct.

Difficulty: **Hard**

16. When an industry is classified as oligopolisitic, it consists of:
A) only one seller.
B) many sellers with similar products.
C) only a few sellers with either standardized or differentiated products.
D) only a few buyers.
E) None of the above is correct.

Difficulty: **Easy**

17. If it is possible for existing firms in an industry to cooperate completely, then we would expect this cooperation to lead to:
A) a market price established close to the competitive price.
B) the production of a monopoly level of output and the establishment of a monopoly price.
C) only a normal profit to be earned by the typical firm.
D) the firms producing that level of output that corresponds to minimum LAC.
E) the firms producing that level of output that corresponds to minimum SAC.

Difficulty: **Moderate**

18. If oligopolies are allowed to fully cooperate, they establish a market price and level of output where:
A) the industry demand and the industry average total cost curves intersect.
B) the industry marginal cost and the industry average total cost curves intersect.
C) the industry marginal cost and the industry average variable costs intersect.
D) the industry marginal cost and industry marginal revenue curves intersect.
E) None of the above is correct.

Difficulty: **Moderate**

19. A problem often encountered when oligopolists try to cooperate is that:
    A) the number of firms in the industry is too small for effective cooperation.
    B) most oligopolists produce highly differentiated products.
    C) some firms might cheat on the established market price.
    D) firms really are not intersected in cooperating with each other.
    E) None of the above is correct.

    Difficulty: **Easy**

20. When we study the Cournot model of duopolistic behavior, one of the behavioral assumption that we make is that:
    A) once it is established, each firm regards its rival's price as being fixed with regard to its own output.
    B) each firm assumes that if it lowers its price, its rival will do the same, but it raises its price, its rival will not follow.
    C) each firm recognizes its mutual interdependence with its rival, and so they agree to cooperate.
    D) once established, each firm regards its rival's quantity as being fixed with regard to its own quantity.
    E) None of the above is correct.

    Difficulty: **Easy**

21. When we study the kinked-demand curve model of oligopolistic behavior, a basic behavioral assumption that we make is that each firm:
    A) assumes that its rival's price does not change with regard to its own price.
    B) assumes that its rival's output, once established, does not change with regard to its own output.
    C) recognizes its mutual interdependence with its rival, and so they agree to cooperate.
    D) assumes that if it reduces its price, its rival will follow, but if it raises its price, its rival will not follow.
    E) None of the above is correct.

    Difficulty: **Moderate**

22. The kinked-demand curve model of oligopolistic behavior is introduced to:
    A) offer an explanation for observed price rigidity of some oligopoly prices.
    B) show the difference between oligopolistics producing standardized products and those producing differentiated products.
    C) show the nature of a zero-sum game.
    D) explain why oligopolies are so common in the U.S.
    E) None of the above is correct.

    Difficulty: **Easy**

23. The kinked-demand curve model of oligopoly behavior is a model of non-cooperating firms. This demand curve arises in oligopolistic markets because rival firms:
    A) will follow only price decreases.
    B) acknowledge that prices are sticky in the neighborhood around the kink.
    C) will follow only upward movements in price.
    D) produce a differentiated product.

E) will follow both price increases and price decreases.

Difficulty: **Moderate**

24. When practicing limit pricing, the oligopolistic firm sets a price at:
A) the monopoly price.
B) the competitive price.
C) the point where marginal cost equals price.
D) the point where average fixed cost equals price.
E) None of the above is correct.

Difficulty: **Moderate**

25. When the oligopolistic producer practices limit pricing, it:
A) sets output price so that maximum profits are made.
B) establishes a price that sets a limit on how much a firm can sell.
C) charges a price just low enough so that new firms do not find it profitable to enter the industry.
D) limits the set of prices from which firms in the industry can choose to sell their product.
E) None of the above is correct.

Difficulty: **Moderate**

26. The price outcome of the Cournot model is a price that:
A) equals the industry marginal cost of production.
B) equals the monopoly price if there are many firms in the industry.
C) equals the industry marginal revenue at the optimal output level.
D) is near the competitive price if there are many firms in the industry.
E) None of the above is correct.

Difficulty: **Moderate**

27. All of the following statements describe some aspect of the Cournot model <u>except</u>:
A) each firm acts in its own best interest, given the assumption of how its competitor will react.
B) there is neither an explicit nor implicit agreement among the firms for joint profit maximization.
C) industry price is established between the monopoly and competitive price.
D) each firm assumes the other will keep its price level constant.
E) each firm believes that the other will keep its output level constant once it established.

Difficulty: **Moderate**

28. An assumption of the Cournot pricing model is that:
A) each firm assumes that its rival will keep producing their original quantity of output.
B) the demand curve faced by the duopolist is highly elastic.
C) each firm assumes that its rival will not change its price, once it is established.
D) each firm assumes its rival will follow a price increase.
E) None of the above is correct.

Difficulty: **Moderate**

29. The major difference between the Cournot model and the Bertrand model is:
    A) the number of firms involved.
    B) the size of the firms involved.
    C) that in the Cournot model the firm assumes its rival will keep its quantity constant while in the Bertrand model the firm assumes that its rival will keep its price constant.
    D) that in the Cournot model the firm assumes its rival will keep its price constant while in the Bertrand model the firm assumes that its rival will keep its quantity constant
    E) None of the above; there is no difference between the two models.

    Difficulty: **Moderate**

30. Suppose that the ABC Corp. practices limit pricing. Which of the following statements does <u>not</u> correctly describe the behavior of the ABC Corp.?
    A) The ABC Corp. practices limit pricing in order to discourage or not attract potential entrants into the market.
    B) When practicing limit pricing, the firm does not set its profit-maximizing price.
    C) The ABC Corp. establishes its limit price where MC = MR.
    D) The ABC Corp. is willing to give up current short-run profits for greater profits in the long run.
    E) When it practices limit pricing, the ABC Corp. will set its price such that P > AVC.

    Difficulty: **Moderate**

31. The Jones Company is the dominant firm in the Widget industry. The industry consists of the Jones Company and five other firms. The Jones Company begins to practice limit pricing, and in order to determine its "limit price" it must consider:
    A) the degree of product differentiation among the widgets produced by the other firms.
    B) the size of new firms that might enter the widget industry.
    C) the rapidity with which new firms may enter the widget industry.
    D) All of the above must be considered.
    E) It is essentially not necessary to consider any of the above because the Jones' Company ATC will determine the limit price.

    Difficulty: **Hard**

32. When an oligopolistic firm practices cost-plus pricing, it will:
    A) set its price to correspond to that output level where P = min ATC.
    B) set its price to correspond to that output level where MC = MR.
    C) add some markup to average total cost that is no greater than ten percent of ATC.
    D) estimate the average variable cost for some normal level of output and then add a particular markup in order to determine its product price.
    E) None of the above is correct.

    Difficulty: **Moderate**

33. The XYZ Co. practices cost-plus pricing. If the AVC of producing its "optimal" level of output is $12 per unit and the XYZ Co. sells its output on the market at a price of $18 per unit, then its markup is:
    A) 50 percent.
    B) 100 percent.

C) 25 percent.
D) 75 percent.
E) Cannot be determined from the information provided.

Difficulty: **Moderate**

34. The price elasticity of demand for widgets is 1.5, and the average variable cost of the firm of producing its optimal level of output is $25 per unit. If the firm producing widgets practices cost-plus pricing, then its per unit price for widgets is approximately:
A) $38.
B) $50.
C) $89.
D) $75.
E) Not enough information is provided to determine and answer.

Difficulty: **Moderate**

35. The ABC Corp. has been designated a barometric price leader in the widget industry. This means that the AB Corp.:
A) must be the dominant firm in the widget industry.
B) is able to accurately gauge conditions in the market, especially changes in demand and cost, and then set price accordingly.
C) is the lowest cost producer in the firm.
D) must have at least one-third of the total market as its own.
E) None of the above is correct.

Difficulty: **Moderate**

36. If the Smith Corp. is a dominant firm in the widget industry and practices price leadership, then we would expect to see:
A) the Smith Corp. set its profit maximizing price.
B) other companies acting as a "competitive fringe" around the Smith Corp.
C) other firms in the industry selling all that they want to at the price established by the Smith Corp.
D) the Smith Corp. satisfying the excess demand that the "competitive fringe" companies cannot satisfy.
E) All of the above to occur.

Difficulty: **Moderate**

37. One of the welfare effects of an oligopolistic industry when compared to a perfectly competitive industry is that:
A) the oligopolistic industry will be productively efficient but not allocatively efficient.
B) the oligopolistic industry will operate in the long run where P < LMC.
C) the oligopolistic industry will produce a lower level of output and charge a higher price than will the competitive industry.
D) the oligopolistic industry will be allocatively efficient but not productively efficient.
E) None of the above is correct.

Difficulty: **Moderate**

38. For the kinked demand curve model, all of the following occur when there is an industry equilibrium <u>except</u>:
A) P > LAC.
B) MR = MC.
C) P > MC.
D) P = MR.
E) LAC > LMC.

Difficulty: **Moderate**

39. Many, if not most, oligopolists participate in nonprice competition, and by doing so:
A) there may be retaliation from producers who did not initially engage nonprice competition.
B) their advertising expenditures can be expected to be greater than if they did not engage in such nonprice competition.
C) the firms may be able to avoid price wars.
D) the firms may try to differentiate their products from those of other firms.
E) All of the above are possible.

Difficulty: **Moderate**

40. In an oligopolistic industry, the typical producer in the industry:
A) can be expected to spend a large percentage of its profits on advertising.
B) will be allocatively efficient in the long run.
C) will earn only a normal profit in the long run.
D) will produce a greater output and at a lower price than the perfectly competitive fir in a long-run equilibrium.
E) None of the above is correct.

Difficulty: **Moderate**

41. Suppose that the XYZ Corp. is the largest firm in an oligopolistic market and is designated as the price leader. This price leadership:
A) will exist under both monopolistic competition and monopoly.
B) is necessary if the industry is to form an effective cartel.
C) is a form of covert collusion.
D) will result in monopoly price as well as monopoly quantity being established.
E) will require all firms to divide and share the market.

Difficulty: **Moderate**

42. All of the following are reasons that help explain the movement toward the globalization of many of the world's largest oligopolistic industries <u>except</u>:
A) that through the process of globalization, the firms in the industries as well as the industries themselves become more competitive, and so price will fall and quantity will rise.
B) that many smaller corporations merge with larger ones because of the fear by the smaller firms that they may be destroyed by global competition.
C) that many firms find it simply irresistible to merge with other firms and get larger.
D) that there have been rapid improvements both in international communication and transportation.

E) that there have been reductions in the barriers to international trade and investment.

Difficulty: **Moderate**

43. From a global perspective, the industrial sector in which the size of the largest firms has grown the most rapidly during the past two decades is:
A) the automobile industry.
B) the telecommunications industry.
C) the electronic data processing industry.
D) the banking industry.
E) the entertainment industry.

Difficulty: **Moderate**

44. As the banking industry has become more globally integrated over the past thirty years or so, the relative importance, in terms of size, within the international banking community has changed. In 1995, the eight largest banks in the world were headquartered in:
A) Great Britain.
B) The United States.
C) Japan.
D) Germany.
E) France.

Difficulty: **Easy**

45. The move toward the globalization of many of the world's largest industrial sectors has been promoted and enhances by:
A) rapid and significant improvements in telecommunications.
B) rapid and significant improvements in the transportation of goods, services, and information.
C) the urge by many of the owners and managers of firms to merge with other firms.
D) the fear by the owners and managers of some firms that if they do not merge and play a more significant role in the global economy, they will become casualties of increased global competition.
E) All of the above are correct.

Difficulty: **Easy**

46. Oligopolistic firms are unique in that they:
A) engage in nonprice competition.
B) may produce differentiated products.
C) may produce product that are very close substitutes for each other.
D) recognize that a mutual interdependence exists among the firms.
E) incur advertising expenses.

Difficulty: **Easy**

47. The Bertrand model of duopolistic behavior among two firms:
A) assumes that one of the firms behaves as described in the Cournot model and establishes its output believing that the other firm will leave its price unchanged.
B) assumes that one of the firms behaves as described in the Cournot model and establishes its output believing that the other firm will leave its output unchanged

C) one firm acts as a leader while the other is a follower.
D) the firm that acts as a leader will have higher profits than is the case under the Cournot model, but these profits are at the expense of the follower.
E) allows one firm to participate in strategic behavior, and so the model is superior to the Cournot model.

Difficulty: **Easy**

48. One of the primary reasons why firms are willing to engage in collusion is that:
A) the current anti-trust laws in the U.S. permit collusion.
B) the firms will earn larger profits than if they did not cooperate with each other.
C) the typical firm is able to expand its level of output.
D) the typical firm will be able to lower its average cost of production.
E) the typical firm will achieve productive efficiency because it will now be able to operate at the minimum point on it ATC curve.

Difficulty: **Easy**

49. On balance, it appears that the use of advertising to make explicit criticisms of the products of one's competitors, and the introduction of advertising into markets where it had previously been prohibited:
A) causes prices to increase and product quality to fall as a consequence of larger advertising expenses.
B) causes prices to fall while maintaining product quality.
C) leads to the development of monopoly power where competition had once prevailed.
D) leads to lawsuits which effectively shut down all advertising in the long run.
E) None of the above is correct.

Difficulty: **Easy**

50. Which of the following is a reason why concentration ratios should be used cautiously in evaluating the degree of competition in an industry?
A) Imports are not included in the concentration ratio.
B) Competition may be localized or regional, whereas the concentration ratio refers to the nation as a whole.
C) The concentration ratio may vary substantially depending on how broadly one defines the good.
D) The concentration ratio does not give any indication of the existence of potential entrants to the industry.
E) All of the above are reasons for cautious use of concentration ratios.

Difficulty: **Moderate**

51. Which of the following might cause a concentration ratio to underestimate the amount of competition in an industry?
A) Imports of the good are substantial.
B) Competition is localized with firms in other regions providing little of the supply of the good outside their own regions.
C) The concentration ratio being used is based on a very broad definition of the good.
D) Very few potential entrants stand ready to enter at any moment.

E) All of the above are correct.

Difficulty: **Moderate**

52. Which of the following was <u>not</u> a short-run consequence of the oil price shocks of the 1970s?
A) The price of petroleum rose from $2.50 in 1973 to $40.00 per barrel in 1980.
B) Efforts to conserve energy use were stimulated.
C) Non-OPEC oil exploration and production were stimulated.
D) Efforts to switch other energy sources were stimulated.
E) OPEC's share of world oil production increased from 30% in 1974 to 55% in 1995.

Difficulty: **Easy**

53. Members of OPEC:
A) have maintained nearly complete agreement about pricing decisions and the need to maximize short-run profits.
B) with high population densities and low petroleum reserves want to charge high prices to maximize short-run profits, but members with sparse populations and large reserves want low prices to maximize long-run prices.
C) with high population densities and low petroleum reserves want to charge low prices to maximize long-run profits, but members with sparse populations and large reserves want to charge high prices to maximize short-run profits.
D) have differed over pricing policy but have always agreed that maximizing long-run profits is the objective.
E) None of the above is correct.

Difficulty: **Moderate**

54. Which of the following suggests that OPEC never really controlled the world crude oil market?
A) OPEC was unable to prevent the decline in petroleum prices in the 1980s.
B) OPEC was unable to prevent widespread cheating by its members in the 1980s.
C) OPEC only succeeded in raising prices when conditions of tight supply prevailed in the 1970s.
D) OPEC was unable to prevent sharp decreases in price when excess supplies arose.
E) All of the above are correct.

Difficulty: **Moderate**

55. For more than 30 years, several Ivy League colleges met to exchange sensitive information about intended tuition increases, the amount of financial aid for students, and faculty salaries. Among other things, they agreed not to outbid each other in granting aid to top students who had been accepted at more than one school. Changes in tuition, student aid, and faculty salaries were also closely bunched. The economic behavior of these colleges is properly described as that of:
A) a pure monopoly.
B) a centralized cartel.
C) a market-sharing cartel.
D) price leadership.

E) a Cournot duopoly.

Difficulty: **Moderate**

56. When the Ivy League colleges signed a consent agreement with the Justice Department prohibiting them from meeting to discuss tuition increases, the amount of financial aid for students, and faculty salaries, the immediate consequence was that:
A) financial aid decreased.
B) tuition increases slowed.
C) faculty salaries fell.
D) MIT joined the consent decree because it could now compete on an even playing field with the other Ivy League colleges.
E) All of the above are correct.

Difficulty: **Easy**

57. According to the empirical studies:
A) the profitability of firms is strongly correlated with size measured by sales.
B) the profitability of firms is weakly correlated with size measured by sales.
C) the profitability of firms shows no correlation with size measured by sales.
D) firm size as measured by sales is strongly correlated with both market power and profitability.
E) None of the above is correct.

Difficulty: **Easy**

58. The adoption of very low discount but refundable air fares by airlines may be expected to:
A) make management of seat inventory easier.
B) decrease the number of no-shows.
C) reduce the amount of overbooking.
D) encourage the earlier sale of discount seats.
E) All of the above are correct.

Difficulty: **Moderate**

59. The practice of reserving block seats for Friday afternoon flights which are to be sold with no discounts even up to the morning of the flight:
A) is a form of price discrimination intended to extract additional revenue from business travelers.
B) is a part of what is more broadly described as yield or inventory management.
C) has the same goal as putting a new batch of cheap tickets that require a 30-day advance purchase on sale 31 days before departure.
D) has the same goal as discounting 80% of the seats on the same flight in the middle of the week.
E) All of the above are correct.

Difficulty: **Moderate**

60. Which of the following statements regarding the practice of yield management for airlines is <u>incorrect</u>?
A) Yield management results in very frequent changes in airfares.
B) Yield management has enhanced airline revenues.

C) Yield management has reduced consumers' confusion about the availability of discounted airfares.
D) Yield management is the single most important technological improvement in airline management in the past decade.
E) Yield management has led to complaints of false advertising which the Transportation Department began to investigate in 1995.

Difficulty: **Moderate**

61. The most innovative banks are:
A) American.
B) European.
C) Japanese.
D) the banks of all these countries have poor records of innovation.
E) banks in all of these countries have equally strong records of innovation.

Difficulty: **Moderate**

62. In the pharmaceutical industry, the cost of developing and bringing new commercial drugs into the market:
A) is the driving force behind the government's efforts to break up large pharmaceutical firms.
B) is causing pharmaceutical firms to reduce their efforts to globalize their operations.
C) is requiring firms to find ways to spread research costs over larger sales and reach a breakeven point on new drugs sooner.
D) has forced companies such as Johnson & Johnson to license drugs to companies abroad in exchange for royalties.
E) All of the above are correct.

Difficulty: **Moderate**

63. If economic profits exist in a monopolistically competitive industry, then:
A) P = MR, MR = MC, and P = SATC.
B) P = MR, MR = MC, and P > SATC.
C) P > MR, MR > MC, and P = SATC.
D) P > MR, MR = MC, and P > SATC.
E) P < MR, MR < MC, and P < SATC.

Difficulty: **Moderate**

64. If economic profits are zero in a monopolistically competitive industry, then:
A) P = MR, MR < MC, and P = SATC.
B) P = MR, MR = MC, and P > SATC.
C) P > MR, MR > MC, and P = SATC.
D) P > MR, MR = MC, and P > SATC.
E) P < MR, MR < MC, and P = SATC.

Difficulty: **Moderate**

65. Under monopolistic competition:
A) it is not possible to define the industry because that term refers to producers of identical goods.

B) there is no single equilibrium price but instead a cluster of prices.
C) sellers of similar goods are lumped together for the purpose of discussion under "product groups" which are casually referred to as an "industry."
D) we cannot derive industry demand and supply curves.
E) All of the above are correct.

Difficulty: **Moderate**

66. Under monopolistic competition, a firm:
A) can affect the volume of its sales by changing price.
B) can affect the volume of its sales by changing the characteristics of its product.
C) can affect the volume of its sales by changing its selling expenses.
D) (A), (B), and (C) are correct.
E) cannot affect the volume of its sales because that would require a "competitive" firm to do something it cannot do, i.e., control the demand curve.

Difficulty: **Moderate**

67. Which of the following statements regarding monopolistic competition is <u>not</u> correct?
A) Product variation and selling expenses can be undertaken with the expectation that in the long run the firm will earn higher profits.
B) Product variation and selling expenses increase the firm's costs.
C) A firm should expend more on product variation and selling efforts up to the point at which MR = MC from these efforts.
D) Selling expenses include advertising costs, costs associated with maintaining a sales force, and costs associated with providing service for a product.
E) All of the above are correct.

Difficulty: **Moderate**

68. Some critics claim that advertising creates false needs and reduces competition. Recent studies indicate that advertising affects brand choices but does not effectively increase the overall consumption of a product, and that industries with higher-than-average advertising expenditures relative to sales have had lower rates of price increases and higher rates of output increases than the average for 150 major U.S. industries. These studies:
A) undermine the critic's claims regarding the creation of false needs but support their claims regarding reduced competition.
B) undermine the critic's claims regarding the creation of false needs and their claims regarding reduced competition.
C) support the critic's claims regarding the creation of false needs but undermine their claims regarding reduced competition.
D) support the critic's claims regarding the creation of false needs and their claims regarding reduced competition.
E) do not offer any clear indication of how advertising affects people's sensed needs and the level of competition.

Difficulty: **Moderate**

69. Which of the following statements regarding monopolistic competition theory are correct?
A) Economists have become disenchanted wit this theory because it is too easy to define a market and industry.

B) Economists have become disenchanted with this theory because in markets where there are many sellers, product differentiation is very slight.
C) Economists have become disenchanted with this theory because in the cases where perfect competition is applicable the monopolistic competition model gives a very good approximation and is much easier to use.
D) Economists have become more appreciative because in markets where there are strong brand preferences there are only a few producers.
E) Economists have become more appreciative because in markets with many sellers the behavior of sellers strongly affects the sellers that are nearby but not the sellers that are far away.

Difficulty: **Moderate**

70. Which of the following could be properly described as the general theory of oligopoly?
A) price leadership
B) kinked-demand curve
C) market-sharing Cartel
D) limit pricing
E) None of the above is correct.

Difficulty: **Moderate**

71. Which of the following is <u>not</u> a source of oligopoly?
A) substantial economies of scale
B) huge capital investments needed to enter an industry
C) a patent for the exclusive right to use a particular production process
D) strong customer loyalty based on product quality and service which is difficult to match
E) All of the above are sources of oligopoly.

Difficulty: **Moderate**

72. A concentration ratio:
A) is the percentage of total industry sales accounted for by the largest firm in the industry.
B) is percentage of total industry sales accounted for by the largest 4, 8, or 12 firms in the industry.
C) of 100% indicates the existence of a pure monopoly in an industry.
D) measures the impact of foreign competitors on the degree of competition in the domestic market of an oligopoly.
E) All of the above are correct.

Difficulty: **Easy**

73. The kinked demand curve:
A) can rationalize the existence of rigid prices.
B) can explain at what price the kink in the demand curve occurs in the first place.
C) is supported by empirical evidence which shows that oligopolists are more reluctant to match price increases than they are to match price decreases.
D) offers an explanation of how price is determined which is consistent with typical oligopoly behavior.
E) All of the above are correct.

Difficulty: **Easy**

74. In a centralized cartel:
 A) the cartel sets the monopoly price, and allocates the monopoly output and profits among all the cartel members.
 B) the cartel minimizes production costs if it shifts production from members with high SMC to members with lower SMC.
 C) the cartel will allocate output on the basis of past output, present capacity, and bargaining ability if the size and costs of the members are the same.
 D) Only (A) and (B) are correct.
 E) All of the above are correct.

 Difficulty: **Moderate**

75. Market-sharing cartels:
 A) are more likely to occur than centralized cartels.
 B) with members which operate in the same geographic area are likely to be more stable than those whose markets are geographically separated.
 C) always produce monopoly outcomes if there are only two sellers, i.e., a duopoly.
 D) find that reaching agreements on pricing and allocating output and profits among members is much easier to do than when the centralized arrangement is attempted.
 E) None of the above is correct.

 Difficulty: **Moderate**

76. The welfare effects of oligopoly:
 A) are difficult to evaluate relative to the perfect competition model because large economies of scale relative to market size make it a impossible for perfect competition to exist there.
 B) are difficult to evaluate because of the possibility that oligopolists use a large portion of incentive to undertake and greater difficulty funding.
 C) include overallocating resources to the industry in order to benefit producers, a practice which only causes P > LMC.
 D) only (A) and (B) are correct.
 E) All of the above are correct.

 Difficulty: **Moderate**

77. The view that cost-plus pricing is <u>not</u> inconsistent with profit maximization:
 A) is true if the markup is varied inversely with the elasticity of demand.
 B) is true if the markup is varied inversely with the elasticity of supply.
 C) is true if the markup is varied directly with the elasticity of demand.
 D) is not supported by empirical evidence which shows that firms in the retail sector increase their markup when demand decreases and becomes more elastic.
 E) (B) and (C) are correct.

 Difficulty: **Hard**

78. Which of the following is <u>not</u> an example of monopolistic competition in the real world?
 A) clothing
 B) food processing
 C) restaurants
 D) newspaper stands

E) None of the above; all are examples of monopolistic competition.

Difficulty: **Easy**

79. Which of the following is <u>not</u> an example of an oligopolistic industry?
A) cigarettes
B) pizza shops
C) automobiles
D) steel
E) breakfast cereals

Difficulty: **Easy**

80. According to the kinked demand curve model, the demand curve facing the oligopolist is _____ above than below the kink.
A) much more elastic
B) much more inelastic
C) slightly more elastic
D) slightly more inelastic
E) just as elastic

Difficulty: **Easy**

Short Essays

Give a brief answer to each of the following questions.

1. **Why might the monopolistic competition model <u>not</u> be very useful to economists?**
Answer: First, it is difficult to define a market product group. Second, in markets with many small sellers product differentiation is slight. Third, markets with strong brand preferences usually have only a few producers and are oligopolistic. Fourth, markets with many sellers often function more like oligopolies because the market is highly localized.

2. **What is the fundamental weakness of the kinked demand curve model?**
Answer: First, the theory itself is flawed because it can explain why oligopoly prices might be rigid due to a "kink" in the demand curve, but it offers no explanation of the formation of the price at which the kink occurs. Second, empirical evidence does not support a basic prediction of the model, i.e., that oligopolists will not match price increases but quickly match price decreases.

3. **What factors contribute to the failure of cartels?**
Answer: They include (1) the difficulty of organizing a large number of sellers, (2) the difficulty in reaching an agreement on how to allocate output and profits when firms' cost curves differ, (3) the incentive to cheat by selling at a lower price in order to make larger profits, and (4) the danger of attracting new firms by earning high profit rates.

4. **Explain why a market-sharing cartel is easier to maintain than a centralized cartel.**
Answer: A centralized cartel has to set a monopoly price and then allocate output and profits based on some criteria. A market-sharing cartel simply allocates market shares and

leaves each firm to operate in its own part of the market as it wishes. Such an agreement is easier, not to say easy, to reach than the agreements required for a centralized cartel.

5. **Explain briefly why cost-plus pricing might be consistent with profit maximization.**
Answer: Cost-plus pricing seems at first to be a kind of fixed rule which implies that pricing decisions simply involve charging whatever the good costs to produce plus some additional amount for a profit. It seems to ignore completely demand conditions. However, empirical studies show that the size of the markup used and prices charged vary with elasticity of demand and with shifts in demand just as profit maximization models suggest will happen.

6. **What difference will it make if duopolists assume that the rival firm will hold its output constant or that it will hold its price constant? (Hint: Contrast the outcome of the Cournot model and the Bertrand model.)**
Answer: The basic behavioral assumption made in the Cournot model is that each firm, while trying to maximize profits, assumes that the other duopolist holds its output constant at the existing level. The result is a cycle of moves and countermoves by the duopolists until each sells one-third of the total industry supply, an outcome that is in between the monopoly equilibrium and the perfect competition equilibrium. In the Bertrand model, each duopolist assumes that the other will hold its price constant at the existing level. A cycle of moves and countermoves again results, but now (assuming the duopolists do not recognize their interdependence) the process will continue until each firm sells one-half of the total industry supply at the perfectly competitive price (assumed to be zero). Thus, under the Cournot model the duopolists each earn positive profits, whereas under the Bertrand model the result for each firm is zero profits.

Chapter 12:

Game Theory and Oligopolistic Behavior

Multiple-Choice

Choose the one alternative that best completes the statement or answers the question.

1. Suppose that Ted and Terry are two individuals who are accused of murder. Both Ted and Terry are able to bribe a jailer in order to establish a channel of communication between them. According to the "prisoner's dilemma", the optimal strategy will be:
A) for Ted to confess and Terry to remain silent.
B) for neither Ted nor Terry to confess.
C) for Terry to confess and for Ted to remain silent.
D) for both Ted and Terry to confess.
E) for both Ted and Terry to hire a good lawyer.

Difficulty: **Easy**

2. A game in which the gain of one player comes at the expense and is exactly equal to the loss of the other player is said to be a:
A) zero-sum game.
B) non-zero sum game.
C) positive-sum game.
D) negative-sum game.
E) None of the above is correct.

Difficulty: **Easy**

3. Suppose we apply game theory to two firms' advertising decisions. If increased advertising leads to higher profits of both firms we would have a:
A) zero-sum game.
B) positive-sum game.
C) negative-sum game.
D) All of the above are correct.
A) None of the above is correct.

Difficulty: **Easy**

4. Suppose that two players are engaged in a game, and it is a zero-sum game. In this type of game:
A) each player will win nothing.
B) the payoff matrix contains zeros.
C) what one individual wins is equal to what the other individual loses.
D) the average payoff for each player is zero.
E) a strategy will be chosen that maximizes the payoff.

Difficulty: **Easy**

5. In game theory, a complete specification of what a participation will do under each possibility in the playing of a game is known as:
   A) a minimax strategy.
   B) a strategy.
   C) a payoff.
   D) a maximum strategy.
   E) a rule of the game.

   Difficulty: **Easy**

6. Suppose that a player in a game has a complete list of the things that he will do under each possible contingency while he is playing the game. This complete list is a:
   A) strategy for playing the game.
   B) determined game.
   C) dominant strategy for playing the game.
   D) payoff of playing the game.
   E) None of the above is correct.

   Difficulty: **Easy**

7. If two individual producers pursue a strategy that ends up as a zero-sum game, then:
   A) the producers will receive no economic profits.
   B) the profit-payoff matrix will consist only of negative numbers.
   C) the average payoff for each producer is zero.
   D) one producer will gain or win exactly the amount that the other producer loses.
   E) None of the above is correct.

   Difficulty: **Easy**

8. The ABC Corp. and the XYZ Corp. are engaged in a non-zero sum game. This means that:
   A) the gains for the ABC Corp. would be exactly equal to the losses for the XYZ Corp. and vice versa.
   B) the gains for the ABC Corp. would be greater than the losses for the XYZ Corp. and vice versa.
   C) the gains for the ABC Corp. would be less than the losses for the XYZ Corp. and vice versa.
   D) Either (B) or (C) could be correct.
   E) None of the above is correct.

   Difficulty: **Moderate**

9. When two firms in an oligopolistic market attempt to determine an optimum pricing strategy in conflict situations, one of the methods that might be used is:
   A) pursuing a policy of constrained optimization.
   B) pursuing a policy of limit pricing.
   C) game theory.
   D) strategic planning.
   E) None of the above is correct.

   Difficulty: **Easy**

10. Game theory was initially developed in the 1940s by:

A) Professor Milton Friedman, formerly of the University of Chicago.
B) John von Neumann and Oskar Morgenstern.
C) John Maynard Keynes and Alvin Hansen.
D) August Cournot.
E) William E. Peacock.

Difficulty: **Easy**

11. If two firms participate in a pricing "game," a Nash equilibrium is attained when:
A) no one can be made better off without making someone else worse off.
B) there is no pressure on prices to change.
C) the quantity demanded in the market equals the quantity supplied.
D) a strategy combination is achieved where no firm has a net incentive to change unless the other firm changes.
E) None of the above is correct.

Difficulty: **Moderate**

12. Which one of the following would result in an infinitely repeated game?
A) a tit-for-tat strategy
B) a dominant strategy by one of the players
C) a positive (win-win) game
D) a zero-sum game
E) a Nash equilibrium

Difficulty: **Moderate**

13. In game theory, the payoff is the outcome or consequence of:
A) a firm's strategy independent of the actions of its rival.
B) the combination of strategies of the firm and its rival.
C) a zero-sum game.
D) a non-zero sum game.
E) None of the above is correct.

Difficulty: **Moderate**

14. For a firm, a strategy could be a choice to:
A) change price.
B) develop new or differentiated products.
C) build excess capacity.
D) introduce a new or a different advertising campaign.
E) All of the above are possible strategies.

Difficulty: **Moderate**

15. Suppose that duopoly exists with firms A and B. If firm A chooses to let firm B be the first in setting a price, then firm A is pursuing a:
A) tit-for-tat strategy.
B) dominant strategy.
C) zero sum game.
D) positive sum game.

E) None of the above is correct.

Difficulty: **Moderate**

16. Generally speaking, economists and policy analysts use game theory to demonstrate that:
A) it is possible for firms in a highly concentrated industry to increase their profits through collusion.
B) if firms in an oligopoly cannot collude, then they may be unable to maximize their overall profits.
C) firms in an oligopolistic industry are mutually dependent on each other.
D) if firms in an oligopolistic industry practice independent pricing, the result will be lower pricing policies.
E) All of the above are correct.

Difficulty: **Moderate**

17. John and Sam have been arrested for armed robbery. They have both tried to bribe the guards in order to establish some type of communication between them; however, they have been unsuccessful. If convicted, both will do a lot of time. If neither confesses, the police do not have enough evidence to make the charges stick. The optimal strategy for John and Sam will be:
A) to both remain silent and admit nothing.
B) for both to confess and implicate the other.
C) for Sam to confess and John to remain silent.
D) for John to confess and Sam to remain silent.
E) for both to make up some wild story and confuse the guards.

Difficulty: **Moderate**

18. Suppose that two firms play a strategic game. The firms have two strategies: they can cooperate with each other or they can not cooperate. The CEO of each firm is the appropriate player, and each is given two slips of paper on which to indicate his/her strategy. The CEOs can either write C for cooperate or N for non-cooperation. If both cooperate and write C, each gets a payoff of $1,000; however, if both write N on each slip of paper, they get nothing. If one CEO tries to cooperate and the other does not, the cooperating player gets a payoff of X dollars and the non-cooperating player gets a payoff of X dollars and the non-cooperating player gets a payoff of T dollars. To defect will be a dominant strategy for both players if:
A) $X < T$ and $T >$ $1,000.
B) $X + T >$ $1,000.
C) $X < 0$ and $T >$ $1,000.
D) $T > 2X$.
E) for any value of X and T.

Difficulty: **Hard**

19. A profit-payoff matrix has the characteristic that:
A) it is usually presented for two players.
B) the payoff shows the outcome of each strategy by the players.
C) the payoff matrix shows the outcome for each combination of strategies for the two players.
D) the payoff is usually expressed in terms of profits or losses for each player.

E) All of the above are correct.

Difficulty: **Moderate**

20. Suppose that you and your friend Charlie make a $100 bet on the outcome of the 1998 World Series. This bet between you and your friend is an example of a:
A) dominant strategy.
B) positive-sum game.
C) nash equilibrium.
D) zero-sum game.
E) tit-for-tat strategy.

Difficulty: **Easy**

21. Suppose that you are the CEO of the Jones Co., and Mr. Smith is the CEO of the AMC Co., and you two are the major players in the Widget industry. If both you and Mr. Smith pursue a dominant strategy in making your decisions, then this strategy will be the one which:
A) results in at least one individual playing a zero-sum game.
B) results in at least one player always losing.
C) results in the best payoff possible.
D) results in neither playing winning.
E) always results in a break-even situation.

Difficulty: **Easy**

22. Which one of the following would be an example of a game involving noncooperative behavior on the part of the players?
A) An accused murderer with a strong likelihood of conviction plea-bargains for something other than the death penalty.
B) A market structure that is purely competitive.
C) Passage of the NAFTA Treaty by the U.S., Canada, and Mexico in 1993.
D) Collective bargaining between autoworkers and General Motors.
E) None of the above is an example.

Difficulty: **Moderate**

23. If a game has a dominant strategy equilibrium, then all of the players:
A) will win no more than they lose.
B) will earn the best possible payoff.
C) recognize that it is in their best interest to cooperate with each other.
D) will face a zero sum game.
E) None of the above is correct.

Difficulty: **Moderate**

24. All of the following conditions are necessary for a tit-for-tat strategy to be effective <u>except</u>:
A) each firm must be able to quickly detect and respond to cheating by other firms in the industry.
B) demand and cost conditions must be relatively stable for the industry.
C) the number of players must be relatively large.
D) the set of players must be stable.

E) the game must be repeated indefinitely.

Difficulty: **Moderate**

25. If an oligopolistic firm adopts a strategy in order to gain a competitive advantage over the other firms in the industry, it means that the firm:
A) must develop a credible policy that is believed by its competitors.
B) may be able to threaten or intimidate its competitors, as long as it is believed by the other firms in the industry.
C) must be committed to see any threat through to the finish.
D) may be able to deter entrance into the market and thereby reduce competition by expanding its productive capacity.
E) All of the above are correct.

Difficulty: **Moderate**

26. Suppose that two players, X and Y, are participants in a game, and player X has a dominant strategy while player Y does not. This means that player X:
A) will always win the game.
B) is not playing a fair game with player Y.
C) has an optimal strategy while player Y does not.
D) should base his strategy on what player Y does.
E) None of the above is correct.

Difficulty: **Moderate**

27. When there are two players in a game and a Nash equilibrium is attained:
A) each player chooses his or her optimal strategy based on the strategy chosen by the other player.
B) one player may have a dominant strategy while the other does not.
C) the Nash equilibrium may not be unique.
D) the goal of each player remains that of choosing an optimal strategy.
E) All of the above are correct.

Difficulty: **Moderate**

28. All of the following statements are correct <u>except</u>:
A) All of the games that can be played between competing firms in a capitalistic market can attain a Nash equilibrium.
B) When a Nash equilibrium is achieved, on player determines her strategy after the other player has chosen her strategy.
C) In the Dell computer case, the Dell Company developed an optimal strategy without regard to what its competitors did.
D) In the prisoners' dilemma, if a line of communication between the prisoners can be established, then it is best if neither confess to a crime.
E) As the number of members of a cartel increases, so is the likelihood of cheating on price.

Difficulty: **Moderate**

29. Suppose that the Widget industry consists of fifteen firms, each producing a homogeneous product, and these firms form a cartel. If each firm had the choice of advertising their product or not, we would expect the members of the cartel to:
    A) spend part of their budget on advertising their product.
    B) spend part of their budget trying to differentiate their product.
    C) collectively advertise their product; that is, advertise as a group.
    D) not spend any part of their budget on advertising.
    E) None of the above is correct.

    Difficulty: **Moderate**

30. If a player of a game issues a threat to another player, then in order for the threat to be taken seriously, the player making the threat:
    A) must be larger than the player threatened.
    B) must have developed a dominant strategy for the game.
    C) must initially be in a Nash equilibrium.
    D) need only to make the threat in order for it to have the desired effect on the other player.
    E) None of the above is correct.

    Difficulty: **Moderate**

31. In a game with two players, if one player issues a threat to another, then in order for the threat to be credibly:
    A) the player issuing the threat must be larger than the player threatened.
    B) the player issuing the threat must be willing to carry out the threat.
    C) the threatened player must not have developed a dominant strategy in the game.
    D) neither player must have a profit-payoff matrix.
    E) None of the above is correct.

    Difficulty: **Moderate**

32. Suppose that a market consists of two players, A and B. Players A and B expect another player, C, to enter the market and take market share from both. If A and B can collude, then which of the following would not be a deterrent to entry for firm C?
    A) Firms A and B threaten to reduce price to only a few cents above ATC at the optimal level of output.
    B) Firms A and B lower price below ATC but maintain it above AVC.
    C) Firms A and B set a price such that profits are reduced in the short run but will be regained in the long run.
    D) Firms A and B set that price associated with the quantity of output where MC = MR.
    E) None of the above is a policy that would deter entrance by firm C.

    Difficulty: **Moderate**

33. All of the following were characteristic of Wal-Mart's rise to its position of one of the largest retail discount chains in the United States except:
    A) Wal-Mart reduced its entry requirement into market areas with at least 100,000 people.
    B) Wal-Mart relied heavily on rapid turnover of inventory.
    C) Wal-Mart relied on size and economies of scale in order to reduce its per-unit costs.

D) Wal-Mart issued a preemptive threat to underprice any potential competitor who might come into the market and threaten its profits.
E) None of the above is correct.

Difficulty: **Moderate**

34. If there are two players from different countries who produce very similar products and then sell their products in the international market, and if the government of one of the players subsidizes its domestic producer, then:
A) the unsubsidized player is placed at a competitive disadvantage.
B) the nation with unsubsidized player could retaliate and offer a production subsidy.
C) the producer that is subsidized may acquire a comparative advantage over the non-subsidized producer by using a strategic trade policy.
D) it is possible that the unsubsidized producer will stop producing the product and leave the market to the subsidized producer.
E) All of the above are correct.

Difficulty: **Moderate**

35. Generally speaking, game theory:
A) is of little use to analysts in the real world.
B) becomes easier and more realistic the more players that are involved.
C) lends itself to the study of competitive markets as well as oligopolistic markets.
D) requires conflict situations and the problem of choice in order to be applicable.
E) None of the above is correct.

Difficulty: **Easy**

36. Which of the following is <u>not</u> a common or shared principle of warfare and business?
A) have a clear objective and explain this objective to all "employees"
B) develop an attack strategy
C) spread command in order to broaden responsibility as much as possible
D) maintain the element of surprise and security
E) All of the above are correct.

Difficulty: **Easy**

37. Before the entry of Dell Computers into the market:
A) all of the other computer companies followed a dominant strategy of selling computers only through retail outlets.
B) all of the other computer companies followed a dominant strategy of selling computers by mail order.
C) none of the other computer companies followed a dominant strategy.
D) the other computer companies followed dominant strategies which never produced a final equilibrium.
E) the number of sellers in the market for computers was not sufficient to generate any competitive behavior.

Difficulty: **Moderate**

38. When Dell Computers entered the market:
   A) Dell developed a dominant strategy that made it sensitive to the responses of its competitors.
   B) Dell developed a dominant strategy of selling computers by mail order in response to the strategic choices of its competitors.
   C) Dell's dominant strategy overwhelmed the dominant strategy chosen by its competitors and generated a Nash equilibrium in the computer market.
   D) Dell's actions along with those of its competitors failed to produce a Nash equilibrium.
   E) (A) and (B) are correct.

   Difficulty: **Moderate**

39. In April 1992, American Airlines initiated a set of price cuts that were followed by other airlines. All of the airlines earned lower profits as a consequence. In the fall of 1992, efforts made by airlines to raise price failed when or more of the carriers did not go along. Which of the following characterizations of these events is <u>not</u> correct?
   A) Whatever were the initial conditions, the price cuts created a prisoners' dilemma for U.S. airline companies.
   B) Efforts to cooperate and return to the position in a payoff matrix that makes all sellers better off were unsuccessful.
   C) Airlines faced heavy losses because the dominant strategy adopted by some of the firms made cooperation impossible.
   D) All of the above are correct.
   E) None of the above is correct because the concept of the prisoners' dilemma is only applicable to the efforts to avoid price cuts and not to efforts to actively raise price.

   Difficulty: **Moderate**

40. The preemptive investment strategy of Wal-Mart does <u>not</u> involve:
   A) adopting an every-day low-price strategy.
   B) relying on size, low costs, and high turnover to earn profits even in relatively small towns.
   C) moving into large markets where competition from another national chain will not make it difficult for both national chains to survive.
   D) moving aggressively to expand into new markets before other national chains are established there.
   E) All of the above are a part of the preemptive investment strategy.

   Difficulty: **Moderate**

41. The strategic mistake made by U.S. automakers in the 1970s was:
   A) not understanding the fundamentals of their business.
   B) inability to foresee serious problems down the road.
   C) loading the firms with heavy debt burdens.
   D) due to strikes and hostilities from unhappy workers.
   E) All of the above are correct.

   Difficulty: **Moderate**

42. In practice, the basic causes of business failure do <u>not</u> include which of the following?
   A) Senior executives do not fully understand the core expertise of their firm.
   B) The inability of top management to anticipate serious problems in the future.

C) The failure to take on sufficient debt so that in economic downturns creditors will help to keep the business afloat.
D) Sticking to obsolete strategies.
E) Strikes and hostilities from unhappy workers.

Difficulty: **Moderate**

43. Which of the following explains why Chrysler was almost driven out of business in the 1980s?
A) Senior executives did not fully understand the core expertise of their firm.
B) Top management failed to anticipate serious problems in the future stemming from new competitors.
C) The failure to take on sufficient debt so that in economic downturns creditors will help to keep the business afloat.
D) Strikes and hostilities from unhappy workers.
E) All of the above are correct.

Difficulty: **Easy**

44. The "virtual corporation":
A) is a permanent network of companies which are merging to form one firm in response to long-term developments in markets.
B) is a temporary network of independent companies cooperating to take advantage of rapidly emerging market opportunities.
C) has not been successfully developed yet because no way has been found to disband the "virtual corporation" after it has outlived its usefulness.
D) is a new method of developing alliances among former rivals that allowed the firms to escape antitrust laws.
E) has yet to be employed successfully because no one has found a way to sustain cooperation among firms at a sufficient level to finish difficult projects.

Difficulty: **Easy**

45. The risks that are faced by the virtual corporation model do <u>not</u> include which of the following?
A) A company losing control of its core technology.
B) A company may be unable to resume its traditional product manufacturing.
C) A company will find itself unable to escape the temptation to merge with the other companies and will lose its own identity.
D) The type of loss IBM suffered by becoming reliant on Microsoft and Intel for quick entry into the personal computer market.
E) None of the above is correct.

Difficulty: **Moderate**

46. In order for a virtual firm to work:
A) the firm will have to be formed by partners that are dependable, but are not the best in their field since the latter would make no gains from cooperating.
B) the network formed must serve the interests of all the partners in a win-win situation.
C) each company must avoid putting its most capable people in the network if it's to preserve the integrity of the network.

D) the objective of the network must be clearly defined, but the gains each partner is expected to make must remain undefined for as long as possible.
E) All of the above are correct.

Difficulty: **Moderate**

47. Suppose that Ted and Terry are two individuals who are accused of murder. Both Ted and Terry are able to bribe the jailer in order to establish a channel of communication between them. According to the "prisoner's dilemma," the optimal strategy will be:
A) for Ted to confess and for Terry to remain silent.
B) for neither Ted nor Terry to confess.
C) for Terry to confess and for Ted to remain silent.
D) for both Ted and Terry to confess.
E) for both Ted and Terry to hire a good lawyer.

Difficulty: **Moderate**

48. Assume that firm A increases its advertising while firm B does not change its advertising. If firm A's gains in market share are all made at the expense of firm B, then firms A and B are engaged in:
A) a zero-sum game.
B) a positive-sum game.
C) a negative-sum game.
D) a nonzero-sum game.
E) behavior which cannot be understood in terms of game theory.

Difficulty: **Moderate**

49. Assume that firm A decreases its price but firm B does not match the price decrease. If firm B loses market share to firm A but their combined sales are unchanged, then firms A and B are engaged in:
A) a nonzero-sum game.
B) a positive-sum game.
C) a negative-sum game.
D) collusive behavior to rig the market.
E) behavior which cannot be understood in terms of game theory.

Difficulty: **Moderate**

50. Assume that firm A increases its advertising and firm B responds by increasing its advertising. If profits of both firms increase, then firms A and B are engaged in:
A) a zero-sum game.
B) a positive-sum game.
C) a negative-sum game.
D) collusive behavior to rig the market.
E) behavior which cannot be understood in terms of game theory.

Difficulty: **Moderate**

51. Assume that firm A decreases price and firm B responds by decreasing its price. If profits of both firms decrease, then firms A and B are engaged in:
A) a zero-sum game.

B) a positive-sum game.
C) a negative-sum game.
D) behavior which cannot be understood in terms of game theory.
E) None of the above is correct.

Difficulty: **Moderate**

The following payoff matrix shows profits in millions of dollars.

	Firm H Advertises F	Firm H Advertises H	Firm H Does Not Advertise F	Firm H Does Not Advertise H
Firm F Advertises	18	14	22	9
Firm F Does Not Advertise	8	17	14	12

52. Given the payoff matrix above which represents how the profits of Firm F and Firm H are affected, according to their decisions to advertise their output,:
A) Firm F has a dominant strategy but Firm H does not have a dominant strategy.
B) Firm H has a dominant strategy but Firm F does not have a dominant strategy.
C) Firms F and H both have dominant strategies.
D) Neither Firm F nor Firm H has a dominant strategy.
E) The payoff matrix yields no strategies.

Difficulty: **Moderate**

53. The outcome of the advertising "game" depicted in the payoff matrix is as follows:
A) neither firm advertises.
B) both firms advertise.
C) firm F advertises, but firm H does not.
D) firm H advertises, but firm F does not.
E) The outcome is conditional on whether the firm with the dominant strategy decides to advertise.

Difficulty: **Moderate**

54. In the advertising "game" depicted in the payoff matrix:
A) the solution requires that Firm F advertise first and Firm H responds because Firm F has a dominant strategy and Firm H does not.
B) the solution requires that Firm H advertise first and Firm F responds because Firm H has a dominant strategy and Firm F does not.
C) the solution requires that Firm F and Firm H begin advertising simultaneously..
D) the solution will emerge regardless of which firm advertises first, and regardless of whether the firms advertise simultaneously.
E) we know in advance whether the solution will emerge without regard to the order in which advertising decisions are made.

Difficulty: **Moderate**

	Firm H Advertises		Firm H Does Not Advertise	
	F	H	F	H
Firm F Advertises	10	8	12	6
Firm F Does Not Advertise	8	10	9	9

55. Given the payoff matrix above which represents how the profits of Firm F and Firm H are affected by, according to their decisions to advertise their output:
A) Firm F has a dominant strategy but Firm H does not have a dominant strategy.
B) Firm H has a dominant strategy but Firm F does not have a dominant strategy.
C) Firms F and H both have dominant strategies.
D) Neither Firm F nor H has a dominant strategy.
E) The payoff matrix yields no strategies.

Difficulty: **Moderate**

56. The outcome of the advertising "game" depicted in the payoff matrix is:
A) neither firm advertises and the solution is not a Nash equilibrium.
B) both firms advertise and the solution is not a Nash equilibrium.
C) neither firm advertises and the solution is a Nash equilibrium.
D) both firms advertise and the solution is a Nash equilibrium.
E) Firm F advertises and Firm H does not.

Difficulty: **Moderate**

Use the payoff matrix to solve the prisoners' dilemma.

	Mr. Y Confesses		Mr. Y Does Not Confess	
	X	Y	X	Y
Mr. X Confesses			1	8
Mr. X Does Not Confess	8	1	2	2

57. Which pairs of values (years of detention) must Mr. X and Mr. Y face, respectively in the upper left hand cell of the matrix, if this matrix is to represent a prisoners' dilemma?
A) 2, 5
B) 4, 4
C) 3, 2
D) 1, 1
E) All of the above are correct.

Difficulty: **Moderate**

58. In a prisoners' dilemma:
A) both "firms" have dominant strategies.
B) both "firms" are better off if they cooperate with one another than if they do not cooperate.
C) a Nash equilibrium is reached.
D) All of the above are correct.
E) Only (A) and (B) are correct.

Difficulty: **Moderate**

59. In the absence of an enforcement mechanism to prevent cheating, cartel members participate in a "game":
A) in which none of the participants have a dominant strategy.
B) which may be described as a prisoners' dilemma.
C) in which cheating is the dominant strategy for all participants.
D) (A) and (B) are correct.
E) (B) and (C) are correct.

Difficulty: **Moderate**

60. In repeated games, the best strategy for firms to follow is to:
A) do to your opponent what your opponent has done to you.
B) tit-for-tat behavior.
C) retaliate for cheating until the cheater begins to cooperate.
D) begin by cooperating in the game.
E) All of the above are correct.

Difficulty: **Moderate**

61. In a non-repeat game, such as the single-move prisoners' dilemma game, in which the decision is whether or not to confess, the best strategy to follow is:
A) tit-for-tat.
B) to wait and see what the other player actually does.
C) to confess.
D) All of the above are potentially successful strategies in the non-repeated game.
E) None of the above is correct.

Difficulty: **Moderate**

62. A "strategic move" by firm Z includes any action that:
A) allows firm Z to make gains in the long run.
B) influences the behavior of firm Z in such a way a to benefit firm Z.
C) alters the expectations of other firms about how firm Z will behave, and thereby causes other firms to make choices which are favorable to firm Z.
D) negatively impacts other firms.
E) None of the above is correct.

Difficulty: **Moderate**

63. Which of the following statements is true?
A) All games have a dominant strategy for each player.
B) All games have a Nash equilibrium.

C) Some games can have more than one Nash equilibrium.
D) All of the above are true.
E) None of the above is true.

Difficulty: **Moderate**

64. Cooperation is more likely to occur in _____ games.
A) repeated or many-move
B) single-move prisoners' dilemma
C) zero-sum
D) positive-sum
E) negative-sum

Difficulty: **Moderate**

65. For a threat to be credible:
A) it must be in writing.
B) it must be strategic.
C) there must be a commitment that the maker of the threat is ready to carry it out.
D) it must result in a positive-sum game.
E) it must result in a negative-sum game.

Difficulty: **Easy**

Short Essays

Give a brief answer to each of the following questions.

1. **Explain how new advertising campaigns by two competitors might constitute a zero-sum game, a negative-sum game, or a positive-sum game.**
Answer: If market share is considered the payoff then if one firm gains market share entirely at the expense of the other it is a zero-sum game. If profits are considered the payoff and both firms' profits fall it is a negative-sum game. If both firms' profits rise it is a positive-sum game.

2. **In a market where there are only two firms, how is it possible for both firms to have "a dominant strategy?"**
Answer: Dominant strategy means that a particular strategy is optimal for a firm no matter what the other firm decides to do. Thus, it is possible for both firms to have a dominant strategy, for neither of them to have a dominant strategy, or for one of them to have a dominant strategy while the other does not. To have a dominant strategy does not mean that one will "dominate" the market.

3. **What is a prisoners' dilemma? (Hint: What has it got to do with dominant strategies and cooperation?)**
Answer: It refers to a situation in which two parties have a dominant strategy, which is not to cooperate when they would both do better if they cooperated. For example, two criminals would be better off if they cooperated with each other by not confessing to a crime they committed together. However, the dominant strategy is to confess first because no matter what the other criminal does, the first person to confess is made better off by confessing first.

4. **Tit-for-tat behavior is the best strategy for what type of game?**
Answer: It is best for a repeated game. Cooperation can be arrived at and can be restored when it is broken by responding in kind to the behavior of other "players," i.e., do not betray a cooperative agreement first, but retaliate until the person who does betray goes back to keeping the agreement. This strategy does not work, of course, if the game is played only once such as in the prisoners' dilemma for two criminals being pressured to confess.

5. **Why do economists hold such a critical view of government policy to develop comparative advantages?**
Answer: Conceptually, it is possible to make a case for a strategic policy to promote international competitiveness in key industries by subsidies, tariffs, and other devices. However, to do so requires such a high degree of knowledge about the outcomes of various strategies that it is likely a government will choose badly and end up promoting the wrong industry. It will be worse off for doing so. Thus, it is preferable simply to promote a free trade policy.

Chapter 13:

Market Structure, Efficiency, and Regulation

Multiple-Choice

Choose the one alternative that best completes the statement or answers the question.

1. Suppose that in the country of Alphania, the production of corn results in an efficient level of output being produced. We can conclude that:
   A) the price of corn is too high to achieve an equilibrium in the market.
   B) the price of corn reflects both the social valuation and the marginal social cost of consuming and producing the last unit of corn.
   C) there will be a positive net benefit to society by producing and consuming an extra unit of corn.
   D) the production of corn does not take place in a competitive market.
   E) None of the above is correct.

   Difficulty: **Easy**

2. Suppose that the production and distribution of widgets occurs in a perfectly competitive market. If, in an attempt to raise revenue, the government places a sales tax of X percent on each widget sold, then:
   A) widgets will be produced at a quantity where the marginal valuation of consuming the last widget is greater than the marginal cost of producing the last widget.
   B) the market will achieve an efficient allocation of resources and widgets more quickly.
   C) the price of widgets will equal the marginal cost of producing the last widget.
   D) widgets will be produced up to the point where the marginal cost of producing the last widget is greater than the marginal valuation of consuming it.
   E) None of the above is correct.

   Difficulty: **Moderate**

3. Suppose that the equilibrium price established in a perfectly competitive market for widgets is $6 per unit. We know that:
   A) the marginal cost of producing the last widget sold is also $6.
   B) consumers would be willing to purchase more widgets at the market price if the firm produced more.
   C) the average cost of producing the last widget sold is greater than $6.
   D) the typical firm earns an excess profit at this market price.
   E) None of the above is correct.

   Difficulty: **Easy**

4. Suppose that a competitive firm and a non-regulated, profit maximizing monopolist purchase their inputs in a perfectly competitive input market. Also, the competitive firm and the monopolist use the same production technology, and so they face the same cost curves.

In the long run, the relation between the competitive price and the monopoly price is such that:

A) **the competitive price will usually be lower than the price established by the monopolist.**
B) it is not possible to determine either the competitive price or the monopoly price without information about product demand.
C) the monopoly price will usually be lower than the competitive price.
D) the competitive price will usually be the same as that established by the monopolist.
E) None of the above is correct.

Difficulty: **Moderate**

5. For the monopolistic producer, resources are inefficiently allocated because:

A) marginal revenue and price are not equal.
B) the monopolist's price demand curve slopes downward and to the right.
C) **the monopolist's price is greater than the marginal cost of producing its optimal level of output.**
D) consumers do not value the last product of output purchased by as much as it costs to produce the unit.
E) None of the above is correct.

Difficulty: **Moderate**

6. The natural monopolist would most likely resist any attempt by government to force it to charge an output price equal to its marginal cost of production because:

A) its marginal cost will be less than its marginal revenue.
B) **its price may very well be less than its average total cost of production, so a loss is incurred on each unit produced.**
C) it will earn only a normal profit.
D) its average fixed cost will increase as output rises.
E) None of the above is correct.

Difficulty: **Moderate**

7. A crude measure of the monopoly power possessed by a firm is the difference between:

A) marginal revenue and marginal cost.
B) demand and the quantity supplied.
C) **market price and marginal cost.**
D) average total cost and average fixed cost.
E) None of the above is correct.

Difficulty: **Moderate**

8. Suppose that a competitive industry and a monopolist face the same input prices and the same production technology. When compared to the competitive industry, the monopolist:

A) is also a price taker like the competitive firm.
B) uses resources more efficiently.
C) improves overall social welfare because it produces more efficiently.
D) **produces less output and charges a higher price per unit of output.**
E) None of the above is correct.

Difficulty: **Moderate**

9. The social cost of monopolization of a competitive industry arises because:
   A) the monopolist raises the price charged for its output.
   B) the monopolist reduces the level of output that it produces.
   C) society values an additional unit in consumption more than it costs the monopolist to produce the extra unit.
   D) market price exceeds the marginal cost of producing an extra unit of the good.
   E) All of the above are correct.

   Difficulty: **Moderate**

10. When a regulated monopoly is compared to an unregulated monopoly, the price charged by the regulated monopolist:
   A) will be that price associated with some point on the inelastic portion of the producer's demand curve.
   B) will generally be less than the price established by the unregulated monopolist.
   C) will generate monopoly profits for the producer.
   D) will usually cause the producer to reduce output.
   E) None of the above is correct.

   Difficulty: **Moderate**

11. The Widget Corp. will be classified as a natural monopoly if:
   A) the government permits the firm to be a monopoly.
   B) the firm owns the patents on the products that it produces.
   C) there are substantial economies of scale that permit the firm to produce its output at a lower per unit cost than could potential rivals.
   D) the demand curve faced by the firm is highly, but not perfectly, elastic.
   E) None of the above is correct.

   Difficulty: **Moderate**

12. Most electric utility companies are natural monopolies, and so only one firm serves a particular area. The reason why the utility companies are natural monopolies is that:
   A) electricity is an inferior good and people must consume a certain amount of it regardless of the product's price.
   B) the firm experiences economies of scale throughout a very large range of output.
   C) the demand curve for electricity is perfectly elastic.
   D) the typical electric utility company experiences constant returns to scale throughout a very large range of output, so the market is best served by only one firm.
   E) None of the above is correct.

   Difficulty: **Moderate**

13. A difficulty often encountered with the regulation of a natural monopoly is that:
   A) social well-being is reduced through the regulation of monopoly.
   B) states do not have the financial means to subsidize regulated monopolies.
   C) the public does not particularly want regulation.
   D) regulators do not have complete information about the monopolist's costs.
   E) None of the above is correct.

   Difficulty: **Moderate**

14. The objective of the antitrust laws in the United States is:
    A) an attempt to reduce the social cost of monopolistic competition.
    B) to prevent firms from merging.
    C) to prevent the monopolization of an industry and to prevent the restraint of trade.
    D) an attempt to promote economic efficiency among competitive firms.
    E) None of the above is correct.

    Difficulty: **Easy**

15. Firms are prohibited from entering into contracts, combinations, and conspiracies that restrain trade because of the:
    A) Sherman Antitrust Act, Section 2.
    B) Clayton Act, Section 1.
    C) Robinson-Patman Act.
    D) Sherman Antitrust Act, Section 1.
    E) None of the above is correct.

    Difficulty: **Easy**

16. If one firm acquires another competing firm so that the concentration in the industry is substantially increased and competition is reduced, the acquisition may be challenged under:
    A) Section 1 of the Sherman Act.
    B) the Robinson-Patman Act.
    C) Section 7 of the Clayton Act.
    D) the Cellar-Kefauver Act.
    E) None of the above is correct.

    Difficulty: **Easy**

17. All of the following statements are correct <u>except</u>:
    A) in the AT&T case, the government charged that AT&T monopolized the telecommunications industry by not allowing other long-distance phone services to have access to AT&T local networks.
    B) a horizontal merger involves the merging of two competing firms.
    C) in the IBM case, the government charged the firm with predatory pricing.
    D) a firm's relevant market is not important in determining whether or not it is a monopoly.
    E) a vertical merger involves two firms merging at different stages of production of a given good.

    Difficulty: **Moderate**

18. An argument often heard against the antitrust laws is that:
    A) the social welfare loss always exceeds any cost savings that result from the increased concentration in an industry.
    B) merged firms are usually larger, so they produce more efficiently and at a lower cost.
    C) since firms are inherently competitive, the antitrust laws waste society's scarce resources.
    D) even if the U.S. economy were perfectly competitive, government would still find reasons to pass antitrust laws.

E) None of the above is correct.

Difficulty: **Moderate**

19. If a regulatory agency imposes marginal cost pricing on a natural monopoly:
A) the firm will always earn a normal profit, but not an economic profit.
B) the marginal valuation by consumers of an extra unit equals the marginal cost of producing the extra unit.
C) the average total cost of production is rising.
D) the firm may earn economic profits.
E) None of the above is correct.

Difficulty: **Moderate**

20. A problem encountered when a regulated natural monopoly is forced to set its price equal to marginal cost of production is that:
A) overall social welfare is not being maximized.
B) average total costs are increasing.
C) the firm may very well suffer losses.
D) more less-efficient firms will enter the industry.
E) None of the above is correct.

Difficulty: **Easy**

21. When a firm earns a "fair" or normal rate of return:
A) its average variable costs are just covered.
B) market price equals average total cost.
C) some economic profits are being made.
D) society's welfare is maximized.
E) None of the above is correct.

Difficulty: **Moderate**

22. Suppose that an electric company (a public utility) has a total cost of production (total variable cost and the opportunity cost of capital) of $1,500 million, and it is expected to produce 22 billion kilowatt hours (kWh) of electricity. What price should customers be charged per kilowatt-hour to ensure that the firm earns a fair return?
A) 10.4 cents per kWh.
B) 7.5 cents per kWh.
C) 6.8 cents per kWh.
D) 4.3 cents per kWh.
E) Not enough information is provided to determine an answer.

Difficulty: **Moderate**

23. When used as a measure of monopoly power, the Lerner Index shows that:
A) as a firm earns more profits, monopoly power increases.
B) the best measure of monopoly power is the four-firm concentration ratio of the largest industries.
C) monopoly power varies inversely with the ratio of profits to sales revenue attained by the firm.
D) as the firm's capital assets increase, so does its degree of monopoly power.

E) None of the above is correct.

Difficulty: **Moderate**

24. Suppose that an imperfectly competitive firm produces and sells widgets. The market price of widgets is $4 per unit, and the marginal cost of producing the optimal output level is $2. The Lerner Index is:
A) 1.00.
B) 2.00.
C) 0.50.
D) 0.25.
E) None of the above is correct.

Difficulty: **Moderate**

25. All of the following statements are correct <u>except</u>:
A) the Lerner Index is a measure of the amount of monopoly power possessed by a firm in the market.
B) if a market is perfectly competitive, it will have a Lerner Index of 1.0.
C) the Lerner Index can be expressed in terms of the price elasticity of demand.
D) the Lerner Index can take a value of between zero and one.
E) if the absolute value of the price elasticity of demand for a product is 4, the Lerner Index is equal to .25.

Difficulty: **Moderate**

26. Suppose that in the market for widgets, the price elasticity of demand at a certain point on the demand curve is equal to 2. The Lerner Index has a value of:
A) 0.50.
B) 2.00.
C) 1.00.
D) 0.75.
E) 0.25.

Difficulty: **Moderate**

27. If a firm is pure monopoly, it will have a Lerner Index of:
A) 0.00.
B) 0.50.
C) 0.25.
D) 0.75.
E) 1.00.

Difficulty: **Easy**

28. When the Lerner Index of monopoly power is used, it is based on the principle(s) that:
A) a low degree of monopoly power is associated with a firms that face a highly elastic demand curve.
B) when a firm can charge a price in excess of its marginal cost, it possesses some degree of monopoly power.
C) monopoly power is always associated with high prices.
D) (A) and (C) are correct.

E) (A) and (B) are correct.

Difficulty: **Moderate**

29. When economists speak of contestable markets, they mean that:
   A) the market is perfectly competitive.
   B) the market is dominated by only one large firm, and that firm earns monopoly profits.
   C) it is difficult for firms to enter or leave the market unless they are willing to incur significant entry and exit costs.
   D) the market is one in which the product being sold is unique.
   E) None of the above is correct.

Difficulty: **Moderate**

30. When economists speak of markets as being contestable, they mean that:
   A) the market is one in which the product being sold is unique.
   B) both entry into and exit from the market is costless.
   C) the market is perfectly competitive.
   D) the market is dominated by a few large firms, and each firm earns an economic profit.
   E) None of the above is correct.

Difficulty: **Moderate**

31. In order for a market to by classified as contestable, it must be true that:
   A) exit from the market is free; there are no costs associated with leaving.
   B) there are no sunk costs that are incurred by the firm.
   C) entry into the market must be free; there are no costs involved when a firm enters.
   D) when price is greater than average total cost, new firms will be more likely to enter the market than they will be if price is less than average total cost.
   E) All of the above are correct.

Difficulty: **Moderate**

32. If a market is a contestable market, then:
   A) newly entering firms can make a profit when price is greater than marginal cost.
   B) newly entering firms can make an economic profit when price is greater than average total cost.
   C) sunk costs in the market are very high.
   D) there are no fixed costs in the short-run faced by the typical firm.
   E) None of the above is correct.

Difficulty: **Moderate**

33. When economic efficiency has been achieved in the market, then:
   A) resources are allocated in the best way.
   B) there is a positive opportunity cost involved in the reallocation of resources.
   C) economic profits are made by the typical firm.
   D) the Lerner Index has a value of 0.50.
   E) it is possible to increase the production if one good without reducing the output of other goods.

Difficulty: **Moderate**

34. The Herfindahl index is calculated as:
A) the ratio of the difference between a firm's price and marginal cost to its price.
B) the difference between the firm's price and marginal cost only.
C) the sum of the squares of the market shares of all of the firms in an industry.
D) can take a value between zero and one.
E) None of the above is correct.

Difficulty: **Easy**

35. Suppose that a Herfindahl index for the widget industry was 50. This would suggest that:
A) there was an absence of monopoly power in the market.
B) the industry consisted of only a few large firms.
C) the firms in the industry try to differentiate their widgets.
D) there is a high variance in the market shares of the firms in the industry.
E) None of the above is correct.

Difficulty: **Moderate**

36. Suppose that in the widget industry, the Herfindahl index was 10,000. This suggests that:
A) the firms in the market have equal market shares.
B) there is a large number of firms in the market.
C) there is a high concentration of market shares in the market.
D) there is only one firm in the industry.
E) None of the above is correct.

Difficulty: **Moderate**

37. If the merger of two firms in the widget industry generated a Herfindahl index of 2,750, then we would expect:
A) the market to remain relatively competitive because this is not a large value for the index.
B) the government to challenge the merger under the nation's antitrust laws.
C) the market to be contestable.
D) the Lerner index to approach zero.
E) None of the above is correct.

Difficulty: **Easy**

38. Generally speaking, X-inefficiency is used to describe the situation where:
A) the actual cost of producing a particular level of output is greater than the minimum cost of producing that level of output.
B) markets are relatively contestable.
C) the Herfindahl index for a particular industry is greater than 2,000.
D) a particular level of output is produced at some point other than the minimum point on an industry's LAC curve.
E) None of the above is correct.

Difficulty: **Moderate**

39. A market exists in which there are 1,000 producers of widgets, and each firm has 0.1 share of the market. Which one of the following statements is correct?

A) The Herfindahl index for this market is 100, and so the government would be indifferent to the merger of two films.
B) This industry would be more productively efficient if it had fewer firms in the industry.
C) Each of the firms in the industry should try to differentiate its product in order to capture more of the market and increase its market share.
D) The Herfindahl index for this market is 10, and so in all likelihood, the government would not oppose the merger of two firms.
E) None of the above is correct.

Difficulty: **Moderate**

40. When a public utility is regulated, it may fall victim to the Averch-Johnson effect. This effect describes:
A) the fall in the economic profits faced by the utility as a result of the regulation.
B) the benefits that accrue to the utility over time.
C) the overspending on plant and equipment by decreasing cost public utilities that results when rates are improperly established by those who regulate the utility.
D) explicit costs that are incurred by the public utility as it attempts to adhere to government regulations.
E) None of the above is correct.

Difficulty: **Moderate**

41. When we study the theory and pricing strategies of firms in contestable markets, their pricing behavior is most like:
A) competitive pricing.
B) limit pricing.
C) predatory pricing.
D) price leadership by a dominant firm.
E) None of the above is correct.

Difficulty: **Moderate**

42. When a constant cost, competitive industry is monopolized, the social cost of the monopolization arises because of:
A) a deadweight social loss in consumers' surplus.
B) the potential for non-minimized costs and the emergence of X-inefficiency.
C) the waste of resources in political lobbying as well as legal fees.
D) the creation of excess capacity to discourage entry.
E) All of the above are correct.

Difficulty: **Moderate**

43. In his work published several decades ago, Schumpeter argued that:
A) the market structure most conducive to economic growth and development was perfect competition.
B) economic profits played no part in the growth and development of capitalist economies.
C) large firms possessing some degree of monopoly power were more likely to engage in research and development than competitive firms.
D) in the long run, economic profits approached zero regardless of the particular market structure.

E) None of the above is correct.

Difficulty: **Moderate**

44. Section 7 of the Clayton Act which addressed the problem of monopolization through merger, was amended by the:
A) Sherman Antitrust Act.
B) Robinson-Pattman Act.
C) Celler-Kefauver Act.
D) Interstate Commerce Act.
E) None of the above is correct.

Difficulty: **Easy**

45. Which one of the following arguments best supports the validity of the Lerner Index of monopoly power?
A) The greater the number and variety of products on the market, the greater will be the level of monopoly power possessed by the firm.
B) The fact that some markets may be contestable is evidence of monopoly power by firms.
C) Industries in which four or fewer firms dominate sales are highly monopolistic.
D) Monopoly power is reflected in relatively greater differences between a firm's price and its marginal cost.
E) None of the above is correct.

Difficulty: **Moderate**

46. All of the following statements are correct <u>except</u>:
A) it is possible that both productive and allocative inefficiencies arise when an industry is regulated.
B) the A-J effect describes the over or under investment in an industry that might arise when the industry is regulated.
C) when a regulatory agency permits a firm to earn only a normal return on its investment, then it will allow the firm to set its price where P = LAC.
D) if the merger of two firms results in a Herfindahl Index that is 100 or less, then the industry is very competitive.
E) if an industry has a Lerner Index of zero, then the industry is a monopoly.

Difficulty: **Moderate**

47. In the following list, the only social cost of monopolizing a competitive industry is:
A) innovations and inventions that reduce the overall cost of production.
B) increased expenditures on research and development.
C) X-inefficiency in production.
D) the presence of increased economies of scale.
E) All of the above are social costs incurred when a competitive industry is monopolized.

Difficulty: **Moderate**

48. Suppose that in Georgia, the state government decides to regulate a public utility that produces and sells electricity. The utility had previously been producing the monopoly quantity, charging the monopoly price, and earning monopoly profits. Which of the following inefficiencies could result from the regulation of the utility?

A) either the over or under investment in the utility because of the regulation
B) reduced incentives for the utility to reduce costs and produce more efficiently
C) a reduced rate of innovations and inventions that might make production more efficient ore introduce new products
D) regulatory lags
E) All of the above are inefficiencies that can occur as a result of regulation.

Difficulty: **Moderate**

49. All of the following can be considered to be a natural monopoly <u>except</u>:
A) Chicago's water system.
B) Pacific Power and Light (a producer of electricity).
C) South-Central Bell Telephone.
D) IBM Corp.
E) garbage collection in Indianapolis.

Difficulty: **Moderate**

50. Beginning in the mid-1970s, there was a movement toward deregulating industries that had previously been regulated. One of the first industries to be deregulated was:
A) the airline industry.
B) gasoline and natural gas production.
C) motor-truck interstate commerce.
D) interstate telephone service.
E) the computer manufacturing industry.

Difficulty: **Easy**

51. Which of the following statements regarding experimental economics is <u>not</u> correct?
A) Experimental economics allows us to test theories and to explore the cause of a theory's failure.
B) Experimental economics allows us to establish empirical regularities that form the basis for a new theory.
C) Volunteers are given money to buy and sell a fictitious commodity within a simple specified institutional framework.
D) Participants are paid to participate, but are not allowed to keep any of the money they earn in the experiment in order to avoid biasing the experiment.
E) Participants attempt to buy fictitious commodities at a low price and sell them at a higher price to other participants in the simulated markets.

Difficulty: **Moderate**

52. In the field of experimental economics, a simple experiment in commodity trading:
A) resulted in price quickly converging to the equilibrium price only when there were a large number of traders.
B) resulted in price quickly converging to the equilibrium price even when there were only a small number of traders.
C) undermined the conclusion of the theory of contestable markets by showing that a large number of competitors must actually be present in a market in order for it to yield to a competitive outcome.
D) suggested that the perfect competition model has a more limited range of applications than had previously been thought.

E) (A) and (C) are correct.

Difficulty: **Moderate**

53. In the field of experimental economics, an important simulated stock market study showed that speculative bubbles:
A) rarely, if ever, develop.
B) are minimized when a rule is in place to stop trading when the market falls by a certain percentage.
C) occur regularly and disappear only after margin trading is allowed.
D) are reduced in size and duration by futures trading.
E) cannot be reduced except by strict rules limiting the trading of shares of stock to a small volume in any given time period.

Difficulty: **Moderate**

54. Which of the following is not a result obtained by experimental economics?
A) Auctions with a larger number of bidders produce more aggressive bidding than with small numbers and result in negative profits (the winner's curse).
B) Consumers more readily accept price increases resulting from rising costs of production then those that arise from higher profits, suggesting that financial disclosure statements of firms can influence consumer behavior.
C) Providing subjects with complete information speeds the convergence to market equilibrium.
D) Participants come to have common expectations regarding the value of a stock by market experience rather than by being given common information.
E) Market efficiency in buying and selling a commodity does not require the complete revelation of buyers' and sellers' preferences.

Difficulty: **Moderate**

55. Which of the following consequences, immediate or longer term, were attributable to the consent decree governing the breakup of AT&T?
A) The emergence of stiff competition and falling prices in the long distance market.
B) A huge increase in marketing expenditures by AT&T and other long distance companies.
C) Monopolies in the provision of local telephone service were permitted to continue.
D) The introduction of advanced services such as customized billing and calling card plans.
E) All of the above are correct.

Difficulty: **Moderate**

56. Which of the following statements regarding the market for transatlantic telephone calls is correct?
A) European telephone companies charge their customers only half of what AT&T charges American customers to make transatlantic calls.
B) European governments have begun to privatize their national telephone companies through stock sales.
C) The European Union has decided not to open its international telephone market to American and British competition for the foreseeable future.
D) European price wars in the provision of the transatlantic calls have made it necessary for AT&T to meet their price cuts if it is to hold on to its American customers.

E) All of the above are correct.

Difficulty: **Moderate**

57. Since the deregulation of the airline industry:
A) most new carriers entering the market have survived with a resulting increase in the total number of suppliers.
B) a large number of relatively small and highly competitive airlines have emerged and are providing a large share of the industry's output.
C) the airline industry has become even more concentrated than it was before deregulation.
D) the market share of the top 5 carriers has fallen from 75% to 61%.
E) None of the above is correct.

Difficulty: **Moderate**

58. Which of the following are practices of established airlines that restrict entry into the market?
A) long-term leasing of the limited number of gates at most airports
B) frequent-flyer programs which increase passenger loyalty to a particular airline
C) computerized reservation systems that give a competitive edge to the airlines owning the system
D) the "hub and "spoke" operations which funnel passengers through centrally located airports where one or two airlines dominate service
E) All of the above are correct.

Difficulty: **Moderate**

59. Which of the following has <u>not</u> occurred in the period following deregulation of the airlines?
A) A 20% reduction of airlines after adjusting for inflation.
B) A near doubling of the number of passengers traveling by air.
C) A loss of air service for most of the small cities that had service prior to deregulation.
D) An increase in the number of airlines competing on many heavy-traffic routes.
E) A decline in the quality of service in the form of lost luggage, cancelled flights, and delays at the airports.

Difficulty: **Moderate**

60. Forces which are contributing to the current merger movement include:
A) massive technological changes.
B) increased international competition.
C) deregulation.
D) Justice Department encouragement of mergers as a means of cutting costs in health and defense fields.
E) All of the above are correct.

Difficulty: **Moderate**

61. In contrast with the mergers of the late 1980s, most mergers today:
A) are strategic alliances among companies in the same line of business.
B) are junk-bond financed leveraged buyouts.

C) merge companies by taking on excessive debt.
D) are not intended to exploit new technologies.
E) are designed to sell the assets of companies being absorbed.

Difficulty: **Moderate**

62. The effects of the "voluntary" export restraints on Japanese automobiles to the U.S. from 1981 to 1985 did not include:
A) Japan gaining by exporting higher-priced autos.
B) U.S. automakers lowering break-even points and improving quality.
C) U.S. automakers passing on cost improvements to their customers.
D) saving 44,000 U.S. auto jobs at a cost of $100,000 each.
E) None of the above was an effect of voluntary export restraints.

Difficulty: **Moderate**

63. From 1977 to 1981:
A) U.S. automobile production fell by about one-third.
B) the share of auto sales taken up by imports increased from 18% to 29%.
C) employment of autoworkers in the U.S. fell by almost 300,000.
D) the Big Three suffered combined losses of $4 billion.
E) All of the above are correct.

Difficulty: **Moderate**

64. The strengths of the Herfindahl index include:
A) it gives more weight to large firms in the industry than to smaller ones.
B) it takes into account all information and the size distribution of firms.
C) it is based on the same view of competition as the four-firm concentration ratios.
D) it attaches more significance to the presence of barriers to entry than do concentration ratios.
E) (A) and (B) are correct.

Difficulty: **Moderate**

65. If a market is contestable, the market will be characterized by:
A) least-cost production methods and a competitive (normal) profit in the long run.
B) high barriers to entry and a small number of suppliers.
C) prices in excess of production costs and mergers leading to monopoly.
D) a large number of suppliers offering a homogeneous product.
E) (B) and (C) are correct.

Difficulty: **Moderate**

66. In a contestable market:
A) sunk costs may be high, but potential entrants are not blocked from entry and thus constitute competition to already existing firms.
B) sunk costs may be high, and therefore entry is blocked unless action is taken to break up existing firms and thereby create a contestable market.
C) zero sunk costs lead to effective competition among already existing firms.
D) free entry is guaranteed by the antitrust division of the Department of Justice.

E) None of the above is correct.

Difficulty: **Moderate**

67. Which of the following market structure descriptions is correct?
A) Monopolistic competition has many firms, a differentiated product, easy entry, and interdependence among firms.
B) Monopoly has one firm, a product with no good substitutes, difficult entry, and direct competition.
C) Oligopoly has few firms, homogenous or differentiated goods, difficult entry, and interdependence among firms.
D) Oligopoly has few firms, homogenous or differentiated goods, difficult entry, and no direct competition.
E) Monopolistic competition has many firms, a differentiated product, easy entry, and no interdependence among firms.

Difficulty: **Moderate**

68. The Lerner index is:
A) (P + MC)/P.
B) (P - MC)/Price elasticity of demand.
C) MC/Price elasticity of demand.
D) (P – MC)/P.
E) None of the above is correct.

Difficulty: **Moderate**

69. For a perfectly competitive firm, the Lerner index number is:
A) = 0.
B) = 1.
C) greater than zero, but less than 1.
D) infinity.
E) None of the above is correct.

Difficulty: **Moderate**

70. Which of the following is <u>not</u> a difficulty associated with the use of the Lerner index?
A) A firm with a great deal of monopoly power may practice limit pricing.
B) The index measures the monopoly power of the industry when what is needed is a measure of the monopoly power of the firm.
C) The index is applicable in a static context.
D) The index is not very useful when a firm's demand and cost functions shift over time.
E) All of the above are correct.

Difficulty: **Moderate**

71. Which of the following statements is correct?
A) The Lerner index measures the monopoly power of the industry.
B) The Herfindahl index measures the monopoly power of the firm.
C) The higher the value of the Lerner index the higher the profits of the firm.

D) The Lerner index may indicate the presence of substantial monopoly power but it should not be understood to imply that the firm is necessarily earning monopoly profits.
E) All of the above are correct.

Difficulty: **Moderate**

72. For a given value for the Herfindahl index, which of the following could cause the index to understate the relative importance of concentration in a domestic industry?
A) Imports are at significant levels in the market for the good being considered.
B) Transportation costs for the good are very high so the relevant market is local.
C) For the purpose of calculating the index, the product has been defined very narrowly.
D) The good is produced in an industry that has very low entry costs.
E) None of the above is correct.

Difficulty: **Moderate**

73. Which of the following statements about duopolists operating in a contestable market is correct?
A) Duopolists behave like perfect competitors facing horizontal demand curves.
B) Duopolists sell at a price that only covers average costs.
C) Duopolists do not collude to charge a higher price.
D) Duopolists face hit and run competition that will eliminate even transitory profits.
E) All of the above are correct.

Difficulty: **Moderate**

74. Which of the following statements about the theory of contestable markets is <u>not</u> correct?
A) The theory is criticized because entry and exit are seldom, if ever, costless.
B) The extreme assumptions of the theory are unrealistic.
C) The importance of the theory lies, in part, in its caution against uncritically accepting the view that a few firms are necessarily noncompetitive.
D) Because of its assumptions, the theory has no real world applications, although it does improve our conceptual understanding of oligopoly.
E) The importance of the theory lies, in part, in its suggestion that easy entry and exit can severely limit the exercise of monopoly power.

Difficulty: **Moderate**

75. The part of the social cost of monopoly which consists of monopolists failing to keep their costs down:
A) is called the dead-weight loss due to monopoly power.
B) is known as X-inefficiency.
C) is believed by economists to belong to a category of social costs which are insignificant in size.
D) are partially offset by the beneficial effect of monopolists installing excess capacity.
E) None of the above is correct.

Difficulty: **Moderate**

76. The thrust of Joseph Schumpeter's argument about the efficiency of oligopoly is that, oligopoly generates:

A) static inefficiency and dynamic efficiency.
B) static efficiency and dynamic inefficiency.
C) static and dynamic inefficiency.
D) static and dynamic efficiency.
E) Either (A) or (B) is correct depending on whether the short run or long run is discussed.

Difficulty: **Moderate**

77. According to Joseph Schumpeter, the process of creative destruction:
A) is attributed to the competition which occurs in markets with a large number of small firms where profits are eliminated rapidly.
B) involves the creation of new products and new production techniques.
C) describes the competition experiences by large firms with some monopoly power.
D) emphasizes the role of technological innovation instead of the entrepreneur.
E) Only (B) and (C) are correct.

Difficulty: **Moderate**

78. According to Joseph Schumpeter's concept of creative destruction:
A) dynamic efficiency is more important to long-term economic growth than static efficiency.
B) the replacement of aluminum with plastic in many uses is an example of creative destruction.
C) monopoly power must be eliminated and replaced with competition if technological innovation is to occur.
D) Only (A) and (B) are correct.
E) All of the above are correct.

Difficulty: **Moderate**

79. Regarding the relationships between monopoly power, technological innovation, and dynamic efficiency:
A) economists are in disagreement about whether monopoly power leads to faster rates of technological innovation and dynamic efficiency.
B) empirical evidence suggests that neither powerful monopolies nor perfect competition are models for dynamic efficiency.
C) empirical evidence suggests that monopoly power is conducive to innovation when technical progress is slow.
D) empirical evidence suggests that monopoly power is likely to retard innovations and growth when technical progress is rapid.
E) All of the above are correct.

Difficulty: **Moderate**

80. Conscious parallelism:
A) is the adoption of similar policies by oligopolists in view of their recognized interdependence.
B) was ruled illegal under section I of the Sherman Antitrust Act of 1890.
C) has been ruled by the courts to be proof of collusion.
D) (A) and (C) are correct.

E) None of the above is correct.

Difficulty: **Moderate**

81. Attempts to monopolize a market by engaging in acts which are aimed at eliminating one's competitors is illegal under:
A) Section I of the Sherman Antitrust Act.
B) Section II of the Sherman Antitrust Act.
C) Section 7 of the Clayton Act.
D) The Celler-Kefauver Act.
E) None of the above is correct.

Difficulty: **Easy**

82. The merger guidelines of the Justice Department includes:
A) challenging most horizontal mergers for which the post-merger Herfindahl index is less than 1000.
B) challenging all mergers for which the post-merger Herfindahl index is between 1000 and 1800.
C) challenging most mergers for which the post-merger Herfindahl index is between 1000 and 1800 and the increase in the post-merger index is more than 10 points.
D) challenging most mergers for which the post-merger Herfindahl index is over 1800 and the increase in the post-merger index is more than 50 points.
E) None of the above is correct.

Difficulty: **Moderate**

83. Which of the following would likely cause the Justice Department to bend its Herfindahl index guidelines?
A) entry into the industry is easy
B) foreign competition is strong
C) the merger will prevent the failure of the acquired firm
D) All of the above are correct.
E) None of the above is correct because the Justice Department does not bend its Herfindahl index guidelines.

Difficulty: **Moderate**

84. Which of the following statements is correct?
A) Empirical evidence suggests that market concentration decreased from the 1950s to 1980.
B) Herfindahl indices for world industries producing autos, petroleum, and aluminum increased between 1950 and 1970.
C) Herfindahl indices suggest the decline of international competition in automobiles and petroleum between 1950 and 1970, and then a resurgence of competition in the late 1980s.
D) Market concentration ratios and Herfindahl indices suggest contradictory or opposite trends in domestic and foreign competition form the 1950s to the 1970s.
E) All of the above are correct.

Difficulty: **Moderate**

85. Voluntary export restrictions:
A) are sometimes called "orderly marketing arrangements."
B) have been negotiated since the 1950s.
C) are administered by the exporting country.
D) encourage product upgrading as a way to get around the "voluntary" restriction.
E) All of the above.

Difficulty: **Moderate**

86. Assume that free trade exists and a country is importing a substantial number of automobiles in addition to producing them domestically. Other things being equal, if voluntary export restrictions (VER) on automobiles are introduced, which of the following will <u>not</u> occur?
A) There will be a decrease in domestic consumption of automobiles.
B) There will be an increase in domestic production of automobiles.
C) There will be a decrease in imports of automobiles.
D) The revenue effect or monopoly profits of the VER will be captured by the domestic government.
E) (A) and (D) are correct.

Difficulty: **Moderate**

87. In general, the practice of peak-load pricing by public utilities providing electricity would <u>not</u>:
A) increase consumer welfare.
B) cause an increase in consumer spending on electricity for peak and off-peak periods combined.
C) reflect the higher marginal cost of producing at peak loads.
D) allow public utilities to build smaller and more efficient plants in the long run.
E) equate the marginal benefit and marginal cost of producing and consuming electricity in peak-load and off-peak periods.

Difficulty: **Moderate**

88. Transfer pricing:
A) refers to the negotiation of a price for transferring shared of stock in one company into shares of stock of another company when a merger is taking place.
B) is required by the movement toward decentralization of large scale enterprises and the establishment of semi-autonomous profit centers.
C) must be done correctly or the Securities and Exchange commission will block the merger.
D) will result in average cost pricing if done correctly.
E) All of the above are correct.

Difficulty: **Moderate**

Short Essays

Give a brief answer to each of the following questions.

1. Why might the Herfindahl index overestimate the importance of concentration?

Answer: It does not take into account the existence of foreign competition and thus may overstate the importance of domestic concentration. It also does not represent the potential for new entrants, which influences the behavior of firms already in the market.

2. **Why might the route two airlines fly between Houston and Chicago approximately be a contestable market?**
Answer: To be contestable, it is necessary that free entry exists. In this case, other airlines could move planes over to this route if the two airlines flying the route began to charge prices for the flight that were well above costs.

3. **Suppose oligopoly sellers of widgets all raise their price in response to an increase in market demand for widgets. What significance does the fact that conscious parallelism is not illegal have in this context?**
Answer: Conscious parallelism means that oligopolists can adopt similar policies or responses to market conditions in view of the firms' mutual interdependence without fear that they will be prosecuted for collusion. In this situation it would mean that all the widget producers raising price simultaneously would not be interpreted as proof of collusive behavior to raise price.

4. **Explain the Averch-Johnson effect that results from public utility rates being set too high.**
Answer: The A-J effect is the overinvestment or underinvestment in plant and equipment resulting from wrong public-utility rates being set. If rates are set too high, public utilities will invest too heavily in fixed assets in order to generate a normal rate of return for the firm.

5. **What are the similarities and differences between the effect of a tariff and a "voluntary export restraint" on the part of another country?**
Answer: Tariffs and voluntary export restraints have the same economic effects. These include a consumption effect, which is the reduced domestic consumption, a production effect, which is the expansion of domestic production, a trade effect, which is the reduced level of imports, and deadweight loss. What is different is that the revenue effect of the restriction will be paid to foreign exporters rather than to the domestic government in the form of revenues from the tariff.

6. **"Peak-load pricing is just another way for public utilities to rationalize a rate hike at the expense of consumers." What is wrong with this statement?**
Answer: The marginal cost of producing electricity, for example, is higher in peak periods and lower in off-peak periods with a given plant size. Average pricing across peak and off-peak periods disguises this and causes resources to be misallocated, i.e., underallocated to electricity in off-peak periods and overallocated in peak-periods. Electricity is overpriced in the off-peak period and underpriced in the peak period. Generally, peak-load pricing would lower the consumer's total electric bill and improve consumer welfare.

Chapter 14:

Input Price and Employment Under Perfect Competition

Multiple-Choice

Choose the one alternative that best completes the statement or answers the question.

1. The demand for a factor of production is a derived demand, and so its demand exists because:
   A) it is not possible to measure the marginal productivity of the factor.
   B) the factor can be used to produce in some, but not all, industries.
   C) the user demands the factor because it will produce something that consumers will purchase.
   D) producers want the factor because it satisfies a consumer want directly.
   E) None of the above is correct.

   Difficulty: **Easy**

2. Suppose that a perfectly competitive firm in the output market hires labor in a perfectly competitive input market. Under which of the following conditions would the firm hire more labor?
   A) The VMP of labor = the price of output sold.
   B) The VMP of labor < the price of output sold.
   C) The VMP of labor > the wage rate paid to labor.
   D) The VMP of labor = the wage rate paid to labor.
   E) The wage rate paid to labor = the price of the output sold.

   Difficulty: **Easy**

3. In a competitive labor market, the industry's demand for labor is not the horizontal sum of each individual firm's demand for labor curve (as it is in the product market). The reason for this is that:
   A) any shift in the demand curve for the industry's output will have little, if any effect on the demand for labor.
   B) each firm in the industry hires labor up to the point where the marginal product of labor is zero.
   C) the demand for labor curves for all firms must be added vertically in order to get an industry demand curve.
   D) a change in quantity of labor used in the industry will cause a change in industry output, and this affects the price of the output sold as well as each firm's demand curve.
   E) None of the above is correct.

   Difficulty: **Moderate**

4. Suppose that you are the manager of the Widget Corp. and you use two variable inputs, X and Y, in the production of widgets. If:

$MP_X = 4$, $P_X = \$2$, $MP_Y = 10$, $P_Y = \$30$, and $MR = \$2$,

then in order to achieve the best profit for the Widget Corp., you should:
A) use more of X and less of Y.
B) use more of Y and less of X.
C) increase the use of both inputs.
D) decrease the use of both inputs.
E) None of the above is correct.

Difficulty: **Moderate**

5. Suppose that you face the situation where, using inputs A and B in production,

$MP_A = 4$, $MP_B = 3$, $P_A = \$12$, $P_B = \$9$, and $MR = \$3$.

In order to reach that combination of inputs A and B that maximizes profits, you should:
A) hire more of A and less of B.
B) hire more of B and less of A.
C) maintain the current level of input usage.
D) hire less of both inputs.
E) hire more of both inputs.

Difficulty: **Moderate**

6. Suppose that you manage the Acme Co. and you are faced with the following information about two inputs, A and B, that you use in the production of your output:

$MP_A = 2$, $MP_B = 8$, $P_A = \$8$, and $P_B = \$32$.

Assuming that you are producing your profit-maximizing level of output, the marginal revenue earned and the marginal cost incurred of producing the last unit of output that you sell is:
A) MR = \$1 and MC = \$5.
B) MR = \$4 and MC = \$4.
C) MR = \$8 and MC = \$8.
D) MR = \$2 and MC = \$2.
E) Not enough information is provided to determine an answer.

Difficulty: **Hard**

7. If a perfectly competitive firm maximizes its profits when the marginal product of the last unit of input is 1/3 and the price of the input is \$9 per unit, then the output price must be:
A) \$10 per unit.
B) \$9 per unit.
C) \$3 per unit.
D) \$27 per unit.

E) Not enough information is provided to determine.

Difficulty: **Hard**

8. The ratio of the wage rate paid to labor (w) and the rental rate paid to capital (r) is a measure of the relative cost of using:
A) both inputs.
B) labor and land.
C) capital compared to labor.
D) labor compared to capital.
E) None of the above is correct.

Difficulty: **Hard**

9. The demand for a factor of production is derived from the:
A) cost of the goods sold on the market.
B) supply of the factors of production.
C) demand for the goods produced by the factors of production.
D) supply of the goods produced by the factors of production.
E) None of the above is correct.

Difficulty: **Easy**

10. Suppose that capital and labor are relatively substitutable in production. A change in the wage-rental ratio will likely cause a change in the:
A) capital-labor ratio.
B) price of capital.
C) price of labor.
D) level of output produced.
E) None of the above is correct.

Difficulty: **Hard**

11. Other things constant, the firm's demand curve for the variable input labor depends on the:
A) marginal cost of the last unit of output sold.
B) marginal product of capital.
C) value of the marginal product of labor.
D) marginal product of labor only.
E) None of the above is correct.

Difficulty: **Moderate**

12. For a firm in perfect competition in the product market, the marginal revenue product of labor falls as more workers are hired because of:
A) diminishing marginal cost of production.
B) falling output price as more of the good is sold.
C) the falling output price of labor.
D) diminishing marginal product of labor.
E) None of the above is correct.

Difficulty: **Easy**

13. The demand for labor as a factor of production is affected by:
A) the productivity of labor.
B) the productivity of capital.
C) the market price of the output produced and sold.
D) changes in the price of capital relative to the price of labor.
E) All of the above affect the firm's demand for labor.

Difficulty: **Moderate**

14. An important determinant of the slope of a firm's demand (marginal revenue product) curve for labor is the:
A) price paid for each additional unit of labor.
B) substitutability between capital and labor.
C) amount of labor available for use in production.
D) price of other inputs besides labor.
E) None of the above is correct.

Difficulty: **Moderate**

15. Suppose that the Acme Corp. sells its output and buys its inputs in perfectly competitive markets. We can conclude that:
A) the wage rate paid to labor will be less than the value of the marginal product of labor.
B) the marginal product of labor times the price at which the firm sells its output is the firm's value of the marginal product of labor.
C) the value of the marginal product of labor is different from the marginal revenue product of labor under perfect competition.
D) the demand curve for the labor input will not be sensitive to changes in the price level.
E) None of the above is correct.

Difficulty: **Moderate**

16. Suppose that you hire labor and capital up to the point where $MP_L / P_L = MP_K / P_K$. If:

$MP_L = 4$, $P_L = \$16$, $MP_K = 5$, and $P_K = \$20$,

then what is the marginal cost of producing the last unit of output that you produce when you use the optimal amounts of capital and labor?
A) $0.25 per unit.
B) $12.00 per unit.
C) $4.00 per unit.
D) $24.00 per unit.
E) Not enough information is provided in order to determine an answer.

Difficulty: **Hard**

17. If a firm uses capital and labor to produce an output and capital is fixed in the short run, then when labor is increased by one additional unit and total revenue rises, the increase in total revenue that results from the additional unit of labor is the firm's:
A) marginal revenue.
B) marginal cost of labor.
C) marginal revenue product of labor.

D) marginal product of labor.
E) None of the above is correct.

Difficulty: **Moderate**

18. For either perfectly competitive or imperfectly competitive markets, the equation w = MR x MP_L, where w is the wage rate paid to labor, tells us that:
A) the price of the labor input is affected by changes in the marginal productivity of labor but not by the price of the output.
B) the firm will earn zero economic profit when the cost of an additional unit of labor equals the value created by the additional unit.
C) the firm hires labor up until the point where the marginal product of labor equals the real wage paid to labor.
D) the firm hires labor up until the point where the value created for the firm by the last worker is just sufficient to pay for the worker.
E) All of the above are correct.

Difficulty: **Moderate**

19. If the Acme Co. produces zaflings and faces a highly (but not perfectly) inelastic demand curve for its product, then an increase in the price of zaflings will, other things remaining constant:
A) reduce the quantity demanded of the labor input used to produce zaflings.
B) increase the quantity demanded for the labor input used to produce zaflings.
C) cause a reduction in the overall marginal productivity of labor.
D) cause an increase in the quantity supplied of labor in the zafling market.
E) None of the above is correct.

Difficulty: **Moderate**

20. Suppose that the demand curve for zaflings shifts to the right. It is most likely that the demand curve for labor used to produce zaflings will:
A) remain unchanged but the quantity demanded of labor will increase.
B) shift inward toward the origin and the wage rate paid to labor will fall.
C) shift to the right.
D) remain unchanged but the quantity demanded of labor to increase.
E) None of the above is correct.

Difficulty: **Moderate**

21. All of the following will increase the elasticity of demand for a factor of production <u>except</u>:
A) it becomes easier to substitute factors of production in the production process.
B) the demand for the product produced by the factor becomes less elastic.
C) it is easy to alter the ratios of the factors used to produce an output.
D) the payments required to secure the factor increase and assume a larger percentage of the firm's total operating budget.
E) None of the above is correct.

Difficulty: **Moderate**

22. The demand for a factor of production used to produce widgets will be relatively inelastic if:
A) there are other factors which can be easily substituted for the factor.

B) the demand for widgets is inelastic.
C) the factor proportions can be easily varied.
D) the market price of widgets is very high.
E) None of the above is correct.

Difficulty: **Moderate**

23. Suppose that there are many substitutes available for input X in the production of widgets. We would expect:
A) the elasticity of demand for input X to be greater than one.
B) a large quantity of input X to be used in the production of widgets.
C) the price of input X to be relatively high.
D) the demand for input X to be inelastic.
E) None of the above is correct.

Difficulty: **Moderate**

24. An individual's decision about the quantity of labor hours to supply for work depends on:
A) the cost of not working an extra hour.
B) the real wage rate.
C) the purchasing power of nominal wages.
D) the work-leisure trade-off.
E) All of the above are correct.

Difficulty: **Moderate**

25. In the short run, the quantity of labor supplied to an industry depends on the:
A) relative strengths of unions within the industry.
B) price of industry output relative to all other industries.
C) type of output produced.
D) wage rate paid in the industry relative to the wage rate paid in other industries.
E) None of the above is correct.

Difficulty: **Moderate**

26. Suppose that you have the choice of two jobs. Job A pays you a 15 percent higher wage than does job B; however, your working conditions in job A are not as desirable as in job B. The 15 percent higher wage is an equalizing differential and it is there to ensure that:
A) your nominal incomes in both job A and job B are equal.
B) your are equally satisfied in job A and job B.
C) your nominal income plus your happiness in job A equals your nominal income plus your happiness in job B.
D) the working conditions experienced in job A are at least as good as the conditions experienced in job B.
E) None of the above is correct.

Difficulty: **Moderate**

27. Suppose that Sam works as an accounting clerk and earns $17,000 per year. Sam has worked as a warehouse manager in the past, so he could manage warehouses again and earn $25,000 per year; however, he does not want to leave his current job. We can conclude that:
A) Sam is an irrational individual.

B) Sam is not maximizing his total utility.
C) Sam would have to be paid some positive equalizing differential to compensate for the perceived differences in job attractiveness.
D) Sam would be willing to pay a compensating differential to work as an accounting clerk.
E) None of the above is correct.

Difficulty: **Moderate**

28. Jan is a pediatrician with a practice in Charleston and earns $110,000 per year. She could move into an already established practice in New York and earn $195,000 per year. Jan remains in Charleston, so we can correctly conclude that she:
A) should move to New York because her salary almost doubles.
B) is not maximizing her total utility in her job.
C) is acting irrationally.
D) does not find the salary differential sufficient to entice her to move to New York.
E) None of the above is correct.

Difficulty: **Moderate**

29. Suppose that you used to work 40 hours per week when the wage rate was $5 per hour but you got a raise to $8 per hour and reduced your work effort to 37 hours per week. We can conclude that:
A) the substitution effect of a wage increase is greater than the income effect.
B) the income effect cancels out the substitution effect.
C) neither the income nor the substitution effect is important to you.
D) the income effect of the wage change is greater than the substitution effect.
E) None of the above is correct.

Difficulty: **Moderate**

30. Suppose that last week you worked 40 hours at your job and earned $4 per hour; however, you received a raise in your hourly wage to $5.50 per hour and now you are willing to work 45 hours per week. We can conclude that:
A) your real wage has decreased because rising wages are usually associated with rising prices.
B) the substitution effect of the wage increase is greater than the income effect.
C) the income effect of the wage increase is greater than the substitution effect.
D) the income and substitution effects of the wage increase cancel each other out.
E) None of the above is correct.

Difficulty: **Moderate**

31. Suppose that the wage rate paid to grocery clerks increases. When we look only at the substitution effect on the quantity of labor supplied, the increase in the wage rate results in:
A) a reduction in the number of hours worked.
B) the reduction in the price of an extra hour of leisure.
C) an increase in the number of hours worked and a reduction in the amount of leisure consumed.
D) a reduction in the price of working an extra hour.
E) None of the above is correct.

Difficulty: **Moderate**

32. Suppose that the wage rate paid workers in the garment industry rises. When we look only at the income effect, an increase in the wage rate:
A) always results in an increase in the amount of leisure consumed.
B) always results in more hours of work being offered.
C) always results in fewer hours of leisure being consumed.
D) results in more leisure being consumed, if leisure is a normal good.
E) None of the above is correct.

Difficulty: **Moderate**

33. Suppose that leisure is an inferior good. An increase in the wage rate will lead to:
A) a reduction in the number of hours worked.
B) an increase in the amount of leisure consumed, always.
C) an increase in the amount of leisure consumed only if the income effect dominates the substitution effect.
D) a reduction in the amount of leisure consumed, always.
E) None of the above is correct.

Difficulty: **Moderate**

34. Assume that leisure is a normal good. An increase in the wage rate will result in:
A) a reduction in the numbers of hours worked if the substitution effect dominates the income effect.
B) an increase in the number of hours worked only if the substitution effect is stronger than the income effect.
C) a reduction in the number of hours worked, always.
D) an increase in the number of hours worked, always.
E) None of the above is correct.

Difficulty: **Moderate**

35. Assume that leisure is a normal good. An increase in the wage rate will lead to:
A) an increase in leisure consumption, always.
B) an increase in the number of hours worked, always.
C) an increase in the number of hours worked only if the income effect dominates the substitution effect.
D) an increase in the amount of leisure consumed only if the income effect dominates the substitution effect.
E) None of the above is correct.

Difficulty: **Moderate**

36. Suppose that labor markets are perfectly competitive and are in equilibrium. If the overall market supply of labor is fixed in the short run, an increase in the demand for labor in one market will most likely result in:
A) an increase in the wages paid to workers in all industries.
B) no effect on the long-run equilibrium wage rate.
C) an increase in the wage rate paid to workers in the one industry but a decrease in the wage rate in all other industries.
D) decreases in the long-run wage rate in all other industries.

E) None of the above is correct.

Difficulty: **Moderate**

37. Suppose that an economy faces a backward-bending supply of labor curve at the equilibrium wage rate. If the government reduces the income tax on wages, we would expect to see:
A) a reduction in the quantity of labor supplied per year.
B) an increase in the quantity of labor supplied per year.
C) a reduction in the average wage rate received per worker.
D) no change in the quantity of labor supplied per year.
E) None of the above is correct.

Difficulty: **Hard**

38. A payment to a factor of production above the amount needed to obtain that factor for a particular task is known as:
A) surplus value.
B) an economic rent.
C) the marginal value product of the factor.
D) a compensating differential.
E) None of the above is correct.

Difficulty: **Easy**

39. In economics, a pure economic rent is a payment:
A) to the owners of a factor of production whose supply is perfectly inelastic.
B) that is made only to landowners.
C) to the owners of a factor of production whose supply is relatively inelastic.
D) only to the owners of land and capital because these are fixed.
E) None of the above is correct.

Difficulty: **Easy**

40. Some superstars in professional baseball and football earn very high salaries. Which one of the following statements is correct?
A) For the players, their economic rent earned is zero.
B) They are paid high salaries because of compensating or equalizing wage differentials.
C) Most of their salaries is an economic rent.
D) The opportunity cost of playing professional sports is equal to their salaries.
E) None of the above is correct.

Difficulty: **Moderate**

41. An economic rent that is paid to a factor of production is:
A) the opportunity cost of using the factor in the best alternative use.
B) **a surplus payment to the factor over its opportunity cost**.
C) a payment for the use of land.
D) payment for the use of factors whose supply is relatively elastic.
E) None of the above is correct.

Difficulty: **Easy**

42. In order for a factor of production to earn an economic rent, the supply curve of the factor must be:
    A) perfectly elastic.
    B) highly, but not perfectly, elastic.
    C) sloping upward and to the right.
    D) perfectly inelastic.
    E) approaching the location of the factor's long-run supply curve.

    Difficulty: **Easy**

43. If the average wage rate is higher in Germany than it is in Mexico and there is free mobility of labor, we would expect:
    A) workers to leave Mexico and move to Germany.
    B) Mexico to have a relative comparative advantage in the production of labor-intensive commodities.
    C) that as workers moved in, the average wage rate would fall in Germany.
    D) that as workers left, the average wage rate would rise in Mexico.
    E) All of the above to occur.

    Difficulty: **Moderate**

44. Which one of the following is most likely to reduce international wage differentials?
    A) limiting the number of immigrants who can come into a nation with relatively high wages
    B) restrictions on trade between nations
    C) an international redistribution of the factors of all of the factors of production except labor
    D) free trade between nations
    E) None of the above is correct.

    Difficulty: **Moderate**

45. The number of physicians per capita in the United States has increased sharply over the past decade. Because of this increase, we would expect to see:
    A) physicians' incomes increasing at a decreasing rate over the next few years.
    B) the price of medical services to decrease, or at least not increase, over the next few years.
    C) more medical services being recommended by physicians.
    D) attempts by physicians to restrict the entry into the medical profession.
    E) All of the above are correct.

    Difficulty: **Moderate**

46. Suppose that the federal government increases the minimum wage rate to $5.50 per hour. The result will be:
    A) an increase in the quantity of labor demanded.
    B) an increase in the demand for labor.
    C) an increase in the disemployment effect.
    D) workers willing to work fewer hours because of the income effect.
    E) None of the above is correct.

    Difficulty: **Moderate**

47. When a worker is paid 1.5 times her regular wage rate when she works overtime:
A) the substitution effect dominates the income effect.
B) the work effort will actually fall.
C) there will be a disemployment effect.
D) the income effect dominates the substitution effect.
E) None of the above is correct.

Difficulty: **Moderate**

48. Suppose that a worker was paid 1.5 times his hourly wage rate in order to entice the individual to work overtime. If the worker had to work ten extra hours per week, week after week, we would eventually expect to see:
A) the substitution effect always dominating the income effect.
B) the individual's work effort to continually rise.
C) the income effect start to dominate the substitution effect, after a period of time and assuming that leisure is a normal good.
D) the individual to reduce the number of hours worked to below those required for a normal work week.
E) None of the above to occur.

Difficulty: **Hard**

49. The marginal productivity theory of income distribution states that each input is paid a factor price that is equal to its:
A) average product.
B) marginal expenditure.
C) marginal product.
D) total product.
E) None of the above is correct.

Difficulty: **Easy**

50. Which one of the following would cause an increase in the unemployment gap?
A) the differences in the marginal productivity of different types of labor diminishes
B) an increase in the minimum wage
C) an increase in the natural rate of unemployment
D) All of the above are correct.
E) None of the above is correct.

Difficulty: **Moderate**

51. The recent trend toward increased hiring of temporary workers rather than permanent employees:
A) has not affected the ranks of professional as of yet.
B) appears to be limited to large firms such as multinationals while the trend in smaller firms has been just the opposite.
C) benefits workers who prefer the flexibility and diversity that temporary jobs provide.
D) is fueled by savings to employers in the form of lower nonwage benefits, but results in no savings in the form of lower wage payments.

E) None of the above is correct.

Difficulty: **Moderate**

52. According to the wage elasticity of demand data in the table below, in which of the following industries is it easier to substitute other inputs for labor?

WAGE ELASTICITY OF PRODUCTION WORKERS IN SOME U.S. MANUFACTURING INDUSTRIES

INDUSTRY	WAGE ELASTICITY
Food	-0.51
Chemicals	-0.65
Petroleum	-1.53
Instruments	-1.69
Stone, clay, glass	-1.97
Electrical machinery	-2.14
Fabricated metals	-2.37

A) Food
B) Chemicals
C) Instruments
D) Electrical machinery
E) Wage elasticity of demand data does not allow one to draw any conclusions about ease of substitution between inputs.

Difficulty: **Hard**

53. For the period 1960 to 1994, changes in labor force participation rates in the U.S. did not include an increase:
A) of about 10% for the population as a whole.
B) of about 11% for males.
C) of about 52% for all females.
D) from 32% to 60% for married females.
E) of about 13% for women not classified as married.

Difficulty: **Easy**

54. The factors driving the change in married female participation rates for the period included changes in:
A) family income.
B) child-rearing practices.
C) female educational levels.
D) relative productivity of married women in market jobs.
E) All of the above are correct.

Difficulty: **Easy**

55. In the face of an elasticity of supply for physicians' services ranging between –0.67 and –0.91, the enactment of Medicare and Medicaid and increased private insurance coverage for medical services led to:
A) price decreases which reduced the quantity supplied of physicians' services.
B) price increases which increased the quantity supplied of physicians' services.
C) price increases which decreased the quantity supplied of physicians' services.
D) price decreases which increased physicians' incomes.
E) physician behavior properly depicted by a positively sloped demand function.

Difficulty: **Moderate**

56. The backward-bending supply curve of labor would be reflected in a price elasticity of labor supply which is:
A) positive.
B) positive, but less than one.
C) zero.
D) negative.
E) Both (A) and (B) are correct.

Difficulty: **Moderate**

57. Empirical studies suggest that the price elasticity of labor supply is:
A) negative for adult males, and positive for adult females, teenagers, and for the total population.
B) positive for adult males, and negative for adult females, teenagers, and for the total population.
C) negative for adult males and adult females, and positive for teenagers, and for the total population.
D) negative for adult males, adult females, and for the total population, and negative for teenagers.
E) negative for the total population and all population subgroups.

Difficulty: **Moderate**

58. It had been argued that a gap which has developed between productivity and real wages in recent years is more apparent than real. Which of the following would justify this skepticism?
A) The gap disappears if one looks at real compensation and productivity over a longer time period.
B) The share of GDP going to labor has been increasing dramatically for several decades.
C) Declining fringe benefits account for the gap so if one looks specifically at real wages there is no gap.
D) Inflation-adjusted wages in recent years have grown at a faster pace than productivity.
E) All of the above are correct.

Difficulty: **Moderate**

59. A labor market is imperfect if:
A) workers lack information on wages in other occupations.
B) workers lack information on job opportunities in other occupations.
C) workers are unwilling to move to other jobs and occupations.

D) There are labor unions and large employers able to affect wages.
E) All of the above are correct.

Difficulty: **Moderate**

60. Which of the following have contributed to international wage convergence among industrial nations?
A) international labor migrations
B) international capital flows
C) international trade
D) All of the above are correct.
E) None of the above is correct because significant wage convergence has been effectively blocked by immigration and trade restrictions.

Difficulty: **Moderate**

61. If trade reduced wages in a high-wage country:
A) then the high-wage country ends up gaining nothing by trading with low-wage countries.
B) labor will still automatically make net gains through market forces just as capital owners do.
C) the high-wage economy will no longer be able to exploit its comparative advantage and that will subsequently lead to lower incomes for owners of both labor and capital.
D) the mechanism of specialization according to comparative advantage will increase the returns to capital by an amount greater than the fall in wages.
E) taxes on capital owners will automatically increase and leave both the owners of capital and labor worse off than they would have been if no trade had taken place.

Difficulty: **Moderate**

62. Which of the following is <u>not</u> correct regarding the research on the impact of the minimum wage conducted by Professors David Card and Alan Krueger (the latter is now chief economist of the U.S. Department of Labor)?
A) They found that the 1990 and 1991 increases in the minimum wage did not reduce employment.
B) They found that an increase in the minimum wage in New Jersey may have actually increased employment.
C) They have been severely criticized in other recent work done by economists at Texas A&M University, the University of Chicago, and the Federal Reserve who support the traditional claims about the expected effect of increases in the minimum wage, i.e., decreased employment.
D) Professors Card and Krueger found that in accordance with the predictions of economic theory, employment fell when the minimum wage was increased.
E) Professors Card and Krueger reached conclusions that are at odds with the employment experience of European countries with much higher minimum wages.

Difficulty: **Moderate**

63. For a firm which is a perfect competitor in the input market, marginal expenditure:
A) is equal to the market price of the input.
B) is the extra cost of hiring another unit of input.
C) is represented by an infinitely inelastic supply curve of the input.
D) All of the above are correct.

E) Only (A) and (B) are correct.

Difficulty: **Easy**

64. Assume the firms in industry X are perfect competitors in the input market and use more than one variable input. Under these circumstances, in industry X.
A) the firm's demand curve for a variable input will not be the marginal revenue curve for the input, and the market demand curve for the variable input will not be the horizontal summation of each firm's demand curve for the variable input.
B) the firm's demand curve for a variable input will be the marginal revenue curve for the input, but the market demand curve for the variable input will not be the horizontal summation of each firm's demand curve for the variable input.
C) the firm's demand curve for a variable input will not be the marginal revenue curve for the input, but the market demand curve for the variable input will be the horizontal summation of each firm's demand curve for the variable input.
D) the firm's demand curve for a variable input will be the marginal revenue curve for the input, and the market demand curve for the variable input will be the horizontal summation of each firm's demand curve for the variable input.
E) the firm's demand curve is indeterminate, but the market demand curve for the variable input will not be the horizontal summation of each firm's demand curve for the variable input.

Difficulty: **Hard**

Assume that a firm is a perfect competitor in the output market and input market, that the firm employs only one variable input, and that the production function for that variable input is set out in the table below. Given that the marginal resource cost of labor is $15 and the price of product x is $5:

L	Q_X	MP_L
2	12	7
3	18	6
4	23	5
5	27	4
6	30	3
7	32	2
8	33	1

65. What is the profit-maximizing amount of labor to employ?
A) 3
B) 4
C) 5
D) 6
E) 7

Difficulty:

66. Using the table above and the assumptions set out in the previous question, what will be the reduction in the firm's profits if it employs two units of labor beyond the level of use indicated by the rule for profit maximization?
A) $5.00
B) $10.00

C) $15.00
D) $20.00
E) $25.00

Difficulty: **Hard**

67. Assume both labor and capital are variable inputs. If they are also complementary inputs:
A) a decrease in the wage rate will cause the firm to hire more labor and more capital.
B) a decrease in the wage rate will cause the firm to hire more labor and less capital.
C) a decrease in the wage rate will cause the firm to hire more labor while leaving the amount of capital employed constant.
D) a decrease in the wage rate will cause the firm to hire the same quantity of labor but more capital due to the effects the status of capital has as a complementary input.
E) None of the above is correct.

Difficulty: **Moderate**

68. Assume both labor and capital are variable inputs. If labor and capital are substitutes:
A) a decrease in the wage rate will ultimately result in a rightward shift of the MRP_L curve.
B) a decrease in the wage rate will cause the firm to hire more labor and less capital.
C) a decrease in the wage rate will ultimately result in a leftward shift of the MRP_K curve.
D) All of the above are correct.
E) Only (A) and (B) are correct.

Difficulty: **Moderate**

69. Assume both labor and capital are variable inputs. If labor and capital are complementary inputs:
A) a decrease in the wage rate will ultimately result in a rightward shift of the MRP_L curve.
B) a decrease in the wage rate will ultimately result in a rightward shift of the MRP_K curve.
C) a decrease in the wage rate will cause the firm to hire more labor and less capital.
D) All of the above are correct.
E) Only (A) and (B) are correct.

Difficulty: **Moderate**

70. A backward-bending supply curve of labor appears when:
A) the substitution effect of a wage increase is greater than the income effect.
B) the income effect of a wage increase is greater than the substitution effect.
C) the income effect of a wage increase exactly offsets the substitution effect.
D) the income effect of a wage increase disappears.
E) (B), (C), and (D) are correct.

Difficulty: **Moderate**

71. In economics a quasi-rent:
A) refers to a payment for the use of a natural resource which also serves as partial payment for capital.
B) is a payment made to a temporarily fixed input.
C) is another name for the returns to fixed inputs in the short run.

D) need not be made in order for fixed inputs to be supplied in the short run.
E) (B), (C), and (D) are correct.

Difficulty: **Moderate**

72. Wage differences associated with different skills and education are:
A) compensating differentials.
B) caused by the existence of noncompeting groups.
C) due to market imperfections.
D) caused by an unwillingness to change jobs or occupations.
E) None of the above is correct.

Difficulty: **Easy**

73. Wage differences which are associated with the nonmonetary differences among jobs are:
A) compensating differentials.
B) caused by the existence of noncompeting groups.
C) due to market imperfections.
D) caused by an unwillingness to change jobs or occupations.
E) None of the above is correct.

Difficulty: **Easy**

74. Which of the following statements regarding potential employer responses to an increase in the minimum wage is <u>not</u> correct?
A) Employers cut fringe benefits.
B) Employers increase on-the-job training to make employment of unskilled workers profitable.
C) Employers increase their use of more capital-intensive production techniques.
D) Employers suspend apprenticeship programs.
E) All of the above are correct.

Difficulty: **Easy**

Short Essays

Give a brief answer to each of the following questions.

1. **In a perfectly competitive input market, if labor is not the only variable input then the firm's demand curve for labor is not the MRP_L. Explain.**
Answer: If labor and capital are complements, the increased use of labor due to a lower wage rate will increase the MRP_K and the firm will purchase more capital. The latter will increase the MRP_L and lead to a greater increase in the use of labor than indicated by the original MRP_L. The same is true if labor and capital are substitutes, because a lower wage rate will shift the MRP curves for other inputs to the left and the MRP_L to the right.

2. **In a perfectly competitive input market, why is the market demand curve for labor not simply the horizontal summation of individual firms' demand curves for labor?**

Answer: Because as the wage rate falls and all firms employ more of this input, the output of the commodity increases and the market price of it falls. This will shift the MRP_L to the left for each firm not because of changes in MP_L with different uses of other inputs, but because in perfect competition P = MR and $MRP_L = MR \times MP_L$.

3. **Explain how a supply curve of labor can be "backward-bending."**
Answer: As wage rate increases it produces a substitution and an income effect. Work time becomes more valuable relative to leisure time so the person substitutes work for leisure. However, the wage increase also produces an income effect, which causes a person to want to "purchase" more leisure time given that it is a normal good. If the income effect is larger than the substitution effect the person will work for fewer hours rather than more hours when the wage rate increases.

4. **If the average professional basketball player would continue to play for one-third of the salary he now earns, then in economic terms what is the athlete earning? What do you think the economic purpose of such payments are, given that they differ greatly in size across all players? (Hint: What determines whether Shaq will play for one team or another?)**
Answer: The player is receiving large economic rents, or the portion of the payment to a supplier that exceeds the amount necessary to keep the input in its present use, i.e., professional basketball in this case. One of the economic functions of rents in professional basketball is to allocate players between teams. Thus, higher rents are paid to some players than to others as a way of placing them on the team where their services are most highly valued.

5. **What is the difference between the disemployment effect and the unemployment gap caused by a minimum wage?**
Answer: The difference is the increase in quantity of labor supplied relative to equilibrium quantity that is due to a minimum wage set above the market clearing level. The unemployment gap (the difference between the supply of labor and the demand for labor at the minimum wage) consists of reduced employment or the disemployment effect (a movement along the demand for labor curve as a result of the wage increase), and the increase in quantity supplied of labor at the higher wage rate (a movement along the supply of labor curve as a result of the wage increase).

Chapter 15:

Input Price and Employment Under Imperfect Competition

Multiple-Choice

Choose the one alternative that best completes the statement or answers the question.

1. The marginal revenue product of labor is the change in the firm's revenue resulting from:
A) selling one more unit of its output.
B) hiring and using one more unit of labor.
C) producing one more unit of output.
D) selling one less unit of the unit.
E) None of the above is correct.

Difficulty: **Easy**

2. The marginal revenue product of labor is found by multiplying the marginal:
A) product of labor time the wage rate.
B) value of the output produced times the number of workers employed.
C) cost of producing an extra unit of output times the number of laborers hired.
D) product of labor times the marginal revenue generated when the extra output is sold.
E) None of the above is correct.

Difficulty: **Easy**

3. The imperfectly competitive firm hires an optimal number of workers when the marginal expense of hiring an additional unit of labor equals:
A) the marginal revenue product of labor.
B) the marginal cost of labor.
C) the marginal product of labor.
D) the market price of the output produced and sold.
E) None of the above is correct.

Difficulty: **Easy**

4. As the marginal expense of hiring labor increases, the typical firm operating in an imperfectly competitive market will employ:
A) more workers.
B) fewer workers.
C) less capital.
D) the same number of workers because the marginal product of labor also changes.
E) None of the above is correct.

Difficulty: **Easy**

5. In the output market, the imperfectly competitive firm's demand for labor curve slopes downward and to the right because:
   A) the wage rate paid to labor falls, so the quantity demanded of labor rises.
   B) in order to sell additional units of its output, the firm must lower output price.
   C) labor's marginal product falls as additional units of labor are hired to produce more output.
   D) (A) and (C) are correct.
   E) (B) and (C) are correct.

   Difficulty: **Moderate**

6. If an industry's demand curve for labor indicates that a change in wages will result in a very small change in the quantity demanded of labor, we would expect:
   A) the demand curve for the industry's output to be inelastic.
   B) a union supply of labor curve of labor to be inelastic.
   C) an attempt by unions to restrict the supply of labor to result in many of its members being laid-off.
   D) the demand curve for labor to be relatively flat.
   E) None of the above is correct.

   Difficulty: **Moderate**

7. Suppose that the Electrical Workers Union requires a five-year apprenticeship period before granting full membership to new workers. The most likely reason for this long apprenticeship period is:
   A) to ensure that some relatively low paid electricians are qualified for jobs that do not require a high degree of specialization.
   B) to restrict entry into the trade and thus maintain relatively high wages.
   C) to assure the market that a large, highly trained supply of electricians will always be available.
   D) to ensure that the quality of electrical work is consistently high.
   E) None of the above is correct.

   Difficulty: **Moderate**

8. Suppose that the labor market servicing the widget industry is initially perfectly competitive but is then unionized. Assuming that the union secures a higher wage, we can expect:
   A) the quantity demanded of labor to fall and the quantity supplied of labor to increase.
   B) both the quantity demanded and the quantity supplied of labor to fall.
   C) the quantity demanded of labor to rise but the quantity supplied to fall.
   D) both the quantity demanded and the quantity supplied of labor to rise.
   E) None of the above is correct.

   Difficulty: **Moderate**

9. If the Acme Co. is the only user of a particular type of labor, then each unit of labor that the company hires adds:
   A) labor's price per unit to the firm's total cost.
   B) less than labor's price per unit to the firm's total cost.
   C) more than labor's price to the marginal revenue of the company when an extra unit of output is sold.

D) more than labor's per unit price to the firm's total cost.
E) None of the above is correct.

Difficulty: **Moderate**

10. For a monopsonist, the cost of hiring an additional unit of labor:
A) is the same as the wage rate paid to the additional worker.
B) is equal to the marginal revenue product generated by the extra worker.
C) is the wage paid to the extra worker minus the charge in the wage expense that is incurred when all previous workers' are raised.
D) is the wage paid to the extra worker plus the increase in wage costs that arises because all previously employed workers must now be paid the higher wage rate.
E) None of the above is correct.

Difficulty: **Moderate**

11. The profit maximizing monopsonist will hire labor up to the point where:
A) the wage rate paid to the last worker equals the marginal revenue generated for the firm by the last worker.
B) the marginal revenue of the last unit of output sold equals the marginal cost of producing the last unit.
C) the marginal revenue product of the last worker hired equals the marginal expenditure on hiring him.
D) the average total cost of producing the optimal level of output is at a minimum.
E) None of the above is correct.

Difficulty: **Moderate**

12. When compared to the wage rate established by a perfectly competitive labor market, if workers begin to compete for the reduced number of jobs offered by a monopsonist, the equilibrium wage will:
A) be lower because the monopsonist will hire additional workers only at lower wages.
B) be lower because the monopsonist will hire fewer workers at its optimal output level.
C) be higher because the monopsonist raises all workers wages.
D) be higher because the firm earns excess profits.
E) None of the above is correct.

Difficulty: **Hard**

13. When there is only one buyer of a particular good or factor of production in the market, the buyer is known as:
A) a monopolist.
B) an oligopsonist.
C) a monopsonistic competitive industry.
D) a monopsonist.
E) an oligopolist.

Difficulty: **Easy**

14. If the ACME Co. is an imperfect competitor in the output market, then it will hire variable inputs up to the point where:

A) the marginal product of each input is equal.
B) the input price equals the input's marginal revenue product.
C) the input price equals the marginal product of the input times the price at which the output is sold.
D) the input price equals the ratio of each input's marginal product to the firm's marginal revenue.
E) the marginal product of each input is zero.

Difficulty: **Moderate**

15. Suppose that the market for input X is imperfectly competitive. The profit-maximizing firm will hire inputs X up to the point where:
A) the marginal product of X is equal to the marginal products of all other inputs.
B) the marginal product of X times the per unit price of X equals the firm's marginal revenue.
C) the marginal product of X times the firm's marginal revenue equals the input price of X.
D) the input price of X times marginal revenue equals the marginal product of X.
E) the marginal product of X equals the input price of X times the firm's marginal cost.

Difficulty: **Moderate**

16. Suppose that the ABC Co. is in a perfectly competitive industry that is suddenly changed into an imperfectly competitive one. The most likely outcome would be:
A) a fall in the level of inputs employed, and each unit of the input would be paid less than the value of its marginal product.
B) the level of inputs employed would not change, but each unit employed would receive less than the value of its marginal product.
C) the level of inputs employed would not change, and each unit of the input would continue to receive the value of its marginal product.
D) the level of inputs employed would fall, but each unit of input employed would receive the value of its marginal product.
E) None of the above is correct.

Difficulty: **Moderate**

17. The Deep Pit Mining Co. owns all of the houses and stores in the small town of Deep Pit, West Virginia. In fact, the Deep Pit Mining Company is the only employer of labor for miles around. This company town is an example of:
A) a pure monopoly.
B) an underdeveloped region.
C) a monopsony.
D) a pure oligopoly.
E) monopolistic competition.

Difficulty: **Moderate**

18. When we examine the model of a monopsonistic buyer, one of the key features of the model is that:
A) the monopsonist can buy all of any input it wants at the prevailing input price.
B) there is no competition in the output market.
C) the output market is characterized by product differentiation.

D) the monopsonist will always pay a higher wage than will the competitive buyer.
E) the supply curve of the input facing the monopsonistic buyer is the market supply curve of the input.

Difficulty: **Moderate**

19. If ten units of labor will be supplied for a wage rate of $10 per unit, and eleven units of labor will be supplied for $15 per unit, we can conclude that:
A) the marginal expenditure on the eleventh worker is less than $10.
B) the marginal expenditure on the eleventh worker is equal to $15.
C) the marginal expenditure on the eleventh worker is between $10 and $15.
D) the marginal expenditure on the eleventh worker is greater than $15.
E) it is impossible to make a statement about the marginal expenditure on the eleventh worker from the information provided.

Difficulty: **Moderate**

20. The marginal expenditure on labor curve is based on the assumption that:
A) all workers are paid the same wage rate.
B) all occupations are equally desirable; there are no equalizing differentials.
C) the market supply curve for labor is perfectly elastic.
D) all workers have the same productivity.
E) None of the above is correct.

Difficulty: **Moderate**

21. A difference between perfect competition and monopsony in the input market is that:
A) it is possible for a monopsonist to buy all of a particular input that it wants without affecting the input's price.
B) under perfect competition, all inputs are the same.
C) under perfect competition, the wage paid to labor, or any other input, is the same.
D) each firm under perfect competition faces a perfectly elastic supply curve for the input.
E) the level of employment of the resource will be less under perfect competition.

Difficulty: **Moderate**

22. Suppose that the market supply curve for a factor of production is an upward sloping straight line. The marginal expenditure curve for the input:
A) is the same as the factor supply curve.
B) lies below the factor supply curve.
C) lies above the factor supply curve and is everywhere steeper than the supply curve.
D) may or may not lie above the factor supply curve.
E) None of the above is correct.

Difficulty: **Moderate**

23. Suppose that a monopsonist practices wage discrimination against its workers. If the employer is able to practice perfect wage discrimination, then the marginal expenditure curve:
A) will lie above the factor supply curve.

B) may be either above or below the factor supply curve.
C) will lie below the factor supply curve.
D) will lie on top of the factor supply curve.
E) None of the above is correct.

Difficulty: **Hard**

24. A monopsonist's marginal expenditure on labor is defined as the:
A) (marginal product of labor) X (output price).
B) (marginal product of labor) X (input price).
C) (change in total cost)/(change in output).
D) (change in total labor cost)/(change in labor usage).
E) (marginal product of labor) X (marginal revenue).

Difficulty: **Moderate**

25. In a market with a monopsonistic buyer, the amount of labor employed and the wage rate will be less than in a competitive market because:
A) the supply of labor is more elastic under monopsony.
B) the monopsonist takes into account that the extra expenditure for the input will be greater than the input price, or ME > W.
C) there is always some excess capacity on competitive markets.
D) in competitive markets, labor is not homogeneous.
E) None of the above is correct.

Difficulty: **Moderate**

26. Suppose that a monopsonist produces one product and uses only one variable input. The firm will maximize its profits when the input is employed up to the point where:
A) the marginal revenue product curve intersects the marginal expenditure curve.
B) the marginal revenue product curve intersects the marginal cost curve.
C) the marginal revenue product curve intersects the input supply curve.
D) the marginal revenue product curve intersects the average total cost curve.
E) the marginal revenue curve intersects the marginal cost curve.

Difficulty: **Moderate**

27. When the monopsonist maximizes profits, it will:
A) pay higher wages than would be the case under perfect competition.
B) pay the same wage rate that the perfect competitor pays.
C) employ less labor than would be the case under perfect competition.
D) employ more labor than would be the case under perfect competition.
E) employ the same amount of labor as does the competitive firm.

Difficulty: **Moderate**

28. Suppose that a market existed where there was only one buyer of a particular product and only one seller of the product. This market would be classified as being:
A) an oligopsony.
B) a monopoly.
C) a monopsony.
D) a monopsonistic competitive.

E) a bilateral monopoly.

Difficulty: **Easy**

29. In an input market that is imperfectly competitive, it is the case that:
A) the marginal expenditure on the input equals the price of the input.
B) the marginal expenditure on the input is greater than the price of the input.
C) the marginal expenditure on the input is less than the price of the input.
D) the marginal expenditure on the input equals the value of the marginal product of the input.
E) None of the above is correct.

Difficulty: **Moderate**

30. The monopsonistic exploitation of an input is equal to:
A) the marginal expenditure on the input minus the competitive price of the input.
B) the competitive price of the input minus the marginal expenditure on the input.
C) the marginal revenue product of the input minus the competitive price of the input.
D) the marginal revenue product of the input minus the marginal expenditure on the input.
E) None of the above is correct.

Difficulty: **Moderate**

31. Suppose that the price of input A rises. Other things constant, we can conclude that:
A) the marginal revenue product of complementary input B falls.
B) the marginal revenue product of substitute input C increases.
C) the marginal revenue product curve for input A shifts to the left.
D) the firm will hire fewer units of input A.
E) All of the above are correct.

Difficulty: **Moderate**

32. Suppose that firm A is a monopsony in the market for input L and the XYZ union is a monopoly is the sale of input L. Other things constant, the equilibrium price and quantity used of input L well depend on:
A) the market forces of demand and supply of input L.
B) the profit maximizing marginal conditions for both the monopolist and the monopsonist.
C) the marginal revenue product of input L.
D) the relative bargaining strength of the monopolist and the monopsonist.
E) None of the above is correct.

Difficulty: **Moderate**

33. Suppose that the government sets the minimum price of an input at the point where the marginal revenue product curve intersects the market supply curve for the input. We can conclude that, other things remaining constant, the monopsonist:
A) will be willing to pay a higher wage than that established by the government in order to get its profit maximizing quantity of the input.
B) hire additional units of the input if MRC > MRP.

C) behave as a perfect competitor in the input market and hire that level of input where MRP = MRC.
D) will always hire labor that results in a surplus of output on the market.
E) None of the above is correct.

Difficulty: **Moderate**

34. If there is free mobility of labor in the international labor markets and the wage paid to labor input A is in the country of Betania is greater than the wage paid for input A in the country of Alphania, then other things constant, we would expect to see:
A) a brain drain from Alphania to Betania.
B) input A would move from Alphania to Betania.
C) eventually wage differentials to disappear.
D) the wage for input A to rise in Betania.
E) All of the above to occur.

Difficulty: **Moderate**

35. Other things constant, a labor union can try to increase the wages paid to its members by all of the following except:
A) making work for some members where there is not really a demand for the members' labor.
B) increasing the productivity of its members.
C) restricting the supply of workers offered to employers
D) bargaining with an employer for a wage rate that is above the equilibrium wage rate.
E) increasing the educational and skill level of its members.

Difficulty: **Moderate**

36. The United Auto Workers Union can increase the average wage rate paid to its members by:
A) increasing the skill level of its members.
B) increasing the demand for its members.
C) restricting the supply of workers to the auto industry.
D) bargaining for higher wages that are above the equilibrium level.
E) All of the above.

Difficulty: **Moderate**

37. Suppose that the ABC Union opposes the increase in the price of complementary labor represented by the XYZ Union. One reason why the ABC Union opposes the increase in the price of complementary labor is that this price increase will:
A) increase the supply of competing inputs because of the output effect.
B) increase the supply of competing inputs because of the substitution effect.
C) decrease the demand for the labor represented by the ABC Union because of the output effect.
D) decrease the demand of the labor represented by the ABC Union because of the substitution effect.
E) None of the above is correct.

Difficulty: **Hard**

38. Suppose that the market for labor used to produce widgets is characterized as a bilateral monopoly. The wage rate for labor used to produce widgets:
A) will be higher than it would be if the marker was perfectly competitive.
B) is indeterminate.
C) will be established at the level desired by the producer of widgets who hires the labor.
D) will be established by the seller of the labor used to produce widgets.
E) None of the above is correct.

Difficulty: **Moderate**

39. If a monopsonist hires labor in a nonunionized market, the employer will:
A) pay a wage that is higher than the marginal revenue product of labor.
B) pay a wage that is equal to the marginal expenditure on the hiring of the last worker.
C) pay the same wage rate but hire fewer workers than if the market was purely competitive.
D) pay a wage rate that is less than the marginal revenue product of labor.
E) None of the above is correct.

Difficulty: **Moderate**

40. An important feature or characteristic of a monopsonistic labor market is that the employer:
A) faces a supply of labor curve that is perfectly elastic.
B) is able to hire as many workers as she wants at the going market wage rate.
C) faces a vertical supply of labor curve.
D) faces an upward-sloping supply of labor curve.
E) pays a wage rate that is equal to the marginal revenue product of the last worker hired.

Difficulty: **Moderate**

41. In many of the urban areas of the United States, the unemployment rate of black youths is three times that of white youths. This is a reflection of:
A) wage discrimination.
B) job discrimination.
C) sexual discrimination.
D) race discrimination.
E) price discrimination.

Difficulty: **Easy**

42. Other things remaining the same, if educational and employment discrimination against minority groups in the United States ended, we would expect to see gross domestic product:
A) decline because minority workers who were trained would force some workers out of their current jobs.
B) decline because of the increased costs from training workers as well as increases in the cost of living.
C) increase because the minorities' spending on consumer goods would rise.
D) increase because of the increased productivity of the labor force.
E) Do none of the above.

Difficulty: **Moderate**

43. To the economist, any type of discrimination:
A) will cause actual gross domestic product to be below its potential level.
B) no longer exists in the United States.
C) will not cause a gap between actual and potential gross domestic product.
D) will serve as an incentive for those discriminated against to work harder and gain more education so that the discrimination will no longer occur.
E) None of the above is correct.

Difficulty: **Moderate**

44. Employers with some monopsony power, unlike perfectly competitive employers, can:
A) pay their workers a wage that is less than their marginal revenue product.
B) always discriminate in the wages that they pay in order to ensure that they gain some monopsonistic exploitation.
C) hire as many workers as they want to at the prevailing market wage rate.
D) be expected to try to hire that quantity of workers that will maximize their profits.
E) always earn an economic profit.

Difficulty: **Moderate**

45. In most states, an employer can legally follow a policy of:
A) refusing to hire female workers.
B) paying workers different wages based on race or sex.
C) discharging workers because they join a union.
D) paying workers different wages based on age.
E) None of the above is correct.

Difficulty: **Easy**

46. If only a few firms buy or hire a particular input that is used in their production process, then the market for the inputs is best described as a(n):
A) monopoly.
B) monopsony.
C) competitive market.
D) oligopsony.
E) oligopoly.

Difficulty: **Easy**

47. Many states require licenses to practice in certain occupations, and do not recognize those obtained in other states. If all states did recognize such licenses from other states, the likely result would be:
A) a decreased degree of competition in these labor markets.
B) a greater degree of variation in the incomes in those occupations across states.
C) less migration of workers in those occupations to other states.
D) the reduction and ultimately the elimination of all interstate differences in fees and incomes in those occupations.
E) None of the above is likely to occur.

Difficulty: **Moderate**

48. The XYZ Co. is an imperfect competitor in the product market. For this company, the profit-maximizing rule requires that:
A) MRP = MC(P) and also that MRP = VMP.
B) MRP = MP(MR) and also that MRP = VMP.
C) MRP = MP(MR) and also that MRP < VMP.
D) MRP = MC(MR) and also that MRP > VMP.
E) None of the above is true.

Difficulty: **Moderate**

49. Suppose that blatant discrimination based on both race and gender exists in the economy of Betania. Other things constant, we would expect:
A) the distribution of national income to be affected, but not the total amount of income.
B) the economy to be operating at some point below its production possibilities frontier.
C) the total size of national income, but not its distribution, to be affected.
D) the overall level of aggregate output to increase.
E) None of the above is likely to occur.

Difficulty: **Moderate**

50. Suppose that ME/MP for labor is greater than ME/MP for capital. Other things constant, in order to maximize profits the firm should:
A) hire less labor.
B) hire or rent more capital.
C) hire more labor and rent less capital.
D) hire more labor as well as more capital.
E) hire less labor and hire or rent more capital.

Difficulty: **Hard**

51. Labor markets experiencing a dynamic disequilibrium:
A) have shortages which lead to relative wage decreases that clear the market in the short run but which also generate such large decreases in supply of this type of labor that in the long run a shortage reemerges.
B) have surpluses which lead to relative wage decreases that clear the market in the short run but which also generate such large decreases in supply of the type of labor that in the long run a shortage emerges.
C) have shortages which lead to relative wage increases that clear the market in the short run but which are insufficient to attract additional labor in the long run thus leading the market back into a shortage.
D) have surpluses which lead to relative wage increases that clear the market in the short run but which are insufficient to reduce the supply of labor in the long run thus leading the market back into a surplus.
E) None of the above is correct.

Difficulty: **Moderate**

52. Labor markets which tend to experience dynamic disequilibriums:
A) involve types of labor which require short training periods.
B) involve low productivity workers who cannot escape the cycle of surpluses and shortages that emerge and reemerge.

C) are populated almost exclusively by married adult females who are heads of households.
D) All of the above are correct.
E) None of the above is correct.

Difficulty: **Moderate**

53. Reciprocity agreements between states which recognize the occupational licenses of each others' dentists and lawyers:
A) have not caused the incomes of dentists and lawyers in these states to be lower than those in states which have no reciprocity agreements.
B) would encourage labor migration and tend to equalize earnings of these professionals across states with reciprocity agreements.
C) would increase the degree of competition in dentistry and law in both states.
D) are opposed by the professional groups involved which lobby to prevent their introduction.
E) All of the above are correct.

Difficulty: **Moderate**

54. In the period in which the "reserve clause" was used in every professional baseball player's contract:
A) baseball teams competed heavily for players driving up their wage rates and necessitating the use of salary caps to save some baseball teams from financial ruin.
B) monopsonistic exploitation by team owners led to all baseball players being paid much less then their net marginal revenue product.
C) team owners maintained, what was in effect, a cartel of employers who paid their better players a wage considerably less than their net marginal revenue products.
D) players became the exclusive property of the teams they played for, after being in the league for seven years.
E) "free agency" was introduced to restrict competition after market experiments allowing movement of players across teams resulted in substantial losses for smaller teams.

Difficulty: **Moderate**

55. The change in the relative salaries and bonuses for CEO's over the past 30 years could be due to a market for CEOs which is:
A) perfectly competitive, paying CEOs in accordance with their marginal productivity.
B) monopolistic, paying CEOs compensation which reflects collusion between CEOs and company compensation committees in the sale of the CEO's services to the company.
C) monopsonistic, paying CEOs considerably less than they contribute to the firm.
D) (A) and (B) are possible.
E) (B) and (C) are possible.

Difficulty: **Moderate**

56. Other things being equal, the brain drain of specialists from Great Britain and Russia to the U.S. results in:
A) net gains for the immigrant, similar specialists already in the U.S., and for the U.S. economy.
B) net gains for the immigrants and for the U.S. economy.
C) net gains for the immigrants, and for the U.S., British, and Russian economies.

D) net gains for the immigrant, similar specialists already in the U.S., and for the U.S., British, and Russian economies.
E) net gains for the U.S., British, and Russian economies.

Difficulty: **Moderate**

57. In the short run, the economic impact of immigration:
A) is positive for the nation as a whole because domestic workers and capital suppliers both experience net gains.
B) is positive for the nation as a whole because domestic workers' losses are exceeded by the gains made by suppliers of capital.
C) is negative for the nation as a whole because domestic workers' losses exceed the gains made by suppliers of capital.
D) is negative for the nation as a whole because domestic workers and capital suppliers both experience net losses.
E) is impossible to evaluate using economic theory, but in the long run it is clearly beneficial.

Difficulty: **Moderate**

58. A recent study on the effects of immigration from the National Bureau of Economic Research indicates that U.S.:
A) domestic workers and firms gain, but the net economic gain from immigration represents only about one-tenth of one percent of the U.S. GDP.
B) domestic workers and firms gain, and the net economic gain from immigration constitutes about one-percent of the U.S. GDP.
C) domestic workers lose while firms gain, but the net economic gain from immigration represents only about one-tenth of one percent of the U.S. GDP.
D) domestic workers gain while firms lose, but the net economic gain from immigration represents only about one percent of the U.S. GDP.
E) it is impossible to measure gains and losses by group, but the net effect of immigration is to increase GDP by about 3%.

Difficulty: **Moderate**

59. Which of the following statements regarding gender and race differentials is correct?
A) For white females and black males, median weekly earnings are approximately 75% of the median weekly earnings of white males.
B) The median weekly earnings of white females are substantially higher than those of black males, but are still only 90% of the median weekly earnings of white males.
C) The median weekly earnings of black females are a higher percentage of white male median weekly earnings than are the median weekly earnings of black males.
D) The difference in median weekly earnings between white males and all other groups decreased between 1983 and 1994.
E) All of the above are correct.

Difficulty: **Moderate**

60. According to empirical studies, most female/male and black/white wage differences are due to:
A) differences in education, training, and experience.
B) differences in hours of work, and difference in firm size.

C) differences in region of employment.
D) All of the above are correct.
E) None of the above is correct since most of the differences are due to wage discrimination.

Difficulty: **Moderate**

61. The fact that the ratio of earnings for black men/white men who have the same productive characteristics:
A) is about 90%, suggests that most of the large wage differential for all black men/white men is due to racial discrimination.
B) is about 90%, suggests that most of the large wage differential for all black men/white men is due to differences in productive characteristics.
C) is about 75%, suggests that most of the large wage differential for all black man/white men is due to racial discrimination.
D) is about 75%, suggests that most of the large wage differential for all black men/white men is due to differences in productive characteristics.
E) None of the above is correct.

Difficulty: **Moderate**

62. The comparable-worth doctrine:
A) proposes the evaluation of jobs in terms of knowledge and skills required, working conditions, and accountability, and the enforcement of equal pay for jobs of "comparable worth."
B) is opposed by many economists who believe that it is impossible to act on this doctrine because many work choices generate wage differences which are based on productivity.
C) is favored by those who argue that gender discrimination affects the types of jobs women are able to enter, and thus makes it possible for women to be paid less than men even though they have similar knowledge and skills.
D) has had little effect to date on female/male wage differences.
E) All of the above are correct.

Difficulty: **Moderate**

63. Assume that a firm with the production function given below is operating as a monopolist in the output market and a perfect competitor in the input market. Assume further that labor is the only variable input.

L	Q_X	MP_L	P_X
4	28	8	$10.00
5	35	7	$9.80
6	41	6	$9.60
7	46	5	$9.50
8	50	4	$9.40

If the wage rate (w) is $33.00, then the profit-maximizing amount of labor to hire is:
A) 4 units.
B) 5 units.
C) 6 units.
D) 7 units.

E) 8 units.

Difficulty: **Moderate**

64. Monopolistic exploitation refers to:
A) the impact which monopoly in an output market has on the firm's demand for inputs.
B) the excess of VMP_L over MRP_L at the point where MRP_L = wage rate.
C) the portion of VMP_L which exceeds MRP_L and is pocketed by the monopoly firm.
D) All of the above are correct.
E) Only (A) and (B) are correct.

Difficulty: **Moderate**

65. Assume male and female workers have the same productivity, and that one industry refuses to hire any females at any wage rate while other industries do not discriminate. This gender discrimination will cause:
A) wage rates of all men to increase.
B) wage rates to increase only for those men employed in the industry practicing discrimination.
C) wage rates of men employed in industries not practicing discrimination to decrease.
D) wage rates to increase only for those men employed in the industries not practicing discrimination.
E) (B) and (C) are correct.

Difficulty: **Moderate**

66. Assume male and female workers have the same productivity, and that one industry refuses to hire any females at any wage rate while other industries do not discriminate. This gender discrimination will cause:
A) wage rates of all women to decrease.
B) wage rates of all men to increase.
C) wage rates of all women to increase.
D) wage rates of all men to decrease.
E) (A) and (B) are correct.

Difficulty: **Moderate**

Use the following assumptions to answer the next 3 questions.

Assume that: 1) all labor is homogeneous and of average productivity; 2) output is produced under conditions of constant returns to scale where labor and capital are the only inputs; and, 3) the supply of labor is perfectly elastic and the demand curve for labor is elastic throughout the relevant range.

67. The area under the demand curve up to the equilibrium employment level represents:
A) the total value of output.
B) the share of income paid to labor.
C) the share of income paid to capital owners.
D) the cost of producing all output.

E) None of the above is correct.

Difficulty: **Hard**

68. The area between the supply curve of labor and the demand curve for labor up to the equilibrium employment level represents:
A) the total value of output.
B) the share of income paid to labor.
C) the share of income paid to capital owners.
D) the cost of producing all output.
E) None of the above is correct.

Difficulty: **Hard**

69. The area under the supply curve of labor up to the equilibrium employment level represents:
A) the total value of output.
B) the share of income paid to labor.
C) the share of income paid to capital owners.
D) the cost of producing all output.
E) None of the above is correct.

Difficulty: **Hard**

70. If immigration of the same type of labor which is already present in the economy occurs, then with an elastic demand for labor the daily wage of the nation:
A) rises and the share of total output going to capital owners decreases.
B) rises and the share of total output going to capital owners increases.
C) falls and the share of total output going to capital owners decreases.
D) falls and the share of total output going to capital owners increases.
E) None of the above is correct.

Difficulty: **Hard**

71. If immigration of the same type of labor which is already present in the economy occurs, then with an elastic demand for labor:
A) total output will increase.
B) there will a net gain from immigration to the economy as measured by the value if total output.
C) the gains of capital owners will be larger than the losses incurred by labor.
D) the immigration of labor with a higher average productivity than that which is already present will generate larger net gains for the economy as a whole.
E) All of the above are correct.

Difficulty: **Hard**

72. Which of the following combinations is not likely to occur?
A) A firm can be a perfect competitor in the output market and an imperfect competitor in the input market.
B) A firm can be a perfect competitor in the output market and a perfect competitor in the input market.
C) A firm can be an imperfect competitor in the output market and an imperfect competitor in the input market.

D) A firm can be an imperfect competitor in the output market and a perfect competitor in the input market
E) All of the above are likely to occur.

Difficulty: **Moderate**

73. The firm's demand schedule for labor is its:
A) MP_L schedule.
B) ME_L schedule.
C) MC_L schedule.
D) MRP_L schedule.
E) None of the above is correct.

Difficulty: **Easy**

74. The excess of the MVP_L over the MRP_L at the point where the MRP_L equals the wage rate is called:
A) monopsonistic exploitation.
B) monopolistic exploitation.
C) bilateral monopolistic exploitation.
D) oligopsonistic exploitation.
E) None of the above is correct.

Difficulty: **Easy**

75. The marginal expenditure on inputs exceeds the input price for:
A) monopsonists.
B) monopsonistic competitors.
C) oligopsonists.
D) All of the above.
E) Only (A) and (C).

Difficulty: **Easy**

Short Essays

Give a brief answer to each of the following questions.

1. **Why is the demand curve for labor of a firm that is a monopolist in the output market, not the same as that of a firm that is a perfect competitor in an output market? Assume that there is only one variable input.**
Answer: The reason is that the monopoly firm recognizes that as it increases production it must cut output price. Thus, marginal revenue is less than price for the monopolist. When that firm faces the input market, its MRP_L is no longer equal to output price x MP_L (value of marginal product) which is the perfect competitor's demand curve for labor, but instead MR x MP_L where $MR < P$ of the output. Thus, the demand curve for labor for a monopolist is different from that of a perfect competitor.

2. **If the local hospital is only one buyer of nurses services in the area and nurses are geographically immobile, what type of labor market will the market for nurses be?**

What will employment and wage rates of nurses be like relative to the standard of a perfectly competitive input market?
Answer: In this case the local hospital is a monopsonist. Consequently it will hire nurses up to the point at which $MRP_L = ME_L$ and pay the wage indicated by the supply curve of labor. The wage rate and the employment level will be lower in the monopsony case than in the case of a perfectly competitive input market in which firms employ labor up to the point at which the wage rate equals the MRP_L, and pay a wage rate equal to the MRP_L.

3. **What methods can a labor union employ to increase the wages of its members? Which method is the most advantageous to a union?**
Answer: Labor unions can shift the supply curve of union labor that the firm must hire to the left, shift the demand curve for union labor to the right, or bargain for an above equilibrium wage rate. The most advantageous method is to shift the demand curve for labor to the right because unlike the other methods this one increases employment of union labor. This is also more difficult to accomplish than raising wages by the other methods.

4. **Explain how the wages of men and women working in industries that do not discriminate against women will be affected if some industries refuse to employ women who have the required education and job skills.**
Answer: The supply of educated and skilled women to industries that do not discriminate will increase. Since the nondiscriminatory industries hire men or women without distinction, the overall supply of labor to industries that do not discriminate will increase. Thus, the wages of men and women working in those industries will be lower than would be the case if no discrimination were taking place in the other industry.

5. **Explain why "brain drain" is so beneficial to the country of immigration and so costly to the country of origin.**
Answer: Brain drain occurs when skilled labor and professionals move from one country to another. This immigration transfers the benefits of education and training to the country of immigration while the costs are born by the country of origin. Most industrial countries favor this type of immigration while imposing obstacles to the immigration of unskilled labor.

Chapter 16:

Financial Microeconomics: Interest, Investment, and the Cost of Capital

Multiple-Choice

Choose the one alternative that best completes the statement or answers the question.

1. When an individual is faced with the choice of various levels of income and consumption this year versus levels of income and consumption next year, a plot of this year's levels on the horizontal axis and next year's levels on the vertical axis yields a budget line. The slope of this budget line for a lender shows:
   A) the rate of interest that the lender receives as a result of not consuming some of his or her initial endowment of income this year.
   B) the rate of trade-off between income and consumption in one period, holding other things constant.
   C) the rate of interest that must be paid to entice an individual to borrow some of next year's income and increase his or her endowment in the current year.
   D) the price of spending relative to the price of borrowing.
   E) None of the above is correct.

   Difficulty: **Easy**

2. As used by an economist, the rate of interest:
   A) cannot really be calculated because of constantly fluctuating prices.
   B) is a measure of the social utility received from current consumption as opposed to future consumption.
   C) is the premium received by an individual next year by lending one dollar today.
   D) is constant in the short run and is equal to the opportunity cost of holding money.
   E) None of the above is correct.

   Difficulty: **Easy**

3. Other things constant, the effect of a change in the interest rate to the budget line faced by the consumer is to:
   A) shift the line outward, parallel to the origin.
   B) alter the slope of the line.
   C) shift the line inward, parallel to the origin.
   D) rotate about a point on either the horizontal or the vertical axis.
   E) None of the above is correct.

   Difficulty: **Moderate**

4. When an individual decides to forego current consumption for future consumption and lend money, an optimal position for the individual is achieved where:

A) the indifference curve between current and future consumption is tangent to the budget line, given an initial endowment.
B) the marginal rate at which an individual is willing to lend another dollar is equal to the marginal rate at which he can lend one in the market.
C) the sum of (1 + r), where r is the market interest rate, equals the slope of the indifference curve between current and future consumption.
D) the MRS between current and future consumption equals (1 + r).
E) All of the above are correct statements for an individual's optimal position.

Difficulty: **Moderate**

5. Suppose that you observe an individual's preference map and budget line, given an initial endowment. Income and consumption next year are plotted on the vertical axis, and income and consumption this year are plotted on the horizontal axis. At some point, an indifference curve will be tangent to the budget line. Suppose, though, that the individual is at a point on his indifference curve where the absolute value of the slope of the indifference curve is less than the absolute value of the slope of the budget line. We can conclude that this individual:
A) will improve his well-being by lending less money so that his current consumption can increase.
B) is initially in a position of equilibrium, so he will neither borrow nor lend an extra dollar.
C) will borrow extra dollars until he has enough funds to attain the highest indifference curve possible.
D) will lend extra dollars until the rate at which he is willing to lend additional amounts equals the rate at which he is able to lend these amounts.
E) None of the above is correct.

Difficulty: **Moderate**

6. Suppose that the market interest rate is currently 12 percent. If you lend your friend $3,000 for one year and charge him 12 percent interest payable at the end of the year, what amount will you receive when the loan is paid off?
A) $3,360
B) $3,600
C) $4,200
D) $3,960
E) Not enough information is provided to determine an answer.

Difficulty: **Easy**

7. Suppose that you observe an individual's preference map and budget constraint for income and consumption this year (plotted on the horizontal axis) versus income and consumption and consumption next year (plotted on the vertical axis). Given an initial endowment of income, if the rate at which a consumer is willing to substitute current consumption for future consumption is greater than the rate at which he can make the substitution, then the individual:
A) will be a net lender and earn some positive interest.
B) will increase his stock of wealth in the future.
C) will be a net borrower and have to pay some positive interest premium.
D) will not be able to achieve an optimal mix of current consumption and saving.
E) None of the above is correct.

Difficulty: **Moderate**

8. Suppose that the current rate of interest is 10 percent simple interest and that you want to borrow $5,000. You find a lender willing to make a loan to you but she wants to deduct the interest you must pay prior to distributing the funds. In other words, although you will have to repay $5,000 one year from now, you will not receive the full amount of the note. How much money will you receive when the loan is made?
A) $5,500
B) $4,000
C) $5,000 - $250
D) $4,500
E) $5,255

Difficulty: **Moderate**

9. Generally speaking, an individual's wealth consists of:
A) the present and future value of all income and income producing assets owned by the individual at a particular point in time.
B) the initial income and asset endowment of the individual plus the present value of any future income or asset endowment.
C) the present value of any future income or asset endowment that the individual is to receive.
D) the present value of all income and asset endowments that the individual currently owns.
E) None of the above is correct.

Difficulty: **Easy**

10. If an individual experiences an increase in his wealth, the increase will:
A) shift the consumer's budget line inward toward the origin.
B) cause the individual to move along some initial indifference curve.
C) other things constant, cause a parallel shift outward of the consumer's budget line.
D) other things constant, change the slope of the individual's budget line.
E) None of the above is correct.

Difficulty: **Easy**

11. Suppose that your current income endowment is equal to $120,000, and you are certain that, in addition, for the next four years you will receive an income endowment of $120,000. If the prevailing interest rate is currently 10 percent and will remain at 10 percent for the next four years, what is the value of your wealth?
A) $600,000
B) $359,000
C) $515,464
D) $500,384
E) Not enough information is provided to determine an answer.

Difficulty: **Hard**

12. When the financial markets are in equilibrium, it is true that:
A) desired borrowing by individuals and firms equals desired lending by individuals and firms.
B) desired savings by individuals and firms equals desired investment by individuals.

C) an interest rate is established so that there is neither a surplus nor shortage of loanable funds.
D) any excess between the savings – investment equilibrium and the lending – borrowing equilibrium refers to the amount of investment that is self-financed from the investor's own savings rather than borrowing in the market.
E) All of the above are true statements.

Difficulty: **Moderate**

13. The present value of the future amount of an asset is the amount of money that must be invested:
A) today to get exactly the future return at some specified future date.
B) at some specified time in the future to get exactly the asset price of the asset today.
C) at specified date in the future to obtain a specified rate of interest today.
D) to keep the value of the asset constant over its useful life.
E) None of the above is correct.

Difficulty: **Moderate**

14. Generally speaking, the present value of an asset is determined by:
A) the prevailing interest rate.
B) the length of time over which payments are made.
C) the market price of the asset.
D) (B) and (C) only.
E) (A) and (B) only.

Difficulty: **Moderate**

15. Suppose that you invest the sum of $2,000 at 10 percent per year, compounded annually. The value of your investment after the first year is:
A) $1,900.
B) $2,200.
C) $1,800.
D) $1,818.
E) Not enough information is provided to determine an answer.

Difficulty: **Moderate**

16. Suppose that you pay $9,000 today for a bond that in one year will be worth $10,000. The return on your investment in the bond is:
A) 10.50 percent.
B) $1,000.
C) 11.11 percent.
D) 8.75 percent.
E) None of the above is correct.

Difficulty: **Hard**

17. Suppose that you purchase an asset for $700 today and one year from now, it will be worth $1,000. The rate of return on your investment in this asset is approximately:
A) 11 percent.
B) 23 percent.

C) 18 percent.
D) 52 percent.
E) 43 percent.

Difficulty: **Hard**

18. Suppose that you purchase an asset that will generate a constant annual income (paid once a year) of $1,400. If the prevailing market interest rate is 7 percent, what is the most that you should pay for this asset?
A) $14,000
B) $20,000
C) $14,980
D) $12,650
E) $12,650

Difficulty: **Hard**

19. Suppose that you are to receive a payment of $10,000 in one year. If the interest rate is 7 percent, the present value to you today of the $10,000 is:
A) $9,300.
B) $10,700.
C) $9,550.
D) $9,345.
E) $9,524.

Difficulty: **Moderate**

20. When the term "present value" is used by economists, they are describing:
A) the value today of a payment that will be made at some date in the future.
B) the price of capital asset.
C) the value that some capital asset will have in the future.
D) the cost of investment spending today as opposed to the cost of investment spending in the future.
E) the present interest rate on capital assets.

Difficulty: **Moderate**

21. Suppose that you are to receive a payment of $8,000 in two years. If the current market interest rate is 10 percent, what is the present value to you today of the $8,000 payment?
A) $5,793
B) $9,680
C) $6,612
D) $7,273
E) $6,011

Difficulty: **Hard**

22. Suppose that you are considering the purchase of an asset that will yield you $50,000 per year (paid on one sum annually) forever. If the current market interest rate is 7 percent, what is the most that you should be willing to pay for the asset?
A) $312,000
B) $927,650

C) $714,286
D) $527,860
E) Not enough information is provided to determine an answer.

Difficulty: **Hard**

23. Suppose that you are to receive a payment of $30,000 at some date in the future. The present value of the payment will be smaller if:
A) the payment is made in the near future.
B) the market interest rate declines.
C) the market interest rate does not change but the length of time until payment is shortened.
D) the payment date is extended into the distant future and the market interest rate does not change.
E) None of the above will affect the present value of the payment.

Difficulty: **Moderate**

24. Suppose that you are the producer of a particular product, say widgets. When you examine the capital value of an asset, you are looking at:
A) the income stream that the asset can generate over a period of time.
B) the present value of the income stream that can be generated by the asset over a period of time.
C) the opportunity cost of buying the asset versus the cost of other assets.
D) the rental price of the capital asset.
E) the future value of the income stream that can be generated by the asset for some specified future time period.

Difficulty: **Hard**

25. If you are a producer and are considering the purchase of a capital asset, the rule that you should follow is purchase the asset if:
A) the present value of the assets future net income stream is less than the purchase price.
B) the present value of the asset's future net income stream is greater than the purchase price.
C) the net income produced per year is less than the purchase price.
D) the net income produced per year is equal to the asset's purchase price.
E) and only if your firm can show a positive economic profit.

Difficulty: **Moderate**

26. Suppose that you are considering the purchase of a capital asset that will yield a return of $5,000 in two years. What is the most that you should pay for the asset (to the nearest dollar) if the market interest rate is 8 percent per year?
A) $4,287
B) $4,479
C) $5,283
D) $3,119
E) $4,109

Difficulty: **Hard**

27. If the prevailing market interest rate is 7 percent, and the most that you are willing to pay for an asset that yields a constant stream of net cash flows in each future year indefinitely is $49,000, then the annual payment from the asset is about:
A) $7,000.
B) $4,900.
C) $5,150.
D) $6,860.
E) $3,430.

Difficulty: **Hard**

28. Other things constant, the demand for capital decreases at higher interest rates because:
A) individuals prefer to place their money and wealth in savings accounts.
B) the number of investment projects with sufficiently high net productivity of capital declines.
C) individuals prefer to purchase stock with their money.
D) the marginal productivity of capital declines.
E) None of the above is correct.

Difficulty: **Moderate**

29. When economists measure the real rate of interest, they are measuring the:
A) rate of return on capital investment projects in terms of dollars.
B) nominal rate of interest plus the inflation rate.
C) the number of dollars that an individual must pay in order to borrow money.
D) the rate at which an individual gives up purchasing power in order to borrow money.
E) None of the above is correct.

Difficulty: **Moderate**

30. Suppose that you, as a typical consumer, expect the inflation rate to increase by 5 percent per year. If everyone expects the same increase, then the real interest rate:
A) will also rise by 5 percent.
B) will rise but by less than 5 percent.
C) will remain unchanged if there is complete adaptation to inflation.
D) will fall because of the increase in the inflation rate.
E) will eventually equal the nominal rate of interest.

Difficulty: **Moderate**

31. Suppose that everyone is given an initial endowment of $10,000 and the real interest rate is a negative 3 percent. We would then expect the typical individual to:
A) increase her wealth over time.
B) invest in projects with a positive nominal interest rate.
C) consume his or her endowment.
D) save more for future consumption because inflation obviously is greater than the nominal interest rate.
E) None of the above is correct.

Difficulty: **Hard**

32. Generally speaking, the beta coefficient:
    A) measures the second most important variable in an investor's stock portfolio.
    B) is large and positive if an asset fluctuates more than and in the same direction as the market for the asset.
    C) is always zero for most preferred investments.
    D) cannot be determined from public information provided about stock prices and rates of return.
    E) None of the above is correct.

    Difficulty: **Moderate**

33. Which one of the following is <u>not</u> a method of estimating the cost of capital for an investment project?
    A) the capital asset pricing model
    B) the full-cost pricing model
    C) the risk-free rate plus premium approach
    D) the dividend valuation model
    E) None of the above is an acceptable method of estimating the cost of capital.

    Difficulty: **Moderate**

34. The Widget Corporation recently issued 5,000,000 new shares of common stock in order to raise additional equity capital. The issue was made through an investment banker and the banker's spread (charge) was 10 percent of the total receipts of the sale. The stock sold on the market for $7.50 per share. If the Widget firm had to incur $250,000 in additional costs to issue the stock, what does the firm receive after the floatation costs are deducted?
    A) $4,500,000
    B) $33,500,000
    C) $33,750,000
    D) $37,250,000
    E) $37,500,000

    Difficulty: **Hard**

35. A firm can raise investment funds:
    A) internally, from undistributed profits.
    B) externally, by borrowing.
    C) externally, by selling stocks.
    D) All of the above are true.
    E) Only (B) and (C) are true.

    Difficulty: **Easy**

36. Suppose that you and many others of your friends buy all of an initial issue of common stock in the Widget Corporation. The investors' required return on the common stock is:
    A) equal to the corporation's cost of new common stock if the flotation costs for the issue are zero.
    B) equal to the corporation's cost of retained earnings.
    C) less than the corporation's cost of new common stock if the flotation costs are not zero.
    D) equal to that return which investors must receive in order for them to purchase the stock.

E) All of the above are correct.

Difficulty: **Hard**

37. Suppose that the Widget Corporation is preparing to float a new issue of corporate bonds. The bonds will have a face value of $1,000, an interest rate of 8.4 percent, a maturity date in ten years, and an issue price of $900.30. The Widget Corporation's marginal tax rate is 34 percent, and interest payments are paid semiannually. The cost of debt (k_d) incurred by the Widget Corporation is approximately:
A) 5.1 percent.
B) 6.6 percent.
C) 3.2 percent.
D) 10.0 percent.
E) Cannot be determined from the information provided.

Difficulty: **Moderate**

38. The Acme Corporation is preparing to issue common stock. The stock will have a face value of $100 and will pay $8 per year in dividends. The Acme Corporation's marginal tax rate is 34 percent, and the flotation costs for the new issue will be $2.38 per share of stock. The anticipated issue price of each new share is $96.50. Given the above information, the cost of Acme's common stock is approximately:
A) 10.8 percent.
B) 5.4 percent.
C) 11.3 percent.
D) 8.5 percent.
E) Not enough information is provided to determine an answer.

Difficulty: **Hard**

39. Which one of the following statements about the beta coefficient is <u>false</u>?
A) If the investment portfolio is well diversified, the beta coefficient will be zero.
B) On the average, the beta coefficient of the market index is one.
C) The beta coefficient of the market index is one.
D) It is possible for a stock to have a beta coefficient that is negative.
E) The beta coefficient of an investment portfolio can take a value greater than or less than one.

Difficulty: **Moderate**

40. Suppose that you are considering two stocks, A and B. The beta coefficient of stock A is .70 and the current price of a share of the stock is $35. The beta coefficient of stock B is 1.3 and its current price is $45 per share. The beta coefficient of a portfolio that consists of only one share of stock A and one share of stock B is approximately:
A) 1.05.
B) 2.55.
C) 1.75.
D) 1.60.
E) 1.15.

Difficulty: **Moderate**

41. Suppose that you are considering the purchase of a piece of property that you can rent for $10,000 per year. If you have to pay $80,000 for the property, what market interest rate must exist for the purchase to be a break-even investment for you?
A) 10 percent.
B) 12.5 percent.
C) 15.5 percent.
D) 20 percent.
E) Not enough information is provided to determine an answer.

Difficulty: **Moderate**

42. Generally speaking, if the preference for present income over future income weakens, then the:
A) present value of income falls.
B) present value of future income increases.
C) interest rate remains unchanged.
D) interest rate rises.
E) None of the above is correct.

Difficulty: **Moderate**

43. Suppose that the present value of the expected future income from an additional dollar of investment spending on a capital project exceeds the current cost of the investment of the additional dollar. We would expect investment spending to:
A) fall.
B) remain unchanged.
C) rise.
D) approach zero.
E) None of the above is correct.

Difficulty: **Moderate**

44. Other things remaining constant, if the nominal interest rate is 12 percent, the present value of $5,000 two years from now is:
A) $5,000.
B) less than the present value of $5,000 received one year from now.
C) $3,210.
D) $2,800.
E) Not enough information is provided to determine an answer.

Difficulty: **Moderate**

45. If the interest rate is represented by r, then in order to discount future income by the interest rate, we must:
A) divide the future income payment by (1 + r).
B) multiply the future income payment by (1 + r).
C) divide the future income payment by 1^r.
D) divide the future income payment by r.
E) multiply the future income payment by r.

Difficulty: **Moderate**

46. Suppose that you purchase a $5,000 bond with an interest rate of 12 percent, and a few months later, you sell the bond when the interest rate is 8 percent. Other things constant, we can conclude that you will receive:
A) less money from the sale of the bond than you paid for it.
B) the same amount of money from the sale of the bond as you paid for it.
C) no interest from the bond because you did not hold it long enough.
D) more money from the sale of the bond than you paid for it.
E) None of the above is correct.

Difficulty: **Hard**

47. A borrower who pays $600 a year interest to a person or firm who lends him or her $5,000 a year pays an interest rate of:
A) 10 percent.
B) 8 percent.
C) 12 percent.
D) 15 percent.
E) 5 percent.

Difficulty: **Moderate**

48. Other things constant, the real rate of interest equals:
A) the nominal rate of interest less the expected inflation rate.
B) the nominal rate of interest plus the expected inflation rate.
C) the expected rate of inflation less the nominal interest rate.
D) the expected rate of inflation plus the nominal interest rate.
E) None of the above is correct.

Difficulty: **Moderate**

49. If both the demanders of investment funds (borrowers) and the suppliers of investment funds (lenders) expect the inflation rate to be 5 percent, the nominal interest rate would exceed the rate that would have prevailed if no inflation had been expected by:
A) 0 percent.
B) 10 percent.
C) 25 percent.
D) 5 percent.
E) 15 percent.

Difficulty: **Moderate**

50. Other things remaining the same, the present value of a stream of future income is:
A) not affected by the rate of interest.
B) not affected by the length of time that the payments are made.
C) higher, the higher the interest rate.
D) lower, the higher the interest rate.
E) None of the above is correct.

Difficulty: **Moderate**

51. Between 1960 and 2000, personal savings as a fraction of disposable personal income has:
A) remained essentially the same at about 4%.

B) fallen substantially to 1%.
C) increased substantially from 4% to 6%.
D) fluctuated greatly and thus it is impossible to identify a trend.
E) fallen almost to zero because higher marginal tax rates have brought about a flight of savings overseas.

Difficulty: **Easy**

52. Which of the following statements regarding the Social Security system and its impact is not correct?
A) The system was established in 1935 as a kind of "forced savings" program in which voluntary saving is replaced by the Social Security tax.
B) For the period from 1960 to 2000, the combination of personal savings plus the revenues collected from the Social Security tax have remained a stable percentage of disposable income.
C) The use of Social Security tax revenues to meet current government expenditures has reduced the nation's savings by a substantial margin.
D) Because the government has saved the Social Security taxes it has levied, net savings (personal plus government) have been more or less unchanged over the past 35 years.
E) For the period from 1960 to 2000, personal savings have fallen as a percentage of disposable income.

Difficulty: **Moderate**

53. Which of the following statements is not correct?
A) In the U.S., business savings much larger than personal savings.
B) Savings impact economic growth, in part, through their use in sustaining and expanding the capital stock.
C) Data from international comparisons suggest that economic growth rates are strongly correlated with net savings rates.
D) It has been estimated that, in the U.S., the impact of the Social Security system on savings has been mildly positive, thus causing the economic growth to be slightly higher than it would have been otherwise.
E) In the period from 1960 to 2000 both personal and business savings have steadily increased.

Difficulty: **Moderate**

The table gives the present value of the difference between the higher yearly salaries with a bachelor's degree in the various fields and the average salary of workers with only a high school diploma. The opportunity costs of obtaining a college degree were not included. Assume that all of the college degrees were obtained at a capital investment (opportunity) cost of $60,000 that was incurred in time period zero.

PRESENT VALUES OF HIGHER LIFETIME EARNINGS WITH BACHELOR'S DEGREE IN VARIOUS FIELDS, 1995

FIELD OF STUDY	HIGHER LIFETIME EARNING
Electrical engineering	$357,240
Computer science	310,500
Nursing	293,000
Mathematics	241,680

Chemistry	223,060
Accounting	194,780
Economics/Finance	189,260
Marketing	144,260
Education	91,800
Communications	90,460

54. Which of the following degree choices left the "investor" with less than simply going to work with a high school diploma?
A) nursing
B) accounting
C) education
D) All of the above are correct.
E) None of the above is correct.

Difficulty: **Moderate**

55. Given the data in the table above and the capital investment (opportunity) costs below, which of the following degrees would have increased the "investor's" wealth by the smallest amount?
A) Electrical engineering, with $200,000 capital investment costs.
B) Nursing, with $150,000 capital investment costs.
C) Economics/Finance, with $150,000 capital investment costs.
D) Education, with $40,000 capital investment costs.
E) Communications, with $40,000 capital investment costs.

Difficulty: **Moderate**

NOMINAL AND REAL INTEREST RATES ON THREE-MONTH U.S. TREASURY BILLS

YEAR	NOMINAL INTEREST RATE	CHANGE IN CONSUMER PRICE INDEX
1990	7.5	5.4
1991	5.4	4.2
1992	3.5	3
1993	3	3
1994	4.3	2.6

56. Given the data in the table above and the assumption that the anticipated rate of inflation was the same as the actual inflation rate, in which year was the real interest rate highest?
A) 1990
B) 1991
C) 1992
D) 1993
E) 1994

Difficulty: **Easy**

57. In comparing the following assets, one finds that the characteristics of common stocks, bonds, and U.S. Treasury bills respectively are:
A) greatest variability risk, greatest default risk, and greatest liquidity.

B) greatest default risk, greatest variability risk, and greatest liquidity.
C) greatest liquidity, greatest default risk, and greatest variability risk.
D) greatest variability risk, greatest liquidity, and greatest default risk.
E) greatest default risk, greatest liquidity, and greatest variability risk.

Difficulty: **Moderate**

58. Which of the following is <u>not</u> a correct statement about derivatives?
A) Derivatives receive their value from the price of underlying financial assets such as stocks, bonds, commodities, and currencies.
B) Derivatives have proven to be a very useful risk-management tool for businesses.
C) Derivatives fell out of favor during the 1992-1993 bull market in bonds.
D) Derivatives include option-type and forward-type contracts.
E) All of the above are correct.

Difficulty: **Moderate**

59. An option contract:
A) gives the owner of the option the right to buy or sell an asset at a specific price over a given time period.
B) obligates the owner of the option to buy an asset at a specified price over a given time period.
C) has not limit to the size of the losses which may be incurred by the owner of the option.
D) has specific limits to the losses which may be incurred by the party which sold the option.
E) All of the above are correct.

Difficulty: **Moderate**

60. Forward-type contracts do not include:
A) forwards.
B) futures.
C) swaps.
D) options.
E) All of the above are forward-type contracts.

Difficulty: **Easy**

61. An agreement to buy or sell a fixed amount of an asset that is not traded on an exchange at a specific price on a specific date is a(n):
A) forward.
B) option.
C) future.
D) swap.
E) None of the above is correct.

Difficulty: **Moderate**

62. An agreement to exchange streams of payments over time according to terms agreed upon today is called a(n):
A) forward.
B) option.

C) future.
D) swap.
E) None of the above is correct.

Difficulty: **Easy**

63. Factors which contribute to the riskiness of derivatives include:
A) very limited leveraging in the purchase of "exotic" derivatives.
B) the imposition of heavy disclosure requirements which reduce profits from derivatives.
C) the treatment of derivatives as "off-balance-sheet" items.
D) the current requirement that banks report the value of derivatives to buyers every day even if not asked for the information.
E) All of the above are correct.

Difficulty: **Moderate**

64. Given an initial equilibrium interest rate in the domestic market for investment funds that is higher than the interest rates in other countries, and supply and demand curves of the usual shape, which of the following is <u>not</u> correct?
A) Foreign investment funds will flow into the domestic market.
B) The equilibrium interest rate in the domestic market will decrease.
C) Total investment in the domestic economy will increase.
D) Domestic investment in the domestic economy will increase.
E) Foreign investment in the domestic economy will increase.

Difficulty: **Moderate**

65. Given an initial equilibrium interest rate in the domestic market for investment funds that is higher than the interest rates in other countries, and supply and demand of the usual shape, which of the following is <u>not</u> correct?
A) There will be a net gain to the country receiving the foreign investment.
B) Domestic labor will benefit due to an increase in the capital-labor ratio.
C) Foreign investors will make gains as a consequence of the return they earn on their investment.
D) The total output of the country receiving foreign investment will increase.
E) All of the above are correct.

Difficulty: **Moderate**

66. In the 1980s the U.S. became a debtor nation, and U.S. benefited from the capital inflow it produced. Which of the following is <u>not</u> cited as a potential danger that can arise from such capital inflows?
A) There is a danger that foreigners may suddenly withdraw their funds and cause higher interest rates and a financial panic.
B) There may be a loss of domestic control over political or economic matters.
C) Foreign companies operating in the U.S. may transfer advanced American technology abroad.
D) There may be an increase in the amount of "crowding out" of private investment spending by government spending.
E) All of the above are correct.

Difficulty: **Moderate**

67. Investment in human capital:
   A) refers to any activity on the part of a worker which increases the productivity of that worker.
   B) includes education, job training, and migration to better job opportunities.
   C) has costs and benefits which may be understood in terms of a present value of a net benefit stream.
   D) produces benefits such as greater enjoyment of one's job which are difficult to measure.
   E) All of the above are correct.

   Difficulty: **Moderate**

68. Given a person's work-leisure preferences and initial endowment of property income, after investing in human capital the person will:
   A) work more hours per day.
   B) work fewer hours per day.
   C) make no measurable changes in hours worked per day.
   D) generally find that the rate of return is negative if the investment took the form of a college education.
   E) (C) and (D) are correct.

   Difficulty: **Moderate**

69. Suppose the price of an exhaustible resource, such as bauxite ore, is $25 per unit today and is expected to be $32 next year. Which of the following market rates of interest will induce the owner to remove the ore from the ground and sell it this year?
   A) 3%
   B) 8%
   C) 12%
   D) 18%
   E) None of the above is correct.

   Difficulty: **Moderate**

70. Suppose the market interest rate increases from 8% to 9% and the current price of an exhaustible resource, such as oil, is $20 per barrel. The lowest expected price of oil for one year from now which can induce the owner to keep in the ground at least some of the oil which he or she currently has plans to sell is:
   A) $20.20.
   B) $21.50.
   C) $21.75.
   D) $22.00.
   E) $22.50.

   Difficulty: **Moderate**

71. In a perfectly competitive market, more of a resource will be sold in the present:
   A) if the net price of the resource is expected to rise faster than the market rate of interest.
   B) if the net price of the resource is expected to rise at a slower rate than the market rate of interest.
   C) until the net price of the resource rises at a rate equal to the market rate of interest.
   D) (B) and (C) are correct.

E) (A) and (C) are correct.

Difficulty: **Moderate**

72. In the real world, the net prices of most resources:
A) increase at a faster rate than the market rate of interest because of technological innovations and new discoveries.
B) increase at a slower rate than the market rate of interest because of technological innovations and new discoveries.
C) do not behave in a way that can be explained by the economic model for exhaustible resources because the model does not take into account extreme shortsightedness of people.
D) increase due to the wasteful manner in which they are employed.
E) None of the above is correct.

Difficulty: **Moderate**

73. If one owns 40 acres of timber, at what point in life of the trees will it be profit maximizing to cut them?
A) When the growth rate in the net value of the trees exceeds the market rate of interest.
B) When the growth rate in the net value of the trees is below the market rate of interest.
C) When the growth rate in the net value of the trees is equal to the market rate of interest.
D) When the trees stop growing.
E) When the growth rate for the trees reaches its peak.

Difficulty: **Moderate**

74. The separation theorem does <u>not</u> require that:
A) capital markets are perfect and costless.
B) borrowers are too small to individually affect the rate of interest.
C) lenders are too small to individually affect the rate of interest.
D) individuals borrow and lend at different interest rates.
E) All of the above are required by the separation theorem.

Difficulty: **Moderate**

75. Differences in interest rates exist because of differences in:
A) risk.
B) duration of the loan.
C) cost of administering the loan.
D) tax treatments.
E) All of the above are correct.

Difficulty: **Easy**

76. All of the following statements are made subject to the *ceteris paribus* assumption. Which is correct?
A) Default risk is the risk associated with the variation in rates of return on stock.
B) The longer the period of the loan, the lower the interest rate.
C) The lower the cost of administering the loan the lower the interest rate.

D) Tax-exempt municipal bonds have higher interest rates than non-tax exempt investments of similar risk.
E) All of the above are correct.

Difficulty: **Moderate**

77. The separation theorem refers to the separation between:
A) individuals' production and consumption decisions.
B) borrowers and lenders.
C) purchasers of bonds and purchasers of stock.
D) domestic and foreign investment markets.
E) All of the above.

Difficulty: **Moderate**

78. If there is no borrowing and lending, the optimal amount of saving and investment for an individual is shown by the tangency between the individual's:
A) indifference curve and budget line.
B) indifference curve and production-possibilities curve.
C) budget line and production possibilities curve.
D) budget line and market line.
E) None of the above is correct.

Difficulty: **Moderate**

79. If there is borrowing and lending, the optimal choice for an individual is shown by the tangency between the individual's:
A) indifference curve and budget line.
B) indifference curve and production-possibilities curve.
C) budget line and production possibilities curve.
D) indifference curve and market line.
E) None of the above is correct.

Difficulty: **Moderate**

80. The risk-free rate used by a firm in estimating the cost of equity capital is usually taken to be the:
A) rate of interest on the firm's own bonds.
B) three-month Treasury bill rate.
C) six-month Treasury bill rate.
D) All of the above can be used.
E) None of the above is correct.

Difficulty: **Easy**

Short Essays

Give a brief answer to each of the following questions.

1. What is net present value and how may it be used to maximize the wealth of a firm?

Answer: NPV is the value today of all the net cash flows of an investment that will be incurred over the life of the investment. A firm maximizes wealth by investigating in projects with the highest positive net present value.

2. **What factors account for the variety of rates of interest that exist at any given moment in time?**
Answer: These factors are risk (including default risk and variability risk), duration of the loan, cost of administering the loan, and tax treatment.

3. **What are some of the favorable effects of foreign investment on domestic economy? What unfavorable effects might it have?**
Answer: Foreign investment can yield a higher rate of capital formation, increase the capital-labor ratio, increase the total output of an economy after paying the foreign investors, increase wage rates, and lower interest rates, to name just some of the benefits. Unfavorable effects include the possible loss of domestic control over political and economic matters, instability should foreign investors decide to withdraw their investments, and the transfer of advanced technology abroad.

4. **In empirical studies calculating the rate of return to investment in a college education, the rate of return to the investment could be exaggerated as a consequence of raw intelligence and work habits. Explain.**
Answer: People attending college may have higher than average raw intelligence that would cause them to have higher wages even if they did not attend college. The work habits of people with college degrees are such that they tend to work more hours per week. This may be due to their college training, but if it were not, then these habits would cause them to have higher wages even if they did not attend college. Both of these factors would make the rate of return to college education appear to be higher than is actually the case.

5. **What effect would a decrease in market interest rates have on the decision to harvest a stand of timber now or allow it to continue to grow for another year?**
Answer: Harvesting the timber and selling it would generate revenue that could be invested at the market rate of interest. On the other hand, the rate of return to keeping the timber stand for another year is determined by the growth rate of the trees and the expected price of timber a year from now. If the market rate of interest increases relative to the rate of return to keeping the timber stand another year, it will be wealth maximizing to cut the timber now rather than waiting.

Chapter 17:

General Equilibrium and Welfare Economics

Multiple-Choice

Choose the one alternative that best completes the statement or answers the question.

1. Suppose that the economy of Alphania consists of two individuals, Ray (R) and Ann (A), and two commodities, X and Y. A general equilibrium in exchange is reached when:
   A) $MRT_{XY} = MRS_{XY}$ for R and A.
   B) $MRS_{XY} = P_X/P_Y$ for R and A.
   C) $MRS_{XY}^{A} = MRS_{XY}^{R}$.
   D) $MRS_{XY} > MRT_{XY}$.
   E) None of the above is correct.

   Difficulty: **Moderate**

2. Suppose that the economy of Betania produces only two commodities (X and Y) and uses only two inputs in its production process, capital (K) and labor (L). Betania reaches a general equilibrium in production when:
   A) $MRTS_{KL} = MRS_{XY}$.
   B) $MRTS_{LK} = P_K/P_L$.
   C) $MRTS_{LK}^{X} = MRTS_{LK}^{Y}$.
   D) $MRT_{XY} = MRS_{XY}$.
   E) None of the above is correct.

   Difficulty: **Moderate**

3. Suppose that in the economy of Alphania, there are only two individuals, Alice (A) and Ben (B), and only two goods, X and Y. A general equilibrium in production and exchange occurs when:
   A) $MRT_{XY} = MRS_{XY}^{A} = MRS_{XY}^{B}$.
   B) $MRS_{XY}^{A} = MRS_{XY}^{B}$.
   C) $MRS_{XY} = P_X/P_Y$.
   D) $MRT_{XY} = P_X/P_Y$.
   E) None of the above is correct.

   Difficulty: **Moderate**

4. For a perfectly competitive economy in an economy-wide general equilibrium, all of the following are correct <u>except</u>:
   A) each firm maximizes its profits, given the level of technology, resource availability, and prices.

B) consumers do not face an income constraining in selecting their optimal combination of goods.
C) each household supplies the factors of production that it chooses, given input prices.
D) all markets for both inputs and outputs clear at the established market prices.
E) individual are efficient in the consumption of goods and services.

Difficulty: **Moderate**

5. Suppose that in the market for widgets, there are hundreds of producers and that each produces the same level of output. The problem, however, is that the same level of output is produced at different marginal costs by the firms. We can conclude that:
A) some firms are making larger profits than others.
B) most firms in the industry will leave and stop producing widgets in the long run.
C) the overall industry cost of producing the same level of widgets could be reduced by reallocating resources among producers.
D) resources are allocated in the best possible manner in the industry.
E) None of the above conclusions can be made.

Difficulty: **Moderate**

6. Suppose that in the economy of Zebania, the marginal rate of substitution for goods does not equal their marginal rate of transformation. We can conclude that:
A) the economy is operating in the best possible manner.
B) it is possible to produce more of both goods.
C) the economy is operating on its production-possibilities curve.
D) it is possible to increase consumer well-being by reallocating resources and changing the output mix.
E) None of the above is a correct conclusion.

Difficulty: **Moderate**

7. In a perfectly competitive economy that achieves efficiency in production, efficiency in consumption, and efficiency in exchange, the marginal rate of transformation between goods A and B will equal the marginal rate of substitution for consumers because:
A) each consumer will face the same set of prices for goods A and B.
B) the prices of good A and good B will equal the marginal cost of producing the last units of the goods.
C) the amount that buyers pay for goods A and B equal the amount that sellers receive for the goods.
D) a point on the production contract curve is also a point on society's production possibilities curve.
E) All of the above are correct.

Difficulty: **Moderate**

8. Given an economy's production-possibilities curve, points along the curve:
A) correspond to input usage for which the marginal rate of technical substitution between any pair of inputs is equal in all uses.
B) are attainable by the economy even though it might have unemployed resources.
C) shows the socially optimal distribution of goods and services produced by the economy.
D) will usually plot as a straight line.

E) None of the above is correct.

Difficulty: **Moderate**

9. Suppose that in the long run, there is a decrease in the supply of input X into an economy's production process. This decrease:
A) will most likely only affect the price of the input.
B) will affect the price of input X as well as the price of any substitute inputs.
C) will affect the price of input X as well as any complementary inputs.
D) will affect the quantity, but not necessarily the price, of input X.
E) (B) and (C) are correct.

Difficulty: **Moderate**

10. Suppose that you have an economy's production-possibilities curve, and the economy produces only two goods, X and Y. The marginal cost of increasing the annual production of good X by moving along the curve is:
A) not calculable because neither the input nor output prices are given.
B) equal to zero because every point on society's production-possibilities curve reflects efficiency in production.
C) the amount of good Y that must be given up per time period in order to gain an extra unit of good X.
D) the amount of good X gained over a given period of time.
E) the marginal rate of technical substitution between goods X and Y.

Difficulty: **Moderate**

11. Suppose that goods X and Y are close substitutes and that the demand for good X increases. Which one of the following might we expect to see occur immediately, or at least in the very short run, in the market for good Y?
A) The supply of good Y will increase.
B) The quantity supplied of good Y will decrease.
C) The quantity demanded of good Y will increase.
D) The demand for good Y will increase.
E) The market equilibrium price of good Y will decrease.

Difficulty: **Moderate**

12. If the marginal rate of substitution of good X for good Y is 6 and the marginal rate of transformation of good X for good Y is 4, then we can conclude that:
A) the output of good X should be decreased and the output of good Y should be increased.
B) the price of good X will always be less than the price of good Y.
C) the output of good X should be increased and the output of good Y should be decreased.
D) the economy exhibits efficiency in production but not in exchange.
E) the price of good X will always be greater than the price of good Y.

Difficulty: **Moderate**

13. Suppose that the marginal rate of substitution of oranges for apples is 2 and the marginal rate of transformation of oranges for apples is 5. Society can be made better off if:

A) fewer oranges and more apples are produced.
B) the price of apples is increased relative to the price of oranges.
C) fewer of both oranges and apples are produced.
D) more oranges and fewer apples are produced.
E) the price of oranges falls.

Difficulty: **Moderate**

14. If the $MRS_{xy} < MRT_{xy}$, then society can be made better off if:
A) it produces more of good X and less of good Y.
B) it increases the price of both goods in order to allocate more efficiently scarce resources.
C) fewer of both goods X and Y is produced.
D) it reduces the output of good X and increases the output of good Y.
E) it reduces the price of good X and increases the price of good Y.

Difficulty: **Moderate**

15. The marginal rate of transformation of good X for good Y:
A) is a measure of the relative satisfaction received from consuming goods X and Y.
B) is the increase in the output of good Y that can be obtained by a one-unit reduction in the production of good X.
C) is of only secondary importance when studying the efficiency of a perfectly competitive market system.
D) measures how many extra units of good Y the consumer must receive in order to be compensated for giving up one unit of good X.
E) None of the above is correct.

Difficulty: **Moderate**

16. When an allocation of resources in a competitive market is efficient in consumption:
A) consumers will be at some point on or below their contract curve for exchange.
B) it cannot be efficient in production and exchange.
C) by rearranging the allocation of consumer goods, someone can be made better off without making someone else worse off.
D) it is not possible to reallocate goods consumed among individuals in order to make one person better off without making someone else worse off.
E) None of the above is a correct statement.

Difficulty: **Moderate**

17. As economists use the term, a general equilibrium exists when:
A) there is an equilibrium in all markets, both goods and factor.
B) there is an equilibrium in the goods markets but not necessarily in the factor markets.
C) there is an equilibrium in the factor market but not necessarily in the goods market.
D) the economy's aggregate demand equals its aggregate supply.
E) an equilibrium exists in at least one goods market and one factor market.

Difficulty: **Easy**

18. The Edgeworth box diagram is used to show trade or exchange between two individual economic units. This diagram:

A) will show how individual households will allocate their given incomes between two goods.
B) shows the degree of income inequality within an economic system.
C) shows in the two-goods case, how much of each good can be produced, given technology and inputs.
D) shows how two economic units interact when the total amount of goods that can be consumed is fixed.
E) shows none of the above.

Difficulty: **Easy**

19. Suppose that the economy of Betania contains only two individuals who each produce a different good. Trade between these individuals will be mutually beneficial as long as:
A) the two individuals do not encounter barriers to trade.
B) the marginal rates of substitution for the two goods are different for the two individuals.
C) the initial allocation of goods results in an inequitable distribution of the goods among the individuals.
D) one consumer has more goods than the other.
E) one of the individuals can be made better off as a result of a trade.

Difficulty: **Moderate**

20. Given an Edgeworth box diagram showing exchange between two consumers, each point in the box reflects:
A) the marginal cost of producing an extra unit of each of the goods represented by the diagram.
B) the best allocation of goods between any two customers.
C) an efficiency in consumption and trade for each individual.
D) an equitable distribution of income and goods between the two consumers.
E) a given allocation of goods between the two consumers.

Difficulty: **Moderate**

21. Suppose that Sam and Jane are free to trade with each other. Sam has apples and Jane has oranges, and so they begin to trade. If both are better off after they trade, it is because:
A) combined aggregate output rises.
B) total consumption of apples and oranges rises.
C) consumption falls because the relative price of oranges in terms of apples is higher than Sam is willing to accept.
D) the total utility of each individual increases.
E) None of the above is correct.

Difficulty: **Moderate**

22. When the allocation of inputs is efficient in the production of two goods, then for this allocation:
A) the marginal rates of substitution between the goods is equal for any two consumers.
B) the marginal rate of technical substitution between any two inputs is the same for any two producers.
C) the marginal products of the inputs used to produce the two goods are constant.

D) the marginal rate of transformation is equal to the marginal rate of technical substitution for the two inputs.
E) None of the above is correct.

Difficulty: **Moderate**

23. Given an Edgeworth box diagram for production, the dimensions of the diagram are determined by:
A) the number of producers in the market.
B) the number and preferences of consumers in the market.
C) the production-contract curve.
D) the total amount of inputs that are available for production.
E) None of the above is correct.

Difficulty: **Moderate**

24. Suppose that you observe a contract curve for production that is a straight line connecting the two origins of an Edgeworth box diagram. You can conclude that the production-possibilities frontier:
A) is convex to the origin.
B) is concave to the origin.
C) is quasi-convex to the origin; that is, the curve falls, rises, and then falls again.
D) is a straight line.
E) None of the above is correct.

Difficulty: **Moderate**

25. When we examine the production-possibilities frontier in general equilibrium analysis, the slope of the frontier provides:
A) the marginal rate of substitution of any two goods.
B) the marginal cost of producing one good in terms of the other good.
C) the marginal rate of technical substitution between the two goods.
D) the ratio of the marginal expenditure on one input relative to another.
E) the real input price ratio.

Difficulty: **Moderate**

26. When a competitive economy is in a general equilibrium in production and exchange, the slope of the production possibilities frontier is equal to:
A) the common slope of the indifference curves faced by consumers.
B) 1 because the prices of all inputs are equal.
C) the marginal rate of technical substitution of one input for another.
D) the ratio of the marginal products of any two inputs.
E) None of the above is correct.

Difficulty: **Moderate**

27. When a competitive economy is in a general equilibrium, a change in the demand for a good in one market will affect:
A) the price and output in the market for the good only.
B) the prices and output in all markets as resources are shifted among markets.
C) the tastes and preferences of all consumers in all markets.

D) only the prices and quantities of inputs used in production.
E) None of the above is correct.

Difficulty: **Moderate**

28. We use partial equilibrium analysis instead of general equilibrium analysis when a change in business conditions:
A) affects all markets instead of just a few.
B) affects either the demand side of the supply side (but not both) of all markets.
C) requires us to study an individual market viewed in isolation.
D) affects many or all markets, but the effects are small.
E) None of the above is correct.

Difficulty: **Moderate**

29. If the country of Zebina has a comparative advantage in the production of wheat over the country of Betania, it means that:
A) Zebina must give up less of other goods than Betania to produce one more bushel of wheat.
B) the raw material costs to produce wheat are less in Zebina than they are in Betania.
C) Zebina is not efficient in the production of wheat.
D) Betania cannot benefit from trade with Zebina.
E) None of the above is correct.

Difficulty: **Moderate**

30. Suppose that the absolute cost of producing all goods is greater in country A than it is in country B. We can conclude that country A:
A) should not engage in trade with country B.
B) could import but will not be able to export anything to country B.
C) will benefit from trade by exporting goods that can be produced with a relatively lower opportunity cost.
D) will gain from trade by exporting those goods to country B that have relative higher opportunity costs.
E) the opportunity cost of producing all goods is also greater than in country A than it is in country B.

Difficulty: **Moderate**

31. In the late eighteenth century, Adam Smith wrote about the competitive economic systems and described the law of the "invisible hand." The law of the invisible hand:
A) plays only a minor role in general equilibrium and welfare theory.
B) states that in a free market society, the individual pursuit of self-interests leads to the promotion of the best interests of society.
C) does not necessarily force business to maximize profits.
D) encourages support of government regulations designed to enhance market efficiency.
E) None of the above is correct.

Difficulty: **Moderate**

32. Which one of the following statements is <u>false</u>?
A) In welfare economics, the relative values placed on commodities are the relative values that are established in the market place.
B) The Pareto criterion is satisfied when it is possible to make at least one individual better off while not making any other individual worse off.
C) Any type of market structure that results in individuals being at a point on the contract curve is Pareto optimal.
D) Generally speaking, if society fails to attain a Pareto optimum, there is some degree of economic inefficiency.
E) It is difficult for economists to make statements or draw conclusions about policies that make some people better off while at the same time making other people worse off because of the required interpersonal comparisons of utility.

Difficulty: **Moderate**

33. All of the following statements are correct <u>except</u>:
A) An allocation of resources that satisfies the Pareto criterion will result from a perfectly competitive price system.
B) Under a competitive price system, an allocation of resources that satisfies the Pareto criterion may result in an inequitable distribution of income.
C) The real world provides few, if any, market structures that are perfectly competitive.
D) Every allocation of resources that satisfies the Pareto criterion is one that will also result in a social welfare maximum because the social welfare function will be optimized.
E) Currently there is no meaningful way to scientifically compare the utility functions among various individuals in society.

Difficulty: **Moderate**

34. One of the basis assumptions of the Kaldor-Hicks criterion is that:
A) any interior point of a utility-possibilities frontier is preferred to any point on the frontier itself.
B) it is possible for an individual who gains in welfare as a result of a reallocation of resources to compensate those who lose.
C) the ability to compensate an individual as a result of a loss in overall welfare is strictly a normative judgement.
D) along any utility-possibilities frontier, it is possible to make on individual better off while not making any other individual worse off.
E) None of the above is an assumption of the Kaldor-Hicks criterion.

Difficulty: **Moderate**

35. In general terms, a "grand utility-possibilities frontier" shows:
A) the maximum combination of utilities for individuals A and B, given a production function.
B) points on the grand utility-possibilities frontier are preferred to any interior points because at least one individual's utility will be reduced.
C) that it envelops all individual utility possibilities frontiers.
D) all of those points that are not inferior to any other points.
E) All of the above are correct.

Difficulty: **Moderate**

36. In studying welfare economics, the Kaldor-Hicks criterion states that:
A) if an individual who benefits from a change can compensate those who lose and still be better off, then the change is desirable.
B) any movement along the grand utility-possibilities frontier does not improve social welfare.
C) if an individual or group of individuals benefit from a change and no one is harmed, then the initial endowment of goods must have been Pareto optimal.
D) any movement along the utility possibilities frontier results in neither a gain nor loss in social welfare.
E) None of the above can be associated with the Kaldor-Hicks criterion.

Difficulty: **Moderate**

37. In Principles of Microeconomics as well as Intermediate Microeconomic Theory, we usually examine the activities of one market at a time and assume "all other things remain the same". This type of analysis is known as:
A) general equilibrium analysis.
B) economic welfare analysis.
C) partial equilibrium analysis.
D) dynamic equilibrium analysis.
E) comparative static analysis.

Difficulty: **Easy**

38. When economists engage in general equilibrium analysis, they develop their models and focus primarily on:
A) the interactions of the economy's product markets, resource markets, households, and business firms.
B) the interaction of both the private sector and the public sector.
C) the interaction of consumers and producers.
D) the firm, its output, its cost of production, its revenue, its profits or losses, and its demand for input.
E) None of the above is correct.

Difficulty: **Easy**

39. Suppose that you observe an Edgeworth box diagram, and the box consists of production isoquants for two producers and two goods. The locus of tangency points between the isoquants within the box is the:
A) product transformation curve.
B) utilities possibilities frontier.
C) production possibilities curve.
D) contract curve for production.
E) Edgeworth contract points.

Difficulty: **Moderate**

40. Every point on a consumption or production contract curve is:
A) a point that maximizes social welfare.
B) a Pareto optimal point.
C) a point that shows both first and second best allocations of resources.

D) can be achieved by the economy, and often some resources are left unused.
E) None of the above is correct.

Difficulty: **Moderate**

41. An endowment or allocation of resources is said to be Pareto optimal if:
A) the assumption of profit maximization does not apply.
B) only government can alter the allocation of resources.
C) it is impossible to alter the allocation of resources without making someone else worse off.
D) it is impossible to alter the allocation of resources without making at least one person better off.
E) None of the above is correct.

Difficulty: **Moderate**

42. Points on the exchange contract curve that are Pareto optimal are also:
A) productive points.
B) efficient points.
C) unattainable points.
D) stable points.
E) contract points.

Difficulty: **Moderate**

43. The Kaldor-Hicks compensation principle is essentially based on the proposition that:
A) the potential gainers in social welfare can compensate the losers so that society is made better off.
B) all costs are minimized, both production and transaction, in society's production, distribution, and consumption of goods and services.
C) the gainers in social welfare are actually able to compensate the losers so that the net change in social welfare is zero.
D) preferences are, when there are more than three individuals and three choices, intransitive when we examine a social welfare function.
E) None of the above is correct.

Difficulty: **Moderate**

44. Suppose that society consists of only two individuals, Bill and Bob. The social indifference curves for Bill and Bob will be downward sloping because:
A) if Bill is made better off, then Bob becomes better off also.
B) if Bob becomes worse off, Bill automatically becomes worse off also.
C) Bill's welfare is independent of Bob's, so any change in Bill's will not affect Bob.
D) any improvement in Bill's welfare will automatically make Bob worse off, assuming that they are on social indifference curve to begin with.
E) None of the above is correct.

Difficulty: **Moderate**

45. When economists engage in general equilibrium analysis and attempt to develop a general equilibrium model, they are attempting to:

A) determine the effect of a policy change or a change in an economic variable on a particular economic unit.
B) compare the different types of market systems; i.e. pure command, mixed, and pure market.
C) determine the effects of a policy change or a change in an economic variable on the competing sectors of the economy.
D) determine the effects of a policy change or a change in an economic variable on the entire, or at least a large part, of the economic system.
E) None of the above is correct.

Difficulty: **Moderate**

46. Given the assumptions that he made, Kenneth Arrow in his impossibility theorem concluded that:
A) the Kaldor-Hicks criterions could be applied in a competitive market.
B) a social welfare function cannot be derived by a democratic vote.
C) it is not possible to evaluate the state of social welfare through democratic voting.
D) given a set of choices, a majority-rule voting process will result in a transitive social welfare function.
E) a dictator cannot impose a social welfare function onto society.

Difficulty: **Moderate**

47. Suppose that you gain $1,000 and as a result, someone loses. Suppose also that you could pay the individual who loses $800, and the individual would be neither better nor worse off once he is compensated. We can conclude that:
A) the Arrow impossibility theorem does not hold in this case.
B) the loser was not a rational individual.
C) the ending distribution of funds is Pareto optimal.
D) the arrangement is optimal according to the Kaldor-Hicks criterion.
E) society faces a Bergson social welfare function.

Difficulty: **Moderate**

48. Given three goods, A, B, and C, which of the following preference rankings would violate Arrow's condition for a democratically determined social welfare function?
A) A is indifferent to B, B is preferred to C, so A is preferred to C.
B) C is preferred to A, A is preferred to B, so C is preferred to B.
C) B is preferred to A, A is indifferent to C, so B is indifferent to C.
D) A is indifferent to B, B is indifferent to C, so A is indifferent to C.
E) None of the above preference rankings violates Arrow's requirement.

Difficulty: **Moderate**

49. Which one of the following best describes the Scitovsky welfare criterion?
A) It is impossible to achieve a social welfare criterion through a democratic voting process.
B) Once a position on the grand utility-possibilities frontier is achieved, there is no compensation principle that will work so that overall social welfare can be increased.
C) An improvement in social welfare that satisfies the Kaldor-Hicks criterion once a change is made does not satisfy the Kaldor-Hicks criterion if the change is reversed.

D) An improvement in social welfare occurs if it is possible for one individual to be made better off and to compensate those who are hurt so that they are neither better nor worse off.
E) Although difficult, it is possible to construct a social welfare function from the explicit value judgements of society, and so a policy increases social welfare if it puts society on a higher social indifference curve.

Difficulty: **Moderate**

50. Generally speaking, we can state that every point on a grand utility-possibilities frontier represents:
A) a Pareto optimum allocation of resources.
B) a particular distribution of goods among individuals.
C) a particular product mix.
D) an efficient allocation of resources.
E) All of the above are correct.

Difficulty: **Moderate**

51. If a firm is a monopolist in the output market, it produces an output level that is less than socially optimal. The reason is that the monopolist charges a price that exceeds its marginal cost of producing the last unit sold. This violates which one of the conditions for optimality?
A) For each and every pair of goods, the marginal rate of transformation must equal the marginal rate of substitution.
B) The marginal rate of substitution for each pair of goods must be the same for all consumers.
C) The firm can't change a price that is higher than it costs to produce the good unless it wants firms to enter the market in the long run.
D) The marginal rate of technical substitution for inputs into the production of all goods must be equal.
E) None of the above is correct.

Difficulty: **Moderate**

52. An explicit social welfare function is assumed to be determined in which one of the following welfare criteria?
A) the Bergson social welfare criterion
B) the Pareto optimal criterion
C) the Kaldor-Hicks criterion
D) the Scitovsky compensation criterion
E) the Arrow impossibility theorem

Difficulty: **Moderate**

53. Suppose that in the country of Alphania, both the input and output markets are perfectly competitive. We can conclude that:
A) the economy will achieve efficiency in production.
B) the economy will achieve efficiency in consumption.
C) the marginal rates of transformation for all goods will equal the ratio of their marginal costs.
D) the marginal rates of substitution for all goods equal the ratio of their prices.

E) All of the above are correct.

Difficulty: **Moderate**

54. When an economic system attains Pareto efficiency, then:
   A) it is operating at a point below its utility possibilities frontier.
   B) it is impossible to make one individual better off without making someone else worse off.
   C) the economy does not achieve efficiency in production.
   D) someone is made better off without making anyone else worse off.
   E) None of the above is correct.

Difficulty: **Moderate**

55. Any point on an economy's grand utility-possibilities frontier:
   A) is not attainable because of the limited resources available for production.
   B) may represent a position of productive inefficiency.
   C) satisfies the requirement of Pareto efficiency.
   D) satisfies the requirement of efficiency in consumption only.
   E) is also some point on a Bergson social welfare function.

Difficulty: **Moderate**

56. Suppose that an economy consists of perfectly competitive markets. When the economic system achieves a long-run equilibrium, it will also achieve Pareto efficiency if:
   A) the difference between the marginal cost to society and the marginal benefit to society of producing and consuming an additional unit of a goods is maximized.
   B) the prices of goods offered on the market equals the marginal cost and the marginal benefits of the goods exchanged.
   C) it is not possible to make anyone better off by allowing them to consume more goods.
   D) all firms in the economy are making positive economic profits.
   E) None of the above is correct.

Difficulty: **Moderate**

57. Given a utility-possibilities frontier, a movement down and along the curve:
   A) makes both individuals better off.
   B) reflects a movement to points that are Pareto efficient.
   C) can be undertaken only if at least one of the individuals is made worse off.
   D) makes individuals worse off and no one is made better off.
   E) does not change the distribution of output produced in the economy.

Difficulty: **Moderate**

58. If no one in an economic system can be made better off without making at least one other person worse off:
   A) the system is said to be Pareto optimal.
   B) the system satisfies the Kaldor-Hicks criterion.
   C) government should increase taxes on the wealthy.
   D) some consumers are below their utilities possibilities frontier.

E) (A) and (B) are correct.

Difficulty: **Moderate**

59. Any point below Ed and Jake's utility-possibilities frontier:
A) is not attainable by either Ed or Jake.
B) reflects those utility combinations that are Pareto efficient.
C) reflects those utility combinations that are efficient in consumption only.
D) reflects a situation in which it is possible to make either Ed or Jake better off without making the other worse off.
E) None of the above is correct.

Difficulty: **Moderate**

60. Although the concept of Pareto efficiency is useful when describing the results of a perfectly competitive model, the main weakness of the concept when examining the utility possibilities frontier is that:
A) it does not indicate how to rank the various efficient points on the frontier.
B) it indicates only the combinations of goods and services that meet the requirements of Pareto optimality.
C) it does not indicate the cost incurred by society in attaining Pareto efficient points.
D) it does not indicate whether society is willing to tolerate a waste of its resources.
E) None of the above is a weakness.

Difficulty: **Moderate**

61. Which one of the following statements is <u>false</u>?
A) Any position on the utility possibilities frontier is Pareto efficient.
B) If a competitive market achieves a Pareto efficient situation, then it also achieves an equitable distribution of income.
C) In a perfectly competitive market, the equilibrium price is equal to both the valuation by consumers of an extra unit of output and the cost of producing the output.
D) Prices signal the market to employ resources in their optimal use.
E) An aggregate social welfare function encounters the problem of the interpersonal comparison of utility.

Difficulty: **Moderate**

62. All of the following are conditions necessary for an economic system to achieve a Pareto efficiency in a general equilibrium <u>except</u>:
A) production has to take place on the possibilities frontier.
B) the MRTS between inputs must be equal for all goods that use the inputs in production.
C) the MRT between any two goods must equal the MRS for all individuals consuming these goods.
D) the MRS between two goods must be the same for all individuals consuming the two goods.
E) All of the above are conditions for Pareto efficiency.

Difficulty: **Moderate**

63. Suppose that two goods, A and B, are produced in a competitive market. A tax on good A results in an inefficient allocation of resources because:

A) the marginal rate of substitution between A and B is not equal to the marginal rate of transformation between A and B.
B) the marginal rate of substitution between A and B is not equal to the ratio of the price of B to the price of A.
C) the marginal rates of technical substitution between the inputs used to produce A and B are equal.
D) the marginal rates of substitution between A and B are equal for all individuals in the economic system.
E) None of the above is correct.

Difficulty: **Hard**

64. The sharp increase in the price of imported petroleum from 1973 to 1980 directly impacted some markets and produced spillover effects in others. These spillover effects included:
A) an increase in demand for domestically produced automobiles.
B) a decrease in demand for auto workers.
C) an increase in demand for steel.
D) a decrease in demand for foreign produced automobiles.
E) (A) and (B) are correct.

Difficulty: **Moderate**

65. Assume a subsidy is in place that causes the price of water for irrigating farms to be lower than for other purposes. In comparison to activities where water is being used with labor of the same skill as that used in farming, one may conclude that the marginal rate of technical substitution (MRTS) between water and labor is:
A) higher in farming than in the other activities.
B) lower in farming than in the other activities.
C) the same in farming as in other activities.
D) not applicable, since one cannot draw any conclusions regarding the MRTS in farming and other activities based on the information given.
E) unaffected by the difference in the price of water for farming.

Difficulty: **Moderate**

66. If one removes a subsidy which lowers the price of water for irrigating farms relative to the price of water which is used for other activities:
A) economic efficiency in production will increase.
B) agricultural output will decline.
C) output in other activities will increase.
D) overall output will increase.
E) All of the above are correct.

Difficulty: **Moderate**

67. In the absence of international trade, if the MRT of X for Y in Country A is lower than the MRT of X for Y in Country B, then:
A) Country A has a comparative advantage in good X.
B) Country A has a comparative advantage in good Y.
C) Country A should decrease its production of good X.
D) Country A should increase its production of good Y.

E) (B) and (D) are correct.

Difficulty: **Moderate**

68. According to recent studies on the work-welfare tradeoff, which of the following statements is not correct?
A) Welfare payments are more generous than commonly believed.
B) Welfare payments provide recipients with higher incomes than they would receive from many entry-level jobs.
C) Welfare payments discourage welfare recipients from finding work and may encourage permanent dependence.
D) All studies indicate that welfare payments reduce work incentives by a large amount.
E) All of the above are correct.

Difficulty: **Moderate**

69. As the degree of income inequality increases:
A) the Lorenz curve has less curvature and the Gini Coefficient increases.
B) the Lorenz curve has more curvature and the Gini Coefficient increases.
C) the Lorenz curve has less curvature and the Gini Coefficient decreases.
D) the Lorenz curve has more curvature and the Gini Coefficient decreases.
E) the Lorenz curve is unaffected but the Gini Coefficient increases.

Difficulty: **Moderate**

70. Given cumulative percentages of total income measured on the vertical axis and cumulative percentages of population measured on the horizontal axis, a perfectly equal income distribution would yield a Lorenz curve which begins at the origin and is a:
A) horizontal line.
B) vertical line.
C) straight line diagonal.
D) line bowed downward.
E) line bowed upward.

Difficulty: **Moderate**

71. If the income distribution is perfectly equal, the Gini coefficient is:
A) equal to 1.
B) greater than 1.
C) less than 1 but greater than 0.
D) equal to 0.
E) less than 0.

Difficulty: **Moderate**

72. As a result of taxes and income transfers programs in the U.S., the after-tax and after-transfer Lorenz curve will:
A) have a smaller curvature and the Gini coefficient will be smaller.
B) have a smaller curvature and the Gini coefficient will be larger.
C) have a greater curvature and the Gini coefficient will be smaller.
D) have a greater curvature and the Gini coefficient will be larger.

E) not be changed but the Gini coefficient will be smaller.

Difficulty: **Moderate**

73. Comparisons of the relevant 1993 Gini coefficients suggest that the after-tax and after-transfer income distribution in the U.S.:
A) is more equal than the average for all industrial countries, and less equal than the average for developing nations.
B) is slightly more equal than the average for all industrial countries, and more equal than the average for developing nations.
C) is slightly less equal than the average for all industrial countries, and less equal than the average for developing nations.
D) is much more equal than the average for all industrial countries, and much more equal than the average for developing nations.
E) is slightly less equal than the average for all industrial countries, and more equal than the average for developing nations.

Difficulty: **Moderate**

74. Empirical studies of trade restriction in textiles and apparel, automobiles, and steel indicate that the largest total welfare gains for the U.S. would be made by:
A) retaining all quantitative restriction and capturing rents from foreigners by auctioning off exports quotas to foreign firms, and retaining all tariffs.
B) eliminating all quantitative restriction but retaining all tariffs.
C) retaining all quantitative restriction and capturing rents from foreigners by auctioning off exports quotas to foreign firms, and eliminating all tariffs.
D) eliminating all quantitative restrictions and tariffs.
E) eliminating all quantitative restrictions and tariffs in textiles and apparel, and in automobiles, but retaining quantitative restrictions and tariffs in steel.

Difficulty: **Moderate**

75. Empirical studies suggest that the employment effects of removing quantitative restrictions on textiles and apparel, automobiles, and steel would be that employment in all three industries would:
A) decrease, and employment in the rest of the economy would increase but by a smaller amount.
B) decrease, and employment in the rest of the economy would also decrease.
C) increase, and employment in the rest of the economy would increase.
D) decrease, but employment in the rest of the economy would increase by a larger amount.
E) increase, and employment in the rest of the economy would decrease.

Difficulty: **Moderate**

76. Which of the following is <u>not</u> a condition Arrow believed to be necessary for a social welfare function to reflect individual preferences?
A) Social welfare choices must be transitive.
B) Social welfare choices cannot move in the opposite direction to changes in individual preferences.
C) Social welfare choices must reflect the relative intensity of individual preferences.
D) Social welfare choices cannot be dictated by anyone inside or outside the society.

E) Social welfare choices must be independent of irrelevant alternatives.

Difficulty: **Moderate**

77. A voting paradox refers to:
A) a situation in which a society cannot derive a social welfare function by democratic voting because individual preferences are internally inconsistent.
B) a situation in which the preference of the majority is inconsistent with the preferences of the individuals making up the majority.
C) a situation in which social welfare choices are intransitive.
D) All of the above are correct.
E) Only (B) and (C) are correct.

Difficulty: **Moderate**

RANKINGS OF ALTERNATIVES BY INDIVIDUALS

	Alternatives		
Individuals	A	B	C
John	1	2	3
Luis	3	2	1
Chloe	3	1	2

78. Given the preferences in the table above, a majority prefers:
A) B to C, C to A, and B to A.
B) A to B, B to C, and A to C.
C) C to A, A to B, and C to B.
D) A to C, C to B, and A to B.
E) None of the above is correct.

Difficulty: **Moderate**

79. Given the preferences in the table above:
A) social welfare choices (rankings of A, B, and C) are intransitive.
B) social welfare choices (rankings of A, B, and C) are transitive.
C) it is not possible to determine whether social welfare choices are transitive or intransitive.
D) social welfare choices cannot be derived because voting in this case would result in a majority imposing its will on a minority.
E) None of the above is correct.

Difficulty: **Moderate**

RANKINGS OF ALTERNATIVES BY INDIVIDUALS

	Alternatives		
Individuals	A	B	C
John	2	3	1
Luis	1	2	3
Chloe	3	1	2

80. Given the preferences in the table above, a majority prefers:

A) B to C, C to A, and B to A.
B) A to B, B to C, and C to A.
C) C to A, A to B, and C to B.
D) C to B, B to A, and A to C.
E) None of the above is correct.

Difficulty: **Moderate**

81. Given the preferences in the table above:
A) social welfare choices (ranking of A, B, and C) are transitive.
B) social welfare choices (ranking of A, B, and C) are intransitive.
C) it is not possible to determine whether social welfare choices are transitive or intransitive.
D) the rankings do not show the intensity of individual choices thus making it impossible to show any rankings at all whether they be transitive or intransitive.
E) None of the above is correct.

Difficulty: **Moderate**

82. The first theorem of welfare economics states that:
A) equilibrium in competitive markets is Pareto optimal.
B) Pareto optimality does not imply equity.
C) when indifference curves are convex to the origin, every efficient allocation is a competitive equilibrium for some initial allocation of goods or of inputs (income).
D) when indifference curves are concave to the origin, every efficient allocation is a competitive equilibrium for some initial allocation of goods or of inputs (income).
E) None of the above is correct.

Difficulty: **Moderate**

83. Which of the following statements is <u>false</u>?
A) Medical care has always been rationed in the United States and elsewhere.
B) The need to ration healthcare exemplifies the great difficulty with interpersonal comparison of utility in making social choices.
C) Health-care costs are likely to continue to fall as a proportion of GDP in the United States in the coming years.
D) All of the above statements are true.
E) None of the above is true.

Difficulty: **Moderate**

84. A point inside the production-possibilities frontier:
A) corresponds to a point off the production contract curve.
B) indicates that the economy is not in general equilibrium of production.
C) is one at which the economy is not utilizing its inputs of labor and capital most efficiently.
D) All of the above are correct.
E) None of the above is correct.

Difficulty: **Moderate**

85. As we move down the production-possibilities frontier:

A) the MRT_{XY} increases, indicating that more and more Y must be given up to produce each additional unit of X.
B) the MRT_{XY} decreases, indicating that more and more Y must be given up to produce each additional unit of X.
C) the MRT_{XY} increases, indicating that less and less Y can be given up to produce each additional unit of X.
D) the MRT_{XY} decreases, indicating that less and less Y can be given up to produce each additional unit of X.
E) None of the above is correct.

Difficulty: **Moderate**

Short Essays

Give a brief answer to each of the following questions.

1. **What is the difference between general equilibrium and partial equilibrium analysis?**
Answer: Partial equilibrium analysis views individual decision-making units and markets in isolation. It shows how equilibrium is achieved in a market independently of other markets. General equilibrium analysis studies the interdependence that exists among all markets and prices in an economy and attempts to explain how the questions of what to produce, how to produce, and for whom to produce are answered in that context.

2. **In order for an economy to be on its production possibilities frontier, it is necessary for it to be on its contract curve for production. Explain.**
Answer: On the contract curve for production the $MRTS_{LK}$ in the production of the two goods are equal. Given the initial endowment of labor and capital in the economy, it is not possible to rearrange the use of labor and capital in the production of either good and produce more of one good without producing less of the other. Given its factor endowment, an economy on its production frontier cannot produce more of one good without producing less of the other. Thus, if an economy is not on its contract curve for production it cannot be on its production frontier.

3. **What is Pareto optimality?**
Answer: A situation in which it is not possible to rearrange the use of inputs among commodities nor commodities among consumers and make some people better off in their judgement without making other people worse off.

4. **What are the first and second theorems of welfare economics? What is their implication for the issue of efficiency and equity?**
Answer: The first theorem is that equilibrium in competitive markets is Pareto optimal. The second theorem is that every point on a contract curve for exchange is a competitive equilibrium for some initial allocation of goods or distribution of inputs. Their implication is that the issues of equity and efficiency are logically separable. Any initial distribution of input ownership (equity) is compatible with an efficient outcome.

5. **What is the Arrow impossibility theorem?**
Answer: It is proof that a social welfare function cannot be derived by democratic vote if social choices: (1) must be transitive; (2) must not be responsive in the opposite direction to changes in individual preference; (3) cannot be dictated by any one individual inside or outside the society; and, (4) must be independent of irrelevant alternatives.

Chapter 18:

Externalities, Public Goods, and the Role of Government

Multiple-Choice

Choose the one alternative that best completes the statement or answers the question.

1. Suppose that in production, a firm generates some external costs. Under perfect competition, the market will produce a level of output:
   A) where the marginal cost of producing the last unit output equals the price of the output.
   B) that is greater than the socially optimal of output.
   C) that results in an underallocation of resources in the production of the good.
   D) that is less than the socially optimal level of output.
   E) where marginal private cost equal marginal social benefit.

   Difficulty: **Moderate**

2. Suppose that in the production of good X, an external benefit is generated. The marginal social benefit of consuming an additional unit of good X will be:
   A) equal to the social cost of producing the last unit of the good.
   B) less than the price that a typical consumer would be willing to pay for the additional unit of the good.
   C) greater than the price that a typical consumer would be willing to pay for the additional unit of the good.
   D) equal to the price that a typical consumer would be willing to pay for the additional unit of the good.
   E) less than the social cost of producing the last unit of the good.

   Difficulty: **Moderate**

3. Suppose that you consume and enjoy widgets. Your consumption of widgets, however, does not reduce the amount of widgets or prevent me from also enjoying them. We can conclude that widgets:
   A) are a free good.
   B) do not involve any resources in production, so they are not a scarce good.
   C) are not an economic good.
   D) are a good which have the characteristic of nonrival consumption.
   E) are subject to the exclusion principle.

   Difficulty: **Moderate**

4. Suppose that good X is produced by the private sector and that it is a good that is nonrival in consumption. We would be correct in concluding that good X:
   A) will not be a scarce good.
   B) will likely be exclusive.

C) will be consumed up to the point where the marginal social benefit of the last unit consumed will be zero.
D) will not command a price in the market place.
E) cannot exist because the private sector cannot produce a nonrivalrous good.

Difficulty: **Moderate**

5. Generally speaking, a public good:
A) involves no external costs or benefits for either private or public consumption.
B) reduces or sometimes eliminates the free-rider problem because users fees are charged for the consumption of the good.
C) is always available for consumption by any individual at any time.
D) is produced in quantities such that the optimal quantity exists when the cost of producing an extra unit of the good equals the extra benefit society receives when it consumes one more unit of the good.
E) at times is subject to the principle of exclusion.

Difficulty: **Moderate**

6. The theory of public choice is designed to:
A) predict how voters within a political system choose to allocate votes among different groups of politicians.
B) predict the effects of public interest groups on the outcome of the governmental processes in a democratic society.
C) predict the goals of voters within a particular political system.
D) predict how voters in a political system and their representatives choose to make decisions and allocate society's scarce resources.
E) determine the optimal mix of goods to be produced by the economy as well as indicate how government can improve overall social welfare.

Difficulty: **Moderate**

7. Suppose that markets are imperfectly competitive and they generate some externalities in both consumption and production. We can conclude that:
A) the intervention by the government will not be able to improve market performance.
B) society's well-being will not be affected by the presence of the externalities.
C) there is an inefficient allocation and use of society's scarce resources.
D) the intervention by the government will always be able to improve market performance when externalities are present.
E) None of the above is correct.

Difficulty: **Moderate**

8. I have an apple orchard on my property, and the trees produce a delicious fruit. In order to produce, though, the blooms have to be pollinated in the spring. My next-door neighbor has three honeybee hives, and the bees sure love the nectar from my apple blooms. The bees provide an uncompensated benefit for me, and this is an example of:
A) getting something for nothing.
B) an external economy in production.
C) an external economy in consumption.
D) an external diseconomy in the production of honey.
E) an external diseconomy in the production and consumption of apples.

Difficulty: **Moderate**

9. After the great Los Angeles earthquake of 1994, many houses in Los Angeles were damaged. John and Ed are neighbors, and John's house was not damaged. Ed, however, suffered major damage to his property. Once Ed had repaired his house and gardens, they looked better than ever. John was very pleased with Ed's repairs, and he enjoyed looking out of his window each morning at Ed's beautiful home and gardens. This is an example of:
A) the free-rider problem.
B) the private sector producing a public good.
C) an external economy in the production of aesthetic value.
D) an external diseconomy in the production of aesthetic value.
E) an external economy in consumption.

Difficulty: **Moderate**

10. At Daytona Beach, I was sunbathing and enjoying the sand and surf. There must have been several thousand other people on the beach, and my enjoyment of the sun did not affect the enjoyment of any other person. Sunshine at the beach is an example of:
A) a good which is rival in consumption.
B) a public good.
C) a private good.
D) a good that generates negative external economies of scale because many people will get sun burned.
E) a normal good.

Difficulty: **Moderate**

11. All of the following may be correctly classified as public goods <u>except</u>:
A) the beach at an exclusive private resort island.
B) fire and police protection in New York City.
C) Yosemite National Park.
D) the sand, surf, and sun at a Virginia Beach state park.
E) the interstate highway system.

Difficulty: **Moderate**

12. The United States Armed Forces stand ready to defend both you and me. Even though you may not pay taxes and I do, the armed forces will defend both of us. This protection is an example of:
A) a nonrivalrous good.
B) a price good or service.
C) an external economy of scale.
D) a public good.
E) a good that is not subject to the free-rider problem.

Difficulty: **Moderate**

13. All public goods share which one of the following characteristics?
A) They are not produced by the private sector.
B) Public goods have the characteristic of nonrival consumption.

C) Consumers must pay for their consumption of public goods based on their ability to pay.
D) The costs of producing public goods by the public sector are higher than they would be if produced by the private sector.
E) None of the above is correct.

Difficulty: **Moderate**

14. Economists recognize that the problem of the free-rider may arise when:
A) a good is provided in quantities greater than the socially optimal quantity.
B) public goods are not subject to the exclusion principle, and so they have to be free.
C) a public good is nonexclusive.
D) there are strong positive external benefits associated with the public consumption of the good.
E) None of the above is an explanation for the free-rider problem.

Difficulty: **Moderate**

15. As economists study the legislative process more and more:
A) we have learned that decisions are made on an issue-by-issue basis only.
B) we question whether the political process results in decisions that reflect society's best interest.
C) we assume that the legislator's goals result in decisions that best reflect society's best interest.
D) we have learned that the process of legislation eliminates the need for compromise and vote trading.
E) bureaucrats have very little power or say-so in the daily operation of the government.

Difficulty: **Moderate**

16. When markets are imperfect and exhibit externalities in either production or consumption:
A) there is an inefficient allocation of resources and use of society's scarce resources.
B) government intervention will not improve market performance.
C) society's well-being will not be affected.
D) government intervention will not always improve market performance.
E) None of the above is correct.

Difficulty: **Moderate**

17. Suppose that in the production and consumption of good X, an externality is generated. We can conclude that:
A) society's scarce resources are allocated efficiently.
B) the market price of the good reflects the presence of an externality.
C) any intervention by government will not be able to improve the market's performance.
D) someone is affected who is not involved in the buying or selling of the good.
E) the quantity produced and the market price charged is Pareto optimal.

Difficulty: **Moderate**

18. The type of externality that arises when declining long-run average costs as output expands lead to monopoly is called:

A) an external diseconomy of production.
B) an external diseconomy of consumption.
C) a technical externality.
D) an external economy of production.
E) an external economy of consumption.

Difficulty: **Easy**

19. In general, a good will be considered a public good if it:
A) is available for my consumption even if you and your friends consume it.
B) cannot be produced by the private sector.
C) is not available for my consumption if you consume it.
D) is usually provided by the private sector.
E) is rivalrous in nature.

Difficulty: **Moderate**

20. Suppose that all television signals in the nation were carried over cable systems, and we had to pay in order to gain access to the cable. In this case, we can conclude that television programs are:
A) public goods since the cable system gets the signals from public airways.
B) goods that are nonrival in consumption because really anyone can watch a T.V. program.
C) subject to the free-rider problem.
D) overproduced because there is a surplus of programs on the market.
E) private goods because they are exclusive.

Difficulty: **Moderate**

21. Which one of the following would most likely be a public good?
A) radio waves broadcasting a New York Yankees baseball game
B) a new video camera system purchased by the local television station to record news stories
C) an airplane flight to Bermuda
D) a lunch at the student union
E) a social security payment to a retired individual

Difficulty: **Moderate**

22. In the production of a good or service that is to be placed on the market, an externality exists when:
A) markets are imperfectly competitive.
B) the marginal cost to society of consuming an extra unit of the good or service equals the marginal benefit society receives when the extra unit of the good or service is consumed.
C) no one can be made better off without making at least one other person worse off.
D) the marginal social cost or benefit in the production or consumption of the good or service differs from the marginal private cost or benefit in the production or consumption of the good itself.
E) the price established in the market equals the marginal social cost or production.

Difficulty: **Moderate**

23. Generally speaking, market failure exists when:
A) the price established in the market equals the total marginal cost of production (both private and social).
B) resources are allocated so that a Pareto optimum is achieved.
C) a competitive market's clearing price equals both the marginal social cost and the marginal social benefits in the production or consumption of the good.
D) the price established in the market does not equal the marginal social cost or the marginal social benefit of producing the good.
E) None of the above is correct.

Difficulty: **Moderate**

24. When an economic system experiences market failure:
A) there is not an optimal allocation of society's scarce resources.
B) government intervention into the market may improve society's overall well-being.
C) someone can be made better off without making someone else worse.
D) markets and prices are not equal to the total marginal cost and benefits (both private and social) of the goods traded.
E) All of the above are correct.

Difficulty: **Moderate**

25. Suppose that the market price of a good does not include any spillover effects (either positive or negative) that exist as the result of the production or consumption of the good. We can conclude that:
A) the market is perfectly competitive.
B) society is consuming and producing the good in optimal quantities.
C) an externality, either positive or negative, exists in the market place.
D) resources are properly allocated in the market.
E) None of the above is a correct conclusion.

Difficulty: **Moderate**

26. All of the following statements are correct <u>except</u>:
A) if there are positive externalities associated with the production of a good, then too little of the good is being produced.
B) an external cost or benefit is not included in the market price of a good or service.
C) if there are external costs associated with a good, then there is an underallocation of resources in the production of the good.
D) the externalities associated with the production or consumption of a good may be either positive or negative.
E) if there are positive externalities associated with the production or consumption of a good, then the good is priced too low.

Difficulty: **Moderate**

27. Suppose that the price of good Y equals the marginal private cost (that cost incurred by the firm only), and that the total marginal cost (both marginal private and marginal social) is greater than the marginal private cost. We can conclude that:
A) the market price of the good is too low.
B) resources are overallocated in the production of good Y.
C) the production of the good imposes a social cost on society.

D) there is a negative externality associated with the production of good Y.
E) All of the above are correct conclusions.

Difficulty: **Moderate**

28. Sometimes an economist will describe a good as being underpriced. When a good is underpriced, it means that:
A) output should be increased because the marginal social benefit in consumption exceeds the marginal social cost of production.
B) there is an under allocation of resources in the production of the good.
C) too much of the good is being produced since a negative externality is associated with the good.
D) resources are properly allocated since society wants more of the good at a lower price.
E) None of the above statements is correct.

Difficulty: **Moderate**

29. All of the following statements are correct <u>except</u>:
A) any market equilibrium price always generates a social optimum and a proper allocation of resources.
B) a social optimum is attained when market price equals the marginal social cost of producing the last output sold, assuming that the private and social benefits are the same.
C) when firms pass on some of their costs of production to society, the market has failed.
D) if a good is overpriced, there is an underallocation of resources in the production of the good.
E) the presence of a positive externality in the production means that in equilibrium, the good is underproduced.

Difficulty: **Moderate**

30. Many economists agree that in a market economy, the ideal solution to the problem of externalities would be to:
A) allow producers to produce the level of output where both the marginal private benefit and the marginal private cost equal the price of the good.
B) charge or tax producers of a good the precise marginal cost of the externality generated in production.
C) regulate both the amount that people consume and the price they pay for goods whose production involves spillover costs.
D) prohibit all production processes involving spillover costs.
E) force the firms that generate negative externalities in production to completely internalize the externality or cease production.

Difficulty: **Moderate**

31. If the marginal social costs of a pollution-abatement program exceeds its marginal social benefits, then:
A) additional resources should be allocated to the abatement program since society can be made better off.
B) the marginal social costs equal the marginal private benefits.
C) resources are overallocated to the abatement program.
D) the correct amount of resources have been allocated to the abatement program.

E) None of the above is correct.

Difficulty: **Moderate**

32. Assuming that a government regulatory agency imposes standards on the production of a hazardous product, we would expect the:
A) industry's marginal cost schedule to shift downward.
B) demand curve for the product to shift toward the origin.
C) market price of the product to fall and its quantity demanded to rise since it is no longer dangerous.
D) industry supply curve to shift upward, market price to rise, and market quantity to fall.
E) market equilibrium price to remain unchanged, but the equilibrium quantity to fall.

Difficulty: **Moderate**

33. In a free market, goods with negative externalities will:
A) be underproduced at the market equilibrium.
B) be overproduced at the market equilibrium.
C) be produced to the point at which marginal social cost equals the marginal social benefit of producing and consuming the last unit.
D) have the marginal valuation of the externality reflected in their price.
E) Not be produced at all.

Difficulty: **Moderate**

34. In the metropolitan area of Los Angeles, smog is an example of:
A) poor planning on the part of the city of Los Angeles.
B) the inefficient operation of the internal combustion engine.
C) an external cost of owning an automobile in Los Angeles.
D) the private cost of owning an automobile in Los Angeles.
E) None of the above is correct.

Difficulty: **Moderate**

35. Suppose that you live in a steel-producing city and you hang out your laundry to dry in the morning sunshine. Upon returning in the afternoon, you find your laundry black from soot. Which of the following statements is correct?
A) There is an overallocation of resources into the steel industry.
B) The price of steel is too low.
C) An external cost has been generated that has spilled over onto you.
D) Steel producers have not paid the full cost of producing their product.
E) All of the above statements are correct.

Difficulty: **Moderate**

36. In the country of Blund, the government has forced the reduction of air pollution to very low level. On economist argued that the level was much too low. Which one of the following do you think was the basis of the economist's argument?
A) It cost more to improve air quality than the total benefits received from controlling pollution.
B) Air pollution damages the environment more than the total cost of controlling pollution.

C) Air pollution damages the environment more than the total benefits gained from controlling pollution.
D) The cost of improving air quality by an extra unit is greater than the reduction in the damages caused by the extra unit of pollution.
E) None of the above provides a good basis for argument.

Difficulty: **Moderate**

37. The Coase theorem postulates that, given no transactions costs and clearly defined property rights, perfect competition results in:
A) the liability of a party when the expected cost of preventing damages is less than the expected cost of the damages.
B) a socially optimal distribution of goods is achieved by the assignment of property rights to either party.
C) property rights that should be assigned to the individual who is hurt most by a negative externality.
D) the situation where, regardless of the endowment of property rights, the output mix for the economy will be identical whether or not there are negative externalities in production.
E) None of the above is correct.

Difficulty: **Moderate**

38. The Coase theorem asserts that:
A) even under conditions of perfect competition and well-defined property rights, it is still possible for negative externalities to exist.
B) the government has a role in reducing negative externalities so that harm to society is minimized.
C) given zero transactions costs and clearly defined property rights, under perfect competition externalities will be internalized, regardless of the assignment of property rights.
D) only in an idealistic state with no transactions costs and clearly assigned property rights, it will be possible to internalize external costs.
E) None of the above statements are correct.

Difficulty: **Moderate**

39. The decision criterion used in benefit-cost analysis when trying to determine whether or not to undertake a particular project is that the project should be undertaken if the present value of:
A) the total net benefits from the project are greater than total net costs.
B) the total net benefits from the project are equal to total net costs.
C) the total net benefits of the project are greater than or equal to the total net costs.
D) the total net benefits from the project are less than the total net costs.
E) the total gross benefits from the project are equal to total net costs.

Difficulty: **Moderate**

40. Generally speaking, an effluent fee will encourage a polluter to:
A) reduce the level of pollution to the point where the effluent fee equals the marginal cost of an extra unit of pollution.

B) reduce the level of pollution to the point where the effluent fee equals the marginal cost of production.
C) increase output and expand profits.
D) reduce the level of pollution to zero because the effluent fee can be very large.
E) go out of business because the total cost of pollution cannot be internalized.

Difficulty: **Moderate**

41. Suppose that the government imposed a per unit effluent fee on the production of good X. The imposition of this fee on the production of good X will most likely cause the supply curve of good X to:
A) become less elastic.
B) become more elastic.
C) shift downward and to the right.
D) shift upward and to the left.
E) intersect the horizontal axis at some point to the right of the origin.

Difficulty: **Moderate**

42. In theory, the imposition of effluent fees on polluters:
A) will cause the level of pollution to eventually fall to zero.
B) will remove all negative externalities in production.
C) will cause the gap between the private cost and the social cost of disposing of pollutants to narrow.
D) will increase the revenue for the federal government.
E) None of the above is correct.

Difficulty: **Moderate**

43. Suppose that you have to decide whether or not to undertake a particular project. You have information on both the cost and benefits of the project. From a social welfare point of view, you should undertake the project if the ration of the present value of benefits to costs is:
A) greater than one.
B) greater than one or equal to zero.
C) greater than zero.
D) equal to one.
E) within the unit interval between zero and one.

Difficulty: **Moderate**

44. Generally speaking, a project makes a positive contribution to overall social welfare if:
A) the benefits from the project equal its costs.
B) net benefits are greater than zero.
C) net benefits are greater than or equal to one.
D) total benefits are equal to total costs.
E) the marginal cost of expanding the project are positive.

Difficulty: **Moderate**

45. A problem often encountered in using benefit-cost analysis is that both direct benefits and direct costs:

A) can never be measured.
B) may be either explicit or implicit in nature.
C) include only those explicit costs, not any implicit costs.
D) include only those explicit benefits, not any implicit ones.
E) Do not reflect any opportunity costs.

Difficulty: **Moderate**

46. Basic research understood as efforts to discover fundamental relationships in nature such as natural laws:
A) produces external benefits.
B) often produces knowledge that does not have immediate commercial application.
C) often has a range of commercial applications which goes beyond what one firm is capable of exploiting.
D) has social benefits which exceed private benefits.
E) All of the above are correct.

Difficulty: **Moderate**

47. Basic research is likely to be:
A) overproduced by one nation because other nations can easily utilize the knowledge it generates.
B) underproduced by a firm because the knowledge it produces can have a range of commercial applications which goes beyond what one firm is capable of exploiting.
C) overproduced because it produces external benefits.
D) underproduced because its private benefits exceed its social benefits.
E) overproduced because it often produces knowledge that does not have immediate commercial applications.

Difficulty: **Moderate**

48. Japan's focus on finding commercial applications for basic discoveries made by other nations is an example of:
A) how cooperative efforts between nations can lead to an increase in basic research.
B) how external benefits may be internalized by entities engaged in basic research.
C) free riding.
D) how the application of the Coase theorem allows nations to escape the dilemma associated with paying for basic research.
E) how external costs may inhibit the conduct of basic research.

Difficulty: **Moderate**

49. In response to the catastrophic overfishing by foreigners in the 1960s, the United States passed a law extending its exclusive economic (fishing) zone from 3 million to 200 miles. This action alone:
A) led to the elimination of overfishing by foreigners in the fisheries affected.
B) substituted overfishing by Americans for overfishing by foreigners.
C) maintained the incentive to overinvest on this industry.
D) did not remove the external costs associated with fishing.
E) All of the above are correct.

Difficulty: **Moderate**

50. Which of the following statements regarding the privatization of fisheries is <u>not</u> correct?
A) Economists believe this is the best solution to overfishing.
B) The cost of catching fish could be reduced far below its current level.
C) The benefits of privatization are so large that an agreement could easily be reached that would induce all parties to abandon the current fisheries management practices.
D) The efficiency of U.S. fisheries would increase substantially if privatization were successfully implemented.
E) All of the above are correct.

Difficulty: **Moderate**

51. Lighthouse signals in England during the 1700s and 1800s were:
A) a private good produced by privately owned lighthouses.
B) a public good with rival consumption.
C) a public good with exclusion.
D) a private good without exclusion.
E) a public good with nonrival consumption and nonexclusion.

Difficulty: **Moderate**

52. Education is:
A) a private good.
B) a public good.
C) a public good with exclusion.
D) a private good without exclusion.
E) a public good with nonexclusion.

Difficulty: **Moderate**

53. Tax reform proposals such as the "flat tax," or the replacement of an income tax with a large retail sales tax and rebate to low income families would shift the focus of the U.S. tax system:
A) from efficiency to equity and promote economic growth.
B) from efficiency to equity and create a more equal income distribution.
C) from equity to efficiency and promote economic growth.
D) from equity to efficiency and create a more equal income distribution.
E) away from the equity-efficiency tradeoff and toward the problem of fairness.

Difficulty: **Moderate**

54. Compared to the United States, European countries have:
A) higher budget deficits (as a fraction of GDP), taxes, and social spending (free medical care, education, etc.), and lower unemployment rates.
B) higher taxes, social spending (free medical care, education, etc.), and unemployment rates, and lower budget deficits (as a fraction of GDP).
C) higher taxes and social spending (free medical care, education, etc.), and lower unemployment rates and budget deficits (as a fraction of GDP).
D) higher taxes, social spending (free medical care, education, etc.), unemployment rates, and budget deficits (as a fraction of GDP).

E) higher taxes and unemployment rates, and lower social spending (free medical care, education, etc.) and budget deficits (as a fraction of GDP).

Difficulty: **Moderate**

55. The French and British governments' decision to develop the supersonic Concorde provides an example of:
A) a successful government response to market failure which occurs when the social benefits of an activity exceed its private benefits.
B) the failure of benefit-cost analysis to lead to optimal decisions due to an overestimation of benefits and underestimation of costs.
C) the failure of benefit-cost analysis to lead to optimal decisions due to an overestimation of costs and underestimation of benefits.
D) how to use subsidies to internalize positive externalities and thereby cause private firms to make socially optimal decisions.
E) (A) and (D) are correct.

Difficulty: **Moderate**

56. Today, the French and British governments' subsidy of the operation of the Concorde:
A) is economically justified because the Concorde's social benefits exceed its private benefits and the subsidy maintains a socially optimal level of Concorde services.
B) is necessary if the Concorde is to continue to fly.
C) is justified by benefit-cost analysis based on current estimates of benefit and cost.
D) has proven that government involvement in the introduction of supersonic transports should have taken place in the U.S. as well as in Europe.
E) All of the above are correct.

Difficulty: **Moderate**

57. The experience of government support for the Semitech consortium:
A) has demonstrated that social benefits of basic research on semiconductors was justified by the existence of large external benefits.
B) suggests that participating firms increased their R&D budgets as a consequence of participating in the consortium.
C) demonstrated that a government strategic trade policy can enable private industry to catch up with foreign competitors when they would otherwise lag behind for many more years.
D) suggests that the resurgence of the U.S. computer chip industry was due more to the drop in the value of the dollar relative to the Japanese yes than it was to Semitech.
E) All of the above are correct.

Difficulty: **Moderate**

58. If a market for pollution is established, the total amount of pollution that occurs is determined by:
A) the government.
B) a market transaction between two or more firms.
C) the price of pollution rights which emerges in the market.
D) how much each firm is willing to pay in order to obtain additional permits which will allow them to increase their level of emissions.

E) None of the above is correct.

Difficulty: **Moderate**

59. In a market for pollution rights, if Firm A can reduce its generation of sulphur dioxide by 1 unit for $10,000, and Firm B can do so for $50,000, then:
A) there will be a mutually beneficial price at which Firm B can sell the right to generate 1 unit of sulphur dioxide to Firm A.
B) there will be a mutually beneficial price at which Firm A can sell the right to generate 1 unit of sulphur dioxide to Firm B.
C) society will gain the same amount regardless of which firm sells and which firm buys.
D) (A) and (B) are correct.
E) All of the above are correct.

Difficulty: **Moderate**

60. In a market for pollution rights, if Firm X can reduce its generation of sulphur dioxide by 1 unit for $20,000, and Firm Y can do so for $60,000, then with a mutually beneficial price of $40,000 for the right to generate 1 unit of sulphur dioxide:
A) Firm X will gain $40,000 by selling the right to generate 1 unit of sulphur dioxide to Firm Y.
B) Firm X will gain $20,000 by selling the right to generate 1 unit of sulphur dioxide to Firm Y.
C) Firm Y will gain $40,000 by selling the right to generate 1 unit of sulphur dioxide to Firm X.
D) Firm Y will gain $20,000 by selling the right to generate 1 unit of sulphur dioxide to Firm X.
E) Neither firm can make gains at the price of $40,000.

Difficulty: **Moderate**

61. According to the Coase theorem, perfect competition results in the internalization of externalities:
A) when property rights are clearly defined, regardless of how property rights are assigned among the parties.
B) when property rights are clearly defined, and are assigned equally among the parties.
C) when property rights are clearly assigned, regardless of whether or not those property rights are clearly defined.
D) if there are only two parties to the transaction.
E) None of the above is correct.

Difficulty: **Moderate**

62. Which of the following is <u>not</u> a type of externality?
A) technical externality
B) external diseconomy of consumption
C) external diseconomy of production
D) external economy of production
E) All of the above are types of externalities.

Difficulty: **Moderate**

63. Special interest groups work in such a way that:
A) a small number of people make small individual gains at the expense of a large number of people suffering small individual losses.
B) a small number of people make large individual gains at the expense of a large number of people suffering small individual losses.
C) a large number of people make small individual gains at the expense of a large number of people suffering small individual losses.
D) a large number of people make large individual gains at the expense of a large number of people suffering small individual losses.
E) None of the above is correct.

Difficulty: **Moderate**

64. For a good to be classified as a public good there must be:
A) nonrival consumption.
B) nonexclusion.
C) rival consumption.
D) negative externalities.
E) (A) and (B) are correct.

Difficulty: **Moderate**

65. Which of the following statements about rational ignorance is <u>not</u> correct? Rational ignorance:
A) refers to voters' tendency to be much less informed about political decision than about their individual market decisions.
B) exists because there is less need for individual voters to be fully informed about public choices for which elected officials act as purchasing agents for the community than private choices where individuals are their own purchasing agents.
C) exists because individuals feel less influential in, and less affected by, public decisions than by their own private market choices.
D) exists because individuals are less influential in, and less affected by, public decisions than by their own private market choices.
E) All of the above are correct statements about rational ignorance.

Difficulty: **Moderate**

66. Assume that the owner of a copper mine is dumping waste into a river and downstream a rancher loses $5,000 worth of cattle each year because the cattle drink polluted water. If the cost of cleaning up the waste at the mine and not dumping it in the water is $2,000 per year, and the mine owner has clearly defined and transferable property rights to the river:
A) the rancher will simply have to go on losing $5,000 worth of cattle every year.
B) the rancher could pay the owner of the mine not to pollute the water if the cost of negotiating a contract is zero or very low, but he would be worse off than if he simply takes his losses in cattle.
C) the mine owner benefits most from the current arrangement and the rancher will be unable to remedy the problem without government action.
D) the socially optimal result is attainable through private negotiation.
E) the only solution is to ride up to that mine and shoot somebody.

Difficulty: **Moderate**

67. Which of the following statements about public sector performance is <u>not</u> supported by public choice theory?
A) It can be improved by contracting out as many public services as possible.
B) It can be improved by allowing private firms to compete with government agencies.
C) It can be improved by encouraging interagency competition.
D) It can be improved by streamlining all government operations to eliminate duplication.
E) All of the above statements are supported by public choice theory.

Difficulty: **Moderate**

68. Strategic trade policy:
A) is based on the idea that government can improve the market outcome in oligopolistic markets which are subject to large external diseconomies.
B) is based on the idea that government can create comparative advantage through temporary trade protection, subsidies, and tax benefits in key industries.
C) is strongly supported by most economists.
D) (A) and (B) are correct.
E) All of the above are correct.

Difficulty: **Moderate**

69. The aggregate demand curve for a public good is:
A) the horizontal summation of the demand curves of the individuals who consume it.
B) the vertical summation of the demand curves of the individuals who consume it.
C) vertical.
D) horizontal.
E) undefined.

Difficulty: **Moderate**

70. Government intervention is required to address the problem of pollution because:
A) there are so many different types of pollution.
B) only the government can know the exact cost of pollution.
C) the external costs of pollution cannot be internalized by the assignment of clear property rights.
D) only the government can negotiate with the large number of parties involved.
E) All of the above are correct.

Difficulty: **Moderate**

Short Essays

Give a brief answer to each of the following questions.

1. **Name and describe the five types of externalities.**
Answer: External economies of consumption are uncompensated benefits conferred on others by the consumption of a commodity by some individual. External diseconomies of consumption are uncompensated costs imposed on others by the consumption of a commodity by some individual. External economies of production are uncompensated benefits conferred on others by the expansion of output by some firms. External diseconomies of production are uncompensated costs imposed on others by the expansion

of output by some firms. Technical externalities exist when declining long-run average costs lead to monopoly.

2. **Assume that transaction costs are zero and that my neighbor plans to add a second story to his house that blocks the view of the mountains from my backyard. Evaluate the following statement in light of the Coase theorem. "The second story will be added if my neighbor 'owns' the right to add a second story regardless of how valuable the view is to me."**
Answer: Given the assumptions, the statement is incorrect. If my valuation of the view is greater than his valuation of a second story, I will be able to pay him not to build the second story.

3. **A television signal relayed by satellite is a public good. Explain.**
Answer: A public good is a good that has nonrival consumption. One person consuming it does not preclude another person from doing so. An unlimited number of people with satellite dishes could receive a signal without preventing someone else from doing the same. It is subject to exclusion, however. Thus, this good falls into the category of a public good that is exclusive.

4. **The free-rider problem arises under what circumstances and has what effect on production of good in a private market?**
Answer: It arises when it is not possible to exclude someone from consuming a good even if he or she refuses to pay for it. In the extreme case a good will not be provided in the private sector if it is nonexclusive. In milder cases where free riding is possible but full benefits cannot be obtained in that fashion, then a suboptimal level of output that is greater than zero will be produced in a private market.

5. **The optimal level of pollution is not zero. Explain.**
Answer: The optimal level of pollution is the level at which the marginal social cost of pollution equals the marginal social benefit (in the form of avoiding alternative and more expensive methods of waste disposal). Zero pollution is an ideal situation, but as long as pollution is the inevitable by-product of the production and consumption of commodities that we want, it is silly to advocate zero pollution. Economists advocate optimal pollution control instead, meaning that amount of pollution, which at the margin, balances the social costs, and social benefits of pollution.

Chapter 19:

The Economics of Information

Multiple-Choice

Choose the one alternative that best completes the statement or answers the question.

1. If either consumers or producers do not have complete information about the safety of a product, then we would expect to see:
   A) a surplus of the good on the market since producers are continuously overproducing the product.
   B) the quantity demanded of the product to exceed the quantity supplied.
   C) the market price to be different from the marginal social cost and the marginal social benefit of the good.
   D) no market price to exist for the good.
   E) the market equilibrium price of the good to be the socially optimal price.

   Difficulty: **Moderate**

2. Suppose that there is incomplete information in the market for widgets. Tests have shown that widgets could be harmful to your health. We can conclude that in the absence of this information:
   A) the marginal social cost of producing the good is less than the marginal private cost.
   B) there is an overallocation of resources in the production of goods.
   C) too few goods are being produced.
   D) the goods are over priced in the market place.
   E) the demand curve for widgets is relatively inelastic.

   Difficulty: **Moderate**

3. Which one of the following would most likely not be included in an individual's search cost as he shops in the marketplace?
   A) physically inspecting products that are potential purchases.
   B) comparison shopping for the lowest price of a good.
   C) reading the newspaper ads in order to determine the availability and price of the goods.
   D) travel time spent going to and from different retail shops.
   E) the cost incurred when the retailer sells a product to a consumer.

   Difficulty: **Moderate**

4. Generally speaking, it is impossible for price differentials to exist in a market economy:
   A) when the market is imperfectly competitive.
   B) when the products sold in the market are relatively homogeneous.
   C) when there is perfect information on behalf of both buyers and sellers in the market.
   D) for any length of time because price differentials will always tend to narrow over time.

E) None of the above is correct.

Difficulty: **Moderate**

5. Suppose that a consumer wants to search the market for a particular product. The price of the product ranges from a low of $100 to a high of $105. If the marginal cost for the typical consumer for a search is $1.70, how many searches will the consumer make?
A) two searches
B) five searches
C) six searches
D) three searches
E) Cannot be determined from the information provided.

Difficulty: **Moderate**

6. If the marginal cost of an additional search for a product is $4, while the marginal benefit gained when four searches are conducted is $6.50, the consumer should:
A) continue to search for the good because the marginal benefit is greater than the marginal cost.
B) stop searching for the good and purchase it at the last determined price because the extra benefit from the search is greater than the cost of the search.
C) continue to search for the good because the marginal benefit of an extra search will rise.
D) stop searching for the good because the marginal cost of an additional search will rise.
E) None of the above is correct.

Difficulty: **Moderate**

7. Suppose that you enter the market for a particular product and, unfortunately, the product that you purchase is a lemon. The purchase of this "lemon" of a product reflects:
A) the moral hazard problem.
B) the problem of adverse selection.
C) speculating on a product and losing.
D) speculating on a product and winning.
E) None of the above is correct.

Difficulty: **Moderate**

8. The source of the adverse selection problem is:
A) the moral hazard problem.
B) the fact that individuals are often more than willing to engage in speculation in the purchase of goods and services.
C) the problem of market-place inertia.
D) the problem of asymmetric information.
E) None of the above is correct.

Difficulty: **Moderate**

9. Which one of the following statements is <u>not</u> correct?
A) Imperfect information generates price differentials in the market place.
B) The existence of price differentials creates the need for consumer search.
C) The number of searches that should be undertaken by a consumer is determined by the marginal benefit and marginal cost of an additional search.

D) The search process tries to solve the problem of how and where to find a particular product at the lowest price.
E) Price differentials exist for only infrequently purchase goods because consumers tend to forget what the price was the last time that they purchased the good.

Difficulty: **Moderate**

10. In your study of the economics of information, you learned that:
A) a consumer should continue the search process until the marginal benefits from an additional search begin to diminish.
B) there exists complete information for both buyers and sellers in some markets.
C) there are essentially no real costs involved in the search process.
D) a consumer should continue to the search process until the marginal benefit from an additional search equals the marginal cost of the search.
E) a consumer should continue the search process until the marginal cost of an additional search is minimized.

Difficulty: **Easy**

11. For the consumer, the search process in the market:
A) tries to answer the question of "how" to find the lowest price of a good.
B) involves some real costs to the individual.
C) results in a declining marginal benefit for each additional search.
D) tries to answer the question of "where" to find the lowest price of a good.
E) All of the above are correct.

Difficulty: **Moderate**

12. Which one of the following does not describe some characteristic of advertising expenditures of an imperfectly competitive firm?
A) The expenditures involve some waste of society's scarce resources.
B) These expenditures lower the consumer's purchase price of the product, assuming that production takes place in a constant cost industry.
C) These expenditures may be a barrier to entry into an industry.
D) These expenditures may provide useful information so that an individual is a more efficient consumer in the market place.
E) These expenditures may be used primarily to try and affect consumers' tastes and preferences.

Difficulty: **Moderate**

13. Generally speaking, the basic principle of insurance is that:
A) it is possible to completely avoid risk and earn large profits.
B) it is possible to identify those individuals with the maximum risk, and so no insurance is sold to them.
C) different insurers can pool risks when the individual risks are larger than the social risk.
D) risk and uncertainty cannot be insured against.
E) None of the above is correct.

Difficulty: **Moderate**

14. Suppose that you go into the market to purchase a commodity, and the seller has more information about the pros and cons of the product than you do. The seller decides not to share this information with you and so you purchase the product, which turns out to be a "lemon." This is an example of:
A) an incomplete search process.
B) asymmetric information.
C) the moral hazard phenomena.
D) the problem of adverse selection.
E) the seller receiving a price that approached the competitive equilibrium price.

Difficulty: **Moderate**

15. In the study of uncertainty, risk, and insurance, the moral hazard phenomenon:
A) is a philosophical approach pursued primarily by risk averters.
B) identifies careless human behavior induced by the security of being insured.
C) is often used to describe the behavior of speculators in the futures market.
D) is a philosophical approach practiced primarily by risk takers.
E) None of the above is correct.

Difficulty: **Moderate**

16. Insurance companies use the method of coinsurance in order to overcome or reduce the problem of:
A) hedging.
B) adverse selection.
C) moral hazard.
D) All of the above are correct.
E) None of the above is correct.

Difficulty: **Moderate**

17. An individual with a long history of serious illness will buy a lot of hospitalization and life insurance. This action is called:
A) risk-neutral behavior.
B) the moral hazard problem.
C) adverse selection.
D) hedging.
E) None of the above is correct.

Difficulty: **Moderate**

18. All of the following statements describe some characteristic or aspect about adverse selection <u>except</u>:
A) asymmetric information is required on the part of buyers and sellers for adverse selection to occur.
B) buying an automobile which is a lemon because of an asymmetric information and so is an example of adverse selection.
C) adverse selection occurs when individuals make the wrong choice because they do not have to bear the entire cost of their decision.
D) adverse selection is a problem in the insurance industry.

E) the presence of adverse selection puts upward pressure on insurance rates.

Difficulty: **Moderate**

19. Suppose that you have an illness and you want to purchase some life insurance. If you conceal your illness from the insurance company, then the insurance company cannot offer fair odds to all consumers because of:
A) the moral hazard problem.
B) the problem of adverse selection.
C) the problem of symmetric information.
D) the inability to equally spread risks.
E) None of the above is correct.

Difficulty: **Moderate**

20. You want to purchase insurance so that you can reduce the risk of certain events occurring to zero. Once the insurance is purchased, you change your behavior and begin to act in a careless manner. The insurance company cannot offer fair odds to all individuals because of:
A) the moral hazard problem.
B) the problem of adverse selection.
C) your speculation about the event occurring.
D) uninsurable risk.
E) None of the above is correct.

Difficulty: **Moderate**

21. One way that insurance companies attempt to reduce the problem of moral hazard is through coinsurance. When an insurance company coinsures, it:
A) spreads the risk among many other insurance companies so that no one company stands to lose a great deal of money.
B) insures only part of the possible loss with the insured bearing part of the risk of any loss.
C) is really acting as a speculator in the futures market because it is not completely certain whether or not a loss will occur.
D) does not face the problem of adverse selection.
E) All of the above are correct.

Difficulty: **Moderate**

22. The process of coinsurance by insurance companies is designed to reduce the problem of:
A) interdependent risks.
B) adverse selection.
C) speculation by the insured.
D) moral hazard.
E) None of the above is correct.

Difficulty: **Moderate**

23. Which one of the following would <u>not</u> be an example of market signaling in an attempt to reduce the effects of asymmetric information?
A) An individual obtains a four-year degree in economics from a state university.
B) Procter and Gamble registers its trademarks and brand names for its laundry detergents.

C) McDonald's sells franchises.
D) A television has a five-year warranty on all components.
E) All of the above are examples of market signaling.

Difficulty: **Moderate**

24. The level of education that an individual possesses serves an important market-signaling device. The signal is one that:
A) notifies producers which workers should be paid higher wages.
B) lets the employer know that if educated workers are to be productive, they need increasing amounts of capital goods.
C) notifies producers that the education level of potential employees provides them with some very firm-specific skill which would be useful in the work place.
D) notifies producers that potential employees possess certain skills and abilities that might be useful in the work place.
E) None of the above is correct.

Difficulty: **Moderate**

25. Most modern-day corporations are operated by:
A) the owners of the firm.
B) the stockholders of the firm.
C) a combination of government planners and stockholders.
D) managers, who may or may not be the owner(s).
E) a group of principles who act in a manner such that their agents' best interests are maximized.

Difficulty: **Moderate**

26. In microeconomic theory, a basic assumption about the behavior of the firm is that its goal is only profit maximization. This assumption, however:
A) is questioned by some economists and business people.
B) is accepted by all economists.
C) is the only rational goal for the firm to pursue.
D) is not relevant for the analysis of the firm's pricing behavior.
E) None of the above is correct.

Difficulty: **Moderate**

27. The fact that there is a separation of ownership and control in modern corporations suggests that:
A) corporations will be controlled by the largest single stockholder.
B) the corporation's profit will not be distributed to the owners.
C) the managers of the corporation, rather than the owners, usually make the decisions of the firm.
D) the corporation is effectively controlled by the stockholders.
E) None of the above is correct.

Difficulty: **Moderate**

28. The principal-agent problem arises when:
A) the goals of the firm are not profit maximization.

B) the managers of the firm do not pursue the best interest of the owners.
C) the firm suffers a loss in the short run, and so some of the workers must be laid-off.
D) the agents want to maximize the principals' total profit.
E) None of the above is correct.

Difficulty: **Moderate**

29. If the principals of a corporation guarantee their agents a golden parachute, the principals are in effect:
A) attempting to purchase the loyalty of agents.
B) assuring the agents that if they are forced out or choose to leave, they will receive a large financial settlement.
C) assuring the agents' approval in the event of a take-over attempt by the firm.
D) trying to assure that the profits of the firm will be maximized.
E) All of the above are correct.

Difficulty: **Moderate**

30. One way that a firm can overcome the principal-agent problem is to:
A) establish profit-sharing programs for their employees.
B) establish deferred-compensation and substantial retirement plans for their middle and upper-level management.
C) make golden-parachutes for top management.
D) All of the above are correct.
E) None of the above is correct.

Difficulty: **Moderate**

31. Each of the following may serve as a market signaling device <u>except</u>:
A) a college education.
B) coinsurance with an insurance policy.
C) guarantees on product.
D) passing a lemon law.
E) None of the above is correct.

Difficulty: **Moderate**

32. One way to reduce the moral-hazard problem is by:
A) co-insurance.
B) placing deductibles on insurance in the even of a claim.
C) insisting that those who buy insurance undertake certain precautions to reduce the risk of occurrence of the event for which they are insured.
D) All of the above are correct.
E) Only (A) and (C) are correct.

Difficulty: **Moderate**

33. Which of the following statements is correct?
A) The moral hazard problem leads to asymmetric information.
B) Adverse selection leads to asymmetric information.
C) Asymmetric information leads to adverse selection.
D) Asymmetric information has no effect on the speculation of commodity brokers.

E) All of the above statements are incorrect.

Difficulty: **Moderate**

34. One price selling:
A) is intended to remove almost all haggling over car prices.
B) when combined with value pricing greatly reduces the benefits to the consumer of continuing to search for a lower price.
C) is a common pricing strategy for General Motors.
D) is a response in part to the perception that many new car buyers attach high costs to the practice of haggling.
E) All of the above are correct.

Difficulty: **Moderate**

35. Which of the following statements regarding the Internet is <u>not</u> correct? The Internet:
A) was started in 1969.
B) was developed from its inception to ensure secure commerce.
C) lays the groundwork for thousands of businesses to deal directly with suppliers, industrial customers, and on-line shoppers.
D) All of the above are correct.
E) (B) and (C) are not correct.

Difficulty: **Moderate**

36. Moral hazard in the Social Security Disability Program:
A) is impossible because only those people who cannot work are covered by the disability program.
B) is possible but is unlikely since both the Social Security disability-recipiency rate and the labor force non-participation rate for men aged 45 to 54 have been falling for several decades.
C) is possible because it contains some incentive not to work, but is not supported by the empirical evidence which shows the Social Security disability-recipiency rate falling in age groups such as men aged 45 to 54 for several decades while the labor force non-participation rate has increased.
D) is likely to have occurred since the program contains some incentive not to work, and the empirical evidence shows significant long-term increases in both the Social Security disability-recipiency rate and the labor force non-participation rate for men aged 45 to 54.
E) has been eliminated by the introduction of welfare programs which are not subject to moral hazard problems.

Difficulty: **Moderate**

In the market for doctors' visits, assume that: (1) supply and demand curves have the usual slopes; (2) Medicare and Medicaid cover all medical costs of the elderly and poor; (3) doctors' visits are the only form of care; and (4) the demand for doctors' visits by the noncovered group is unchanged.

37. Given the above information, the introduction of Medicare and Medicaid can be expected to cause (respectively) equilibrium price, equilibrium quantity, the quantity of doctors' visits consumed by the covered group, and the quantity of doctors' visits consumed by the noncovered group to:

A) decrease, decrease, decrease, and decrease.
B) increase, increase, increase, and increase.
C) increase, increase, increase, and decrease.
D) increase, decrease, increase, and decrease.
E) increase, decrease, decrease, and decrease.

Difficulty: **Moderate**

38. Given the above information, the introduction of Medicare and Medicaid can be expected to cause (respectively) the price of doctors' visits to the covered group, the price of doctors' visits to the noncovered group, and the income of the noncovered group after the payment of taxes and subsidies associated with these programs to:
A) decrease, increase, and decrease.
B) decrease, decrease, and decrease.
C) increase, increase, and increase.
D) increase, increase, and decrease.
E) decrease, decrease, and increase.

Difficulty: **Moderate**

39. The use of golden parachutes:
A) decreased during the 1980s after an explosive growth in their use in 1981.
B) have been extended only for top executives because use of them for middle level management is simply too expensive.
C) have escaped careful scrutiny of stockholders because there is no legal requirement to report them.
D) must now be approved by a vote of stockholders according to Securities and Exchange Commission rules.
E) All of the above are correct.

Difficulty: **Moderate**

40. The consequences of Henry Ford implementing an efficiency wage for assembly line workers in 1914 did not include:
A) increased worker loyalty.
B) decreased worker absenteeism.
C) increased labor turnover.
D) increased labor productivity.
E) decreased cost of producing each automobile.

Difficulty: **Moderate**

41. Which of the following may be used to calculate the approximate lowest price expected with each additional search?
A) Lowest Price + Range of Prices / 2.
B) Lowest Price x Number of Searches.
C) Lowest Price + (Range of Prices / Number of Searchers + 1).
D) (Highest Price + Lowest Price) / Number of Searchers.
E) None of the above is correct.

Difficulty: **Moderate**

42. Which of the following statements is <u>not</u> correct?
A) Search goods are goods whose quality can be evaluated by inspection at the time of purchase.
B) Experience goods are goods that can only be judged after using them.
C) Advertisements of search goods require little informational content.
D) Large expenditures buy a firm on advertising an experience good are indirect evidence that the claims made in the seller's advertisements are valid.
E) All of the above are correct.

Difficulty: **Moderate**

43. The efficiency wage:
A) is the wage which emerges in a perfectly competitive labor market.
B) results from a principal-agent problem rooted in asymmetric information.
C) is paid to induce workers to avoid shirking.
D) Only (B) and (C) are correct.
E) All of the above are correct.

Difficulty: **Moderate**

44. The efficiency wage:
A) increases as the unemployment rate increases.
B) decreases as the unemployment rate increases.
C) is not related to the unemployment rate.
D) is paid in order to reduce unemployment.
E) (A) and (D) are correct.

Difficulty: **Moderate**

45. The most important component of search costs is the:
A) money spent on information to aid in the search.
B) time spent learning about the attributes of the product.
C) difference in the price that is ultimately paid for the product.
D) All of the above are equally important components of search costs.
E) None of the above is a component of search costs.

Difficulty: **Moderate**

46. In the formula used to obtain the approximate lowest price expected with each additional search, the expected price will be lower the:
A) lower is the "Lowest price".
B) smaller is the "Range of Prices".
C) greater the number of searchers.
D) All of the above are correct.
E) (A) and (B) are correct.

Difficulty: **Moderate**

47. Even though consumers will search for the lowest price, producers can charge different prices to different consumers because:
A) some consumers will stop searching before others and will therefore pay a higher price.

B) some consumers will stop searching before others and will therefore pay a lower price.
C) the marginal costs of search are the same for all consumers.
D) the marginal benefit of search increases.
E) None of the above is correct.

Difficulty: **Moderate**

48. Which of the following is an example of a search good?
A) fresh fruits and vegetables
B) apparel
C) greeting cards
D) All of the above are examples of search goods.
E) (A) and (B) are correct.

Difficulty: **Moderate**

49. Which of the following is not an example of an experience good?
A) automobiles
B) canned foods
C) laundry detergents
D) computers
E) All of the above are examples of search goods.

Difficulty: **Moderate**

50. As a result of the adverse selection problem in the used car market:
A) there will be relatively more low-quality cars than high-quality cars.
B) there will be relatively more high-quality cars than low-quality cars.
C) there will be about the same number of low-quality cars as high-quality cars.
D) fewer people will buy cars.
E) buyers will engage in less search.

Difficulty: **Moderate**

Short Essays

Give a brief answer to each of the following questions.

1. **How do brand names reduce the problem of adverse selection?**
Answer: Adverse selection arises because of the existence of asymmetric information about product quality. Brand names and the expense that firms incur to insure that they are proof of high quality tend to reduce this asymmetry and thus the problem of adverse selection.

2. **Paying higher starting salaries to people with college degrees than to those without a degree, and then paying all employees according to actual on-the-job productivity is an example of market signaling. Explain.**
Answer: In this case educational attainment is being used as a market signal of higher quality labor because the firm lacks a better signaling device. Later, better information about worker productivity is obtained on the job and salaries reflect that.

3. **How can coinsurance reduce the problem of moral hazard?**

Answer: Moral hazard refers to the situation in which insuring against the costs of an outcome increases the likelihood of that outcome, e.g., fire insurance causing people to be less careful about the use of fire. Coinsurance refers to insuring against only part of the loss and leaves a greater incentive to avoid loss.

4. **How do golden parachutes help to overcome the principal-agent problem?**
Answer: The principal-agent problem arises when managers of a firm have different goals from the owners. In the case of takeover bids, managers may fear for their jobs and thus resist a takeover that is in the owner's best interest. Golden parachutes buy the approval of managers for takeovers by reducing the cost associated with losing their positions in the firm. The benefit to the owners of the takeover is larger than the cost of overcoming management opposition.

5. **What is an above efficiency wage rate paid to avoid shirking or slacking off on the job?**
Answer: It is an above-equilibrium wage rate paid to avoid shirking or slacking off on the job. It reduces shirking because individuals will not want to risk being fired and then not be able to find a similarly rewarding job. If all firms paid an efficiency wage, the unemployment associated with it would induce workers not to shirk because of the concern that they might not be able to find employment again if they are fired.